ᘓ

The Making of Early
Chinese Classical Poetry

Harvard East Asian Monographs 261

CᎡ

The Making of Early Chinese Classical Poetry

Stephen Owen

Published by the Harvard University Asia Center
and distributed by Harvard University Press
Cambridge (Massachusetts) and London 2006

Printed in the United States of America

The Harvard University Asia Center publishes a monograph series and, in co-ordination with the Fairbank Center for East Asian Research, the Korea Institute, the Reischauer Institute of Japanese Studies, and other faculties and institutes, administers research projects designed to further scholarly understanding of China, Japan, Vietnam, Korea, and other Asian countries. The Center also sponsors projects addressing multidisciplinary and regional issues in Asia.

Library of Congress Cataloging-in-Publication Data

Owen, Stephen, 1946–
     The making of early Chinese classical poetry / Stephen Owen.
          p. cm. -- (Harvard East Asian monographs ; 261)
     Includes bibliographical references and index.
     ISBN-13: 978-0-674-02136-5 (hbk. : alk. paper)
     ISBN-10: 0-674-02136-3 (hbk. : alk. paper)
     1. Chinese poetry--221 B.C. - 960 A.D.--History and criticism. I. Title. II. Series.
     PL2313.O94 2006
     895.1'1309--dc22

                                                                          2006013697

Index by Christopher J. Dakin

⊛ Printed on acid-free paper

Last figure below indicates year of this printing
16 15 14 13 12 11 10 09 08 07 06

In memory of my teacher

Hans Frankel

Contents

ᘉ

The Making of Early
Chinese Classical Poetry

Introduction

In his monumental *Poetry of the Pre-Qin, Han, Wei, Jin, and Northern and Southern Dynasties*, Lu Qinli, one of the preeminent scholars of this period, follows established custom in arranging poems by author in chronological order. The earliest appearance of the mature five syllable line, the form that was to dominate the rest of Lu's compendium, was a poem on a fan, attributed to Lady Ban, who lived in the reign of Emperor Cheng of the Han (r. 32–7 B.C.). After giving the text of the poem with extensive notes on its sources and variants, Lu Qinli concludes: "This poem was probably written by a professional musician of the Wei Dynasty (A.D. 220–65)."

There is nothing surprising here for those long accustomed to working with Chinese sources, so much so that the scholar might wonder why we mention it at all. Indeed, all anthologies place the poem under Lady Ban's name in the last part of the Western Han, though very few modern scholars and anthologists actually believe that the poem was written by Lady Ban or written in that period. The chronological placement of the poem and the attached notes—which discredit the attribution and give the poem a much later date—do, however, beg a very simple question on which some important issues hang. If the author of the book and the probable consensus of scholars of poetry of this period agree that the poem was composed about two and a half centuries after Lady Ban, why is the poem placed here, in the reign of Emperor Cheng in the Western Han, rather than given as a poem of unknown authorship from the Wei, many pages later?

The answer to this question comes in several layers. The easy, pragmatic answer is not to be lightly dismissed: this is where a reader of Lu Qinli's compendium or of any anthology of early poetry would look for the poem. We may now disbelieve, for good reason, that the poem was written by Lady Ban, but the poem has been associated with her name for the past fifteen hundred years. Even a reader who did not believe in her authorship of the poem would still expect to find her name in the usual chronological position in the table of contents of the compilation and to find the poem under her name. A more interesting reason is the inability to securely place the poem if we were to detach it from Lady Ban's name. It could be placed among the anonymous poems of the Wei Dynasty, but even Lu Qinli would probably admit that it could perhaps come from the Jian'an Reign of the Han (196–220) or from the Western Jin in the last part of the third century. That is, if one acted on the conviction that this famous poem was written later than Lady Ban, it would have no secure place in a compilation that is chronologically organized.

These two points may be generalized: what we will call early Chinese "classical poetry" has over the centuries become embedded in a chronological account, an account with great cultural historical resonance. Modern scholarship has seriously questioned some of the components of that account, such as Lady Ban's poem. No one, however, knows quite what to do with a poem that has been detached from the account; it no longer has a "place"; it is no longer fully meaningful because it cannot fit into the historical network that confers meaning. The poem therefore is wisely kept close to Lady Ban's name, even though we know that it doesn't truly belong there. A famous poem that had had a home for at least a millennium and a half would otherwise become a vagrant.

Lu Qinli's compilation by and large follows tradition in attaching early classical poems to authors and arranging those authors in chronological sequence. At the same time, the high quality of his scholarship on the sources, alternative attributions, and textual variants often destabilizes the very history implied in the organization. This is particularly true of poetry before the second half of the third century.

•

In the present study I will adopt a dual approach, two lines of inquiry that can never be perfectly disentangled. First, I will look at the surviving material from this early period synchronically, as if it were not historically arranged, with some poems attached to authors and some not. Second, I will consider how the current account of the origins of classical poetry was constructed out of this material in the late fifth and early sixth centuries (which I will call the "Qi and Liang," the two dynasties in the South during which the greater part of extant literary scholarship on early poetry took place). The advantage of the first approach is that by setting aside a putative history of differences of genre and author, we can see that in many ways this was "one poetry," created from a shared poetic repertoire and shared compositional procedures. The second line of inquiry is also necessary because the textual medium through which we have received this material has been selected and sometimes radically reshaped to produce our standard account of the origins of classical poetry.

To examine the formation of the standard account of the origins of classical poetry is not to disbelieve the possibility that it *might be* historically true. What we offer is a critique of the assumptions and the evidence used to prove that it is historically true. What we must conclude is that we do not know when a large number of poems were composed and, perhaps more important, how they changed over the centuries before entering the textual record that we now have. It is possible, as is commonly believed, that the anonymous "Han" *yuefu* predate or are contemporaneous with the anonymous "old poems," which in turn predate the Jian'an Reign. It is, however, no less possible that our current "old poems" postdate the Jian'an and that our current versions of anonymous *yuefu* postdate the "old poems." There *are* poems by known authors in this corpus that we can date roughly or precisely, but we will discuss the fallacies by which those datable texts are deployed to historically position the much larger body of texts whose dating is uncertain.

•

This study has two historical centers. The first is, of course, the period of the poetry under discussion, stretching from uncertain beginnings (no earlier than the end of the first century B.C.) to the last part of the third century. The second historical center is the literary world of Jiankang, the capital of the Southern Dynasties, from the late fifth to the middle of the sixth century, the "Qi and Liang." The scholars of this latter period edited, anthologized, and offered critical judgments on the poetry of the first period. They were the primary mediators through whom later ages received this poetry, and it is no exaggeration to say that the beginning of Chinese classical poetry is as much their creation as it is the creation of poets working two and a half to three centuries earlier. In some cases it is clear that literary men of the Qi and Liang attributed, knowingly or not, more recent poems to the early period in order to flesh out the corpus of early poetry.

To understand both our early "historical centers" and how this poetry reached the Qi and Liang, it is essential to keep in mind that we are talking not so much about poems and poets as about manuscripts. It is easy to overlook this because those manuscripts no longer exist. The modern notion of the "text" as a disembodied thing that transcends any particular paper version is very much the consequence of print culture and mass reproduction. These texts, however, existed in physical manuscripts, some no doubt in unique copies at some stage of their transmission. Judging from our knowledge of Tang practice, poems were often written down from memory, where the production of variants and variation was the norm. Manuscripts were copied and recopied with different degrees of care, also introducing variants. The "text" was highly flammable. We know that central libraries were plundered and burned. We know that the status of poetry in the five syllable line attained unprecedented heights in the Qi and Liang, and the scholars of the period showed an interest in the beginnings of classical poetry, an interest for which we have little earlier evidence. We can assume with some confidence that the court literary circles of the Qi and Liang produced beautiful and careful manuscripts of early poetry. We have, however, far less confidence in the quality of the manuscripts they were copying, and we have good evidence that they "fixed" texts according to their own standards of taste.

The only extensive Chinese manuscript library that survives is that of Dunhuang, many centuries later. It is such a peculiar case—a provincial Buddhist library on the margins of Chinese civilization—that it cannot serve as a perfect model, but it is the only model we have. What we find there is what might be expected: there is great variety in the quality of manuscripts, ranging from those prepared with meticulous care to barely literate manuscripts riddled with mistakes. To a large degree the level of care taken is proportional to the "importance" accorded the work being copied. It is an unfortunate fact of cultural history that what was unimportant in one age may become very important in another. Historians of song lyrics (*ci* 詞) surely would wish that those copyists had taken the same care in copying early songs that others took in preparing a fine copy of the eighth-century poet Gao Shi's works.

If we carry this lesson back to the earlier period under discussion, we know that Qi and Liang scholars did feel that early poetry was important. The manuscripts with which they worked, however, had to pass through generations of copying, and, as we said, we are ignorant of the scholarly care with which those earlier manuscripts were prepared. The Liang monk Sengyou at one point gives us eloquent testimony to the terrible textual state of the Buddhist manuscripts he was working on.

We do have some evidence—though, like much of the material from this period, it is open to varying interpretations. A group of the early anonymous song lyrics and lyrics by Cao princes appears in the "Treatise on Music" ("Yuezhi" 樂志) of the *Song shu* 宋書, compiled by Shen Yue 沈約 (441–513). While the greater part of the *Song shu* was completed in 488, the "Treatise on Music" was not finished until the early sixth century, perhaps at the beginning of the Liang.[1] This work grows out of a tradition of commenting on music (and perhaps preserving lyrics) for court performance, and it is valuable precisely because its motive is conservation rather than pleasing readers interested in poetry. Anyone who has worked with this material

---

1. In his introduction to a scholarly edition of the "Yuezhi," Su Jinren suggests that the final form was not completed until the Liang.

(without the various later emendations) knows that it is filled with errors, transpositions, loan characters, and missing words, along with passages and sometimes whole poems that are utterly incomprehensible. One way to account for this is oral transmission by performers, but Shen Yue's version either is a manuscript transcription or faithfully copies manuscript transcriptions. (Indeed, the only way to account for one of the most learned men of his age writing down texts in this way is a commitment to the exact reproduction of his sources.) Some other early poetry probably also circulated orally before it was transcribed; we can never perfectly distinguish the changes to a text that occur in oral transmission, in transcription of oral texts, and in manuscript transmission. Shen Yue's very fidelity to transcribing texts as he had them (including one poem so unreadable that modern scholars do not even venture punctuation) gives us an image of one stage and level of received manuscripts in the late fifth century. The fact that these must have been court manuscripts with a long history of scholarship behind them does not inspire confidence in the quality of manuscripts for less "significant" texts.

The *Yutai xinyong* 玉臺新詠, compiled toward the middle of the sixth century, was intended for readers of poetry who already had an interest in early poetry. A number of poems from the "Treatise on Music" reappear there, albeit often in a very different guise: incongruous passages are dropped; rhyming lines that do not rhyme are made to rhyme; incomprehensible passages are made comprehensible. In *Yutai xinyong* early poetry is stylistically distinct from more recent poetry, but it is poetically comprehensible by early sixth-century and later standards. Some Chinese scholars have argued that the *Yutai xinyong* versions are the original poems and that the versions in the "Treatise on Music" were modified by singers (though why singers would drop rhymes is incomprehensible). The alternative, championed by Jean-Pierre Diény, seems more plausible: in these cases Xu Ling 徐陵, the editor of *Yutai xinyong*, took texts from the "Treatise on Music" and edited them for contemporary poetic taste. If we believe that Xu Ling did this with the handful of texts with alternative versions in the "Treatise on Music," what are we to think of the large number of other early texts for which *Yutai xinyong* is the only primary source? As we will see, we have some other traces of sixth-century editorial practices, traces that remind us that the production of anthologies and manuscript texts was an active procedure rather than a passive copying of received manuscripts.

We know Xu Ling's name, and we can guess his role in shaping many of the texts that have come to represent early classical poetry. In that era, however, there are also many forgotten names of editors and scribes—all doing little things to texts. We know that scholars then believed in fixing errors in manuscripts, but a sixth-century scholar's "error" might be precious evidence to the scholar of the twenty-first century. We can imagine how they tinkered as they copied, changing this, reshaping that, writing down a plausible author. And if this is so, the texts we have do not come from some early moment of "authorship" but from a complex history of changes. Thus, the story of the beginning of Chinese classical poetry is not just a story of the "Han and Wei" but a story of how the Qi and Liang, the late fifth and early sixth centuries, shaped the evidence for a story of "Han and Wei."

As I said above, this study has "two historical centers," but we can never entirely disentangle the first center—classical poetry up to the last part of the third century—from the second center—the Qi and Liang. The two centuries in between our two historical centers also obviously played a very large role, both in transforming received materials and "supplementing" them.

•

The basis of our inquiry begins with the material sources and their nature rather than the usual questions of "genre," "author," or "poem." There are many relatively stable texts: stable in the degree of variation, in the ascription of authorship, and in the title that eventually determined a genre or subgenre. There are, however, just as many or more texts that are fluid in all these essential qualities. Although there was certainly a very loose sense of poetic genre in the third century, the genre system that we now know was a product of the Qi and Liang and remained relatively fluid even through the Tang. If we think of "authorship" as a property of a text, like a title, then we can see that in many cases it was something added by inference, just as titles so often were. We can also see the point at which anonymity came into being as a value in its own right. A poetic text that simply circulates without a name does not become "anonymous" until it enters a literary regimen where names are assigned, decided, and arranged in chronological order.

A primary focus on sources rather than genre allows us to see *yuefu*, a genre on which much ink has been spilled, first and foremost as a bibliographical category. If there is a *yuefu* "genre," it is to some degree a genre of manuscript rather than of poetry. Certain kinds of poetic texts were preserved primarily or exclusively in this bibliographical category, but many texts could appear in other kinds of manuscripts as well (such as "poetry" anthologies). Its lore of musical categories and their origins—transmitted long after the music was lost—was a particular—and, one might even say, peculiar—tradition of scholarship with its own protocols. Some part of that manuscript tradition survived to inform Guo Maoqian's great compendium, the *Yuefu shiji* 樂府詩集, completed around the turn of the twelfth century. Guo clearly relied heavily on the mid-sixth-century *Gujin yuelu* 古今樂錄, which postdates the age of scholarly consolidation of early sources in the Qi and Liang. This was but one work among many, which leads to the disturbing question: To what degree is one important part of our knowledge of early *yuefu*—a field rich in disputed lore even in the early period—a function of the chance survival of one or a few works into the Song? The lore we derive is interesting, sometimes useful, and often ambiguous. And what do we do when a passage of a *yuefu* is cited in a seventh-century encyclopedia under a different title from a different musical category? We might wishfully attribute this to the carelessness of the encyclopedist. We might also see this as the trace of one of the other manuscripts of texts in the musical tradition, lost before the Song. Or, just as likely, we might infer that the same passage occurred in several different *yuefu*.

•

Delimiting the scope of material for this study presents certain problems, which I will hide in the term "classical poetry." By classical poetry, I mean a kind of shared poetic practice of uncertain origin but which appears in history in the last part of the second century in the informal poetry of the elite. Until the end of the third century, it remained fundamentally poetry in a low register, though, as we will see, it took on relatively high register forms on certain social occasions. It never acquired the allusiveness or lexical range of archaizing poetry in the four syllable line or of ambitious poetic expositions (*fu* 賦). Its conventions also differ from the "Chu style" lyrics (two hemistiches divided by *xi* 兮) that were relatively common in the Eastern Han.

Classical poetry in this sense centers primarily on verse in the five syllable line, though meter must be understood as a contingent form of realization; we can find the same material realized in four syllable lines, six syllable lines, seven syllable lines, and in verses with lines of irregular length. What this poetry shares are themes, topics, sequences of exposition, templates, and a range of verbal habits that we will discuss at length in the course of this study. Thus it includes a large part of the anonymous *yuefu*—though not, say, the *yuefu* category "Naoge," whose poems share almost none of those conventions we mentioned. It includes the anonymous "old poems," the pieces from the Li Ling corpus, and much of the five syllable verse by known poets through the first part of the third century.

This poetry has a low register base that is, in some sense, "popular." I am not unaware of the irony in calling this poetry classical poetry; and yet that is part of the story of this book: how low register poetry was preserved and made "classical."

•

In the first chapter we take up the issue of "Han" poetry, including the evidence that the anonymous *yuefu* and old poems date from the Han, and the issues around the manuscript transmission of this material. Then we will trace how a literary historical account of classical poetry before the Jian'an Reign took shape in the fifth and early sixth centuries, including the deployment of the "old poems" in that story. Finally, we will consider the evidence for the early use of the five syllable line.

The second chapter treats compositional practice, from common "topics" (*topoi*) to themes to the way in which pieces are combined and borrowed in different poems. "Historicizing" can also mean escaping from untenable constructions of history. By treating this corpus as "one poetry" in varying realizations, as if synchronic, we find that problem passages and poems become clear within sets of other poems of the same kind. At the end of this chapter, we show how material from outside "classical poetry" is integrated into it.

In the third and fourth chapters we take up two related themes: immortals and the feast. The procedures for attaining immortality had fixed sequences, and we show how those sequences became mapped onto the sequences of topics within a theme. Here we also will begin to probe the margins of this poetry, how it went beyond convention in some pieces by Cao Cao and Cao Zhi. The themes of the feast and immortality were very close, along with meditation on mortality; in the following chapter we will see the thematic crossovers. Finally, we look at a high register composition by Wang Can and see how a shared poetic language of low register poetry was the model for the creation of high register poetry.

Questions of authorship and persona are the concern of the fifth chapter. We begin with some texts of questionable attribution as a way of thinking of authorship less as a verifiable historical truth than as a property of a text, part of the way in which it comes to be read, even to the extent that it becomes part of the work's textual evolution. We close with a short reception history of what is now one of Cao Zhi's best-known *yuefu*, tracing it from its first appearance in *Yuefu shiji* around the turn of the twelfth century through a series of critics who gave it a secure place in the "Cao Zhi story."

Finally, we come to the "imitations" of the "Nineteen Old Poems," primarily those of Lu Ji at the end of the third century. After discussing the specific meaning of *ni* 擬, "imitation," we use those texts to reflect on the "old poems" as Lu Ji knew them, over two centuries before the texts that we have, dating from the first part of the sixth century.

•

To write on this period is to engage a mass of scholarship that is formidable—in Chinese, in Japanese, and in European languages. I recall a legendary Harvard Chinese dictionary project of many decades past; in its desire to be truly comprehensive, it never got past the first word: *yi* 一, "one." The present work could have been much longer, but I yielded to more moderate ambitions. This work intersects with the work of a number of scholars, including that of my teacher Hans Frankel, who has been a seminal figure in the study of early poetry. This present work grows out of his teaching, slowly germinating over the course of three decades. It was he who taught me to begin to think of poetry as a shared practice rather than as a collection of "creations" by individual poets. To anyone reading these pages the debt is clear. I think the changes that have occurred over those decades are no less clear. These changes in large measure follow from scholarship on manuscript traditions during the past decades, breaking down the boundary between written and oral and between "folk" and literati. We do indeed have clear traces of "orality" in the most basic sense—a consonantal final influencing the following initial—but this could as easily be the trace of Chinese editing practice (one scholar reading and the other, sitting facing him, writing) as of the transcription of singers' practice.

Suzuki Shūji's *Kan Gi shi no kenkyū* (A study of Han and Wei poetry) is another work to which I owe a great debt. Rereading it after three decades reminds one that scholarship of a certain depth does have permanence. Quite apart from his immense erudition, he long ago opened my eyes to the conventionality of the material, how passages move back and forth, and how versions change in different sources. Coming back to this book after trying to work things out on my own, I see how clearly I am following directions he set. My third great debt is to the work of Jean-Pierre Diény. Many of the wheels I thought I invented were first invented by him; his willingness to set aside old assumptions and think about the material afresh, combined with erudition and meticulous scholarship, should be a primary guide for any student in this field. Finally, every scholar of the poetry of this period owes a debt of dependency to Lu Qinli (1911–73), both for his vast efforts in compiling the sources and for the critical intelligence that informed his learning. Many of us first studied this period using Ding Fubao's compendium (based on Feng Weine's *Gushiji* of the mid-sixteenth century) and looking at indices or encyclopedias and the Li Shan commentary to find sources and variants. When Lu Qinli's work, with its meticulous notation of sources and variants, appeared in 1983, it truly changed the field.

The arguments made in this book have some resonance with oral formulaic theory. In *The Bell and the Drum:* Shih Ching *as*

Formulaic Poetry in the Oral Tradition, Wang Ching-hsien applied Parry and Lord's oral formulaic theory to the *Shijing*. Hans Frankel was primarily responsible for proposing an oral formulaic base for anonymous *yuefu*. Gary Shelton Williams's 1973 dissertation, "A Study of the Oral Nature of the Han Yüeh-fu," offers a more fully developed discussion of *yuefu* based on oral formulaic theory, but he takes the received texts as stable transcriptions of Han materials, as do some theoretically sophisticated discussions, such as those in Christopher Connery's *Empire of the Text: Writing and Authority in Early Imperial China*. Much thoughtful work was done along oral formulaic lines, but from a contemporary perspective it is often based on assumptions that no longer seem tenable.

Since even in their putative Han origins *yuefu* appeared in the context of a moderately literate culture, the anonymous *yuefu* are either attributed to the "folk" or, in Frankel's far more plausible suggestion, professional singers. The need for the "folk" or professional singers was one legacy of Parry's and Lord's versions of oral formulaic theory, presuming an absolute barrier between the literati and the preliterate or illiterate singer. Walter J. Ong's 1982 study *Orality and Literacy* helped to bridge this division by means of a notion of "secondary orality," reflecting on how the processes of orality continued to function in a literate world. Although he tries to address the very long periods of transition between preliteracy and modern literacy, modern literacy remains the standard by which he conceives of literacy.[2] In two important recent articles, "Were *Yüeh-fu* Ever Folk Songs? Reconsidering the Relevance of Oral Theory and Balladry Analogies" and "Reconsidering the Role of Folk Songs in Pre-T'ang *Yüeh-fu* Development," Charles Egan surveys the scholarship, reexamines the evidence, and comes

---

2. In some other venue there would be much to address in detail in these questions, such as the narrative of progress or fall from grace implied in terms like "preliterate" and "secondary orality," and their relation to a lapsarian myth of writing, begun by Plato and retold in different guises across millennia in the European tradition. One of Ong's chapters echoes the weight of this myth very well: "Writing restructures consciousness." It would be best to reconsider the matter with a fuller range of particular cases. What is true of Homer or an illiterate Serbian singer of tales may not be true of an equally illiterate but highly professional medieval Welsh bard, composing an *awdl* under severe formal restrictions for a court presentation.

to a number of conclusions that overlap with those of the present study. Egan, as I do, questions the Han dating of the anonymous *yuefu* and their association with the "folk." In the first of these articles, Egan provides a survey of earlier and more recent scholarship on oral formulaic theory and its application to the case of *yuefu*. In the second of these studies, Egan links the Shen Yue material specifically with performance traditions and the state support for reviving orthodox music.

Understanding the complex interplay between literacy and orality (and adding generations of scribes between some hypothetical moment of origin and the texts we have), oral formulaic theory now becomes important primarily as the ancestor of diverse lines of inquiry regarding the production and circulation of texts in manuscript culture. In the present study, I would like to set aside oral formulaic theory, along with its baggage focusing on the question of literacy. Working under the assumption that writing has important consequences but does not "restructure consciousness," I will try to account for the historical nature of variation and reproduction in written texts, which are all we have. At different moments and in different cultural venues, we can see free variation, transformation according to different needs, forces for conservation, and the modification of texts for changed literary values.

•

Discussing this poetry inevitably involves covering ground that has been covered before. However, I think the differences should also be clear. By thinking of manuscripts and manuscript traditions, we escape from some of the artificial boundaries of genre as later conceived and from assumptions of historical priority that change the way we understand differences between texts as part of a narrative of change. We can think of the encyclopedia sources not as excerpts but as versions, accepting that in manuscript culture texts usually changed wording and size whenever they were written down. One of the most telling moments in Suzuki's *Kan Gi shi no kenkyū*, to which I will return, are the nine occasions of citing the final lines of Li Yannian's song for Lady Li, none of which are identical. Decisions about "correct versions" are largely functions of an age of literary scholarship and print culture and of compendia (like *Yuefu shiji*) that place different versions side by side.

One theoretically informed recent work also deserves mention. Joseph Allen's *In the Voice of Others* generously includes the "Nineteen Old Poems" within the scope of *yuefu*, but his is a study of genre and how a genre and its subfamilies are constructed by later works that align themselves in relation to earlier works. I do not dispute his general insights. However, I am concerned with early poetry and how it is organized into a history of poetry in the Qi and Liang. Although Allen agrees that the genre of *yuefu* underwent a slow process of formation, he looks at it from the later period when the genre was well formed enough to be called such. Although he raises the question regarding the assumption that early anonymous works in the *yuefu* tradition are "Han," he adopts a later perspective that grants those poems priority. Most of all, Allen accepts the texts and attributions as they are preserved in the dominant sources and does not address the fluidity of the material, which is a central concern here.

Coming to Terms with Early Poetry

Many of the discussions in this study involve recurring patterns in groups of texts. I sometimes call these patterns "compositional technique"—not because we have any historical knowledge of how poems were actually composed but because, in their relative predictability, these patterns seem to guide the composition, offering templates for how to phrase lines and anticipating "what to say next." This is a useful way to think of this poetry because it involves a repertoire of knowledge that is not restricted to writers of poetry alone; those who heard and passed on the poetry had the same competence. Perhaps some of the extant texts of Jian'an and early Wei poems are indeed exactly as a poet wrote them down, but we are considering poetry that has come to us through layers of reproduction—by those who repeated poems, by those who wrote the poems down, and by those who copied manuscripts. We have considerable evidence that the texts of poems changed in this process—in some cases significantly. But insofar as the early participants in this process shared a competence—what I am calling "compositional technique"—such textual change still was part of an ongoing practice. When we arrive at the sixth century we can see other kinds of changes introduced into textual reproduction, changes that reveal a very different sense of how poetry works; not surprisingly, the poetics of reproduction here is consistent with the way poems were written in the sixth century.

We may eventually want to return to consider "poets" and "poems" as fixed texts, but it is useful to begin by thinking of "poetic material," with particular texts not as independent "creations" but as realizations of one piece of a shared repertoire. Any particular realization is not stable over time. The text itself changes; its title or category often changes; sometimes its meter changes; sometimes it loses or gains or changes an author. Sometimes by the good fortune of reputation—but far more often by chance—a manuscript with one particular version of a text survived. People interested in literature read those manuscripts from the fifth century on to the end of manuscript culture in the early Northern Song. It is through these mediators that we possess the poetry we do have. When they read, they were looking for something—and they were overlooking texts that did not suit their purposes. In compiling the *Wen xuan*, Xiao Tong was looking for texts that were "important"— his sense of literary importance—guided by a new critical interest in literary history in his day. Xu Ling, while compiling the *Yutai xinyong*, was looking for texts that were enjoyable to a contemporary audience. The Sui and Tang encyclopedists were looking for texts with material that addressed a predetermined set of headings. Guo Maoqian was saving everything he could from the remnants of collections of musical poetry, *yuefu*—but, working in the late Northern Song, he had only chance survivals from what had once been an extensive corpus of texts. Both our current canon of early classical poetry and pieces we neglect are only remnants, surviving into the mass reproduction of print culture through accident and the motives of later ages.

The term "intertextuality" is probably inappropriate for early classical poetry. Intertextuality presumes a relationship between "texts." We can safely assume that many more poems were composed in the early period than have been preserved. Except for a very few exchange poems and poems presented in the presence of Cao Cao or Cao Pi, we have absolutely no idea who, in this period, heard or read which other poem. If a surviving poem was indeed responding to some particular other contemporary poem, we probably don't have that poem. The kind of intertextuality that is so important in later Chinese poetry is usually inaccessible here—and perhaps even irrelevant. A poet did not need to think of any particular prior case because he had read or heard many poems "of the same kind" and knew many lines that followed a certain pattern. As in language acquisition itself, the multiplication of particular utterances leads to language as a virtual set of possibilities, rules, and habits. What we are describing here is neither "oral formulaic" theory nor the poetics of stable textuality. We might describe this as something in between the two, but it has elements distinct from both.

I need words to describe this practice. No terminology can be used with perfect consistency, and no terminology is precise. Terminology is a way of enforcing a set of conceptual relations that become persuasive by becoming habitual. Some prefer the promise of radical difference in neologisms; some like the resonance of borrowing old words with histories and semantic depth. I tend toward the latter practice, though I need to be explicit about how I am twisting old words. I will return to refine some of these terms in the main body of the study as they are used in particular cases.

The easiest and perhaps best way to think of this practice is "composition by theme." We can easily list a limited set of themes that account for most of the poems in the five syllable line (probably) composed before the last decades of the third century—as well as a significant body of poems in irregular lines and a smaller corpus of poems in four syllable lines. In thinking of themes, the figure of the roadmap is useful. Some themes seem to lead easily into other themes; sometimes at a particular point one could go in various directions—these are contiguous thematic "territories." Some themes never cross. As we will see later in this study, meditation on human mortality can lead to the quest for immortality, to the feast, or to encouragement to "work hard." These can crisscross in interesting ways. "Sleepless on an autumn night," however, is a very common theme, but it leads to none of the sets of themes just mentioned. It does, however, easily connect with the theme of separation, which in turn has a route connecting it to the feast poem. Just as maps are possible itineraries, a sequence of themes is a potential narrative.

I use the term "theme" in a large and general sense, as it is commonly used. To name some of the usual themes in this poetry is at the same time to remind us how limited the range of themes actually is. The thematic range of later classical poetry is vastly broader. Early classical poetry has a limited scope, but its limitation is part of its appeal.

The second term I use is "topic." Let me first explain the history behind this choice. The English topic is a derivative of the Greek *topos*, "place." The Greek term was brought back into critical usage because of the unfortunate fate of its expanded Latin translation, *locus communis*, which in English literally became a "commonplace." In rhetoric it simply means something often repeated, but it acquired in English pejorative associations. I prefer a twisted sense of the English "topic" to the revived Greek *topos* as a technical term because I want us to think of the phenomenon somewhat differently. A *topos* is a "figure of thought"; it is one particular kind of utterance one recognizes within a larger discourse. That is, we think of it as one possibility within discourse rather than the fundamental constituent of discourse. (If I am talking about something else and add "Ah, but life is short," that is a *topos*.) "Topics," as I am using the term, are pervasive; they are the constituent components of themes in early poetry. Another way of putting this is that a "theme" is essentially a series of habitually associated topics. In their thematic unfolding, topics have a sequence that is more or less variable, but the process involves expectations that certain things will be mentioned in a roughly predictable order. Topics sometimes also have "templates," line patterns with certain words in fixed positions expressing roughly the same semantic content.

This brings us to variation, which is one of the most difficult issues. To one who is used to this poetry, the significance of variation is not difficult at all; one recognizes immediately different kinds of variation. The difficulty is to describe those differences on a general level. Lines are always varied: they are varied by poets, by hypothetical transmitters who repeat the line, and by scribes.

Given five syllables with a caesura after the second syllable and a limited number of grammatical functions in a positional language, it is not surprising that early poetry in the five syllable line had a limited number of grammatical patterns. Some lines became what I will call "template" lines: this is a grammatical pattern, often with one or two words in the same position, with the other positions in the line variable by synonyms or by conceptual class (for example, "I hitch up my robes," "I put on clothes," "I wear my shoes," "I tie up my belt"). Some template lines are strongly linked to topics within a particular theme, while some serve functional positions in the taxis of a poem. An example of the latter is opening a poem with the following pattern: "At place X there is, *you* 有 (or 'there is much,' *duo* 多), Y," in the form XX *you* YY.

Although it is not at all uncommon to find the same lines and phrases in a wide variety of poems, these patterns were "templates" for variation of the sort described. As poetry moved up the social hierarchy—not necessarily by the social position of the poet but often by the formality of the circumstance—lexical register became an important part of variation. A range of words were marked as "elevated." We will thus speak of "low register" poetry and "high register" poetry, referring to the way education, social status, and the public gravity of the moment can be encoded in lexical choices and, increasingly, in grammatical patterns.

•

One other kind of recurring sequence is important; it is related to habitual sequences of topics but can exist independently. These are sets of words appearing in roughly the same sequence in different lines. That is, in a standard sequence of topics "A then B," we often find word X in topic A, and word Y in topic B. Even if the poem varies the topic or changes its theme, we may still find the sequence of word X followed by word Y.

Another related phenomenon is the return of a displaced word. If a poet rephrases a common line and omits an anticipated word for the sake of variation or the need of rhyme, the displaced word will often appear, sometimes in a different sense, in the following line or couplet.

These two cases of recurring pattern on the level of particular words, independent of the meanings of the lines in which the words are used, are reminders of the degree to which this poetry can be purely *verbal* as well as thematic. Although such word sets often occur with themes, their recurring presence is independent of the sense of the lines in which those words are used.

One conclusion I have reached in the course of this study is that sequences, whether of topics or words, often have an inertia that transcends poetic argument and, at best, drives it. When I read a Cao Pi *yuefu* that closes with paired birds flying away and cannot understand what that image has to do with the long poem preceding it, I have learned to look for some habitual sequence of topics that would call for those birds: in this case the poem contained a long passage on music, which is commonly followed by an image of paired birds flying away. To those who would believe that a verbal poem is the expression of some prior concern or "poetic idea," we must respond that here poetry is to a large degree a verbal mechanism that often creates beautiful poetry unreflectively.

•

Variation can occur in the length of a text as well as in the words. Poets can, of course, vary the treatment of a theme between terseness and copiousness. But in reproduction as well, poems can grow and shrink. We can see this commonly in texts where several versions survive and in comparing "originals" with line-by-line imitations. Scholarly habits firmly in place in both the "West" and East Asia look for the text as it existed in the moment of production. Nothing could be more misleading in understanding early poetry: this was a poetry that existed and comes to us through reproduction—by those who knew the poem and passed it on, by musicians who performed the poem, and by scribes and literary anthologists of a later era. All of these people in situations of reproduction took the liberty to change the text to suit their needs, and, as we will see, the traces of those changes are often still quite visible. Poems grew and shrank with some freedom.

We can see what the boundaries of a single theme are, but we don't know what the boundaries of a single "poem" are. In many works we see what we will call "segmentary composition," that is, combining formally distinct segments into a longer text.[3] This is clearest in a kind of *yuefu* that we will call "compound *yuefu*," whose sections are often marked by musical terminology in the tradition of manuscripts of musical poetry. Many such compositions have only two distinct segments, sometimes with a couplet wishing blessings on the audience added (there are some that mix many segments, however). In musical terminology there are three predominant section terms: the *yan* 豔, or "prelude," the *jie* 解, or "stanzas," and the *qu* 趨, or "coda." Sometimes we see only one of these; sometimes we see them combined.

In some cases the segments are combined with close thematic coherence, but in other cases the two components have no clear relation to one another. In some cases distinct components have been combined, and the long interpretive tradition has been able to reconcile them into a single "poem."

Although segmentary composition is clearest in *yuefu*, and explicit in those *yuefu* where sections are marked, we also see it in material preserved as "poetry." The markers of transition are a recognizable closing couplet followed by a recognizable opening couplet, usually with a shift of theme.

As we think of early poetry not as a text determined by a moment of production but rather as something continually reproduced, it might be best not to think of "poems" but rather of "poetic performances" in which received material was often combined and recombined.[4] We have a number of cases in which the same segment is reused in different "poetic per-

---

3. See Yu Guanying's "Yuefu geci de pincou he fen'ge" 樂府歌辭的拼湊和分割. Yu Guanying, *Han Wei liuchao shi luncong* 漢魏六朝詩論叢 (Beijing, 1962): 26–38.

4. When I use "performance" in this study, I am not referring to musical performance of song except where specified. I am using the term as a way of thinking of the commonalities in the processes of textual production and reproduction. A useful term needs an opposite. The opposite here would be the exact textual reproduction of a textual original, whether in the conservatory textual practice of compiling the *Song shu* or later scholarly practice—the scribal equivalent of photocopying.

formances." Combining segments may have been the norm not only in musical performance but also in recitation; and we cannot decide if two segments joined together are "two poems" or "one poem." If we have a *yuefu* preserved under Cao Pi's name with a segment on becoming an immortal, followed by a second segment in a different rhyme attacking belief in the immortals, there is something at stake in this question of "one poem" or "two poems." If we suppose a single author composing such a poem with a purpose, then the closing critique of the cult of immortality is the "meaning"; if, however, compounding segments was indeed the norm, as it often seems to have been in musical presentation, then might not a poet also have combined two segments in the "moment of production"? In this second case we would have a medley. What survives is only the form in which poetic material entered manuscript traditions and was transmitted in manuscript traditions. The bibliographical genre of manuscripts of musical poetry often preserved compound segments. Manuscripts of poetry seem to have preferred single segments—or they preserved "sets."

•

One other kind of variation needs to be addressed, namely, metrical variation. The same poetic material could be realized in different meters. Any poet, performer, or editor-scribe could change the meter of many kinds of texts. We can see this clearly in different versions of the same poem. This invites us to think of meter as a possible form in which to realize poetic material. The material itself is formally variable. Here, however, there is a clear tendency later in the tradition to regularize meters (including complaints recorded in the *Song shu* of the variety of meters in received song materials). Scholars often treat *Shijing* lines redone in five syllables as "allusions." They may be full "allusions" in some cases, but there is a range of possibilities: the *Shijing* still existed as an oral repertoire (at the very least "performed" in school recitation and in public situations demonstrating elite learning). There were habitual ways to make a four syllable *Shijing* line into a five syllable line. There is also well into the third century a "popular" four syllable line, which we can see in *yuefu*.

In the five syllable line we can see a rough distinction between low register verse, which can often be redone in four syllables without significant change, and high register verse, which cannot easily be reformulated without significantly changing its semantic value. It is, perhaps, at this moment that we can begin to think of meter as defining "genre."

•

In many ways this book presents the unlovely side of the study of literature, examining both poetry's internal mechanisms and how its broken pieces were singled out and configured to create a luminous whole. The anonymous "old poems" already had an aura by the early fifth century. By the early sixth century they still had an aura, but the nature of that aura was profoundly changed: it was an aura in part produced by their very anonymity, within a new literary historical narrative that set them in a vague Han past. It is hoped that by demystifying both the texts and the cultural narrative in which they have been set, their aura will not diminish but change again into a different kind of beauty.

ONE

*"Han" Poetry and
the Southern Dynasties*

Our current account of poetry in the Han generally mixes together ritual texts, verses, and short songs from texts reliably datable to the Han with a large body of poetry that does not begin to appear securely in the textual record until the early sixth century—and in many cases much later. In the formation of classical poetry, it is this latter body of poetry that is considered by far the most important. Scholars of the poetic category known as *yuefu* 樂府 ("music bureau") poetry inevitably begin with an account of the Western Han institution of the "Music Bureau," sometimes considering the handful of ritual and other verses that can be legitimately associated with the Western Han institution; they then usually move to a kind of verse associated with song but not commonly classified as *yuefu* until perhaps as late as the end of the late fifth or early sixth century.[1] Another body of early texts, the anonymous "old poems" (*gushi* 古詩), shows in the name given them that their categorization is retrospective.[2] There are also a modest number of poems and *yuefu* attributed to Han authors with

---

1. See Appendix A.

2. The history of the use of the term *gushi* 古詩 and what it refers to is complex. Early usages always referred to the poems of the *Shijing*. In a letter to his brother Lu Ji, Lu Yun 陸雲 (262–303) has to specify otherwise: "One day I saw you and Zhengshu [Pan Ni 潘尼] reciting old five-syllable-line poems" 一日見正叔與兄讀古五言詩. Lu Yun 陸雲, *Lu Yun ji* 陸雲集, ed. Huang Kui 黃葵 (Beijing: Zhonghua shuju, 1988), 135. It is possible that this refers to the anonymous "old poems" that Lu Ji imitated. Since the contrast is with current compositions, however, we cannot be sure what is being referred to.

varying degrees of credibility. At the very end of the Eastern Han is the Jian'an Reign (196–219) followed by the Wei Dynasty (220–65), with a far larger number of poems that can be credibly attributed to known authors—though later centuries play an equally important role in their transmission.

We do not, in fact, know when the anonymous "Han *yuefu*" (meaning not the ritual songs but the secular material) or the anonymous "old poems" took their present forms.[3] There is much faith in the Han dating of such texts and little reliable evidence; faith can endure a negative claim (viz. that these texts are *not* Han) more comfortably than the agnostic claim made here. We have a few rough parameters for dating some elements of this corpus. We know from several verses preserved in the *Han shu* that the five syllable line, with its characteristic rhythms, existed in the first century A.D. and perhaps as early as the late first century B.C. We know from a poem preserved on a stele inscription that some of the conventions of such poetry already existed soon after the middle of the second century A.D.[4] On the other end, we have late third-century imitations of particular anonymous "old poems" that follow the current versions line by line; this tells us, with some degree of confidence, that our versions of these particular poems were in circulation in the late third century A.D.

•

Rather than beginning with claims about the putative origins of classical poetry, either in the Western or Eastern Han, and its early development in the third century, the best way to sort out this problematic material might be to look first at the later period which preserves it and comments on it. Our knowledge of early classical poetry comes primarily through the literary scholars of that later era: we still largely follow their judgments,

---

3. See Joseph Allen, *In the Voice of Others* (Ann Arbor: University of Michigan Center for Chinese Studies, 1992), 47–52. Allen points out that the conviction that such poems are Han is a mere assumption; since his interest is in the ways in which later poems need an "original," he does not question the assumption further. See also Charles Egan, "Reconsidering the Role of Folk Songs in Pre-T'ang *Yüeh-fu* Development," *T'oung Pao* 86 (2000): 47–99. Egan questions the evidence for Han dating of *Yuefu* in detail. See Appendix B.

4. Lu Qinli 逯欽立, *Xian-Qin Han Wei Jin Nanbeichao shi* 先秦漢魏晉南北朝詩 (Beijing: Zhonghua shuju, 1983), 175–76. The five syllable line as a set meter can be dated back to the late Western Han, but the examples of certain authenticity use none of the conventions of "old poems" and some *yuefu*.

based on the texts they chose to be remembered, the texts they edited and organized according to their values. We pretend to read the poetry of the "Han and Wei," but we have no direct access to the "Han and Wei": a long history stands between us and that age, and the dominant mediators were the literary communities of the sixth century in Jiankang, the capital of the Southern Dynasties.

Of this later period much more is known—though much still remains uncertain. The literary regimen of the early sixth century was concerned with preserving fixed texts, ascribing authorship (enabling the characterization and judgment of authors), and describing chronological filiations and literary historical changes. This scholarly and critical activity was the foundation for cultural narratives by which these Southern Dynasties literary men defined their own age. This is to say that our understanding of early classical poetry through the last part of the third century is radically mediated by the values of a very different cultural world two centuries later.

Manuscripts

Weighty claims about large cultural or literary changes and smaller claims about the tone and opinions of poets in particular works are based on the continuity of fragile manuscripts. Reflection on the literary history of the early medieval period invites us to think back on what we know about the transmission of texts. Scholars often treat this process as if it were transparent; and when a supposedly Han text appears for the first time in Guo Maoqian's *Yuefu shiji* around the turn of the twelfth century, most scholars do not wonder what happened to that text in the intervening millennium. The literary scholarship that developed in the eleventh century was intensely concerned with sources and accurate texts; since such care generally became the high scholarly norm up to the present, modern scholars generally impute similar care to earlier editors and copyists. And yet, when we look at the different texts that have survived from the age of manuscript culture (through its preservation in print culture), we see little evidence (apart from the canonized *Wen xuan*) of a commitment to exact reproduction of texts. Generally speaking, the more sources we have, the more variations. The song attributed to Li Yannian 李延年, a singer in the court of Emperor Wu of the Han, was often quoted in our various sources; despite the fact that a stable and easily accessible "original" text was preserved in the *Han shu*, the last lines were quoted in nine different variations.[5] These particular variations all preserve roughly the same "sense," but this is not always the case. Our evidence for textual variability begins at the beginning of the sixth century, when the material we are considering—"popular" poetry in the five syllable line and irregular lines—had already achieved the status of a serious genre. We have every reason to wonder about the textual condition in which such material reached the literary world of the early sixth century, especially considering the immense loss of manuscripts with the fall of the North in 317 and uncertain care in transcription.

The "Treatise on Music," *Yue zhi* 樂志, of the *Song shu* represents the careful conservatorial work of generations of scholars of musical poetry; the resulting text has been relatively stable since the early sixth century. Yet anyone who has worked with those early texts in the *Song shu* recognizes all the standard problems of manuscript transmission: loan characters, transpositions, dropped lines, wrong words. It represents exactly the textual problems of which the Liang monk Sengyou 僧祐 complained in Buddhist manuscripts.[6] Rather than a "problem text," the *Song shu* materials probably represent the most accurate representation of the *best* manuscript traditions of transmission of early poetry. The very conservation of their imperfections is a mark of their special status. This, in turn, invites us to think of the processes that shaped the other, textually more perfect poetic material that has survived. The obvious transformation of *Song shu* texts into "poetry" in its early sixth-century sense in *Yutai xinyong* and elsewhere encourages us, at the very least, to ponder the textual condition of other sources no longer extant. It also reminds us that most sixth-century editors and copyists—not working under the special protocols of those charged with preserving imperial musical traditions—changed texts as they saw fit. Literary

---

5. Suzuki Shūji 鈴木修次, *Kan Gi shi no kenkyū* 漢魏詩の研究 (Tokyo: Taishūkan shoten, 1967), 81–82.
6. *Quan Liang wen* 71.12b.

scholarship from the Northern Song on was far closer to the constraints of the scholars of the musical tradition; it is anachronistic, however, to assume the same constraints on Xu Ling, compiling the *Yutai xinyong* as an anthology for reading pleasure.

The critical and editorial work of the early sixth century was based on a rich manuscript culture. Our understanding of the range of that manuscript culture largely derives from the "Bibliography" ("Jingji zhi" 經籍志) of the *Sui shu*, which was compiled in the early seventh century, but which incorporates what is clearly a bibliography from the Liang (502–54).[7]

Zhi Yu's 摯虞 *Wenzhang liubie* 文章流別 from the late third century is generally considered the first general anthology of belles lettres.[8] Fragments of its general discussions and genre headings survive, and it seems to have begun with poetic expositions and poetry, like its extant sixth-century descendant, the *Wen xuan*. While Zhi Yu must have included examples of poetry in the five syllable line in a range of poetic meters,[9] his extant comments on poetry strongly favor the archaic four syllable line: not only did he consider the four syllable line "correct" (*zheng* 正), but his only surviving comments on particular poems name five praiseworthy pieces by Wang Can, all in the four syllable line.[10] It seems quite possible that this

---

7. An account of the libraries and bibliographical work of the period is given in the introduction to the "Classics" section of the "Bibliography" of the *Sui shu* (pp. 906–8). Although numerous bibliographies are listed there, the *Sui shu* "Bibliography" itself generally notes some versions as "Liang" and sometimes also as "lost." This indicates that the "Bibliography" is not simply a catalogue of texts extant at the time of composition but is comparing extant texts with an earlier bibliography.

8. For a discussion of a roughly contemporary anthology, *Shanwen* 善文, see Deng Guoguang 鄧國光, *Zhi Yu yanjiu* 摯虞研究 (Hong Kong: Xueheng chubanshe, 1990), 175–76. See also David Knechtges, *Wen xuan or Selections of Refined Literature*, vol. 1 (Princeton: Princeton University Press, 1982), 3–4. For a discussion of other lost early anthologies, see Fu Gang 傅剛, *Zhaoming wenxuan yanjiu* 昭明文選研究 (Beijing: Zhongguo shehui kexue chubanshe, 2000), 17–100.

9. See Yan Yanzhi's comment, cited in Deng Guoguang, *Zhi Yu yanjiu*, 174. See also Yu Yuan 郁沅 and Zhang Minggao 張明高, *Wei Jin Nanbeichao wenlun xuan* 魏晉南北朝文論選 (Beijing: Renmin wenxue chubanshe, 1996), 273.

10. See Deng Guoguang, *Zhi Yu yanjiu*, pp. 185, 191. It is possible to read the fragment of Yan Yanzhi's *Tinggao* 庭誥 (*Taiping yulan* 586.3a) as praising the Li Ling poems, thus implying their inclusion.

anthology excluded poetry in a lower register, and thus all anonymous poems. We can infer only a few of Zhi Yu's selections from his critical comments, and we know almost nothing of the contents of the general anthologies between *Wenzhang liubie* and the *Wen xuan*. We can only speculate that they certainly must have gradually come to include more poetry in the five syllable line as the form gained prestige over the course of the fifth century.[11]

Poetry anthologies (as opposed to broader anthologies of all literary genres) are grouped together in the "Bibliography." The first two titles strongly suggest collections of poetry in the four syllable line, perhaps technically "hymns," *song* 頌. The third poetry anthology was done by the poet Xie Lingyun 謝靈運 (385–433) and was clearly a foundational text for subsequent poetry anthologies. Given its size and apparent popularity, Xie's anthology must have been largely of poetry in the five syllable line; Zhong Rong 鍾嶸, who restricted his interests to poetry in the five syllable line, referred to it in his preface to *Gradations of Poetry, Shipin* 詩品, criticizing it for a lack of selectivity.[12] Listed after Xie's anthology is *The Beautiful Writing of Ancient and Modern Poems in the Five Syllable Line, Gujin wuyanshi meiwen* 古今五言詩美文, in five scrolls, attributed to Xun Chuo 荀綽.[13] At the very least the form of the title suggests a descriptive title added much later. (A review of the "Bibliography" suggests that anthologies changed size and title, and Sengyou noted of Buddhist manuscripts that "sometimes one book has several names and sometimes several books share a

---

11. Many of these anthologies begin with the term *ji* 集, a "[literary] collection," which possibly suggests that they are drawn entirely from the collections of known authors; e.g., *Jilin* 集林, *Jiyuan* 集苑, *Jichao* 集鈔, and *Jilüe* 集略. But we might note Fu Gang's speculation that *Jilin* included tales; see Fu Gang, *Zhaoming wenxuan yanjiu*, 40.

12. Xie Lingyun twice worked in the imperial library, and Zhong Rong criticized Xie for including every poem he happened on. Since the "Bibliography" lists numerous expansions and anthologies that seem to be selective condensations of Xie's anthology (judging from the shorter length and the term "flower," *ying* 英, in the title), we get a sense of its popularity. It is tempting to link the appearance of this anthology with the resurgence of interest in early poetry in the mid-fifth century, when we find the first imitations of "old poems" after a century and a half, along with a large increase in literary *yuefu*.

13. See Appendix C.

single name" 或一本數名, 或一名數本.)[14] There was a Xun Chuo
who was a distinguished scholar of the Western Jin, and no-
where else is such an anthology credited to him. If the an-
thology was indeed late Western Jin, it would certainly have
been the earliest anthology of poetry.

Immediately after Xun Chuo's anthology, Xie's anthology,
and the spin-offs of Xie's anthology, we see a suggestive title,
the anonymous *Collection of Old Poems, Gushi ji* 古詩集.[15] Such
a collection may have included the anonymous "old poems,"
but it would have had to also include poems by known "old"
authors through the third century and perhaps later. In short,
we know very little. We do know, however, that the loss of texts
when the Jin fled south in 317 was immense.[16] We can feel

---

14. *Quan Liang wen* 71.12b.

15. Most anthologies cannot be dated except by their position in a roughly
chronological sequence in the *Sui shu* "Bibliography." Suzuki believes this work
was the source for the anonymous "old poems" (Suzuki, *Kan Gi*, 301), but this
is by no means certain, and it probably postdates Xie Lingyun's anthology.
With nine scrolls, it must have contained far more than the fifty-nine "old
poems" mentioned by Zhong Rong; if nothing else, this shows us that the usage
"old poem" was not restricted to anonymous poems.

16. The Wei and Western Jin library contained almost 30,000 scrolls; in the
early Eastern Jin only 3,014 scrolls survived (though some others were re-
covered later). Before he took the throne and founded the Song in 420, Liu Yu
was supposed to have brought back 4,000 scrolls from his northern campaign.
When Xie Lingyun served in the imperial library, he listed over 64,000 scrolls.
Xie Lingyun was probably counting duplicate titles (i.e., a "catalogue" rather
than a "bibliography"), because in a bibliography of 473 Wang Jian listed only
15,704 scrolls. A Qi bibliography listed 18,010 scrolls, and a Liang bibliogra-
phy, 23,106 (*Sui shu*, 906–7). Setting aside Xie Lingyun's inflated numbers,
this sounds like a reasonable growth curve, allowing for the recovery of texts
after the beginning of the Eastern Jin and increased activity in the Liang. Even
the Liang library, however, had not reached the size of the Wei library cata-
logue. We might set these figures beside the *Sui shu* bibliography itself, which
gives 14,466 titles in 89,666 scrolls. Most of these were in areas other than
literature (individual collections totaled 4,381 scrolls and anthologies of all
sorts 2,213 scrolls). That is, only somewhat over 7 percent of the works listed
were in the category of belles lettres. If such proportions held roughly true in
earlier periods, not much literature survived the transition to the Eastern Jin
(the Sui ratio of literary texts to nonliterary texts would mean that only 220
scrolls of literary works initially survived into the Eastern Jin); and it is quite
possible that Liu Yu's captured manuscripts provided a major impetus to the
interest in poetry in the fifth century. The imperial libraries of the Southern
Dynasties obviously gradually rebuilt the collection of early works from private
libraries and probably from trade with the North; but if the proportions hold (in
the case of individual collections, about 4.8 percent of the whole), the *Sui shu*

some confidence in works that were recopied in the setting of an imperial library. When the imperial library is lost, however, and works must be recovered from other sources, such confidence is lost. The number of occasions on which central libraries were destroyed between the fall of the Western Jin and the print culture of the Northern Song should be kept in mind.

When we look at the possible bibliographical sources for early anonymous poetry, we note that one important distinction is made in the *Sui shu* "Bibliography": "poetry" anthologies and anthologies of verse in the musical tradition (containing the material we now identify as *yuefu*) are grouped separately.[17] When we find, as we often do, the same material realized differently in "poetry" and anonymous *yuefu*, we may be seeing not a "generic" distinction in the purely literary sense but a difference in the textual conventions of those distinct venues of preservation. If the fifteenth of the "Nineteen Old Poems" reappears almost verbatim in the *yuefu* "West Gate" 西門行, it might be anachronistic and unhelpful to ask (as scholars sometimes have) whether singers have expanded an "old poem" for the needs of song or a "poet" has reworked lines from an earlier *yuefu*. Rather, we might think of poetic "material" that is realized differently in terms of different kinds of conventions of textuality.

Collections of lyrics in the musical tradition grew out of a long interest in conserving old ritual and court music; the anonymous, apparently "popular" lyrics that are now so prized were probably once pieces performed for informal court occasions and part of a repertoire preserved from this essentially conservatorial impulse. Whatever the possible or imagined "folk" origins of some of these anonymous *yuefu*, it is important to keep in mind that these survived as court traditions for centuries.[18]

One apparent feature of such collections—at least judging from the "Treatise on Music" of the *Song shu* and the *Yuefu shiji*

---

bibliography records only about half as many pre-317 collections as would have been held in the Wei and Western Jin imperial library. The assumptions made in arriving at such figures render them highly dubious; I include them simply as a supplement to the argument.

17, See Appendix C.

18. Suzuki Shūji is one of the few earlier scholars who insistently remind us of the point; see, e.g., *Kan Gi*, 186. Charles Egan also stresses this point.

citations from works such as the *Yuanjia zhengsheng jilu* 元嘉
正聲技錄 by Zhang Yong 張永 (410–75), the "Record of Per-
formers," *Jilu* 技錄 (or 伎錄) by Wang Sengqian 王僧虔 (426–85),
and Zhijiang's 智匠 *Gujin yuelu* 古今樂錄 of 568—was the in-
clusion of lore about these songs.[19] This reminds us of the
fundamental difference between the poetry anthologies and
these collections of lyrics in the musical tradition: the poetry
anthologies were intended for reading pleasure, while collec-
tions of lyrics in the musical tradition seem to have been in-
tended to correct and conserve court musical traditions with
their lore. Certainly the "Treatise on Music" in the *Song shu*,
our one complete extant early source in this tradition, was
conservatorial. None of these collections of verse in the musical
tradition have titles such as we find in poetry anthologies: the
"flower" (*ying* 英 or *yinghua* 英華), suggesting selection of the
"best" for the pleasure of readers. Our two extant literary an-
thologies of the period, both Liang, do include anonymous
yuefu with poetry (though the *Wen xuan* has very few); however,
comparison of these with versions in the "Treatise on Music"
suggests that in most cases the versions in the musical tradi-
tion were modified for literary taste when included in literary
anthologies.[20]

The tradition has divided anonymous works into "*yuefu*" and
"old poems"; this has been understood as a "generic distinc-
tion," but, as we observed earlier, this may largely be a con-
sequence of the primary venue of preservation of the text under
consideration. When we look at how such works have been
cited in other early sources, we see that passages of *yuefu* are
very commonly cited as "old poems" and passages of "old po-
ems" are just as often cited as *yuefu*.[21] The only significant

---

19. For information on Zhijiang and the *Gujin yuelu*, see Nakatsuhama
Wataru 中津濱涉, *Gafu shishū no kenkyū* 樂府詩集の研究 (Tokyo: Kyūko shoin,
1970), 614–15. *Gujin yuelu* is listed under the "Music" 樂 heading in the Clas-
sics section of the treatise, rather than with anthologies of musical poetry. It
should be noted that Zhijiang was not operating under the constraints of the
imperial musical establishment, and by 568 many of his sources may have
undergone serious editing.

20. See Appendix D.

21. For example, the large majority of the "Nineteen Old Poems" have
sometimes been cited in passages as *yuefu* in Sui and Tang sources, with their
access to a much larger manuscript tradition. Even if we ascribe this to a lack
of precision on the part of the person citing the text, it still shows that the

distinction is that passages in the five syllable line may be cited either as a *"yuefu"* or as an "old poem," whereas passages in irregular line lengths are always cited as *yuefu* or some other term referring to the musical poetry (irregular lines are very rarely cited). I refer here specifically to "passages cited": the same material can easily appear in different meters. *Yuefu* and "old poems" also have different conventions of titling (though some *yuefu* are known by their first line, like "old poems"); but these are merely conventions of titling: these early verses are commonly found cited under different titles.[22]

Certain kinds of texts (narratives using a conventional persona distinct from the poet) tend to be preserved primarily in *yuefu* venues, but we can see similar texts also preserved as "poems." A concluding invocation of blessings on the audience may characterize professional singers and thus *yuefu*; but in a situation in which texts are highly fluid, this signals a form of presentation, textually preserved either from a desire to accurately transcribe the practice of singers or from a nostalgic gesture to such practice. As is well known, the term *"yuefu"* is too capacious, and some of the anonymous early *yuefu* that first appear in the sixth century do not overlap with anonymous poetry. A truly "generic" distinction does indeed eventually come into being; but it is a slow process, beginning perhaps as early as the late third century (well before there was an idea of *yuefu* as a genre in the later sense) and finally realized only in the Tang.

In short, before we have "poems" we have "sources," and each source has its own interests and customs. Those sources are all bibliographical types, defined by their self-statements or membership in a family of other works of the same type. The early texts we have are mediated by the interests of those sources. Not until *Yuefu shiji*, around the turn of the twelfth

---

distinction remained a fuzzy one through the Tang and was not considered essential information about a text.

22. The best case for an earlier distinction between "old poems" and *yuefu* can perhaps be made in Lu Ji's "imitations," *ni* 擬, of the "old poems" and his versions (without the *ni*) of *yuefu*. The problem case here is Lu Ji's "Jiayan chu beique xing" 駕言出北闕行, preserved as a *yuefu* in *Yiwen leiju* as well as in *Yuefu shiji*, which is a line-by-line "imitation" (*ni*) of "Nineteen Old Poems" XIII (Lu Qinli, 662). Here we are left with a distinction that is merely in conventions of titling.

century, and later Feng Weine's 馮惟訥 *Gu shi ji* 古詩紀 (completed between 1544 and 1557) do we have compendia dedicated to preserving what survives as it survives. A great deal of history, however, lies between those later scholarly moments and the time when early poetry was first composed and circulated.

Canonizing the "Old Poems"

Toward the end of the third century Lu Ji 陸機 (261–303) clearly admired some of the anonymous "old poems" enough to imitate them; and if these are the "old five-syllable-line poems," *gu wuyan shi* 古五言詩, to which Lu Yun 陸雲 (262–303) was referring in his letter to his brother, then that admiration was shared with others.[23] Lu Yun's usage, however, is descriptive rather than the name of a corpus. Our earliest evidence that one could refer to the "old poems" and expect others to know what one was talking about can be found in Liu Yiqing's 劉義慶 *Shishuo xinyu* 世説新語, compiled around 430. Here we find an anecdote of an event that supposedly occurred in the late fourth century:

王孝伯在京行散，至其弟王睹戶前，問：“古詩中何句爲最？”睹思未答. 孝伯詠 “‘所遇無故物，焉得不速老！’ 此句爲佳.”

Wang Xiaobo [Gong] was walking off his medicine when in the capital and he came to his younger brother Du's [Wang Shuang] door. He asked: "Which are the best lines in the 'old poems'? Du pondered without answering. Then Xiaobo recited: 'Whatever I encounter, there are no familiar things, / how can one help growing swiftly old?' These are the finest lines."[24]

As is usually the case with *Shishuo xinyu* anecdotes, we cannot be sure that the events occurred at the time and in the way described; nevertheless, the anecdote is significant in presuming a shared knowledge of the "old poems," and it has the same form as the anecdote in which Xie An asked Xie Xuan

---

23. See note 2.

24. Yu Jiaxi 余嘉錫, *Shishuo xinyu jianshu* 世説新語箋疏 (Shanghai: Shanghai guji chubanshe, 1993), 276. Liu Yiqing (Liu I-ch'ing), *A New Account of Tales of the World*, trans. Richard B. Mather (Minneapolis: University of Minnesota Press, 1976), 143. The translation is my own.

which was the finest passage in the *Shijing*.[25] Some set of the "old poems" was a corpus that could be called upon to provide a touchstone for judgment.[26] The term *gushi* 古詩, which once meant the *Shijing* (the "old poems" [of the *Shijing*]), had come to refer to a corpus of "classical poetry." At the same time we should no less take note that of the 104 entries in the chapter on "Learning / Belles-Lettres," *Wenxue* 文學, in the *Shishuo xinyu*, only four touch on poetry in the five syllable line.[27]

While the "old poems" were known and admired, they as yet had no place in a cultural history of poetry: they were simply "old." When they were imitated in the first half of the fifth century, they were "improved," raised in register. It is during the course of the fifth century that we see the first accounts of the history of classical poetry and the beginning of understanding poetic style historically.[28] We do not know what was included in Xie Lingyun's apparently influential poetry anthology from the first third of the fifth century, but we can learn something of his relation to the poetic past from his imitations of the Jian'an poets in *The Collection at Ye, Yezhong ji* 鄴中集.[29]

---

25. Yu Jiaxi, *Shishuo*, 235; Liu Yiqing (Mather), *New Account*, 118.

26. One problem, however, does arise. We are so accustomed to the term *gushi* referring to the anonymous "old poems" that when Wang Shuang answers with a couplet from one of the anonymous "old poems," we presume that Wang Xiaobo was referring to such a corpus. It is not impossible that Wang Xiaobo was simply referring to some vaguely defined "earlier poetry" and that Wang Shuang's choice of an anonymous couplet from the canonical "Nineteen Old Poems" was fortuitous.

27. In addition to the Wang Xiaobo anecdote, there are: IV.66, 85, and 88. Two of these are on figures whose works are largely lost and never entered the canon. IV.66 is the famous apocryphal "Seven-Step Poem" attributed to Cao Zhi. See Joe Cutter, "On the Authenticity of the 'Poem in Seven Paces,'" in Paul W. Kroll and David R. Knechtges, eds., *Studies in Early Medieval Chinese Literature and Cultural History: Dedicated to Donald Holzman and Richard B. Mather* (Boulder: T'ang Studies Society, 2003), 1–26. Some other notes touch generally on the styles of Western Jin writers, but their prose and poetic expositions are probably the primary frame of reference.

28. Obviously literary history (or the history of poetry) in this period does not accord with modern definitions of the field. One element of the critical work of the Southern Dynasties was establishing chronological sequences that enabled genealogies; however, even in their earliest forms, these chronological sequences were also mapped onto arguments about large cultural changes or the development of literary forms.

29. For an extensive discussion, see Mei Jialing 梅家玲, *Han Wei Liuchao wenxue xinlun: nidai yu zengda pian* 漢魏六朝文學新論: 擬代與贈答篇 (Taibei: Liren shuju, 1997), 1–92.

This is a peculiar work, in which Xie Lingyun adopts the persona of Cao Pi in the preface, ostensibly imitating a collection of poems not otherwise known to exist.[30] In these imitations Xie Lingyun writes very much as an early fifth-century poet: he "translates" the lines and concerns of earlier poetry into a higher poetic register, much as Lu Ji had rewritten anonymous "old poems" and *yuefu* over a century earlier. Here is the opening of Wang Can's 王粲 original poem, preserved as the first of a group under the title "Sevenfold Sorrows" 七哀詩; the date is probably the late 190s:[31]

西京亂無象	The Western Capital was in unparalleled turmoil,
豺虎方遘患	jackals and tigers were wreaking havoc.
復棄中國去	So I abandoned the heartland and went away,
遠身適荊蠻	going to Jingman to be far off.
親戚對我悲	My kin faced me in sadness,
朋友相追攀	my friends went after me clinging.
出門無所見	Going out the gate I saw nothing,
白骨蔽平原	just white bones covering the plain.

The following is the opening of Xie Lingyun's imitation:[32]

幽厲昔崩亂	Of old You and Li fell in times of Troubles,
桓靈今板蕩	now Huan and Ling met revolt and upheaval.[33]
伊洛既燎煙	The Yi and Luo were razed in smoke,[34]
函崤沒無象	Han and Yao passes' fall was unparalleled.
整裝辭秦川	I prepared my gear, took leave of Qin's rivers,
秣馬赴楚壤	to pasture my horses I headed to Chu's soil.

---

30. Xie may be thinking of Cao Pi's 218 "Letter to Wu Zhi" 與吳質書, in which he speaks of compiling the works of the Jian'an Masters, most of whom had died in the plague of the preceding year. If so, it is a nice example of the beginning of the fifth century privilege accorded to five-syllable-line poetry, since Cao Pi was probably thinking of other writing.

31. Lu Qinli, 365.

32. Lu Qinli, 1182.

33. These are the Zhou kings You and Li, whose misrule supposedly hastened the end of the Western Zhou. Emperors Huan (r. 147–67) and Ling (r. 168–89) likewise saw the ruin of the Eastern Han.

34. This refers to Dong Zhuo's destruction of Luoyang.

沮漳自可美	Though the rivers Ju and Zhang be beautiful,
客心非外奬	a sojourner's heart is not attracted by outer things.
常歎詩人言	Ever I sigh at the word of the poet:
式微何由往	"Brought low!" but what means have I to go on?[35]
上宰奉皇靈	The High Minister serves the Imperial Numen,[36]
侯伯咸宗長	the counts and earls all revere him.

The difference here is not simply in the additional references, though they contribute to rhetorical "elevation," but a much higher register of diction. As Xie's imitation continues, the rhetoric grows even more turgid.

When, however, we come to Jiang Yan's 江淹 (444–505) thirty "Various Forms" (*zati* 雜體), probably written toward the end of the fifth century,[37] we find a poet attempting to capture the historical difference of individual and period styles. Here is the opening of Jiang Yan's imitation of the same Wang Can poem:[38]

伊昔值世亂	Long ago I met times of turmoil,
秣馬辭帝京	to pasture my horse I left the imperial capital.
既傷蔓草別	Having felt the pain of parting "among the creepers,"[39]
方知杕杜情	I understand the feelings of the "lone pear tree."[40]
崤函復丘墟	Yao and Han passes return to wasteland,[41]
冀闕緬縱橫	I look hopefully toward the palace, spread out in the distance.
倚棹汎涇渭	Leaning to the oars, I sail on the Jing and Wei,
日暮山河清	at sunset the mountains and rivers are clear.

---

35. *Shi* 36, supposedly composed to exhort the Count of Li to return from his refuge in Wei.

36. Cao Cao.

37. We do not know when the collection of "Various Forms" was written; but since Jiang Yan was famous for the fading of his poetic talent in old age, we assume they are late fifth century.

38. Lu Qinli, 1572.

39. *Shi* 94. According to the Mao interpretation, "There are creepers in the wild" 野有蔓草 refers to times when the people suffer from warfare.

40. *Shi* 119. "Lone pear tree" 杕杜 suggests turmoil and the separation of kin.

41. Reading *fu* 復 with the *Wen xuan*, rather than *dang* 蕩.

蟋蟀依桑野	There are crickets among mulberry trees in the wilds,[42]
嚴風吹枯莖	harsh winds blow the dry, leafless stalks.

Although Jiang Yan uses two allusions to the *Shijing*, they are particularly straightforward and of exactly the same form Wang Can himself used later in the poem cited above. While Xie Ling-yun consistently holds to a high register, Jiang Yan moves to simple descriptive lines. When Jiang Yan imitates Xie Lingyun, however, he keeps to the high register.

This represents a profound change in the understanding of the poetic past. All but one of Jiang Yan's thirty poems imitate specific authors arranged in chronological order; the exception is the first poem, which is entitled simply "Old Parting" (*Gu libie* 古離別). It appears to be an imitation of an anonymous "old poem," though it could just as easily be understood as a *yuefu*.[43] Here for the first time we see how the solution to a formal problem insinuates itself into the account of the history of poetry: the anonymous poem is placed first in an otherwise chronological sequence of authors; it is "old"; therefore it seems to be the earliest, the beginning of a historical process of poetic variation and change.

Some decades after Jiang Yan's "Various Forms," Zhong Rong composed the *Gradations of Poetry* (*Shipin* 詩品). We do not know the particular sources he had at his disposal, but he probably had access to the imperial library and a range of books at least something like what we see in the "Bibliography" of the *Sui shu*. He does not even mention the anonymous *yuefu*, perhaps suggesting that these were not yet fully considered "poetry." Zhong Rong does, however, take up the anonymous

---

42. Reading *sang* 桑 with the *Wen xuan*, rather than *su* 素.

43. The transformations of the term *gu* 古, "old," deserve study in their application to the literary tradition. In the *yuefu* tradition by Wang Sengqian in the middle of the fifth century, we have the term "old lyrics," *guci* 古辭, used in contradistinction to lyrics with known authors (since all the "known authors" are members of the Wei imperial house, we must grant the possibility that *guci* may not have originally implied anonymity and may have included other "old lyrics" by commoners). Since Shen Yue also uses *guci*, we may assume that it had already become a technical term for scholars working with lyrics in the musical tradition. Then we have this "old parting" used by Jiang Yan, situated ambiguously between what we would now call an "old poem" and a *yuefu*.

"old poems," which he places at the beginning of the highest category.[44]

其體源出於國風. 陸機所擬十四首, 文溫以麗, 意悲而遠, 驚心動魄, 可謂幾乎一字千金. 其外, "去者日以疏" 四十五首, 雖多哀怨, 頗爲總雜, 舊疑是建安中曹王所製. "客從遠方來," "橘柚垂華實," 亦爲驚絕矣. 人代冥滅, 而清音獨遠, 悲夫!

The source of the form came from the "Airs of the States." The fourteen pieces that Lu Ji imitated are rich and beautiful in style, and in their sense, moving and far-reaching. They startle mind and spirit—one may even claim that each word is worth a thousand pieces of silver. As for the forty-five others, including "Those departed grow daily further from us," even though they are filled with painful resentment, they are very much a mixed bag. People used to suspect that they were written by the Caos and Wang [Can] in the Jian'an.[45] "A traveler came from afar" and "The orange shows flower and fruit" are also quite remarkable. How sad it is that the times of these people are lost in obscurity, yet their clear tones alone have lasted so long.

We might first note that we see here the core of the "Nineteen Old Poems," *Gushi shijiushou* 古詩十九首, the *Wen xuan* selection of anonymous "old poems" that has become a foundational text in the history of Chinese poetry.

Zhong Rong's comments tell us much. First, we know that in the early sixth century there was a manuscript with fifty-nine anonymous "old poems."[46] The phrasing suggests that the first fourteen poems in that manuscript were those imitated by Lu Ji.[47] Unless we make the highly unlikely assumption that Lu Ji decided to imitate the first fourteen in some early version of the same manuscript text, we must conclude that an anthologist or copyist gave first place to versions of those anonymous "old poems" imitated by Lu Ji. In other words, it was the imitations that drew attention and gave prominence to the "originals." If

---

44. Wang Shumin 王叔岷, *Zhong Rong* Shipin *jianzheng gao* 鍾嶸詩品箋證稿 (Taibei: Zhongyang yanjiuyuan, Wenshizhe yanjiusuo, Zhongguo wenzhe zhuankan, 1992), 129; Cao Xu 曹旭, *Shipin jizhu* 詩品集注 (Shanghai: Shanghai guji chubanshe, 1994), 75.

45. There is some debate whether this is one particular Cao, such as Cao Zhi, or the Caos as a group, effectively Cao Pi and Cao Zhi.

46. This was probably not a separate manuscript but rather a section in an anthology, perhaps Xie Lingyun's (which Zhong Rong knew). Anonymous "old poems," from one or diverse sources, would necessarily have been put together in a structure arranged chronologically by author.

47. Zhong Rong's phrasing (其外, "去者日以疏" 四十五首) gives the impression that the remaining forty-five poems begin continuously from "去者日以疏."

many now read the "originals" and few the imitations, it is worth remembering why we have these texts. We think of poetic history in terms of chronological sequence and discover continuity; at this formative moment in the tradition, however, the recognition of continuity was the ground on which particular early texts merited attention and, through attention, preservation.

For his "Nineteen Old Poems" Xiao Tong would select twelve of the "old poems" imitated by Lu Ji, along with two of the other three "old poems" that Zhong Rong mentioned above, and the poem quoted in the *Shishuo xinyu* anecdote.[48] This is to say that for fifteen of the canonical "Nineteen" we have some form of extant prior testimony to their value. Perhaps there were also lost testimonies to the value of the missing four. Much of the rest of this corpus of fifty-nine "old poems" clearly did not entirely satisfy early sixth-century standards of what an "old poem" should be: they seemed, as Zhong Rong said, a "mixed bag," *zongza* 總雜. Although we need to exercise caution not to read too much into such terms, *zongza* suggests impurity, an admixture of elements not proper to what an "old poem" should be.[49] That is, the early sixth-century critic had his own idea about what "old poems" should sound like, and he selected and praised works from a much larger corpus according to how well such works conformed to that ideal.[50] There is perhaps no more

---

48. Xiao Tong selected only twelve of the fourteen Lu Ji imitations mentioned by Zhong Rong; one of the others is extant and is an imitation of "Nineteen Old Poems" XIII. The one case in which we have a Lu Ji imitation in the *Wen xuan* without the corresponding "old poem" included among the "Nineteen" is "Orchid and *duruo* grow in spring light" 蘭若生春陽, which is included in *Yutai xinyong* under the name of Mei Sheng. I suspect that the missing Lu Ji imitation is "Nineteen Old Poems" XVII because there is a later imitation by Liu Shuo (Lu Qinli, 1215), who is probably redoing Lu Ji's imitations. Xiao Tong also included 迴車駕言邁, whose couplet was quoted in the *Shishuo xinyu* anecdote above, as the ninth in his selection.

49. *Zongza* was also the term used by Yan Yanzhi to describe the Li Ling corpus: 總雜不類，是假託，非盡陵制 "a mixed bag and not of a piece—there are false attributions, and not all were composed by Li Ling" (*Taiping yulan* 586.3a).

50. We do not know the qualities that made some of the other "old poems" objectionable to Zhong Rong. We may suspect that such poems had marks of "literary" composition in a higher register. Here again we come to the potential confusion between lexical register and literary historical change. In Zhong Rong's age (and often in our own) a less elevated register suggested an earlier (purer) period.

striking evidence of the degree to which the "early poetry" that survives is a motivated, even ideological, selection of available material.

The second issue is dating. In the main entry Zhong Rong cites a speculation that places the authorship of the "old poems" in the Jian'an but does not offer a date. In one of the prefaces to *Gradations of Poetry* Zhong Rong restates his uncertainty about authorship and makes an inference that the "old poems" (presumably the "pure" ones) are Han (rejecting an otherwise unknown suggestion that they might date from the Warring States). One thing is clear: Zhong Rong did not know when these poems were composed, and attributions of authorship and date were matters of speculation. Zhong Rong may have insisted on a Han date, but his judgment rests not on tradition or manuscript authority but on stylistic inference. Such stylistic inference is based on comparison to poems by known poets and presumes that stylistic difference is best explained in literary historical terms, as the historical movement from a simple style to a more literary style, rather than a roughly synchronic difference of register.

Zhong Rong's *Gradations of Poetry* is arranged chronologically within each of its three categories of evaluation; the *Wen xuan* is arranged chronologically in its subsections; *Wenxin diaolong* often runs through chronological sequences of authors and works in its chapters. Chronological sequence also dominates the arrangement of works by sections in *Yutai xinyong*. This was an age in which chronology, as the foundation of genealogy and cultural history, had become the most important conceptual frame for organizing material—whether the larger and ostensibly more important principle of organization was gradations of quality (*Gradations of Poetry*) or genre (*Wen xuan* and *Wenxin diaolong*). To establish chronology names are necessary. As we suggested earlier in Jiang Yan's "Various Forms," anonymous texts of uncertain date present a special formal problem in a chronological structure. They can be placed first or last; however, placing them first in a chronological sequence gives the impression that they are necessarily earlier than works by known poets. This was the impression about the "old poems" that has lasted. It is, however, only an impression that follows from the solution to a formal problem.[51]

In many ways this brief passage from *Gradations of Poetry* is one of the clearest traces of the way late Southern Dynasties literary men worked upon their manuscript heritage. They selected and sometimes rewrote according to their strong sense of "how it should have been." This is not to say that what we have does not authentically represent early poetry; it suggests only that what we have is a selective and modified part of a manuscript tradition. Some core of the material is authentic: the precise textual form of the material and its dating is open to question.

Stories of Origins

The selection and canonization of the "Nineteen Old Poems" was a key component in a larger process of conceptualizing literary history in general and providing an account of pre-Jian'an origins for poetry in the five syllable line, the dominant poetic form in the fifth century. Prior to the Qi and Liang, we frequently have judgments about authors, often comparative judgments made in reference to who is earlier and who is later. The earliest attempt at a historical account of poetry is organized around the change in poetic fashion that occurred with the waning of Neo-Daoist *xuanyan* 玄言 poetry. This is found in Tan Daoluan's 檀道鸞 *Xu Jin yangqiu* 續晉陽秋, a work of the first half of the fifth century and thus earlier than the works of Jiang Yan and Shen Yue 沈約 (441–513) treated below. The discussion focuses on the fourth-century *xuanyan* poet Xu Xun 許詢. I give Richard Mather's translation with *pinyin* Romanization:

---

51. Li Shan recognized the problem of assumed priority because of sequence, noting that the "Nineteen Old Poems" make reference to Eastern Han sites and suggesting that it was only because of the poems' anonymity that Xiao Tong placed them before Li Ling (昭明以失其姓氏, 故編在李陵之上). If these poems refer to imperial Luoyang before its destruction, it does not mean the poems are from that era; they refer to a poetic Luoyang whose specific places are also mentioned in other datable poems written long after the destruction of the city. And, of course, Luoyang was repopulated when it became the capital of the Wei and Western Jin.

Xu Xun possessed ability and style and was skilled in literary composition. Ever since such worthies as Sima Xiangru (ca. 179–117 B.C.), Wang Bao (d. 61 B.C.), and Yang Xiong (53 B.C.–A.D. 18), the world has esteemed the poetic essay (*fu*) and hymn (*song*), and everyone imitated the "Songs" (*Shi*) and "Elegies" (*Sao*), gathering from every quarter the words of a hundred authors.

During the Jian'an era (196–219), lyric poems (*shi*) and essays (*zhang*) enjoyed a great florescence, and even as late as the Western Jin (265–316) people like Pan Yue (247–300) and Lu Ji (261–303), although from time to time they produced substantial writings, never departed from the old models and sources.

During the Zhengshi era (240–249), Wang Bi (226–249) and He Yan (ca. 190–249) had favored mysterious and transcendent (*xuansheng*) conversation about *Zhuangzi* and *Laozi*, and after that the world set great store by them. But at the time of the crossing of the Yangzi River (307–312) Buddhist doctrines became especially flourishing.[52] So Guo Pu (276–324), in his five-word poems [poems in the five syllable line], began gathering together the words of Daoist masters and setting them to rhyme. And Xu Xun and Sun Chuo (active between 330 and 365), each in turn, were taken as models and admired, and moreover, they used Buddhist terms like "the three times" (past, present, and future), and thus the imitation of the "Songs" and "Elegies" came to an end. Xun and Chuo both became literary models for the entire age, and from their time onward all writers imitated them. It was not until the Yixi era (405–418) that Xie Hun initiated a change.[53]

This represents something like an authoritative consensus on poetry of the third and fourth centuries, and it was commonly repeated by the critics of the late fifth and early sixth centuries. In this context the account is given to contextualize a particular poet, Xu Xun; as we will see, Shen Yue's very similar account is to contextualize an issue in poetics, namely, euphony. Yet, as in Shen Yue's later and more detailed account of the history of poetry, "poetry" (probably but not certainly meaning poetry in the five syllable line) begins with the Jian'an reign. The "old poems" (however many) may have been popular and widely known, but they were not yet part of the "history" of poetry.

Literary history implies a coherent sense of differences of style and interests; in order to understand, it implies sympa-

---

52. The manuscript *Wen xuan jizhu* 文選集注 cites this passage as "Li Chong was particularly flourishing [popular]" 李充尤盛. Yu Jiaxi, *Shishuo*, 264 (author's note).

53. Liu Yiqing, trans. Mather, *New Account*, 136–37; Yu Jiaxi, *Shishuo*, 262.

thetic acceptance of difference in values. We earlier compared Xie Lingyun's imitations of the Jian'an poets with Jiang Yan's "Various Forms." Xie Lingyun makes no attempt to recreate the style of the Jian'an poets; rather, he takes what he understands as the situations and concerns of particular poets and represents them in the very thick style of the early fifth century. For Xie poetry has a past, but not a history.

Writing in the latter part of the century, Jiang Yan is attempting to imitate a style, within a set of different styles, determined by author and period. In the interval between Jiang and Xie Lingyun something important has happened in the understanding of the poetic past; and while Jiang Yan's series of imitations are not in themselves a history of poetry, they represent the condition within which a history of poetry is possible. It is clear from Jiang Yan's preface to the series that he is thinking of his enterprise in terms of literary history: "Chu's lays and the airs of Han are not of a single frame; also Wei's products and what was fashioned in Jin were absolutely two [different] forms" 夫楚謠漢風, 既非一骨; 魏製晉造, 固亦二體.[54] This same preface argues another important case for literary historical understanding: the reader must not judge only according to the standard of his own time, but must have a sympathetic openness to differences. That is, Jiang Yan is in some ways responding to earlier critical practice based on passing judgments and calling for an understanding and appreciation of period difference that does not call for comparative judgment.

Judgment is, of course, never far from accounts of literary history and canon formation—both judgments of what is valuable within a period and the relative judgment of periods themselves. The uneasy relation between a degree of historical relativism and the impulse to pass judgment was to remain throughout the literary scholarship of the Qi and Liang. The implied argument in Jiang Yan's preface may be seen in the following passage.

故蛾眉詎同貌, 而俱動於魄; 芳草寧共氣, 而皆悦於魂, 不其然歟? 至於世之諸賢, 各滯所迷, 莫不論甘而忌辛, 好丹而非素. 豈所謂通方廣恕, 好遠兼愛者哉?

---

54. Hu Zhiji 胡之驥, *Jiang Wentong ji huizhu* 江文通集彙注 (Beijing: Zhonghua shuju, 1984), 136.

How can lovely women each have the same face?—yet all can stir the spirit. How can aromatic plants share the same aroma?—yet all are pleasing to the soul. Is it not so? When it comes to worthy men of the age, each is mired in what beguiles his fancy, yet all favor the sweet and shun the bitter, love the cinnabar red and reject the plain white. How could this be what is known as "being comprehensive and broadly tolerant" or "liking what is far and loving equally"?[55]

In the first example Jiang Yan sets up a model of simple difference within the categories of "lovely" and "aromatic"; he does not suggest that we also appreciate the ugly and the foul smelling. Yet he comes close to just such a position in the second phase of his argument, where he suggests that people should also appreciate the bitter and the plain. Emerging from an age, the Liu-Song, that loved rich poetic ornament (often figured as rich colors), Jiang Yan seems here to be arguing for the value of the poetically "plain"; that is, for the value of the relative straightforwardness of earlier poetry.

•

In accounts of literary history it is sometimes difficult to separate what is specific to the history of classical poetry from a more general history of belles-lettres or poetic writing. Like Tan Daoluan, Shen Yue, in his "Postface" to the "Biography of Xie Lingyun" in the *Song shu* of 488, moves from Han poetic expositions (*fu*) directly to poetry in the Jian'an, without reflecting on the difference of genre.[56] Like Tan Daoluan, Shen Yue has specific motivation for this larger literary historical account of poetry; in Shen Yue's case it is the issue of poetic euphony, which was specifically an issue for poetry in the five syllable line. Poetic euphony, was, as Shen Yue recognized, a modern issue at the end of the fifth century; and it led Shen Yue to look at the literary past in terms of linear change: a privileged moment of an instinctive sense of poetic euphony in the Jian'an, a period of falling away, and an implied recovery of the principles of euphony in the present.

In the first section of his account, Shen Yue begins with the *Shijing*, goes to the *Chuci*, then to the poetic expositions (*fu*) of

---

55. Hu Zhiji, 136.

56. *Song shu*, 1778–79; translation in Richard B. Mather, *The Poet Shen Yüeh (441–513): The Reticent Marquis* (Princeton: Princeton University Press, 1988), 40–44. The text is also included in *juan* 50 of the *Wen xuan*.

the Han, and finally to the Jian'an. Shen Yue clearly is here working with an idea of "poetic writing" in a very broad sense—though when he comes to the Jian'an there is little doubt that he is thinking primarily of poetry in the five syllable line.[57] The discussion of the Jian'an is the foundation for the second section which discusses the history of poetry, primarily poetry in the five syllable line, from the Jian'an into the fifth century.

In the third section Shen turns to principles of euphony through the alternation of pitches. Speaking from an age that was developing systematic principles of euphony, Shen Yue praises the Jian'an poets (and he makes reference to specific poems in the five syllable line) as having achieved euphony "without prior awareness" (*wu xianjue* 無先覺). The history of poetry from that moment through the first half of the fifth century is a story of falling away, of deviation from this basic intuitive principle—and this is a loss to poetry that his own age will repair, though consciously, "with prior awareness."

It is significant here that even though the central issue of structured euphony was one strongly associated with poetry in the five syllable line, Shen Yue does not make any explicit differentiation of genre. In his account poetry in the five syllable line seems to have no origin; in the Jian'an it simply appears, replacing the Sao and *fu* that were the focus of attention in an earlier era.

Genre was indeed an issue for most of the critics of the Qi and Liang. We cannot date Jiang Yan's "Various Forms" in relation to Shen Yue's "Postface," but in his preface Jiang Yan acknowledges that "the rise of the five syllable line is indeed not of remote antiquity" 五言之興，諒非夐古. Here in the specific authors and works imitated, however, we have the first outline of a lineage: first the anonymous "Ancient Parting" 古離別 mentioned earlier, then Li Ling 李陵 (d. 74 B.C.), Lady Ban 班婕妤, Cao Pi 曹丕 (187–226), Cao Zhi 曹植 (192–232), Liu Zhen 劉楨 (d. 217), Wang Can 王粲 (177–217), and then on to Xi Kang

---

57. The poetic expositions of the Jian'an, so prominent in earlier critical comment, were clearly not even in Shen Yue's mind here. Mather translates Tan Daoluan's *shizhang* 詩章 as "lyric poems and essays." This may also be understood simply as "poems," in which case Tan, too, is moving to lyric poetry as the representative form of the Jian'an.

嵇康 (223–62) and Ruan Ji 阮籍 (210–63), before moving into the Western Jin.

There is much of interest in Jiang Yan's list. As we discussed earlier, the formal problem of anonymous poetry in a chronological sequence invited its placement before the first named poet, Li Ling.[58] A Li Ling collection was in circulation in the first half of the fifth century, when the authenticity of some of its poems was doubted by Yan Yanzhi 顏延之 (384–456). Li Ling was the failed Han general who was captured by the Xiongnu; the poems under his name were primarily parting poems and perhaps became attached to his name because of the famous scene of his parting from Su Wu, an emissary to the Xiongnu from the Han court. The poems naturally acquired the title "To Su Wu" 贈蘇武; perhaps because it was somewhat incongruous to have one person composing so many farewell poems on a single occasion, some of the poems were eventually ascribed to Su Wu himself, with the title "To Li Ling."[59] These poems use the common material of the anonymous *yuefu* and "old poems," but many have the clear marks of a basic literary education, and it is hard to believe that some are earlier than the third century. Here, however, was a known and datable figure to serve as the earliest poet in the five syllable line.

Continuing in Jiang Yan's list, Lady Ban was a court lady of the late first century B.C. Only one poem has been attributed to her, the poem on the circular fan that Jiang Yan imitated. Jiang Yan then moved directly from Lady Ban to four of the Jian'an poets. If the Jian'an was the first great moment of poetry in the five syllable line for Shen Yue, Jiang Yan provided prior history for the Jian'an moment—though from our contemporary perspective, at least two of those three pre-Jian'an moments (Li Ling and Lady Ban) now seem to postdate the Jian'an—the third (that is, the anonymous "old poems") has no author and is merely "old."

In his account of the history of poetry Shen Yue had moved

---

58. Since Zhong Rong accepts Li Ling as the author of the poems attributed to him, the anonymous "old poems" must be placed earlier. This is perhaps why, in his preface, he has to limit their antiquity by rejecting any attempt to date them from the Warring States.

59. Tang commentators have some of the Su Wu poems as parting from his wife and brother.

directly from the Jian'an to the second generation of the Western Jin poets, Pan Yue 潘岳 (247–300) and Lu Ji, without mentioning Ruan Ji and Xi Kang. Jiang Yan, who did a separate set of imitations of Ruan Ji, included both Xi Kang and Ruan Ji in his series. We might simply conclude that Shen Yue did not think Ruan Ji important, but the evidence is quite to the contrary: Shen Yue wrote a commentary on Ruan Ji's poetry, parts of which have been preserved. Why Shen Yue omitted Ruan Ji in his account of the history of poetry is a question we cannot answer (in the context of 488 his omission of Tao Qian is understandable); in the next generation Zhong Rong would place Ruan Ji in the highest category in his *Gradations of Poetry*. The best explanation is perhaps that for Shen Yue, Ruan Ji represented an important personality embodied in poetic texts, deserving of commentary but not deserving of mention in an account of poetry conceived in terms of euphony and rhetoric. The following generations would see the breakdown of such a distinction, with Ruan Ji rising to the first order in Zhong Rong, and Tao Qian rising to the first order in Xiao Tong. Anonymous *yuefu*, belonging to a bibliographically proximate but distinct category, seem to have made the crossover into the realm of literary "poetry" first in the *Wen xuan* and, on a large scale, in *Yutai xinyong*. This seems to have been a general process of reconceptualizing poetry more broadly in the Qi and Liang, and that process was based on the principles enunciated by Jiang Yan: if one can see the value of the "pale" as well as the "cinnabar colored," then one can see the value not only of the "straightforward" old poems and *yuefu*, but also of less rhetorical poets like Ruan Ji and Tao Qian.

It is clear that in the Qi and Liang there was an extensive social discourse about poetry, both "ancient" and "modern." Traces of that social discourse are apparent in a wide range of texts. There were important disagreements and disputes, but we see a degree of consensus—a consensus on which authors and texts were important, even if one disagreed on how to interpret such importance or disagreed in relative terms. We come now to the critics Liu Xie 劉勰 and Zhong Rong, both writing prior to the compilation of the famous anthologies that have preserved our canonical texts. Both give full histories of the beginnings of poetry in the five syllable line.

Here it is important to keep in mind that poetry in the five syllable line did not yet have a history of origins. There was a body of texts in circulation to which names had become attached, and anonymous poems seem to have acquired authors with some ease. The sense that a particular person in history would have been an appropriate speaker for a poem was so close to a claim of authorship that the transition between the two was imperceptible. As large anthologies of poetry in the five syllable line began to appear in the fifth century, the authors, both credible and imputed, would be arranged in chronological order. The material for a history was probably already in place.

Let us return to Liu Xie's chapter "Elucidation of Poetry" 明詩 in *Wenxin diaolong*. Here we have a full history of poetry in the five syllable line, including a discussion of its origins. The following passage begins after a discussion of other poetic forms in the Han.

至成帝品錄, 三百餘篇, 朝章國采, 亦云周備, 而辭人遺翰, 莫見五言, 所以李陵, 班婕好見疑於後代也. 按召南行露, 始肇半章, 孺子滄浪, 亦有全曲; 暇豫優歌, 遠見春秋; 邪徑童謠, 近在成世; 閱時取證, 則五言久矣. 又古詩佳麗, 或稱枚叔, 其孤竹一篇, 則傅毅之詞, 比采而推, 固兩漢之作也. 觀其結體散文, 直而不野, 婉轉附物, 怊悵切情, 實五言之冠冕也. 至於張衡怨篇, 清典可味; 仙詩緩歌, 雅有新聲. 暨建安之初, 五言騰踊, 文帝陳思, 縱轡以騁節; 王徐應劉, 望路而爭驅; 並憐風月, 狎池苑, 述恩榮, 敘酣宴, 慷慨以任氣, 磊落以使才, 造懷指事, 不求纖密之巧; 驅辭逐貌, 唯取昭晰之能; 此其所同也. 及正始明道, 詩雜仙心, 何晏之徒, 率多浮淺. 唯嵇志清峻, 阮旨遙深, 故能標焉. 若乃應璩百一, 獨立不懼, 辭譎義貞, 亦魏之遺直也. 晉世群才, 稍入輕綺, 張潘左陸, 比肩詩衢, 采縟於正始, 力柔於建安, 或析文以為妙, 或流靡以自妍, 此其大略也.

When we come to the record of bibliographical categories in Emperor Cheng's reign, there were more than three hundred pieces, both court works and those selected from the domains, which may well be said to be comprehensive.[60] Yet in those works by writers remaining, we see no works in the five syllable line; and for this reason the pieces attributed to Li Ling and Lady Ban have been doubted by later ages.[61]

---

60. This refers to the *Yiwen zhi* 藝文志 of the *Han shu*, based on Liu Xin's 劉歆 catalogue of the imperial library in Chengdi's reign (32–8 B.C.), the *Qilüe* 七略. This lists 314 "poems and songs" 歌詩.

61. We have earlier mentioned Yan Yanzhi's doubts regarding the authenticity of all the Li Ling pieces. We have no other extant record of contemporary doubts regarding the authenticity of Lady Ban's fan poem.

I would venture that "Hanglu" in the "Shaonan" began it [five syllable verse] in half of a stanza,[62] and from the child at Canglang we even have a whole song.[63] The Bard singing of "Leisure" appeared far back in the Spring and Autumn Annals period;[64] the children's ditty on "warped paths" is found more recently, in the age of Emperor Cheng.[65] Examining different ages for evidence, we find that the five syllable line has existed for a long time.

Some claim that Mei Sheng is responsible for the beauty of the "Old Poems";[66] the one on "solitary bamboo" is the writing of Fu Yi.[67] When we investigate by comparing stylistic qualities, they are from the Western or Eastern Han.[68] When we observe the construction of their form and their deployment of phrases, they are direct without being uncouth, and are subtle in the way they make comparisons with things,[69] deeply saddening and touching the affections sharply—these are truly the crown of works in the five syllable line.

When we consider Zhang Heng's "Reproach," it has a lucid gravity that may be savored;[70] his "Poem on the Immortals" and "Slow Song" have a popular style with dignity.[71]

---

62. Four lines in the second stanza of "Hanglu" 行露 in the *Shijing* are in the five syllable line. These are the lines cited by Zhi Yu to prove the antiquity of the five syllable line. Deng Guoguang, *Zhi Yu yanjiu*, 185.

63. *Mencius* IVA.8.2. This same verse also appears in the "Fisherman," *Yufu* 漁父 in the *Chuci*.

64. This refers to a song cited in "Jinyu" II 晉語 in the *Guoyu* 國語 sung by Bard Shi 優施. Three of its four lines are five syllables in length. *Guoyu* 國語 (Shanghai: Shanghai guji chubanshe, 1978) 286.

65. This is cited in the "Treatise on the Five Phases" 五行志 of the *Han shu*.

66. Or "responsible for the most beautiful of the 'Old Poems.'" Mei Cheng died around 140 B.C. Zhong Rong and Xiao Tong took all the "old poems" as anonymous, but some included in the *Yutai xinyong* carry the Mei Sheng attribution.

67. Fu Yi 傅毅 lived in the first century A.D. This attribution of the eighth of the "Nineteen Old Poems" to Fu Yi is otherwise unattested.

68. The text as given follows the now widely accepted reading of the Tang manuscript edition, concluding the sentence with 也. The received text concludes with the interrogative 乎, leading to the possible interpretation that Liu Xie doubted the Han dating.

69. *Fuwu* 附物 is literally something like "match" or "conjoin" with things. This usage strongly suggests Liu Xie's definition of "comparison" 比 in the 比興 chapter: "Comparison is that which conjoins" 故比者, 附也. Liu is clearly referring to *jituo* 寄托, "investing one's feelings in things," using description of external things to convey one's feelings.

70. A version of this poem has been preserved in later sources; it is, however, in a four syllable line, and Liu Xie has been consistently talking about poetry in the five syllable line.

71. If Liu Xie is referring to poems attributed to Zhang Heng, nothing is known of them.

At the beginning of the Jian'an poetry in the five syllable line bounded upward: Wendi [Cao Pi] and Prince Si of Chen [Cao Zhi] let the reins go and set a galloping pace. Wang Can, Xu Gan, Ying Yang, and Liu Zhen set their eyes on the course and raced each other.[72] In each other's company they were fond of the breeze and moonlight, felt easy familiarity with pond and park, gave account of the glories of enjoying favor, told of festively tipsy banquets. Moved to passion, they gave free rein to their energies; and they employed their talents with expansive grandeur. Without trying to achieve a dense and delicate artfulness, they fashioned their concerns in reference to what really happened; they employed phrasing to catch the appearances of things, preferring only skill in luminous lucidity. In these things they were the same.

When we come to the elucidation of the Way in the Zhengshi Reign, poetry became involved with the mind set on the immortals. He Yan and his ilk are generally very shallow and insubstantial. Yet Xi Kang's aims were pure and lofty, and Ruan Ji's import was far-reaching and deep; thus we can take them as standards. When we have something like Ying Qu's "One of a Hundred," we find someone who fearlessly stood alone; the diction is weird but the sense of right is unsullied.[73] He too can represent forthrightness surviving from the Wei.

The many talents of the Jin rather tended to lightness and ornament: the Zhangs, the Pans, the Lus, and Zuo stood shoulder to shoulder on the thoroughfares of poetry. The colors of their diction are flashier than the poetry of the Zhengshi Reign, and their force is weaker than the poetry of the Jian'an. Sometimes they took passages of antithetical divisions as the greatest finesse; at other times they used an insinuating fluency to make themselves appear attractive. This generally sums them up.[74]

If a chronological sequence of texts and names is the basis for a history, our first account here of the origins of poetry in the five syllable line appears when many of the authorial attributions from before the Jian'an are in question. As is sometimes the case with Liu Xie, we are often unsure of where he stands on these questions.

He begins with a critique of the earliest attributions. It may be his own critique, but more probably it was a critique current

---

72. This echoes the figure of competition as racing in Cao Pi's "Discourse on Literature," "Lunwen" 論文.

73. Ying Qu's series was satirical.

74. Zhan Ying 詹鍈, *Wenxin diaolong yizheng* 文心雕龍義證 (Shanghai: Shanghai guji, 1989), 185–204.

in contemporary literary discussions. Liu Xiang's catalogue of the imperial library has over three hundred poems and songs enumerated under twenty-eight writers, who include neither Li Ling nor Lady Ban.[75] Early in the fifth century Yan Yanzhi had raised doubts about the authenticity of some of the poems in the Li Ling corpus on stylistic grounds; the critique here, however, is of the Li Ling corpus as a whole. Considering the apparent countermove in the passage that follows, we do not know whether Liu Xie accepts this as a valid critique or not; but these are the only occasions on which he mentions Li Ling and Lady Ban.

Liu Xie next offers proof of the existence of the five syllable line in antiquity, perhaps answering Jiang Yan's statement that the form was "not of remote antiquity," and following the example of Zhi Yu, who traced all the possible line lengths of poetry to examples from the *Shijing*. As Liu Xie was quite aware, the irregular verse forms of antiquity used many line lengths, and it is hardly surprising that sometimes one finds passages in the five syllable line; moreover, the three examples from the pre-Qin period are obviously different in rhythm and style from the five-syllable-line poetry that Liu Xie was discussing. The fourth and final example was a peculiar inclusion: this was a children's song attributed to the reign of Han Emperor Cheng (the emperor whom Lady Ban served and who ordered the catalogue of the imperial library). This is indeed in the five syllable line as it was practiced in later poetry, and we don't know what Liu meant by including such an example.

The anonymous "old poems" come next. Here for the first time we see attribution of "old poems" to Mei Sheng 枚乘 (d. ca. 140 B.C.)—before Li Ling. These attributions were accepted by Xu Ling 徐陵 (507–83) in the *Yutai xinyong*. The fact that Jiang Yan did not include Mei Sheng in his imitations suggests either that he did not take the attribution seriously or that it had not yet been made.[76] Liu Xie mentions the attribution to Mei

---

75. Modern scholars can easily dismiss this critique because the low status of the five syllable line made it highly unlikely that such works would be included in the imperial library. To Liu Xie, however, this would have been a weighty critique.

76. The choice of Mei Sheng as an author for the "old poems" does suggest a rather late date for the attribution: it seems to follow an arrangement in which the "old poems" come first, followed by Li Ling as the first known

Sheng, but it is unclear whether it was believed that Mei Sheng wrote the entire corpus or just some (as in *Yutai xinyong*). Then he mentions Fu Yi as the author of "Nineteen Old Poems" VIII, but we cannot tell if this is Liu Xie's own conviction or another opinion of "some." In short, all the early names are here, but all are under a half-cloud of suspicion and uncertainty.

At last Liu Xie expresses his own opinion, based on inferential investigation (*tui* 推). Any hope for clarity here is, unfortunately, soon lost for reasons beyond Liu Xie's control. We have a textual problem, a variant in the final character which renders the sentence alternatively affirmative or interrogative. Later critics have very much wanted Liu Xie to affirm a Han date for the old poems (one version of the affirmative text includes *gu* 固, "most certainly!"); but the interrogative version is that of the received text. If we accept the interrogative particle, we could read this as a mildly rhetorical interrogative, suggesting assent; but it could also be a true question, suggesting doubt about the Han dating. Such a grammatically natural reading might echo Zhong Rong's comment that some believe the "old poems" were composed by the Caos and Wang Can in the Jian'an.[77] If Liu Xie was indeed tactfully expressing doubts about an early dating for the "old poems," his doubts were soon interpreted away.

We do know one thing for certain. The anonymous "old poems" had been unmentioned by Shen Yue and were simply the first "form" imitated by Jiang Yan (without the categorical term "old poems"); a few decades later in Liu Xie they have already achieved a canonical stature equal to that of the Jian'an poets: they are the "crown of works in the five syllable line." In his account Liu Xie praises only the "old poems" and the

---

author. Anonymous poems were magnets for authors, and here contemporary critics would automatically be looking for an author earlier than Li Ling (apart from those who believed a Jian'an date). Because Sima Xiangru also served Han Wudi, he would probably have seemed too close to Li Ling (despite the fact that Wudi's long reign left room for several distinct generations). That left Jia Yi and Mei Sheng as famous "poetic" names in the Western Han, and the shadowy figure of Mei Sheng probably seemed the better choice.

77. While the Jian'an is technically still the Han, it was generally referred to as a separate period and would not have been designated under the broad rubric "Western or Eastern Han," *liang Han* 兩漢.

Jian'an poets without reservation (and the mid-Wei poets Xi Kang and Ruan Ji, though less fulsomely).

We find the next account of the origins of poetry in the five syllable line probably shortly after *Wenxin diaolong* in the preface to Zhong Rong's *Gradations of Poetry*. The account appears in a linear form in Zhong Rong's preface and piecemeal in the comments appended to individual poets. Unfortunately the preface and the individual comments in the main body are sometimes strikingly at odds, especially in the early period through the third century. The following is the account in the preface.

逮漢李陵, 始著五言之目矣. 古詩眇邈, 人世難詳, 推其文體, 固是炎漢之製, 非衰周之倡也. 自王揚枚馬之徒, 辭賦競爽, 而吟詠靡聞. 從李都尉迄班婕妤, 將百年間, 有婦人焉, 一人而已. 詩人之風, 頓已缺喪. 東京二百載中, 惟有班固詠史, 質木無文. 降及建安, 曹公父子, 篤好斯文; 平原兄弟, 鬱爲文棟; 劉楨王粲, 爲其羽翼. 次有攀龍託鳳, 自致於屬車者, 蓋將百計. 彬彬之盛, 大備於時矣. 爾後陵遲衰微, 迄於有晉. 太康中, 三張二陸兩潘一左, 勃爾復興, 踵武前王, 風流未沫, 亦文章之中興也.

When we reach Li Ling in the Han, the category of the five syllable line appears for the first time. The "old poems" are so far in the past they are unclear, and the times of their authors cannot be ascertained fully; yet when we investigate their form, they are obviously the work of the Han and not the songs of the moribund Zhou.

Poetic expositions of the likes of Wang Bao, Yang Xiong, Mei Sheng, and Sima Xiangru competed in vigor, yet we know nothing of their chants and songs. From Defender Li Ling down to Lady Ban, for an interval of almost a hundred years, there was a woman, and she was the only one. The influence of the poets of the *Shijing* was all at once gone.

During the two centuries in which the capital was in the east there was only Ban Gu's "On History," which was plain wood lacking adornment.

But when we come down to the Jian'an Reign, the lords Cao, father and sons, were steadfastly fond of literary culture. Pingyuan [Cao Zhi] and his brother burgeoned as a beam of letters. Liu Zhen and Wang Can formed the wings. Beyond that there were those who "clung to the dragon and rode the phoenix" [rose by the power of their masters], and those who brought themselves to the level of attendants can be reckoned at almost a hundred. The glory of pattern and substance in balance was fully achieved in those times.

Thereafter things went downhill and grew feeble all the way until the Jin. In the Taikang Reign [280–89] were three Zhangs, two Lus, a

pair of Pans, and a Zuo who burst forth in a renewal and followed in
the footsteps of the former princes [Caos], ease and fluency were not
yet attenuated, and this too was a restoration of literature.[78]

If Liu Xie makes his way tentatively through a series of
problematic attributions of pre-Jian'an poems in the five syl-
lable line, Zhong Rong firmly believes the attributions to Li Ling
and Lady Ban. Belief, however, creates a new problem: Zhong
Rong wants to write a history and there are too few names. He
expresses something of a *horror vacui* at the Western Han after
Li Ling and at the entire Eastern Han. He mentions Lady Ban
and Ban Gu as the "only ones"—and we should point out here
that each of these two figures is credited with only one poem.
Zhong Rong does affirm unambiguously that the anonymous
"old poems" are Han, but his preface leaves us with just two
known poets and two poems for the three centuries between Li
Ling and the Jian'an.

The main body of *Gradations of Poetry* fills that void a little,
though creating some troubling contradictions with the pref-
ace.[79] Ban Gu is indeed included in the judgments, in the
lowest category, where he is grouped with two other late
Eastern Han figures, Li Yan 酈炎 and Zhao Yi 趙壹, both un-
mentioned in the preface, and both of whose poems are so stiff
that they were clearly mentioned only to add to the count of
Eastern Han poems in the five syllable line. We also have the
inclusion, in the middle category, of Xu Shu 徐淑, Qin Jia's wife,
also unmentioned in the preface.[80] The Eastern Han may still
have been relatively empty, but now it had about six poems
rather than one.

---

78. Wang Shumin, *Zhong Rong*, 50–62; Cao Xu, *Shipin*, 8–23.
79. One contradiction between the preface and the comments occurs in the
Wei. The preface treats this as a period of decline, followed by a Jin "restora-
tion." Ruan Ji, who belongs to that period, is accorded a place in Zhong Rong's
highest category, while Xi Kang is placed in the middle category. Moreover, at
the end of the preface Zhong Rong includes a select list of the "very best po-
ems," a list that includes Ruan Ji's "Yonghuai," but none of the "old poems," of
which he says in his comment that "every word is worth a thousand in silver" —
字千金.
80. The case of the Qin Jia poems is a fascinating one. We have some reason
to believe that Zhong Rong knew of only the poem attributed to Xu Shu, the wife,
and that his comments apply only to her one poem. It is possible that the "Qin
Jia" poems included in *Yutai xinyong* were composed after *Gradations of Poetry*
to fill in the gap. See the discussion on pp. 248–54.

Zhong Rong picks up many of the issues raised by Liu Xie. It is likely that Zhong Rong had read Liu Xie's account of the early history of poetry in the five syllable line; but rather than taking Zhong Rong's comments as a direct response to Liu Xie, we might understand both critics as participating in a widespread contemporary discourse on poetry and its history. Liu Xie notes that authors in the five syllable line are not included in the catalogue of the imperial library; Zhong Rong names the famous writers of *fu* and says "we know nothing of their chants and songs." Mei Sheng's name is pointedly included only in the list of *fu* writers. It is hard to believe that Zhong Rong did not know of the attribution of "old poems" to Mei Sheng; apparently he thought this was not worth mentioning. He does believe in Li Ling's authorship of the poems attributed to him, though in his note on Li Ling he qualifies his praise of Li Ling's poetic success as being contingent on his misfortunes ("Had Ling not encountered bitter hardships, how could his writing have been able to reach this level?" 使陵不遭辛苦, 其文亦何能至此).[81]

Although Zhong Rong mentions the "old poems" after Li Ling in the preface (where he wants a datable moment of origin), he places his comments on the "old poems" first in the main body of the work. In the preface there is no uncertainty in ascribing the "old poems" to the Han (presumably the Western Han); in his comments in the main body of the work he cites the opinion that they came from the Caos and Wang Can, after which he leaves the question open. Next we have Lady Ban's poem, with Zhong Rong troubled by the thinness of the record, but with no doubts of Lady Ban's historical authorship of the poem.

Like Liu Xie, Zhong Rong offers one representative of poetry in the five syllable line for the Eastern Han. Perhaps Ban Gu's "On History" replaces Zhang Heng's "Reproach" (Liu Xie's Eastern Han choice) because Zhang Heng's poem was in the four syllable line. Zhong Rong then leaps across a century to get to the Jian'an, which he praises as fulsomely as Liu Xie does.

A "canon" consists of texts and authors whose value almost everyone agrees on—though they may interpret the value differently. By this standard the "old poems" and the main Jian'an

---

81. Wang Shumin, *Zhong Rong*, 140; Cao Xu, *Shipin*, 88.

poets have indeed become part of the canon.[82] After the Jian'an we see a real divergence between Liu Xie and Zhong Rong. For Liu Xie there is a general decline in the Wei, salvaged by the excellence of Xi Kang and Ruan Ji; the situation in the Jin is even worse. For Zhong Rong there is a decline in the Wei, but the Western Jin restores the glories of the Jian'an (Zhong Rong places four of the Western Jin poets in the highest category). Xiao Tong was obviously persuaded by Zhong Rong's point of view.

In terms of constituting canon, the interesting case here is that of Ruan Ji. He had become one of the "great names." For Liu Xie the "great name" had to be a central part of the literary historical account: there are inferior poets in the Wei, but the greatness of Ruan Ji (along with Xi Kang and Ying Qu) salvages the era. The era overall was inferior to the Jian'an precisely because the Jian'an "genius" seems to have touched almost everyone then writing; the Wei was a period of a few solitary talents and general mediocrity. In his preface Zhong Rong, by contrast, is telling a story of the "genius" of the times rather than individuals; he may truly disagree with Liu Xie about the Western Jin, but the two critics are in essential agreement about the Wei. For Zhong Rong the place to acknowledge Ruan Ji is in the litany of great names and great poems; though he is the best poet of his age, he is not treated as central to the history of poetry of his age.

•

Despite their differences, the two critics have much in common; and, judging from comments on earlier poetry by their contemporaries, what they hold in common was shared by the cultural elite in Jiankang in the early sixth century. When describing early poetry in the five syllable line, there is already a canon of names that must be mentioned, including the poets before the Jian'an.

After the "old poems" Liu Xie seems to come to a new level of certainty in the Eastern Han. There is no hesitancy in attributing the poem "Reproach" to Zhang Heng; but "Reproach"—at

---

82. In addition to the *Shishuo xinyu* anecdote, the fact that we have a number of fifth-century imitations might suggest their importance earlier; however, we have those fifth-century imitations thanks to the *Wen xuan* and *Yutai xinyong*, when the "old poems" were formally established.

least in the current version—is a poem in the four syllable line (of which there are a great many examples in the Eastern Han). The inclusion of the Zhang Heng poem, like Zhong Rong's inclusion of Ban Gu's poem, is a modest gesture to satisfy the *horror vacui* of Jiang Yan's two-century leap from Lady Ban to the Jian'an.

Horror vacui is a useful concept here. The early history of poetry in the five syllable line was terribly thin (a thinness that is unsurprising if we are not dealing with a real history of works in a certain form, but simply a few later poems that had picked up early names). New attributions appeared to fill this void. Perhaps old attributions, less widely known, were given new prominence—we know that Ban Gu's "Poem on History" was known already in the time of Shen Yue because Lu Jue mentioned it favorably in his rejoinder to Shen Yue. In addition to Ban Gu, Zhong Rong added Xu Shu, Li Yan, and Zhao Yi. Of these the Li Yan and Zhao Yi poems are credibly Eastern Han poems in the five syllable line, but, as we said earlier, of a quality that suggests Zhong Rong was including whatever he could. Had those poems been written after the middle of the third century, such poets and such work would not have attained even Zhong Rong's lowest category.

The process is obvious. Critics and anthologists were scanning the extant record to supply a corpus of poets and poems from before the Jian'an. The anonymous "old poems" could no longer be "possibly Jian'an" because they were urgently needed elsewhere, in the earlier period. Although he accepted the authenticity of the Li Ling poems, Xiao Tong was generally very scrupulous about problematic attributions and exercised fair judgment in not including some of the dullest but very credibly Eastern Han poems written in the five syllable line.[83]

In compiling the *Yutai xinyong*, however, Xu Ling felt no such scruples. He was, after all, composing an anthology of poetry for reading pleasure. In this anthology the Jian'an was provided with a rich ancestry. Almost an entire *juan* is given to

---

83. For an extensive discussion of Xiao Tong's and Xu Ling's roles as anthologists, see David R. Knechtges, "Culling the Weeds and Selecting Prime Blossoms: The Anthology in Early Medieval China," in Scott Pearce et al., eds., *Culture and Power in the Reconstitution of the Chinese Realm 200–600* (Cambridge: Harvard University Asia Center, 2001), 200–241.

works implicitly pre-Jian'an: anonymous "old poems" and "Mei Sheng's" poems, anonymous *yuefu*, Lady Ban's fan poem, along with a poem from the Li Ling corpus now attributed to Su Wu. Li Yannian's song on Lady Li is included from the *Han shu*. Zhang Heng was improbably credited with an erotic poem in the five syllable line (the "Tongsheng ge" 同聲歌); we have a full set of the poems between Qin Jia and his wife (Qin Jia's poems may well have been composed for the anthology); "Watering My Horse by the Great Wall" 飲馬長城窟行 ceased to be anonymous (as it was in the *Wen xuan*) and became the work of Cai Yong. In addition two charming ballads attributed to otherwise unknown "Han" figures Xin Yannian and Song Zihou were added.[84] Last but not least, there was the very long narrative ballad "Old Poem: On the Wife of Jiao Zhongqing" 古詩爲焦仲卿妻作, of much debated date, but whose current version is probably Southern Dynasties. Where there had been lamentably few poems before, now there were many—not a few of which seem to have been recent compositions donated by an age rich in poems to an age poor in poems. A remarkable number of these poems have remained in every modern anthology of early classical poetry—always in roughly the same order. In place of a void we have a "canon."

We do indeed have a "history," but this history is not of poetry in the five syllable line before the Jian'an; the history we are discovering takes place between the completion of the *Song shu* in 488 and the compilation of the *Yutai xinyong* about half a century later. In 488 the history of poetry in the five syllable line was not an issue: there was a larger history of "poetic writing," with poetry in the five syllable line as the final phase in the larger history, a phase that begins a second history of poetry, this time primarily of poetry in the five syllable line. But for Shen Yue, the Jian'an had no significant previous history in five-syllable-line poetry.

Jiang Yan's imitations of famous poetry in the five syllable line were organized chronologically and had to take into ac-

---

84. In an unpublished paper Tian Xiaofei has shown that, apart from some Southern *yuefu* of dubious date, the falling of spring flowers does not appear in poetry until the turn of the sixth century; since this is the topic of the Song Zihou "Dong Jiaorao," we can reasonably suspect that this was a Qi or Liang poem.

count the early attributions of a few famous poems in circulation as well as the anonymous "old poems." This was not a history of poetry in the five syllable line before the Jian'an; it was simply the consequence of organizing names chronologically. Liu Xie did want to write a brief history of poetry in the five syllable line, but there was much about poetry before the Jian'an of which he was uncertain. The one thing of which he was certain was that the "old poems" were as important as the Jian'an poets. Zhong Rong added a few more names and affirmed the reliability of the attributions that Liu Xie doubted. Xu Ling finished the task with a wide range of anonymous poems and a considerable set of verses by named poets. This canon has survived.

•

The anthologies and critical works of the Southern Dynasties preserved, organized, and perhaps radically edited a selective portion of older poetic material preserved in manuscript. Later ages received that selection of material and elaborated their own accounts of "Han and Wei" poetry. The mid-Ming raised to canonical status the anonymous *yuefu* and Cao Cao (placed in Zhong Rong's lowest category as an example of "old directness," *guzhi* 古直).[85] Traditional literary history resembles a queue in which sequence remains constant, while dates change. The anonymous "old poems" occupied a place in the queue before the datable poems of Li Ling and Lady Ban. When Li Ling's and Lady Ban's poems lost credit, the anonymous "old poems" kept the place in the sequence, moving forward into the Eastern Han to serve as the poetic monuments prior to the Jian'an. At the same time the anonymous *yuefu* entered the queue at an earlier position.[86] This essential sequence is maintained in virtually every anthology and textbook and literary history, as if it were a historical fact beyond question. Out of this sequence is constructed a habitual account of literary and cultural history: once upon a time there was a simple and direct poetry of the "folk"—these poems are the anonymous *yuefu*, belonging to the Western Han or to a relatively early period in the Eastern Han. These were followed by the more regular poems of unknown

---

85. Wang Shumin, *Zhong Rong*, 324; Cao Xu, *Shipin*, 362.

86. We should note that in *Yutai xinyong* the anonymous "old poems" precede anonymous *yuefu*.

literary men toward the end of the Eastern Han, the "old po-
ems." Building on this basis, the Jian'an poets wrote a more
literary, yet still vigorous poetry. In many ways this standard
modern account recapitulates the claims of the Qi and Liang
critics: that poetry begins in simplicity and moves to ever
greater complexity and literary embellishment.

Even as the assumed dates of anonymous poems float across
centuries, the assumed sequence remains quite stable. What is
remarkable is the absence of any indication, beyond sixth-
century guesses, that the anonymous "old poems" predate the
Jian'an. The early evidence that the anonymous *yuefu* are Han
(apart from some fanciful etiologies of particular songs) is a
single, brief statement by Shen Yue:

凡樂章古詞, 今之存者, 並漢世街陌謠謳, 江南可采蓮, 烏生十五子, 白頭吟之屬
是也.

In general, the old lyrics of musical pieces that survive today are jointly
street songs of Han times. These are the sort of "In the Southland you
can pick lotus," "The crow bore," "Fifteen,"[87] and "Song of White
Hair."[88]

This is indeed a "claim" by Shen Yue—though we are uncertain
both to the extent of the claim and the basis of the claim.[89]
Compared to his careful and extensive documentation of the
history of ritual song, with lists of all titles and period dates, it
is remarkably vague ("the sort of," *zhishu*). When he has a
specific fact he knows, like Xun Xu's 荀勖 "compilation" of the

---

87. The Chinese text given is the original. The editors want either to remove
the *zi* 子 to give the poem "Fifteen," mentioned in the *Jilu*, but not included by
Shen Yue (*Sung shu*, 561, note 14) or to change "fifteen" to "eight or nine," *bajiu*
八九, giving "The crow bore eight or nine young," the first line of that *yuefu*. Su
Jinren 蘇晉仁 and Xiao Lianzi 蕭煉子, *Song shu Yuezhi jiaozhu* 宋書樂志校注
(Ji'nan: Qi Lu shushe, 1982), 59, 62.

88. *Song shu*, 549. Charles Egan bases his argument that the texts of the
"Treatise on Music" were transcribed from performance practice on a slightly
different translation of this passage. He understands *yuezhang guci* 樂章古詞 as
"the musical pieces and old lyrics" rather than "the old lyrics of musical pieces."
See Egan, "Reconsidering the Role of Folk Songs in Pre-T'ang *Yüeh-fu* Devel-
opment," 69.

89. See the thoughtful discussion in Masuda Kiyohide 増田清秀, *Gafu no
rekishiteki kenkyū* 樂府の歷史的研究 (Tokyo: Sōbunsha, 1975), 79–83. Masuda
argues that the passage has been misinterpreted. He is, however, interested in
the category *xianghe geci* 相和歌辭, arguing that popular music was selected
and modified for court performance in the reign of Wei Mingdi.

Qingshang sandiao 清商三調, he mentions it. His claim here raises more questions than it answers and is an exceedingly unsound basis on which to ascribe all texts characterized as "old lyrics" to sometime in the four centuries of the Han.[90] Even if we understand Shen Yue as claiming that all the "old lyrics" he includes are Han (whether we believe the claim or not), that does not mean that texts called "old lyrics" in other sources should be presumed to be Han.[91]

•

Our common account of the beginnings of classical poetry, an account covering at least several centuries, is based on texts whose dates are far from certain. It is possible that the historical sequence is indeed as commonly described; it is possible that there is a historical sequence that is far more complicated; it is no less possible that all these texts are roughly from the same period, the first part of the third century. What is clear, however, is that variation in stylistic register—with implications of class, literacy, and venue of presentation—has been transposed to a historical sequence, in which texts in a lower register are presumed to precede texts in a higher register. We have no evidence of real history here; rather, we have a belief about historical process, in which the simple moves to the complex, the less literary to the more literary. Such belief made it possible to account for undatable poetic material in a history of poetry.

---

90. The first question we would ask is: How does he know this? Perhaps it is "tradition," but we do not know in this case if "tradition" means a continuous account or a vague way of accounting for early texts. This brings us back to the formal problem of anonymity. Shen Yue had no other term but "old lyrics" to classify anonymity or unknown authorship in a collection where most other texts are marked by dynasty. We need to situate Shen Yue's judgment of a Han date in the context of the "Treatise on Music," most of which is devoted to preserving ritual texts in the highest register. What are these anonymous poems doing here and how can we value them, given the compiler's commitment to preserve the received court manuscript tradition as he has it? What are obviously secular texts doing among high ritual texts? "Old" becomes a justification. "Street songs," with its *Shijing* associations of collecting popular lyrics, explains the difference of such texts from the ritual songs. It is, indeed, true that these seem like popular songs, but we have no certainty when they entered the court repertoire.

91. A survey of the use of the term in encyclopedias, not to mention indecision in the sources of musical poetry, shows us that it is used very vaguely.

We can indeed see, on the level of specifically elite poetic practice, a rough process of increasing ornamentation in poetic language through the course of the third century. This does not mean, however, that lower register poetry disappeared, somehow "replaced" by higher register poetry. Indeed, we have good evidence that lower register poetic composition continued throughout the third century.

•

This fundamental problem about the dating of anonymous poetry begs a number of other valid questions that make an account of the origins of classical poetry even more problematic. Most of these are questions for which we can provide no good answers, but we have ample evidence in the textual record to keep them open as questions. How stable were the texts of early poetry? We have, of course, numerous variants, as well as texts that survive in quite different versions. Adding and subtracting couplets and using different lines seem to have been common, not only in later manuscript venues, but also in the manuscript tradition before the sixth century. We have persuasive evidence that some texts were modified to suit sixth-century poetic standards in *Yutai xinyong* and in the *yuefu* sources used by Guo Maoqian in *Yuefu shiji*. If we find this commonly in a handful of song texts where we can compare versions with those in the *Song shu*, what are we to assume about other early texts in *Yutai xinyong* and *Yuefu shiji* for which no other version exists for comparison? We have seen in this chapter how the "old poems" became classics; some of the anonymous *yuefu* became classics later. Yet these texts were being done in different versions and modified to suit the norms of the venue in which they appear, even in the early sixth century.

What is the nature of "authorship" in early poetry? Certainly there were some circumstantially occasional poems that persuade us to trust attributions of authorship; yet there were also persona poems, no less circumstantial, in which someone assumed the role of a speaker in a particular circumstance. There was a fine line between the intuition that a known poet would have been an appropriate author for an anonymous poem and actual attribution of authorship. Poems seem to have gathered to Cao Zhi, swelling his collection. Multiple attributions of poems are not uncommon. Secure knowledge of authorship may no longer be accessible, and in a world where texts were always changing, it may be irrelevant.[92]

We must also ask questions more specifically about writing. What was written down, when, and why? Were texts written or transcribed from oral recitation? How much care was taken in copying these kinds of texts? We know that in the case of the imperial library only a very small part of the manuscript tradition in Luoyang was carried to Jiankang, when the Jin reestablished itself in the South. What part of that manuscript tradition was selected by Six Dynasties anthologists, and to what degree did they change the texts they selected to conform to an imagined standard of difference and change?

We need to radically rethink our account of the beginnings of classical Chinese poetry in the third century and earlier. It is worthwhile raising these questions, questions often overlooked, but important questions; at the same time, we should avoid trying to give definitive answers for which the evidence is inadequate. We should not try to give an account of literary history based on texts whose attribution and dating are highly uncertain, nor should we try to define clear genres when there were none. We should, rather, look at the material we have as the surviving traces of a much larger world of poetry and song, traces mediated by the interests of later ages in their preservation, and see what those texts can tell us.

•

Every pre-Tang text must be considered in relation to its provenance. Each source has its own peculiar features and its own motives, motives that shape both the selection and the form of the text. This is not to say that some of these texts do not represent an accurate lineage of manuscripts going back to the Han or Wei—the question is that we simply do not know.

The "Treatise on Music" of the *Song shu* did not "select" poems for readers; it conserved. It conserved material of an imperial musical repertoire that included both ritual and secular texts. The "Treatise on Music" is a precious survivor because it preserves texts from a performance tradition, with

---

92. For the question of authenticity, see Hans H. Frankel, "The Problem of Authenticity in the Works of Cao Zhi," in Chan Ping-leung et al., eds., *Essays in Commemoration of the Golden Jubilee of the Fung Bing Shan Library (1932–1982)* (Hong Kong: Hong Kong University Press, 1982), 183–201.

all the extraneous lines and textual problems, without making those texts fit the shape of "poetry" as it appeared in the sixth century.[93] This is the court ritual tradition, with a long history of care and probable textual conservation. As suggested earlier, if this is the manuscript tradition of poetry in the court, we cannot but wonder about other manuscripts of poetry.

The *Wen xuan* chose texts to represent "the best" and instantiate tradition; Xiao Tong may have accepted the judgments of people like Zhong Rong regarding the anonymous "old poems," but he was clearly someone who favored good texts. If we believe the preface (and there is no reason not to), *Yutai xinyong* chose texts because they gave pleasure. We don't know what was in Zhijiang's *Gujin yuelu* from 568; because this work is commonly cited by Guo Maoqian, we presume that its contents were copied into *Yuefu shiji*, and it seems the most likely source for many of the anonymous early *yuefu* that did not come from *Song shu*. On the whole these other early *yuefu* present fewer textual difficulties than the *Song shu* texts; this may reflect sixth-century editing and a degree of freedom from the constraints that compelled Shen Yue to copy out the manuscripts as he had them.[94] And we should mention the Tang anthology *Guwen yuan* 古文苑, which gives its own selection from the manuscript tradition that survived into the Tang, including some of the "old poems" and Li Ling poems that were omitted by the sixth-century anthologies.

The Sui and Tang encyclopedias—Yu Shinan's 虞世南 (558– 638) *Beitang shuchao* 北堂書鈔, Ouyang Xun's 歐陽詢 (557–641) *Yiwen leiju* 藝文類聚, and Xu Jian's 徐堅 (659–729) *Chuxue ji* 初學記—along with the Li Shan 李善 commentary on the *Wen*

---

93. Any reading of the "Treatise on Music" has to situate such a real interest in preserving court song in the context of acknowledged change and loss. We can only guess from where and by what accidents Shen Yue had the texts he recorded. In a treatise whose primary concern is court ritual music, why do we have decidedly social verses by Cao Cao and Cao Pi, but not Wang Can's *Poems for Bringing Peace to the Age, Anshi shi* 安世詩, ritual poems with immense resonance? These are, as Shen Yue says, "now lost" 今亡 (Su Jinren, *Song shu*, 21). So many of the ritually important pieces Shen Yue mentions are lost, even in the context of anxious conservation of ritual texts, that we must wonder why we have the texts that have survived.

94. If the *Gujin yuelu* was the source for the alternative version of the anonymous "Full Song," "Man'ge xing," discussed in Appendix C, we have a comparative case.

xuan—are as invaluable as they are problematic. The compilers still had access to the older manuscript tradition, including an unknown range of materials that were preserved in the North; their motives for selection (examples for encyclopedia headings and source passages for commentary) were very different from the motives of the anthologists, and they preserved many texts not preserved elsewhere. They sometimes copied carelessly and often gave only passages and excerpts, to provide examples that suited their rubrics. At the same time these works were not subject to the same level of "correction" that was commonplace in editions mediated by literary scholarship; in recent times such "corrections" are often scrupulously noted, but we have clear evidence that editors in early print culture (and in manuscript culture) simply changed texts to fix what they saw as errors or to make a passage conform to a standard text. The extent of citations in the encyclopedias and commentaries also reminds us of the range of material that did not get anthologized. That same manuscript tradition was preserved through the Tang, reemerging in later encyclopedias like Bai Juyi's 白居易 (772–846) *Baishi liutie shilei ji* 白氏六帖事類集 and the massive 1,000-*juan Taiping yulan* 太平御覽, completed in 983, compiled from previous, often lost encyclopedias.

Considered as a whole, these sources are all different "takes" on manuscript traditions that survived into the late Southern Dynasties and beyond, through serial burnings of the imperial libraries and recollecting manuscripts, perhaps from inferior sources. We see the poetry of the third century and earlier (poetry in the five syllable line and *yuefu* in irregular lines) through accidents of transmission of a literary form that was not accorded fully serious "literary" status until the fifth century. We still have much, but we cannot forget the intermediaries through whom we have what we have.

While we may question specific attributions, we will try to treat this body of material—anonymous *yuefu*, anonymous "old poems," and a body of verse attributed to known authors from the end of the second century through the first part of the third century—as "one poetry"; that is, as if it were synchronic. Where historical differences are clear from credibly datable texts, we may comment on them; but we will always try to remember that other kinds of composition continued and were not necessarily older. We will attempt to set a parameter for the origins of this poetry; we will not try to define when such poetry ceased to be written. This enables us to look at what this poetry has in common in terms of shared compositional techniques. We will try to describe differences in terms of register rather than historical change or authorial style.

Early Traces

Most of the rich body of verse surviving in sources that can be credibly dated to the Han is in the four syllable line or in the longer irregular line sometimes called the "Chu song" form. Our purpose here is not to survey this material, however interesting it is, but to look for texts in the five syllable line, datable to the Han, along with irregular texts that already use the conventions and patterns that characterize both the "old poems" and most of the anonymous *yuefu*. This will permit us to establish how early the more uncertain texts could be.

One important grouping of songs is of the eighteen "Naoge" 鐃歌, preserved in the *Song shu*. Unlike the "old lyrics," Shen Yue specifies these as "Han" in the title. Some of these are so textually corrupt that they are either unreadable or readable only in part. Although some of the "Naoge"—those textually best preserved—treat "popular" motifs, many of these pieces belong to a court context.[95] What is remarkable about those we can read is that they show no traces of the conventions and line patterns so widely shared among the other anonymous *yuefu*, "old poems," and literary poems. This negative evidence does imperfectly suggest that these are the earliest texts we have preserved in the later sources.[96] The five syllable line is used sometimes, but the poems are largely irregular. However interesting these pieces are, we will place them outside the scope of our study.

Apart from the random appearance of lines with five syllables in early texts, our first texts in the five syllable line (with its

---

95, We know this from the titles and from readable passages. This probably represents a court performance repertoire, combining explicitly imperial occasions with less formal pieces probably used in banquet performance.

96. Many scholars, including Lu Qinli, consider these to be authentic Western Han survivals. This is quite possible, though there is no real evidence to assume this is the case.

characteristic 2:3 rhythm and grammatical patterns) appear in the *Han shu* of Ban Gu 班固 (32–92), that is, toward the end of the first century. These are songs ascribed to Lady Qi 戚夫人, imprisoned by Dowager Empress Lü after the death of the Han founder, Gaozu, in 195 B.C., and to the singer Li Yannian 李延年 in the reign of Emperor Wu (140–87 B.C.), along with two street songs making figurative reference to political events in the reign of Emperor Cheng (Han Chengdi).[97] One of the street songs has only a few lines in the five syllable line. We might add that all but Lady Qi's song, along with some songs in other meters, were included in *Yutai xinyong* (removing a moralizing couplet in one of the street songs).

The sources are widely known. The question is how the sources are used. Since the *Han shu* is a very "serious" history, earlier scholars have tended to accept the dates it assigns to works. We have many Western Han texts containing verse of various kinds. When we note that the five syllable line is represented as being used by an imperial concubine, a professional singer, and in prophetic children's street songs, we must at least suspect that in Ban Gu's map of styles, five-syllable-line verse belongs to "women and children" and upstarts from the lower class. That is, in the *Han shu* the five syllable line is a discursive "sumptuary" sign marking one's social place, just as mastery of an archaic lexicon marks another class.

Lady Qi's song is part of the sensational narrative of Empress Dowager Lü taking revenge on her rival Lady Qi after Gaozu's death. In the first stage of her humiliation, she is chained, her head is shaved, and she is dressed in the red robes of a criminal, forced to hull grain. She sings:[98]

子爲王	The son is a prince,
母爲虜	the mother is a slave.
終日舂薄暮	All day long she hulls grain until dusk,
常與死爲伍	ever the companion of those condemned to die.
相離三千里	We are three thousand leagues apart:
當誰使告女	who can I have tell you?

---

97. Lu Qinli, 91, 102, 126. See Donald Holzman, "Les premiers vers pentasyllabiques datés dans la poésie chinoise," *Mélanges de sinologie offerts à Monsieur Paul Demieville* (Paris: Presses universitaires de France, 1974), 81–84.

98. *Han shu*, 3937.

On hearing of this song, the Dowager Empress has Lady Qi's limbs cut off; she is blinded, deafened, and made mute, becoming "the human swine." As with the other verse in the five syllable line quoted in the *Han shu* the rhythms are right, but only a few of the conventions of later five-syllable-line verse can be seen. In this case, it is the common measure of distance, with the first hemistich using various formulations of "apart" (*xiangli* 相離 in this case), and the second hemistich measuring that distance.

It is always worth asking how we come to have such a text. We cannot reject out of hand the possibility of some listener who heard this song and passed it on to Empress Lü. Somehow the verse continued to be transmitted verbatim, at some point entering the written record that appeared in transmitted texts two centuries later. It is, however, clearly the song Lady Qi "should have" sung, a voice of protest that serves as the etiology of having her tongue cut out. Although we cannot absolutely reject the possibility that Lady Qi did indeed recite these verses, they have all the marks of historical romance, in which the protagonist, at an intense emotional moment, bursts into song.

Few still believe that the Li Yannian song actually dates from the reign of Emperor Wu; rather, it probably comes from the historical romances that grew up around Emperor Wu later in the Han.[99] It is possible that the street songs do indeed come from the reign of Emperor Cheng; but one refers to the notorious Zhao Feiyan and her sister, also a favorite topic of historical romance, and the other supposedly anticipates Wang Mang's usurpation of the Han throne. We do not know when any of these poems originated; they even could have been invented by Ban Gu or reformulated by Ban Gu. All we can say with certainty from these examples is that the five syllable line was in use in the second half of the first century and was then associated with low social status.

---

99. David Knechtges argues for the link between the Lady Li biography and the legends growing up around Emperor Wu in "Han Wudi de fu" 漢武帝的賦, in *Disanjie guoji cifuxue xueshu yantaohui lunwenji* 第三屆國際辭賦學學術研討會論文集 (December 1996), 1–14.

The song ascribed to Li Yannian 李延年 in the *Han History* (*Han shu* 漢書) is set in a narrative in which the famous musician praises his sister to Emperor Wu.[100]

Emperor Xiaowu's Lady Li originally entered the court as a performer. Earlier Lady Li's brother Li Yannian had an innate understanding of music and was skilled at singing and dance. Emperor Wu [Xiaowu] was quite fond of him. Whenever he did his variations on popular songs, the audience never failed to be stirred. Once when attending on the Emperor, Li Yannian rose to dance and sang:

北方有佳人	In the north country is a lady fair,
絕世而獨立	she stands alone beyond compare.
一顧傾人城	She glances once, a city falls;
再顧傾人國	a kingdom falls when she glances again.
寧不知	Surely you know that a lady so fair,
傾城與傾國	she for whom cities and kingdoms fall,
佳人難再得	will never be found again.

The Emperor heaved a great sigh: "Wonderful! But could there really be such a woman in this day and age?"[101]

The song alludes to the *Shijing* (264, "Look Up" 瞻卬), where the destructive power of the woman is not yet a standard figure for beguiling beauty:

哲夫成城	The smart man builds a city,
哲婦傾城	The smart woman brings the city down.

Since the anecdote clearly plays on Emperor Wu's blindness to the warning of the allusion in the song, it could possibly have been a fabrication of Ban Gu himself, imitating what he understood as a singer's style.

Only the first line can be recognized immediately as using a template familiar in the corpus of "old poems" and *yuefu*. The rest of the poem does not use familiar templates and mixes true five syllable lines (ll. 1, 3, 4, and 6) with four syllable lines expanded to five syllable lines by the addition of a particle.[102] This

---

100. Lu Qinli, 102; *Han shu*, 3951; *Ytxy* 1; *Ywlj* 18; *Cxj* 10, 19.

101. *Han shu*, 3951.

102. Rather than think of such lines as "expanded," it might be best to think of them as lines that can be realized in either four or five syllables by the subtraction or addition of a particle. This was, of course, a useful technique for integrating *Shijing* lines into five syllable verse. Since there was also a popular four syllable verse style in the early period, such flexible lines could be used in either of the two meters. This song could easily be entirely rewritten into

absence of the familiar phrases and patterns of five-syllable-line verse, both in this song and in the street songs, is significant: these were so much a part of later poetry in the five syllable line that we might conclude either that these poems come from a time when such conventions did not exist or that they were composed by someone of a social class who was not familiar with them (like Ban Gu).

Moving roughly a half century into the future, we see those missing conventions very much in place in a stele inscription for one Fei Feng 費鳳, mentioning the date A.D. 143, but probably composed in the second half of the second century.[103] The commemorative verse is in the five syllable line. We can only wonder what peculiar circumstances led to this unique case of inscribing five syllable verse on a stele. Parts are stiff and narrative, offering a precedent for some of the *yuefu* attributed to Cao Cao. This verse includes both metrically variable lines (often varied from the *Shijing*) and template lines characteristic of the *yuefu* and "old poems." When southeastern bandits foment troubles, we read: "In Danyang there were Yue brigands," *Danyang you Yue kou* 丹陽有越寇.[104] In the middle, with Fei Feng's death, we have some very familiar lines:

不悟奄忽終	Before we were aware, he was suddenly gone,
藏形而匿影	his form, hidden, and his shadow concealed.
耕夫釋耒耜	The plowman sets aside his plow,
桑女投鉤筥	the mulberry picker drops her handled basket.
道阻而且長	The road is blocked and long,
起坐淚如雨	rising or sitting, my tears are like rain.[105]

The poem closes:

壹別會無期	Once we part, there is no date set to meet,
相去三千里	three thousand leagues apart.

---

smooth four syllable lines without any loss to the sense: 北方佳人, 絕世獨立. 一顧傾城, 再顧傾國. 傾城傾國, 佳人難得.

103. Lu Qinli, 175–76. Parts of the verse are first quoted by Ouyang Xiu in the *Jigu lu* 集古錄, *Ouyang Xiu quanji* (rpt. Taibei: Shijie shuju, 1963), 1120–21.

104. Cf. Cao Cao describing the coalition against Dong Zhuo in "The Land of the Dead" 蒿里行: "In Guandong there were righteous gentlemen" 關東有義士 (Lu Qinli, 347).

105. In this line I follow the reading in the *Jigu lu*, rather than the *Li shi* 隸釋, the source for Lu Qinli's version, which reads the first two characters of the line as 望遠.

絕翰永忼慨	I stop my brush, ever overcome with feeling,
泣下不可止	tears fall and cannot be stopped.

For the reader familiar with the *yuefu* and "old poems," this is remarkable. From the famous anonymous *yuefu* "Moshang sang" 陌上桑 we have "the plowman forgets his plow" 耕者忘其犁, a gesture that follows from his amazement at Luofu's beauty. In Fei Feng's stele virtually the same gesture is from grief at Fei Feng's passing. We have, in effect, a topic (*topos*) that can be rephrased and applied in very different contexts: the death of an important man or awe at a beautiful girl.

Other lines recall numerous instances in the *yuefu* and "old poems." We need only quote lines from the first of the "Nineteen Old Poems":

相去萬餘里	More than ten thousand leagues apart,
各在天一涯	each at an edge of the sky.
道路阻且長	The road is blocked and long,
會面安可知	how can we meet face to face again?

Perhaps the best indication that Fei Feng's stele verse has been realized through a body of lyric convention is the line "three thousand leagues apart," in which a line appropriate to "parting when still living" has been appropriated for "parted by death," but measuring the exact distance from the dead.

Fei Feng's stele inscription closes with the speaker too overcome by emotion to continue, which is perhaps the most common form of poetic closure in the corpus of "old poems." There is, however, one detail that deserves note: the speaker *jue han* 絕翰, "stops his brush," gesturing to composition specifically in writing. This is something we do not find in the received corpus of early poetry. It is, moreover, not simply writing a text down, but a process of composition represented as carried out in writing, perhaps suggesting the less painstaking scripts that accompanied the spread of paper.[106] Orality is certainly somewhere behind this text, but it is worth keeping in mind that the first roughly datable poem using many poetic conventions

---

106. It is worth noting that in the second half of the second century we begin to find comments on "draft script," *caoshu* 草書. This kind of script enabled a more fluid kind of writing whose speed could more closely approach an oral compositional practice.

which endured into later datable poetry declares itself to be a written text, not simply a text preserved in writing.

To point out these correspondences is *not* to suggest that the "old poems" or anonymous *yuefu* in their present versions can be necessarily dated to the first or second century; rather it tells us that by the middle of the second century we can already see the existence of a body of lyric conventions that were the basis on which many of the "old poems" were composed. Those same conventions were still in use throughout the third century.

TWO

A *"Grammar" of*
Early Poetry

When we set aside questions of the "original text," authorship, and relative dating, we can think of each extant text as a single realization of many possible poems that might have been composed. What survives is certainly only a small fraction of all the poems actually composed and of different realizations of the texts that survive. We have textual variants, texts given as "variant versions" of the "same" poem, and poems considered "different" but which have lengthy passages in common. When we think of this as a spectrum of variation, we realize there is no absolute boundary separating another version of the "same" poem from a "different" poem. When we imagine the variations that no longer survive and segments combined in different ways, we begin to think of this as "one poetry," as a single continuum rather than as a corpus of texts either canonized or ignored. It has its recurrent themes, its relatively stable passages and line patterns, and its procedures.

Some of the individual poems that emerged from this "one poetry" possess a singular beauty; all have an aura. In this chapter we will discuss the common ground from which these poems emerged—its "language," the shared rules by which poems were produced. From the surviving corpus we can learn much about its building blocks and its compositional procedures. Lexical register, varying between a plain style and a learned or literary style, is one important component of this "language"; to those who believe that such difference represents historical change, moving from the plain and popular to the learned and elite, we should note that the Fei Feng stele, our earliest datable example of the characteristic material of the "old poems," is both learned and explicitly written.

Commonplace Lines and Variation

We might first consider a line that occurs in Fei Feng's stele inscription and one in the first of the "Nineteen Old Poems": the former reads *dao zu erqie chang* 道阻而且長, and the latter reads *daolu zu qie chang* 道路阻且長; both can be translated as "the road is blocked and long." The line would surely have been intelligible even to an illiterate listener, but anyone with a modest education would have recognized behind this a line with the same meaning from "Jianjia" 蒹葭 in the *Shijing* (Mao 129): *dao zu qie chang* 道阻且長. Both five-syllable-line versions represent common techniques for expanding a four syllable line: adding a particle (especially in the third position of the five syllable line) or turning a single syllable noun into a compound noun. Fei Feng's stele follows the former technique, adding the particle *er* to the *qie* ("and") to form the compound particle *erqie*, while the "Nineteen Old Poems" line expands the monosyllabic *dao* ("road") to the common compound *daolu*.[1]

We do not know enough to decide whether this qualifies as an "allusion" to the *Shijing* or has entered the contemporary poetic repertoire so fully that it exists independently as a commonplace.[2] What we can say, however, is that both of these five-syllable-line versions are essentially the "same" line, realized differently. This kind of difference is one of the most common kinds of textual variant within a single text.

---

1. If the Fei Feng stele version sounds more awkward and "primitive," then that moves the first of the "Nineteen Old Poems" to a later period when the stylistic patterns of five syllables were more regularized.

2. The Fei Feng stele verse is filled with references to the *Shijing*, and we are tempted to take it as an "allusion" of sorts. The context of the line's use in the *Shijing* and in the Fei Feng stele inscription is, however, so different that it is best to consider it, like many pieces of the *Shijing* that crop up in the old poems, as a "tag"; that is, a freely floating line, detached from its original context, that can be applied to any appropriate occasion. In many ways this follows the ancient tradition of *Shijing* citation, "taking a passage out of context" (*duanzhang quyi*). We should also keep in mind the degree to which the *Shijing* was still a voiced and performed text in the Eastern Han; pieces of poems could be heard, circulate, and enter an oral repertoire without implying "learning."

When we come to the "Song of Grief" ("Beifen shi" 悲憤詩), attributed to Cai Yan 蔡琰 but probably composed sometime between the mid-third and the early fourth century, we can see what deserves to be called a "variation" on the line: *jiong lu xian qie zu* 迥路險且阻, "the distant road is dangerous and blocked."[3] "Long," *chang* 長, has been replaced by a higher register synonym, *jiong* 迥, and transposed to modify "road"; moreover, "dangerous," *xian* 險, has been added as a new attribute. The basic form of the line, however, remains exactly the same as its realization in the first of the "Nineteen Old Poems."

We would also call Cao Zhi's version, in the second of his two poems on "Sending Off Mr. Ying" 送應氏二首, a variation. Here we should quote the full couplet:[4]

山川阻且遠	The mountains and rivers are blocked and distant,
別促會日長	parting presses us, the day of our meeting is far off.

Here we see the same sequence of topics as in the first of the "Nineteen Old Poems":[5]

道路阻且長	The road is blocked and long,
會面安可知	how can we meet face to face again.

In Cao Zhi's version the *chang* 長 ("long," translated above as "far off" in context) has been removed from the commonplace line on the blocked interval between those parting, but has returned in the following line. The use of *chang* in the phrase *hui ri chang* 會日長, "the day of our meeting is far off," is slightly odd (it could mean "the day of our meeting lasts long"); but the meaning is governed both by an expectation of what should be said under the circumstances and by the sense of *chang* in the more usual phrasing of the topic of the preceding line, "blocked and long."[6]

When we come to the latter part of the third century, we can see a new principle in variation, to which we can give the term "copiousness" (*copia*) used in traditional European poetics:

---

3. Lu Qinli, 199. For the question of attribution, see pp. 232–43.
4. Lu Qinli, 454–55.
5. Ibid., 329.
6. Cao Zhi cannot, of course, use *chang* as the final word in the first line of his couplet because of the rhyme he has established.

what was one line is stretched into two or more lines. Cao Zhi can replace the "road" with "mountains and rivers"; in the fourth of his poems "On Feeling" 情詩, Zhang Hua keeps Cao Zhi's variation but restores the road in another line:[7]

懸邈修塗遠	So remote, the lasting road is distant,
山川阻且深	mountains and rivers are blocked and deep.

Even with this expansion, the form of the base line is retained. Again, in Zhang Hua's younger contemporary Lu Ji, in "Imitating 'I Crossed the River to Pick Lotus'" 擬涉江采芙蓉:[8]

故鄉一何曠	How widely divided he is from his homeland!—
山川阻且難	mountains and rivers are blocked and difficult.

So far we have been talking about different realizations and variations of what we can call a single "topic."[9] The line can also provide a formal template for a different though related meaning, as in the first line of the twelfth of the "Nineteen Old Poems": *dongcheng gao qie chang* 東城高且長, "the eastern wall is high and long."[10] The template line can also suggest other adjacent components of a theme, as in the following passage from one of the poems in the Li Ling corpus:[11]

良友遠別離	Parted far from my good friend,
各在天一方	each of us on a different side of the sky.
山海隔中州	Mountains and seas cut me off from the heartland,
相去悠且長	our being apart is lasting and long.
嘉會難再遇	A fine meeting is hard to encounter again,
歡樂殊未央	our pleasure and joy is not yet done.

For the sake of comparison, let me quote the opening of the first of the "Nineteen Old Poems":

行行重行行	On and on, and once again on and on,
與君生別離	parted from you when still living.

---

7. Lu Qinli, 619.
8. Ibid., 687.
9. See Introduction.
10. Lu Qinli, 332.
11. Ibid., 339.

相去萬餘里	More than ten thousand leagues apart,
各在天一涯	each at an edge of the sky.
道路阻且長	The road is blocked and long,
會面安可知	how can we meet face to face again?

Here we begin to get a sense of the "mix and match" element of early poetics. In both the first of the "Nineteen Old Poems" and the Cao Zhi passage quoted above, the topic "the road is blocked and long" is followed in the same couplet by the topic "when will we meet again?" In this poem from the Li Ling corpus, a similar line, with the familiar pattern in the second hemistich, ends a couplet and clearly evokes the topic of meeting again in the first line of the next couplet.

The wrong lesson to draw from this series of examples is that everyone is imitating the first of the "Nineteen Old Poems" as we now have it.[12] This is not impossible, but it is not the point: the poems of this period are part of a fluid repertoire of loosely associated topics and line templates that could be realized in many different ways. There is a virtual network of topics and linkages that transcends any particular realization. We will later see cases in which a text is clearly echoing a prior text, but that works very differently from these habitual and often repeated patterns.

Topic and Theme: Sleepless at Night

In the realm of "old poems," as well as many anonymous *yuefu* and poems by known authors, the forms of poetic utterance are largely conventional. We can roughly set out a range of themes, each theme linked to a set of topics addressed in a fluid sequence. Whenever a given topic appears, it may draw in other, associated topics. Each topic has a lexicon, a register of articulation that varies from "plain" to "ornamented." The higher the lexical register, the more likely there will be variation. To these compositional principles we must add another. We must understand these thematic units as segments, which can either stand alone or be compounded in *yuefu* and some poems.

---

12. Indeed, our current version of the first of the "Nineteen Old Poems," "On and on," may not have been the one most commonly in circulation in the third century; see pp. 285–95.

Themes often intersect with other themes. As we will see, the theme of immortals can lead to the feast or vice versa; in another direction, the feast can lead to the theme of parting and separation (in this case, for the obvious social role of the parting feast). A theme can be extensively treated or appear as a single couplet, the extensiveness of treatment often varying in different versions and citations of a single text.

Let us address these elements one by one, beginning with the smallest unit, the "topic." We have already looked at a small set of these above in "the road is blocked and long." One of the finest examples, however, can be found in Suzuki Shūji's *Kan Gi shi no kenkyū* in a list of lines from the poetry of the period on the brevity of human life.[13] This topic could be used in a wide variety of themes, from a general *carpe diem* to more particular occasions, as in the lament for the death of a child, attributed to Kong Rong. The topic is usually initiated by the phrase *rensheng* 人生 ("human life") followed by variable predicates declaring life's brevity or limits, and sometimes supplying a simile. *Rensheng* could be varied with other roughly synonymous compounds: *shengnian* 生年; *nianming* 年命; *renshou* 人壽; *minsheng* 民生; *renming* 人命. The topic can be done in a single line or a couplet, or later expanded to two couplets.

•

It is sometimes useful to think of a theme as the larger, organizing principle; however, one may also conceive of it as a cluster of topics that commonly occur together. Such an aggregation of topics outlines a situation that may be general or made specific in an occasional context. Topics associated with a theme can cluster together without any specific order, but often we can observe loosely defined sequences recurring. Since some topics can be shared by many different themes, the introduction of particular topics within a given theme may set up associations that can lead to the introduction of a new theme.

In the following pages I will give some examples of a common theme in early poetry, which can be called "sleepless at night." Among the topics that cluster around this theme are: putting on clothes, pacing about, moonlight, breeze, birds singing, and sometimes playing music (or singing). Although these are

---

13. Suzuki Shūji, *Kan Gi*, 364–72. See Appendix E.

mostly normal things one might expect if one were sleepless in the third century, other equally normal responses to sleeplessness are not included. Poetic convention may be based in experience of the natural world, but it has a literary life apart from the actual contingencies of experience: the moon, when present, is always bright, and never appears as a sliver or a quarter or even a half moon; the poet is never, in this period, sleepless on a rainy night; it is usually autumn; there is never anyone else in the bed. Speakers in poems of sleeplessness are always by themselves. Hence the theme is often associated with the absence of another person; sometimes it is the sleepless woman missing her beloved.

Not all the associated topics occur in every instance of the theme. Some topics involve a direct or implied claim, such as "human life is short." Other topics are images or even words which can be deployed differently according to the situation; the moon is shining, but sometimes it is shining on the bed, apparently contributing to sleeplessness, while at other times the moon is observed only on going outside. If the moon is not full and bright, it is not mentioned; but if the occasion is not toward the middle of a lunar month (with a full moon), the speaker may comment on brightly shining stars rather than the moon.

The first two examples are the most famous: the last of the "Nineteen Old Poems" and the first of Ruan Ji's (210–63) series preserved under the title "Singing of My Cares," "Yong huai" 詠懷. While it is generally assumed that the last of the "Nineteen Old Poems" is earlier than Ruan Ji's poem, there is no evidence that this is the case.

Nineteen Old Poems XIX[14]

明月何皎皎	How the bright moon glows so!—
照我羅床緯	it shines on my gossamer bed curtains.
憂愁不能寐	I cannot sleep from worries,
攬衣起徘徊	I pull on my clothes, rise and pace.
客行雖云樂	Although they say that travel brings joy,
不如早旋歸	it is best to turn home as soon as one can.

---

14. Lu Qinli, 334; *Wen xuan* 29; *Ytxy* 1 (attributed to Mei Sheng). Sui Shusen 隋樹森, *Gushi shijiushou jishi* 古詩十九首集釋 (Beijing: Zhonghua shuju, 1955), 27–28; Jean-Pierre Diény, *Les dix-neuf poèmes anciens* (Paris: Presses universitaires de France, 1963), 45–45, 154–57.

出戶獨徬徨	I go out the door, walk around alone,
愁思當告誰	to whom can I tell my sad thoughts?
引領還入房	I crane my neck, go back into the room,
淚下沾裳衣	tears fall, soaking my clothes.

As often in the "Nineteen Old Poems," we cannot identify the position of the speaker: it could be either the person traveling or the person staying at home. Although commentators often prefer a female speaker here, there is nothing to indicate the gender of the speaker. We will see that in other, more specific poems it can be either the traveler or the person at home, male or female.

阮籍, 詠懷 Ruan Ji, Singing of My Cares I[15]

夜中不能寐	In the night I could not sleep,
起坐彈鳴琴	rising, then sitting, I plucked my zither.
薄帷鑒明月	The thin curtain gave the image of the bright moon,[16]
清風吹我襟	a cool breeze blew on the folds of my robes.
孤鴻號外野	A lone swan cried out in the wilderness,
翔鳥鳴北林	winging birds sang in the woods to the north.
徘徊將何見	I paced about, what might I see?—
憂思獨傷心	worried thoughts wounded my heart alone.

Ruan Ji includes more of the topics of the theme: playing the zither, the breeze, and birds; this version does not, however, bring up the theme of travel, either of the speaker or of someone absent. Because of assumptions that Ruan Ji must be responding to the decline of the Wei imperial house and the rise of the Sima clan, this poem has been made to bear a heavy weight of figurative reference. It is possible that such a poem could have been used to refer figuratively to contemporary events; this remains, however, only a hypothesis that cannot be proved or disproved by anything in the text or by any certain historical circumstance that grounds the text. Perhaps his "worried thoughts" (*yousi* 憂思) were indeed for the fate of his dynasty, but no one suspects such a cause for the "worries"

---

15. Lu Qinli, 496; *Wen xuan* 23; *Ywlj* 26. Huang Jie 黃節, *Ruan bubing Yonghuai shi zhu* 阮步兵詠懷詩注 (Beijing, 1957), 1–2; Donald Holzman, *Poetry and Politics: The Life and Works of Juan Chi (A.D. 210–263)* (Cambridge: Cambridge University Press, 1976), 229–32.

16. *Jian* 鑒, literally "mirror" and translated as "gave the image of," may be also "caught the light of."

(*youchou* 憂愁) or "sad thoughts" (*chousi* 愁思) that bring sleep-
lessness in the "Nineteen Old Poems" or for the "sad thoughts"
(*beisi* 悲思) in the Cao Pi poem that follows.[17]

We might next consider a longer and more elaborate treat-
ment in an "unclassified poem" (*zashi* 雜詩) attributed to Cao
Pi.[18] Here the "breeze," now a cold autumn wind, precedes the
moonlight and seems to contribute to the poet's sleeplessness.
The topic of travel returns, in this case with the speaker clearly
the person traveling.

曹丕, 雜詩 Cao Pi, Unclassified Poem[19]

漫漫秋夜長	Gradually the autumn nights grow long,
烈烈北風涼	fierce and sharp, the north wind 　　brings chill.
展轉不能寐	I toss and turn and cannot sleep,
披衣起彷徨	I put on my clothes, rise and pace about.
彷徨忽已久	Suddenly I find I have paced about long,
白露沾我裳	silvery dew is soaking my robe.
俯視清水波	I look down on the waves of clear water,
仰看明月光	I look up to the light of the bright moon.
天漢回西流	The River of Stars turns flowing west,
三五正縱橫	spread across sky in threes and fives.
草蟲鳴何悲	How sadly the insects in the plants 　　cry out!—
孤鴈獨南翔	a lone goose soars southward alone.
鬱鬱多悲思	Many sad thoughts well within me,
綿綿思故鄉	continuously I long for my home.

---

17. In *Poetry and Politics*, Donald Holzman admits that every image has
"precedents," but strenuously argues that Ruan Ji "has breathed new life into
the tradition" (230). The disposition to follow the strained commentarial tradi-
tion takes over and leads to such implausible claims as "the 'northern wood'
does suggest the emperor" (231). I will refrain from citing all the poetic in-
stances of "northern" that are hardly imperial—including a "lady fair." In the
Li Ling corpus we have "the dawnwind hawk cries out in the northern woods"
晨風鳴北林 ; and we begin to realize that forests tend to be poetically
"northern"—not eastern, southern, or western—just as poetic birds prefer to fly
south, seasonally in this case, but not in all cases.

18. The classification "unclassified" may have been initially given to poems
that survived, like the "Nineteen Old Poems," without titles, but attributed to
known authors. Once the classification was fully established, poets wrote
"unclassified poems" intentionally, usually gesturing back to the poetic world of
the first part of the third century.

19. Lu Qinli, 401; *Wen xuan* 29.

願飛安得翼	I want to fly off, but how can I get the wings?—
欲濟河無梁	I want to cross, but the River has no bridge.
向風長歎息	Facing the wind I give a long sigh,
斷絕我中腸	it breaks apart my heart within.

As examples multiply, we begin to notice not only the shared topics but also the template lines associated with some. "Sleep" may be *mei* 寐 or *qin* 寢 or *mian* 眠, but the "cannot," *buneng* 不能, occupies the third and fourth position in the five syllable line. The sleepless speaker clothes himself, rises, and paces around: 攬衣起徘徊 ("Nineteen Old Poems" XIX), 披衣起彷徨 (Cao Pi), 攬衣起躑躅 (Ruan Yu, below), 躧履起出戶 (Xu Gan, below); 攬衣起西遊 (Cao Zhi, "To Wang Can" 贈王粲); then expanded in the Cao Rui "Yuefu Poem" cited below:

攬衣曳長帶	I put on my clothes, trailing a long sash,
躧履下高堂	in sandals I go down the high hall.
東西安所之	In which direction shall I go?—
徘徊以彷徨	I pace about and wander around.

The template line is indeed so common that when we read the version from the Li Ling corpus cited below, 褰裳路踟躕 "I lift my robes and hesitate on the *road*," it is possible to suspect that "road," *lu* 路, in the third position is a mistake for "rise," *qi* 起, which is the normative word in the third position of the line.[20]

In the first "Singing of My Cares," much interpretive weight has been invested in the "lone swan," particularly in contrast to the other bird(s) singing in the woods. The lone bird reappears as a wild goose in Cao Pi's poem, contrasted with the "singing" of the insects (note that in both cases the "singing," *ming* 鳴, occupies the third position in the line).[21] As we will see, it is one of the standard topics of the theme. The theme is commonly associated with autumn, and Cao Pi's bird, like Ruan Ji's, is appropriately flying south. In a version sometimes attributed to Cao Rui, the bird is going in the expected poetic direction, but

---

20. We do, however, have another example from the Li Ling corpus that tends to support the usage: in the first poem, "holding hands we hesitate in the wilds" 執手野踟躕.

21. Note in the Cao Rui poem below the (then) phonologically identical *ming* 命 in the third position of the line 悲聲命儔匹.

as an explicitly "spring bird" it is apparently suffering a certain seasonal confusion.

[曹叡,] 樂府詩 [Cao Rui,] Yuefu Poem[22]

昭昭素月明	Shining, the white moon is bright,
暉光燭我牀	its glowing light illuminates the bed.
憂人不能寐	The careworn person cannot sleep,
耿耿夜何長	restless, how long night lasts!
微風衝闈闥	A light breeze strikes the bedchamber,
羅帷自飄颺	gossamer bed curtains toss and flutter.
攬衣曳長帶	I put on my clothes, trailing a long sash,
屣履下高堂	in sandals I go down the high hall.
東西安所之	In which direction shall I go?—
徘徊以彷徨	I pace about and wander around.
春鳥向南飛	A springtime bird flies toward the south,
翩翩獨翱翔	flapping its wings, soaring about alone.
悲聲命儔匹	Its sad voice calls to companions,
哀鳴傷我腸	its mournful singing wounds my heart.
感物懷所思	Stirred by things, I think on my loved one,
泣涕忽沾裳	suddenly tears soak my skirts.
佇立吐高吟	I stand long, giving forth loud chanting,
舒憤訴穹蒼	venting these passions, I complain to the blue vault.

When we find a bird flying south in spring, we can either understand this as intentional or unintentional. This is the sort of contradiction that often alerted traditional commentators to figural readings. This seems most unlikely here. The referential coherence which was so important in later poetics does not matter much here; poetic birds of the third century are generally disposed to "fly south," *nan fei* 南飛 (and sometimes, to "fly southeast," *dongnan fei* 東南飛) in the final syllables of a five syllable line. There are variant verbal ways of flying south in poems, but only in the "toward," *xiang* 向, in the third position.

---

22. Lu Qinli, 418; *Wen xuan* 27; *Ytxy* 2; *Yfsj* 62. Huang Jie 黃節, *Wei Wudi Wendi Mingdi shi zhu* 魏武帝文帝明帝詩注 (Beijing, 1958), 71–72. *Wen xuan* and *Yfsj* take this as anonymous. Lu Qinli rejects the *Yutai xinyong* attributions of "old poems" to Mei Sheng and takes them as anonymous, but here he chooses to accept the *Yutai xinyong* attribution of the poem to Cao Rui, rather than taking the poem as anonymous. This suggests the ideology of register. The register here is clearly higher than that of the "Nineteen Old Poems." Thus, when the tradition provides him a possible author for the poem, Lu Qinli prefers that choice. Wu Qi 吳淇 (cited in Huang Jie, *Wei Wudi*, 72) takes this as having been elaborated from "Nineteen Old Poems" XIX.

If the nights seem to be growing long (l. 4), that is consistent with an autumn setting in which birds should fly south, as is the bright moon, which is poetically brightest in autumn. This invites the question why we have a "springtime bird." There is no clear answer to our question, but the unseasonable modifier reminds us that we are reading representations of scenes that are poetically, rather than empirically coherent.[23]

If one reads the many variations on this theme, one recognizes immediately what is wrong with the version above. The poem should end with the penultimate couplet and the speaker soaking his or her clothes with tears. The high register final couplet seems tacked on. This is the version in the *Wen xuan*. Indeed that final couplet is absent in the Song edition of the *Yutai xinyong* version of the poem. Xiao Tong and Xu Ling may have had different versions; Xiao Tong or some later editor may have added the last couplet because the ending seemed too abrupt; Xu Ling may have deleted the couplet instinctively, sensing that it did not belong. We cannot know what happened, but we can see that textual variation often appears where elements do not fit a standard pattern.

•

In Cao Rui's "Long Song," the lone bird is specifically one that has lost its mate (more later on a bird losing a mate), and the topic is expanded in this relatively high register version to become the focus of the poem. The lone bird is always potentially the analogue of a human situation (thus occupying the functional role of a person away on travels in other versions of the theme), and it is explicitly so in both Cao Rui versions.

曹叡, 長歌行 Cao Rui, Long Song[24]

靜夜不能寐	In the stillness of night I could not sleep,
耳聽眾禽鳴	my ears listened to flocks of fowls singing.
大城育狐兔	The large wall fosters foxes and rabbits,
高墉多鳥聲	the high ramparts have many voices of birds.
壞宇何寥廓	How vast and dreary, broken roofs,

---

23. The Wuchen commentary does not address this issue. I suspect the reason is because the poem is given as anonymous in the *Wen xuan*. The seasonal incongruity matters only if one can impute to it covert authorial intention.

24. Lu Qinli, 415; *Yfsj* 30. Huang Jie, *Wei Wudi*, 63–64.

宿屋邪草生	evil plants grow in way station chambers.
中心感時物	My heart is stirred by the things of the season,
撫劍下前庭	hand on sword, I descend into the front yard.
翔佯於階際	I roam about by the edge of the stairs,
景星一何明	How bright is the Shadow Star.[25]
仰首觀靈宿	Looking up, I view the divine constellations,
北辰奮休榮	the Polestar stirs its glorious splendor.
哀彼失群燕	I lament the swallow that has lost the flock,
喪偶獨煢煢	its mate gone, lonely and isolated.
單心誰與侶	Who will be companion of its solitary heart?
造房孰與成	who will join it to construct a chamber?
徒然喟有和	In vain I heave a great sigh,
悲慘傷人情	its sadness wounds a man's feelings.
余情偏易感	My feelings are all too easily stirred,
懷往增憤盈	thinking of those gone increases my swelling passions.
吐吟音不徹	I utter my chant, the notes don't conclude,
泣涕沾羅纓	tears soak my gossamer hat-ribbons.

The memorable contradiction in the first couplet is a match for the spring bird flying south: this is a very noisy stillness. It reminds us that this poetry is not referential, even in a piece like this elaborated with many specifics that are not part of the common theme. If the preceding poems were "versions" of the theme, we can call this a "variation." Most of the same elements are present, but they occur in changed versions and without the familiar line templates. There is no moon, but the Shadow Star and the Pole Star are bright. The breeze is missing, but there are ample birds and tears. Instead of putting on his clothes, he puts his hand on his sword; instead of "rising," he "descends"; but, displaced into the next line, he still "roams about."

Loneliness because of parting from a loved one is one of the topics of the theme, though it can also be expanded to a theme in its own right. When separation is the initial theme, it can

---

25. The "Shadow Star" was an auspicious asterism whose appearance was understood as a sign of a world in which the Way prevailed.

easily incorporate or merge into the theme of sleeplessness. Template lines can be echoed in other meters, but they are relatively tied to a single meter; topics, however, can be realized in a variety of meters.

曹丕, 燕歌行 Cao Pi, Banquet Song II[26]

別日何易會日難	Days of parting come all too easily, days of meeting are hard,
山川悠遠路漫漫	mountains and rivers stretch far, the road extends on and on.
鬱陶思君未敢言	With pent-up feeling I long for you and dare not tell,
寄書浮雲往不還	I send a letter by the floating clouds, they go and don't return.
涕零雨面毀形顏	Tears fall upon my face, harming both form and complexion,
誰能懷憂獨不歎	who can harbor such cares and not also heave a sigh?
耿耿伏枕不能眠	Restless, I lie on my pillow and cannot sleep,
披衣出戶步東西	I put on my clothes, go out the door and pace east and west.
展詩清歌聊自寬	I deliver a verse and sing unaccompanied to give myself ease the while,
樂往哀來摧心肝	joy goes and grief comes, ruining heart and liver.
悲風清厲秋氣寒	Mournful winds are sharp and clear, the autumn air is cold,
羅帷徐動經秦軒	the mesh curtain stirs gently, passing the Qin balustrade.
仰戴星月觀雲間	Looking up with moon and stars overhead I gaze among the clouds,
飛鳥晨鳴	a flying bird calls out in the morning,
聲氣可憐	the tone of its voice touches me,
留連懷顧不自存	I linger on, looking with care and lose all sense of myself.

Here the three syllable marker of the theme ("cannot sleep" 不能寐/寢/眠) is retained in the second hemistich of the seven

---

26. Lu Qinli, 395. This is the version in the *Song shu*; there is another in *Ytxy* 32. Huang Jie, *Wei Wudi*, 49–51. The title is often interpreted as "Song of Yan," reading 燕 as *yān* rather than *yàn*. Note that the *Yutai xinyong* version omits ll. 11–12.

syllable line; putting on clothes, marking a template line at the beginning of a five syllable line, is retained at the beginning of its line. The zither is replaced here by song. What is remarkable, however, is that once the theme of "sleeplessness" is announced in the poem, its expected topics follow in close succession (clothing oneself, pacing, music, wind, bed curtain, moonlight, and bird).

The following version by Xu Gan (170–217) begins as a general poem of autumn melancholy, longing for the absent beloved, then slips into an abbreviated version of the theme of sleeplessness.

徐幹, 室思 Xu Gan, Chamber Thoughts IV[27]

慘慘時節盡	Gloomily the seasons draw to an end,
蘭葉凋復零	leaves of the orchid wither and then fall.
喟然長歎息	With a moan, I heave a long sigh,
君期慰我情	meeting you will console my heart.[28]
展轉不能寐	I toss and turn and cannot sleep,
長夜何緜緜	How the long night stretches on.
躡履起出戶	I put on my slippers, rise and go out the door,
仰觀三星連	and looking up I see the Three Stars joined.
自恨志不遂	I feel distressed that my goals are not fulfilled,
泣涕如涌泉	my tears are like a gushing spring.

In very abbreviated versions like this it is interesting to note which topics are preserved and which are omitted. Here we have sleeplessness, clothing oneself, and going out, the bright heavenly body, and the tears. To some degree we must accept the texts as we have them, and we are more inclined to believe in the integrity of a "poem" in the *Yutai xinyong* than in an encyclopedia. If, however, this poem were preserved in an encyclopedia, we could easily imagine the omission of couplets mentioning birds, breeze, and playing music.

---

27. Lu Qinli, 377; *Ytxy* 1. Han Geping 韓格平, *Jian'an qizi shiwenji jiaozhu yixi* 建安七子詩文集校注譯析 (Changchun: Jilin wenshi chubanshe, 1991), 352; Wu Yun 吳雲, *Jian'an qizi ji jiaozhu* 建安七子集校註 (Tianjin: Tianjin guji chubanshe, 1991), 296–97.

28. As Lu notes, citing the *Yutai xinyong kaoyi*, 君期 ("meeting you") is a problem. Ji Rongshu wants to transpose the characters to 期君. Han Geping takes it as "the date of your return." Wu Yun takes the 期 as 其, an optative: "May you console my heart." We might note that transposition of characters was a common problem in manuscript transmission.

Although the "cannot sleep" template line is the most common way to announce the theme, as long as sleeplessness is indicated and the usual topics are present, the compositional principle is the same. The following version from the Li Ling corpus includes the basic topics without the "cannot sleep" template line.

from the Li Ling corpus[29]

晨風鳴北林	The dawnwind hawk sings out in the northern woods,
熠燿東南飛	flashing brightly, it flies southeast.
願言所相思	I want the one I am longing for,
日暮不垂帷	at twilight I don't draw down the bed curtain.
明月照高樓	The bright moon shines into the high mansion,
想見餘光輝	I imagine seeing its lingering rays.[30]
玄鳥夜過庭	By night the swallows pass by the yard,
髣髴能復飛	a vague semblance, they can fly on further.
褰裳路踟躕	I lift my robes and hesitate on the road,
彷徨不能歸	in troubled uncertainty, unable to return.
浮雲日千里	The drifting cloud goes a thousand leagues each day—
安知我心悲	how can it know the grief in my heart?
思得瓊樹枝	I long to get a branch of the alabaster tree,
以解長渴飢	to resolve this continual hunger and thirst.[31]

Although commonly repeated themes with their associated topics are easily identified in their full form, they can be invoked in truncated and partial form—or perhaps cited in manuscript in truncated form. In the following poem, probably an excerpt, attributed to Ruan Yu in the detritus of the manuscript tradition that survived into the seventh century, an autumn poem slips into the adjunct topics of the theme of sleeplessness (putting on clothes, rising, pacing, moonlight); they seem to create a pressure to somehow indicate that the

---

29. Lu Qinli, 340; *Guwen yuan* 4; *Ywlj* 29. Rather than assign particular poems to Li Ling or Su Wu, I will simply call this group of old poems "the Li Ling corpus."

30. Yu Guanying interprets this as the speaker imagining other places on which the moonlight falls.

31. Yu Guanying understands this as a tree of the immortals, with the power to cure sorrow.

speaker could not sleep, which is realized in the question: "When will the cock crow?" When we look at the gap between the situation in the second couplet and the third couplet, it seems what is missing is precisely the statement "at night I could not sleep."

阮瑀, 詩 Ruan Yu, Poem[32]

臨川多悲風	By the river is much mournful wind,
秋日苦清涼	autumn days are terribly clear and cool.
客子易爲戚	The traveler is easily made sorrowful,
感此用哀傷	and stirred by this, feels pain thereby.
攬衣起躑躅	I take hold of my gown and rise pacing,
上觀心與房	view the Heart and Chamber constellations above.
三星守故次	The Three Stars hold their former positions,
明月未收光	the bright moon has not withdrawn its rays.
雞鳴當何時	When will the cock crow?—
朝晨尚未央	the dawning is still not over.
還坐長歎息	I sit back down and heave a long sigh,
憂憂安可忘	how can I forget these continuous cares?

In my comment above I suggested that in the beginning of the poem Ruan Yu could have been outside during the day, then moved in and found himself unable to sleep. Let me offer yet one more example of sleeplessness, in a famous and beautiful poem by Wang Can, dated to the turn of the second century. The poet has fled the collapse of Dong Zhuo's regime in Chang'an to Jingzhou (Jingman). At dusk (far too early to declare sleeplessness) he gets off his boat and roams around on the shore. Certain elements are present in what I am willing to believe was an actual experience: he is pacing in the growing darkness, birds are flying, there is a breeze, dew soaks his clothes. He then returns to his quarters. The "poetic topics" he has experienced need their theme: "Alone at night I cannot sleep" 獨夜不能寐. And once the theme line is announced, Wang Can completes the appropriate topics by putting on his clothes and rising (qi 起 in the expected third position of the line), and playing his zither. The poem is not, like most of the others we have read, a simple performance of a standard poetic

---

32. Lu Qinli, 380; *Ywlj* 27, 34 (the second citation entitled *Qi'ai shi* 七哀詩). Han Geping, *Jian'an*, 369–70; Wu Yun, *Jian'an*, 327.

theme; rather, the appearance of the usual topics in a different context seems to demand the declaration of the theme of "sleeplessness."[33]

王粲, 七哀詩 Wang Can, Sevenfold Sorrow II[34]

荆蠻非我鄉	Jingman is not my native land,
何爲久滯淫	how can I linger here long?
方舟泝大江	My catamaran goes up the great River,
日暮愁我心	and the twilight makes my heart sad.
山崗有餘映	On the mountains and hills is a lingering light,
巖阿增重陰	while the folds of the cliffs increase layered shadows.
狐狸馳赴穴	Foxes and badgers rush to their lairs,
飛鳥翔故林	flying birds soar around former groves.
流波激清響	Waves in the current stir clear echoes,
猴猿臨岸吟	gibbons whine looking down from the slopes.
迅風拂裳袂	A swift wind brushes my skirt and sleeves,
白露沾衣襟	the silvery dew soaks my gown's folds.
獨夜不能寐	Alone at night I cannot sleep,
攝衣起撫琴	I lift robes, get up, and strum the zither.
絲桐感人情	The silk and tung wood stir a man's feelings,
爲我發悲音	on my behalf it makes mournful tones.
羈旅無終極	Being on travels never ends,
憂思壯難任	the prick of worried thoughts is hard to bear.[35]

Many of the poems above cannot be roughly dated, and some of the attributions are dubious. We can, however, place this poem

---

33. See Itō Masafumi 伊藤正文, "Ō San shi ronkō" 王粲詩論考, *Chūgoku bungaku hō* 20 (1965): 38–42. I differ from Itō in interpreting this relationship to the conventional tradition not as a movement toward originality, but rather the force of poetic convention working within a poem that begins "originally." We might also note the similar movement in "In the Army" III 從軍詩, "In the army I march on the far-off road" 從軍征遐路: here, too, the poet goes on shore and encounters the topics appropriate for sleeplessness on an autumn night; in this case, however, the poet dismisses his cares out of a sense of duty toward military service.

34. Lu Qinli, 366; *Wen xuan* 23. Wu Yun 吳雲 and Tang Shaozhong 唐紹忠, *Wang Can ji zhu* 王粲集注 (Henan: Zhongzhou shuhua she, 1984), 16–17.

35. *Zhuang* 壯 here could simply mean "strong." Some commentators, however, prefer a regional northeastern usage, cited in Yang Xiong's *Fangyan*, where it describes the prick of a thorn.

at the end of the second century and Ruan Ji's poem above sometime around the middle of the third century. The theme, with its constituent topics, is already established at the beginning of this interval and still very much alive at the end of the interval.

•

It is instructive to quote again the final lines of this small sampling of poems on "sleepless at night."

淚下沾裳衣	tears fall, soaking my clothes. ("Nineteen Old Poems" XI)
憂思獨傷心	anxious thoughts wounded my heart alone. (Ruan Ji, "Singing My Cares" I)
斷絕我中腸	it breaks apart my heart within. (Cao Pi, "Unclassified Poem")
舒憤訴穹蒼	venting these passions, I complain to the blue vault. (Cao Rui, "Yuefu Poem")
泣涕沾羅纓	tears soak my gossamer hat-ribbons. (Cao Rui, "Long Song")
留連懷顧不自存	I linger on, looking with care and lose all sense of myself. (Cao Pi, "Banquet Song" II)
泣涕如涌泉	my tears are like a gushing spring. (Xu Gan, "Chamber Thoughts" IV)
思得瓊樹枝 以解長渴飢	I long to get a branch of the alabaster tree, to resolve this continual hunger and thirst. (Li Ling corpus)
憂憂安可忘	how can I forget these continuous cares? (Ruan Yu, Poem)
憂思壯難任	the prick of worried thoughts is hard to bear. (Wang Can, "Sevenfold Sorrow" II)

First we note how the example from the Li Ling corpus stands out as an anomaly. As for the others, it may be that we simply have a group of very unhappy poets; but an examination of the corpus of early poems will reveal that the majority of poems of a certain kind end with a similar declaration of misery or tears. We begin to see that such lines, while they do retain semantic meaning (they are always in sad poems) occupy an essentially positional function in a poetic "grammar": this is a way to announce that a poem is over. This positional function of the declaration of misery invites comparison with a very different kind of closure that is sometimes preserved in *yuefu*. At the same time we can revisit the topic of the solitary bird.

Segments: The "Prelude: O When"

The following is the text of the anonymous *yuefu* "Prelude: O When" as it is preserved in the "Treatise on Music" in the *Song shu*.

豔歌何嘗行 Prelude: O When[36]

飛來雙白鵠	Pairs of white swans came flying,
乃從西北來	it was from the northwest they came,
十十五五	ten by ten and five by five,
羅列成行	all arrayed in lines.[37]
妻卒被病	The mate of one was sick
行不能相隨	and couldn't keep up.
五里一返顧	Every five leagues he looked back once,
六里一徘徊	every six leagues he paused.
吾欲銜汝去	"I want to carry you in my beak,
口噤不能開	but my mouth is closed, I can't open it.
吾欲負汝去	I want to carry you on my back,
毛羽何摧頹	but how ruined are my feathers!
樂哉新相知	Happy indeed is a newfound love,
憂來生別離	sorrow comes with parting in life.
躇躊顧群侶	I pause and look around at the flock,
淚下不自知	tears fall without my knowing it."
念與君離別	Thinking on parting with you,
氣結不能言	breath knots within, I cannot speak.
各各重自愛	Let each take heed to take care of self,

---

36. Lu Qinli, 272; *Song shu, Yuezhi*; *Yfsj* 39. The first twelve lines are cited as an "old poem" in *Yiwen leiju*; a somewhat different version is found in *Ytxy* 1. Huang Jie 黃節, *Han Wei yuefu feng jian* 漢魏樂府風箋 (Hong Kong: Shangwu yinshuguan, 1961), 43–44; Jean-Pierre Diény, *Aux origines de la poésie classique en Chine: étude sur la poésie lyrique à l'époque des Han* (Leiden: E. J. Brill, 1968), 142–46; Anne Birrel, *Popular Songs and Ballads of Han China* (London: Unwin Hyman,1988), 53–57.

37. Something is obviously wrong with this line in that it does not rhyme. In "Yuefu geci de pincou he fen'ge" (30) Yu Guanying argues that *lai* 來 and *hang* 行 are old rhymes. The first example he gives (see Lu Qinli, 286–87), evidently taken by Guo Maoqian from *Taiping yulan*, does not rhyme *fang* 方 and *lai* 來 in the *Taiping yulan* version, where both first lines end with *lai*. This is apparently not an "old rhyme" but an emendation on the part of Guo Maoqian. Yu's second example is from *Kongque dongnan fei*, perhaps not a text that should be used to prove old rhymes, and one that has strange rhyming patterns at certain points.

道遠歸還難	the journey is long, return will be hard.
妾當守空房	I must keep to my empty chamber,
閑門下重關	the idle gate doubly barred.[38]
若生當相見	If you live, we will see each other again;
亡者會重泉	if you die, we will meet in the world below.
今日樂相樂	This day joy upon joy,
延年萬歲期	may you live ten thousand years.

We should say from the outset that the "Prelude: O When," as an anonymous *yuefu*, is not usually considered in the same context as the anonymous old poems, much less Jian'an and Wei poems.[39] In this particular case the conventional segregation of "poems" (*shi* 詩) and *yuefu* is interesting in that a version of the first twelve lines are, in fact, quoted as an "old poem" 古詩 in the seventh-century encyclopedia *Yiwen leiju*, while lines 17–24, using a different rhyme, are an abbreviated realization of a standard "old poem" theme.[40] This is a common type of *yuefu*, which I call a "compound *yuefu*," composed of distinct segments which can often circulate independently. This probably represents performance practice in which at least two relatively independent segments were conjoined. The first segment often represents something other than the human world, such as birds or immortals; the second segment is a human situation, usually parallel, but sometimes in a problematic relation to the opening segment.

In this, the earliest recorded version of "Prelude: O When," the poem is divided by rhyme and sense into three distinct segments: lines 1–16, 17–24, and 25–26 (marked by an added space between lines in the translated version above).[41] The final

---

38. Although I have kept the received text here, *xian* 閑, "idle," was a common scribal mistake for *bi* 閉, "to close." *Bimen* 閉門, "to close one's gate," was a common term for living in seclusion.

39. There are many scholars who attend to the overlaps between the forms, but most still accept a difference of genre. Diény sometimes assumes the priority of the *yuefu*, but in discussing *yuefu* he also draws on the "old poems" as if providing topics for use in *yuefu*.

40. See Diény, *Aux origines de la poésie classique*, 145.

41. Diény notes the conventional nature of ll. 13–16 and takes them as a separate section. I believe, rather, that ll. 13–16 are the necessary closure for a complete segment. I do not believe there are "fixed texts" in the background of this piece: rather, each thematic core is expanded to suit the situation of reproduction: a segment needs closure, and this closure provides a transition to the next segment.

couplet, with an isolated rhyme, is the professional singer's formulaic marker for closure, wishing blessings on the audience. It serves exactly the same positional function as the expression of misery and tears in the previous set of poems on sleeplessness, but with one important distinction: it is thematically incongruous, declaring the heights of joy right after the pathos of the farewell of a wife and her husband. If the test case of true oral formula is incongruity (the Homeric "cloud-gathering" Zeus dispersing the clouds), then this couplet passes the test (though the function here is positional rather than metrical): in effect the last couplet simply carries the message that the song is now completed.

A standard literary historical account will treat this poem as earlier than Ruan Ji and the Jian'an poets, earlier even than the last of the "Nineteen Old Poems."[42] Such a historical deployment of the texts comes from the intuition that "Prelude: O When" is somehow more primitive or closer to the "folk." This intuition derives in part from the formulaic ending and the padded verse. If we take these qualities as traces of a professional performance tradition rather than the "folk," that immediately complicates the cultural assumptions behind the standard sequence (first, poetry of the "folk," followed by literati appropriation). But even if we grant that a poem like this bears traces of the "folk," there is no natural or historical law that proves that the poem is, thereby, early. We can immediately grant a difference in register, but there is no real evidence (apart from Shen Yue's general characterization of the "old lyrics" as being from the Han) that the "Prelude: O When" antedates any of the poems quoted above.

When we compare the "Prelude: O When" to Wang Can's second "Sevenfold Sorrow," we can see that in terms of compositional practice it differs in degree but not in kind. In both cases an initial theme is developed, in the process of which topics shared with another theme are used. The accumulation of such topics leads the poet to the second theme. We have already seen this in the Wang Can poem, where topics from "sleeplessness" appear before the poet declares that "at night I

---

42. Most accounts prefer the somewhat later version in *Yutai xinyong* which excludes ll. 17–24, the wife's farewell, because it interrupts the rhyme.

could not sleep." In "Prelude: O When" the pathos of the male swan's address to his mate, clearly a figure for a human situation, increasingly uses topics that are appropriate only for humans. Line 16 ("tears fall without my knowing it" 淚下不自知) is not only a purely human phenomenon (most inappropriate for swans), it is also, as we have seen, the marker of poetic closure in an old poem. It is at this point of closure that the "singer" shifts to a parallel, explicitly human situation in a new rhyme.

If we take the "Prelude: O When" as a base level in performance practice, then we see both the continuity and the differences of Wang Can's poem. About two thirds into his poem Wang Can writes:

獨夜不能寐	Alone at night I cannot sleep,
攝衣起撫琴	I lift robes, get up, and strum the zither.

He is "announcing" a familiar topic in familiar template lines, giving the reader the pleasure of shift and recognition. The difference is, of course, that Wang Can keeps everything on a level of representational coherence: his sleeplessness is the continuation of his earlier experience of the outside scene rather than a distinct but analogous poetic segment. The rhyme is also maintained.

Thus we can see three levels in compositional practice: topics, themes, and the combination of themes, sometimes in independent segments as in the "Prelude: O When" and sometimes woven together into a coherent representational whole, as in Wang Can's poem. These simple principles will help to explain many particular cases in early poetry.

"Poems" and Extant Texts:
More on the Swans (or Cranes)

"Prelude: O When" has no real name, but is called by several different names in different places. In addition to the "Treatise on Music," the poem appears in several other earlier sources, whose sharp differences invite the question: Which is the real poem? Perhaps when we ask the question as baldly as this, we can see that it might be the wrong question.

We are moving toward a notion of a text as a particular realization of material, some of whose parts may be relatively

determined but still variable to some degree. As we have sug-
gested, from a broad perspective this fluidity is common to both
performance practice and manuscript transcription. Here,
however, we must make a distinction between a realization in
performance or in the act of first writing down a text (in both
cases we have indirect traces only) and its realization in a later
manuscript that survives in some extant printed text. In these
later cases there is still considerable latitude, but the textual
realization is mediated by the protocols of a particular textual
venue and its sense of what the poem should be. That is, many
particulars in these early texts, as we have them, are a function
of the nature of the written sources.[43]

There are a remarkable number of variations of this poem,
including whether the birds are swans or cranes (*he* 鶴). Before
turning to these variations, we should point out that there is no
evidence that these different versions were ever set side by side
until the *Yuefu shiji* in the Northern Song, an age that had
begun to concern itself with literary scholarship and "correct"
titles and texts. Only in recent times have all the variations
been viewed together. This means that while certain texts were
variable, variation was not an issue that called for a reader's or
scholar's attention—until the advent of a certain kind of literary
scholarship in the Song. Such freedom of manuscript variation
seems to have been the norm in such texts, and each particular
realization "was" the text.

There are three extant primary sources for "Prelude: O
When": the "Treatise on Music" (*Yuezhi*) based on fifth-century
materials; the *Yutai xinyong* from the early sixth century; and
the encyclopedia *Yiwen leiju* of the early seventh century. Here
we must acknowledge that it is sometimes impossible to sort
out the complexity of variations among the sources from the
complexity of textual variations in printed editions of the

---

43. Again, in a general sense the essential principle is no different among
composition, performance, and manuscript transcription. We can assume, for
example, that in non-ritualized performance (that is, not exactly reproducing a
text court performance) a singer or reciter would vary or amplify according to
his sense of the needs of the moment. The difference is that in the particular
versions of manuscript transcription that have survived, we can clearly see how
a particular venue has shaped the form of the text.

sources, particularly in the case of *Yutai xinyong*.[44] Looking at the three distinct extant versions, here is roughly what we get.

豔歌何嘗行 (or 雙白鵠??) 大曲白鵠豔歌何嘗行 古詩

Yutai xinyong	Song shu	Yiwen leiju
飛來雙白鵠	飛來雙白鵠	飛來白鶴
乃從西北來	乃從西北來	從西北來
十十將五五	十十五五	十五十五
羅列行不齊	羅列成行 (rhyme X)	邐迤成行
忽然卒被病	妻卒被病	妻卒被病
不能飛相隨	行不能相隨	不能相隨
五里一反顧	五里一返顧	五里一反顧
六里一徘徊	六里一徘徊	六里一徘徊
吾欲銜汝去	吾欲銜汝去	吾欲銜汝去
口噤不能開	口噤不能開	口噤不能開
吾欲負汝去	吾欲負汝去	吾欲負汝去
羽毛日摧頹	毛羽何摧頹	毛羽日摧頹
樂哉新相知	樂哉新相知	
憂來生別離	憂來生別離	
跚蹰顧群侶	躇躊顧群侶	
淚落縱橫垂	淚下不自知	
	念與君離別	
	氣結不能言	
	各各重自愛	
	道遠歸還難	
	妾當守空房	
	閉門下重關	
	若生當相見	
	亡者會重泉	
今日樂相樂	今日樂相樂	
延年萬歲期	延年萬歲期	

As we suggested earlier, the "Treatise on Music" is unique among our extant texts in its conservatorial function, preserving a text as it appeared in earlier manuscripts or as it was performed. Insofar as "Prelude: O When" belonged to the category "great song," *daqu* 大曲, it probably required more than

---

44. To give but one example, the *Siku quanshu* version of *Yutai xinyong* gives the bird in question as a "swan," *hu* 鵠, but Ji Rongshu's 紀容舒 textual study of the collection, *Yutai xinyong kaoyi*, also in *Siku quanshu*, gives the primary reading as "crane," *he* 鶴. Even more strange, *Yiwen leiju* gives the bird as a "white crane," *baihe*, but includes the poem under the category "black swan," *xuanhu* 玄鵠 (even though there is a category for "white cranes" in the encyclopedia).

one segment, though we may reasonably doubt whether, apart from this particular occasion of preservation, the segment on the pair of white swans was necessarily paired with a version of the wife's speech on parting.[45]

Yutai xinyong's inclusion of the singer's closure does suggest that this anthology took its base text from the 漢 musical repertoire in the "Treatise on Music." The *Yutai xinyong* removed the segment on parting (producing a satisfying mono-rhyme), normalized the meter, repaired the dropped rhyme in the fourth line, and changed line 16 to "tears fall, dropping wildly" 淚落縱橫垂, avoiding the repetition of "know," *zhi* 知, as a rhyme word. In other words, this version has been realized in a way to suit the standards of what a "poem" should be in the context of early sixth-century poetics, while still retaining its "archaic" flavor. It would be wrong, however, to see this transformation as in some way "inauthentic." Rather, until the period when texts would be reproduced exactly, realizations of a text would always vary to suit the period and venue.

The *Yiwen leiju* often cites only passages (though it would be equally fair to say that *Yutai xinyong* has only cited a passage of the "Prelude: O When"). In addition to the fact that it is cited as an "old poem," which might suggest that this segment circulated independently, the *Yiwen leiju* version is a particularly interesting realization. First, it makes all of the first six lines four syllable lines, just as the *Yutai xinyong* made them all five syllable lines. This reminds us how easily four and five syllable lines can be interchanged in early poetry. Meter and text are not bound tightly together; rather, a meter is one possible form within which material can be realized (as we saw the topics of the theme of "sleeplessness" realized in a seven syllable line in Cao Pi's "Banquet Song"). The second observation we might make is that the *Yiwen leiju* version breaks off at precisely the point where the poem moves from statements appropriate for birds to statements appropriate only for human beings. In part this is a function of the venue of the encyclopedia (*leishu*), including literary material under the category of a bird (albeit the

---

45. See Piao Yingji's theory of complexity of perspectives as a motive for compounding segments. Piao Yingji 朴英姬, "Cong 'Yange hechang xing' lun Han Wei Jin yuefu shi de jige wenti" 從豔歌何嘗行論漢魏晉樂府詩的幾個問題, *Zhongguo wenhua yuekan* 中國文化月刊 193 (November 1995):103–23.

wrong bird in this case). The *Yiwen leiju* version stops (l. 12) before one of the standard marks of poetic closure in early poetry (l. 16); the omitted material (ll. 13–16) is precisely the humanization of the birds that creates the pressure for the human segment in the "Treatise on Music" version of "Prelude: O When."

In short, each version is a realization of the material that is "right" for its own venue. Each version is "complete" in different ways. If we are looking to establish historical priority, clearly the "Treatise on Music" version represents the earliest textual realization; but that version may be no earlier than court performance traditions in the fourth or fifth century; it gives us no access to some earlier "original."

There is yet another version of our birds, a short segment tagged onto a version of "Looking Down from the High Terrace," *Lin gao tai* 臨高臺, improbably preserved under the name of Cao Pi.[46] The first part of "Looking Down from the High Terrace" is a variant version of the anonymous piece preserved in the *Naoge*.[47] In the anonymous version there is a "yellow swan" 黃鵠 flying and someone shooting at it. In the version preserved under Cao Pi's name there is no shooting—that would be most unkind in the *yuefu* context.

臨臺行高	[Looking down from the high terrace,]
高以軒	high and lofty;
下有水	below are waters
清且寒	clear and cold.
中有黃鵠往且翻	There we find a yellow swan, going then turning back.
行爲臣	To act as an officer
當盡忠	one must show loyalty to the utmost.

---

46. Lu Qinli, 395. *Ywlj* 42; *Yfsj* 18. Huang Jie, *Wei Wudi*, 51–52. I follow Lu Qinli's punctuation; Huang Jie punctuates this piece rather differently. The *Wen xuan* commentary cites this as "original lyrics," quoting a couplet from the swan segment. This piece clearly cannot be by Cao Pi, unless we imagine him composing it for the last Han emperor. One of the transformations worked here on the *Naoge* version is changing the simple *zhu* 主 to "His Imperial Majesty," *huangdi bixia* 皇帝陛下. Christopher Connery discusses this poem in *Empire of the Text* (166–68). He is certainly correct here to dispute historically grounded subjectivity in such a poem; however, if we are to consider this poem in terms of "intertextuality," the concept is greatly in need of nuanced distinctions.

47. Lu Qinli, 161.

願令皇帝陛下三千歲	I wish His Imperial Majesty three thousand years!
宜居此宮	He should dwell in this palace.
鵠欲南遊	The swan was traveling south,
雌不能隨	his mate could not follow.
我欲躬銜汝	"I want to personally hold you in my beak
口噤不能開	my mouth is closed, I cannot open it.
我欲負之	I want to carry you on my back,
毛衣摧頹	but my feathers are ruined."
五里一顧	Every five leagues it looks back once,
六里徘佪	every six leagues it lingers.

It is testimony to the conservatorial nature of at least some of the anthologies of musical poetry that such an almost incoherent conjunction of segments could be textually preserved. It is hard to guess how the associations produced this conjunction, unless it came from the swan's "turning back," *fan* 翻 (also simply "fly"), used as a rhyme both in this version and in the muddled version of the line in the version preserved in the *Song shu*. A "yellow swan turning back" would immediately recall the song material discussed above, whose opening core is preserved here, with one of the couplets transposed. In this we are coming to the edge of "medley," where associations of one verse segment move into another verse segment in another context. "Medley," however, may be a useful concept by which to think of the combination of segments.

Birds

Xu Ling, the editor of the *Yutai xinyong*, was probably working with the "Treatise on Music" version of "Prelude: O When" and removed the segment on the husband and wife parting because it was discordant and interrupted the rhyme.[48] Even the modern scholar Lu Qinli wants to divide the "Prelude: O When" into two pieces.[49] It is fair then to ask how anomalous this is. We know that segments can be expanded and shortened.

---

48. We cannot be sure, but this seems the likely case because Xu Ling preserves the singer's closing blessings on the audience, not a usual practice with *yuefu* in *Yutai xinyong*. In this case the final couplet of blessing rhymes with the first segment and can be integrated smoothly.

49. Lu Qinli, 272.

Would one feel the same unease at the combination if the "bird" segment had the same rhyme and were shortened—say to one couplet?

from the Li Ling corpus[50]

雙鳧俱北飛	A pair of ducks both flew to the north,
一鳥獨南翔	one bird soared off south alone.
子當留斯館	You must remain in this lodge,
我當歸故鄉	I must return to my homeland.
一別如秦胡	Once parted we will be as Qin and Turkestan,
會見何詎央	[when will we meet again?][51]
愴恨切中懷	Sorrow cuts at my feelings within,
不覺淚沾裳	unawares, tears soak my skirts.
願子長努力	I want you to always strive hard,
言笑莫相忘	and don't forget our laughter together.

I hope it will not seem too extravagant to say that this is a different realization of the "Prelude: O When," albeit a radically different realization. The bird segment is now only a couplet—though it could easily have been elaborated into a longer passage. The couple parting is now probably two men, rather than a man and his wife. In this version the poem is spoken from the point of view of the person going off rather than the person staying; but in the citation of these lines in the Song encyclopedia *Taiping yulan*, the "you" and "I" of the second couplet are reversed. And, of course, if the poem is uttered by the person staying rather than the person leaving, the pronouns will be reversed in just that way. That is, the text is not fixed but open to variation in circumstantial performance (including textual as well as oral performance). The "tears coming unawares" is shared with the "Prelude: O When." The ending is different, but the exhortations to strive and not forget are also closure devices in other "old poems."

If we accept that the long segment on birds parting in "Prelude: O When" can be done simply as a couplet, then we can add other examples that begin to suggest marks of the "literary" beyond simple variation in lexical register.

---

50. Ibid., 341; *Guwen yuan* 4; *Ywlj* 29.

51. This is what the line ought to mean, but there is something very wrong. Lu proposes emending *ju* 詎 to 遽 ("how swiftly our meeting ended"), but this is not entirely satisfying.

from the Li Ling corpus[52]

黃鵠一遠別	Once the yellow swan parts for far away,
千里顧徘徊	it looks back and hesitates at a thousand leagues.
胡馬失其群	When the Tartar horse loses its herd,
思心常依依	its longing heart is ever filled with yearning.
何況雙飛龍	Even more so [we], a pair of flying dragons,
羽翼臨當乖	whose wings are on the verge of separating.
幸有絃歌曲	Luckily we have songs and string music
可以喻中懷	which can figure forth our feelings within.
請爲遊子吟	I would have you sing the Traveler's Lay—
泠泠一何悲	how sad its ringing notes are!
絲竹厲清聲	The strings' and pipes' clear notes grow intense,
慷慨有餘哀	in their strong feeling is ample sorrow.
長歌正激烈	Now the Long Songs are urgently stirring,
中心愴以摧	the heart within is depressed and broken.
欲展清商曲	I would perform a tune in the clear Shang mode,
念子不得歸	thinking on how you will not be able to return.
俛仰內傷心	In a moment the heart feels pain within,
淚下不可揮	tears fall, I cannot wipe them away.
願爲雙黃鵠	I wish we were a pair of yellow swans,
送子俱遠飛	I would send you on your way, both flying far.

This is the yellow swan rather than the white one, but it still "looks back"—though after a thousand leagues rather than the five or six in the "Prelude: O When." We recognize the "bird segment," though it has been reduced to a mere couplet. In this case, however, the "bird couplet" is followed by another parallel example, the Tartar horse. The first of the "Nineteen Old Poems" offers the well-known parallel:

| 胡馬依北風 | The Tartar horse leans into the north wind, |
| 越鳥巢南枝 | the Yue bird roosts in the southernmost branches. |

The Li Ling poem is explicit about why the Tartar horse leans into the north wind; but the most revealing transformation is the *yi* 依, which as a single character means "to lean against,"

---

52. Lu Qinli, 338; *Wen xuan* 29, *Ywlj* 29.

but doubled as *yiyi* 依依 is a sound compound meaning "yearning." What is shared between the two versions is the sound syllable (and perhaps the character), rather than the meaning—though in this case the particular realization of the monosyllable *yi* 依, "leaning into," implies *yiyi*, "yearning." We sometimes see not a continuity of meanings becoming words realized in sounds, but of sounds taking form in words with the larger meanings adapting to account for such purely verbal continuity.

We now have two parallel cases in the animal world, the parted swan and Tartar horse, but it turns out that they are inadequate: the human case is figured in yet a third (albeit mythical) creature, compared to which the situations of animals in the *yuefu* and "old poem" traditions are merely less intense and less elevated examples. The traces of rhetorical training are clearly evident (and perhaps most evident in the redeployment of analogy as hierarchy).

何況雙飛龍	Even more so [we], a pair of flying dragons,
羽翼臨當乖	whose wings are on the verge of separating.

Granted that most *yuefu* and "old poems" do not use two parallel cases, nor do they bring up dragons; however, the clearest marker of rhetorical education is "even more so," *hekuang* 何況, turning poetic parallels into an explicit comparison of degrees. This *hekuang* has no place in the conventions of low register poetic language. We have the cases of two ordinary creatures (drawn from the "lower" poetic tradition) who feel separation strongly; therefore dragons, the most elite of creatures, will feel separation even more strongly; and we humans find adequate analogy for our situation only in "dragons." The dragons become by synecdoche "wings," which, in a high register, *guai* 乖, "come apart."

We do however find a close parallel in Cao Zhi's "Dew on the Onion-Grass" 薤露行:[53]

鱗介尊神龍	Among scaly and shelled creatures we honor the divine dragon,
走獸宗麒麟	among beasts that run we revere the unicorn.

---

53. Lu Qinli, 422.

蟲獸猶知德　　　　　If we recognize virtue even among beasts and
　　　　　　　　　　cold-blooded creatures,
何況於士人　　　　　how much more so among gentlemen.

The parallel tells us less about precise dating than about register; both texts not only use an elite register but also make the distinction of "eliteness" a theme.[54]

We see clearly here how the material of poetry, elsewhere realized according to the "grammar" of "old poetry," has been appropriated for something that looks like elite literary argument. We will return to this poem from the Li Ling corpus since it later draws on elements of the low register poetic repertoire in interesting ways. But here we can clearly see an elite transformation of the material in the "Prelude: O When."

We have seen the theme of the birds parting as a fully developed segment in "Prelude: O When," a segment that could stand as an autonomous poem in its *Yiwen leiju* version. We have seen it done as a single opening couplet, announcing the theme of parting as with the "affective image," *xing* 興, in the *Shijing*. In the final variation, the couplet on parting birds migrates from the beginning to the middle of the poem, like the figural couplet on "Tartar horse" and "Yue bird" in the first of the "Nineteen Old Poems."

from the Li Ling corpus[55]

陟彼南山隅　　　　　I ascended a nook of South Mountain
送子淇水陽　　　　　and send you off on the north bank of
　　　　　　　　　　the Qi.
爾行西南遊　　　　　You are traveling to the southwest,
我獨東北翔　　　　　I alone will fly off to the northeast.
轅馬顧悲鳴　　　　　The coach horse neighs sadly, looking
　　　　　　　　　　around,
五步一彷徨　　　　　it pauses, uncertain, at every five steps.
雙鳧相背飛　　　　　The pair of ducks fly apart,
相遠日已長　　　　　daily increasing the distance from
　　　　　　　　　　each other.
遠望雲中路　　　　　I look afar in the road through
　　　　　　　　　　the clouds

---

54. Though it is not the issue we are following here, we might note how the hierarchical taxonomy of parallel cases is followed by a taxonomy of musical types.

55. Lu Qinli, 340; *Guwen yuan* 4; *Ywlj* 29.

想見來圭璋	and fancy I see jade tablets coming.[56]
萬里遙相思	I long for you, ten thousand leagues afar,
何益心獨傷	what good that my heart is pained all alone?
隨時愛景曜	Cherish the light as the seasons go,
願言莫相忘	and I want you not to forget me.

This is by no means an erudite poem, but it gestures toward elite literary education throughout. The opening gestures to the *Shijing*, and high register terms appear here and there. Beneath the superficial polish, however, the author of this version is obviously deeply familiar with the low register poetic repertoire and follows its sequences of topics. The horse neighing on parting is a relatively elevated image, but the poet caps the line: "it pauses, uncertain, at every five steps." This calls to mind our parting birds:

五里一反顧	Every five leagues he looked back once,
六里一徘徊	every six leagues he paused.

The line on pausing at an interval, from a familiar sequence of topics, naturally leads to the image of a pair of birds, now ducks.

雙鳧相背飛	The pair of ducks fly apart,
相遠日已長	daily increasing the distance from each other.

Since the requisite "pausing" has already taken place in the horses, these ducks simply keep flying. This leads to the second line of the couplet, a version of the topic "daily farther away," as in the first of the "Nineteen Old Poems": "we grow daily farther apart" 相去日已遠. If at this point we look at the first of the "Nineteen Old Poems" and other poems on separation, the rest of the poem is quite predictable: there is looking toward the one absent, there are clouds, there may be a letter received or expected or a message sent; the closing is a statement of love and care, either in the letter received or in the message sent to the faraway person or the person leaving.

This is truly "poetic material," themes and topics open to multiple variations: it can be redone in many ways: it can be expanded or contracted; it can be done in different registers; it

---

56. That is, letters.

can be done alone or linked to other, parallel themes. Whenever the theme is realized, topics and template lines are available. The theme is most at home in the five syllable line, but it could be expanded to seven syllable lines or contracted to four syllable lines. If the birds must part, the speaker can assume the position of the person going or the person staying. And, most important, it could be applied to a specific context. This is "virtual" poetic material that is always realized differently, modified for the situation—whether that situation is oral performance or the proprieties of a particular transcriptional venue in manuscript.

Once we grasp the significance of this as virtual poetic material (as grammar is virtual), it profoundly changes the way we read the tradition of early poetry. Scholars have tended to treat these early poetic texts as if they were unique and stable and thus open to chronological comparison: scholars will say that poem Y borrowed from or recast lines from poem X. If that third-century poet did yet another version of the theme, he was probably not responding to any particular prior text, but rather making use of a shared range of topics and procedures of variation. Thus we understand not by identifying "precedents," but by looking to the commonalties through what survives.

We might here contrast a reliably Western Han version of the parting birds. We cannot expect the complex relation of elements in the gnomic verses of the *Jiaoshi Yilin* 焦氏易林; however, all we have is the hen bird that could not keep up.[57]

九雁列陣	Nine wild geese formed a line,
雌獨不群	only the hen bird could not join the flock.
為罾所牽	She had been taken by the net
死於庖人	and died at the hands of the cook.

On this level we can call the hen bird that could not keep up with the flock simply a "motif," and like many of the images in *Jiaoshi Yilin*, a motif probably with some popular currency. We frequently find images and motifs that appear in early classical poetry in the *Jiaoshi Yilin*: but we never find them with the associated topics, the sequences, and the template line pat-

---

57. Chen Liangyun 陳良運, *Jiaoshi Yilin shixue chanshi* 焦氏易林詩學闡釋 (Nanchang: Baihuazhou wenyi chubanshe, 2000), 251.

terns that distinguish the poetics of early classical poetry. If the
motifs themselves are older, they are only raw material for the
poetics of *yuefu* and the "old poems."

The Parting Segment

Here we might turn back to the parting segment from "Prelude:
O When," the segment that so many later scholars want to
remove.

念與君離別	Thinking on parting with you,
氣結不能言	breath knots within, I cannot speak.
各各重自愛	Let each take heed to take care of self,
道遠歸還難	the journey is long, return will be hard.
妾當守空房	I must keep to my empty chamber,
閑門下重關	the idle gate doubly barred.
若生當相見	If you live, we will see each other again;
亡者會重泉	if you die, we will meet in the world below.

The parallel realization of the theme of the parting of man and
wife is easily found in one of the most famous of the old poems.

from the Li Ling corpus[58]

結髮為夫妻	When I bound up my hair, we became man and wife,
恩愛兩不疑	neither doubted the love that we shared.
歡娛在今夕	Joy and pleasure are for this evening,
燕婉及良時	intimacy must be had when the chance comes.
征夫懷往路	The traveler thinks on the journey ahead,
起視夜何其	he rises to see what time of night it is.
參辰皆已沒	Shen and Chen have already set,
去去從此辭	he goes off, taking leave from this moment on.
行役在戰場	He goes to serve on the battlefield,
相見未有期	there is no time set to meet again.
握手一長歎	We clasp hands and heave a long sigh,
淚為生別滋	tears heavy because of being parted while alive.
努力愛春華	Try to make your best of the glory of spring,
莫忘歡樂時	but do not forget our times of joy.

---

58. Lu Qinli, 338; *Wen xuan* 29, *Ytxy* 1.

生當復來歸   If you live, you will come back again;
死當長相思   if you die, I will long for you always.

To suggest that this loosely defined "old poetry" shares a common language and compositional practice is not to imply that all such poems are aesthetically equal. This is as good an example as any that great poetry can emerge out of this common language. And yet the common language remains the best place to begin to consider what can be achieved.

Here we have another parting of man and wife; and if it be objected that only the ending is a close verbal echo of the parting segment in "Prelude: O When," we can easily supply parallels for the missing pieces.

Anonymous Old Poem[59]

悲與親友別	In sadness I take leave of my dear friend,
氣結不能言	the breath knots within me, I cannot speak.
贈子以自愛	I enjoin you to take care of yourself,
道遠會見難	the journey far, it will be hard to meet.
人生無幾時	Human life does not last long,
顛沛在其間	upsets occur in its course.
念子棄我去	I brood on how you abandon me and go,
新心有所歡	the heart may change and one may find someone to love.
結志青雲上	Your aims are set high, above the blue clouds,
何時復來還	when will you come back again?

The first four lines here are variations on (or, in the case of the second line, a duplication of) the first four lines in the parting segment of "Prelude: O When." This leaves only the third couplet without a close parallel or template line:

妾當守空房	I must keep to my empty chamber,
閉門下重關	the idle gate doubly barred.

In the poetry of this period close parallels can usually be found. We can begin with Cao Zhi's famous "The Beauty" 美女篇:[60]

---

59. Lu Qinli, 335; *Ytxy* 1. There is a note that this was not in the original version of *Yutai xinyong*; but there is no other known early source.

60. Lu Qinli, 432.

青樓臨大路	Her green mansion stands by the great road,
高門結重關	her high gate is bound by double barrings.

And in the first of Cao Pi's "Banquet Songs":[61]

君何淹留寄他方	Why do you linger, lodging in a strange land?
賤妾煢煢守空房	I, a poor woman, all alone, keep to my empty chamber.

Or the third of Cao Zhi's "Unclassified Poems":[62]

妾身守空閨	I keep to my empty chambers,
良人行從軍	and my man has gone off with the army.

Nor should we overlook Fu Xuan's 傅玄 "Ballad of Qiuhu" 秋胡行, after Qiuhu has to leave his wife:[63]

皎皎潔婦姿	Gleaming was the figure of his chaste wife,
冷冷守空房	cold and alone, she kept to her empty chamber.

One could move from poem to poem, multiplying parallels, in which not only the same phrases recur in the same situations but the same words appear at the same positions in lines. Poetic composition in the third century and perhaps earlier was probably frequent and ephemeral; few poems were written down, and of those that were written down, fewer still survived in the Southern Dynasties manuscript tradition; of that number fewer still were selected and recorded in our sources. Apart from the conservatory "Treatise on Music," the poems were selected and edited according to later criteria of good "poetry" and an image of what early poetry should have been. Considering the extensive loss of texts and motivated selection, the fact that such a large proportion of these extant poems shares so much material suggests topics and templates that were continually reused, sometimes in habitual combinations and sometimes in variation.

---

61. Ibid., 394.
62. Ibid., 457.
63. Ibid., 556.

Another "Prelude: O When"

If the versions of the "Prelude: O When" we have been discussing present us with interesting questions about "which is the real poem," its problems are small compared to the second anonymous "Prelude: O When" 豔歌何嘗行 in the "Treatise on Music." The first problem follows from a general conviction that for every *yuefu* title there should be only one set of *guci* 古辭, literally "old lyrics," but eventually understood as "original lyrics." This shift in the implications of the term follows from a desire to establish chronology and priority, at the beginning of which must be only a single "original."

The existence of two different anonymous "old lyrics" under the same *yuefu* title was an unstable situation: one of those lyrics needed an author. The *Yuefu shiji* gives a relatively long discussion at the head of the first version of "Prelude: O When," a discussion whose ambiguities create as many problems as they try to solve. Guo Maoqian begins by citing the sixth-century *Gujin yuelu*, which in turn cites Wang Sengqian's "Record of Performers," *Jilu* 技錄, which says (without giving modern punctuation):

豔歌何嘗行歌文帝何嘗古白鵠二篇

"Prelude: O When" ballad song Emperor Wen [Cao Pi] "O When(")" Old (")White Swans" two pieces

We do not know Wang Sengqian's claim to authority here, nor can we be sure which poems he is referring to (some version of "White Swans," discussed above is probably one of them). Sometime in the fifth century Wang Sengqian knew what he meant and perhaps knew the texts to which he was referring; quoted out of context in *Gujin yuelu*, which is in turn quoted in *Yuefu shiji*, we can only guess. The way the passage has been understood is: "two pieces: Emperor Wen's 'O When' and the old/original 'White Swans.'" This solves the problem of two sets of anonymous lyrics as given in the "Treatise on Music" and still referred to as anonymous in the Tang *Yuefu jieti* 樂府解題.[64]

---

64. Diény reads this passage in another way, attributing both pieces to Cao Pi. Diény, *Aux origines de la poésie classique*, 148.

Guo Maoqian solves the contradiction by this reasonable interpretation of Wang Sengqian's comment: taking the second version as Cao Pi's.[65] When we read this second version of "Prelude: O When," however, it is even more of a "mixed bag" than our "White Swans" version; and while we may reasonably suspect that Cao Pi, by repeated experience of song performances, could have composed "as" a professional singer, the speaking voice here is far less personal than many other pieces more credibly attributed to Cao Pi. In the context of traditional poetics the song is something of an embarrassment—unless, of course, we think of poetic composition in a very different way.

[曹丕,] 豔歌何嘗行 Cao Pi (*Yuefu shiji*) or
Anonymous (古辭, *Song shu*), Prelude: O When?[66]

何嘗快獨無憂	O when will we have perfect joy, without cares?[67]
但當飲醇酒	One should just drink pure ale,
炙肥牛	and roast a fat ox.
長兄爲二千石	The eldest brother gets two thousand gallons of grain,
中兄被貂裘	the middle brother wears sable furs,
小弟雖無官爵	the youngest brother has neither office nor title,
鞍馬馺馺	his mounts are fleet,
往來王侯長者遊	he moves among princes, counts, and the great.
但當在王侯殿上	In the palaces of princes and counts one should just
快獨拷蒲六博	take perfect joy in dice and toss-sticks
對坐彈棋	and playing go with an opponent.
男兒居世	In his times each and every man
各當努力	should strive hard.

---

65. This presumes, of course, that the "Prelude: O When" under discussion is the same as the Cao Pi piece to which Wang Sengqian referred.

66. Lu Qinli, 397; *Song shu*; *Yfsj* 39. Huang Jie, *Wei Wudi*, 56; Diény, *Aux origines de la poésie classique*, 146–50; Birrel, *Popular Songs*, 87–89.

67. Some modern versions break this into two lines of three characters: "O when will there be joy, / without any cares at all?" This is a very attractive solution in that it makes the line easy to read; however, the problematic phrase *kuaidu* 快獨 reappears in line 10. Therefore breaking the compound apart in the opening seems unlikely.

憂迫日暮	Twilight presses hard on his heels,
殊不久留	and he will hardly long remain.
少小相觸抵	From youth we have been in conflict,
寒苦常相隨	poverty and pain have been with us long.
忿恚安足諍	Why fight in such furious rage?—
吾中道與卿共別離	I am going to part from you mid-course.
約身奉事君	I bound myself to serve my lord/you,
禮節不可虧	no fault can be found in my principles or behavior.
上慚滄浪之天	Feel shame before the gray heavens above;[68]
下顧黃口小兒	look to your infant babe below.
奈何復老心皇皇	How can I bear to turn old with my heart always uneasy,
獨悲誰能知	who can understand my solitary grief?

There is now a canon of *yuefu* and "old poems," intensively interpreted to yield an iconic image of "Han poetry." For those who know that image, this verse (now safely attributed to Cao Pi and thus rarely read, as being "later," a less successful work by an inferior poet) is an almost incoherent pastiche of all too familiar poems.

If we suppose, however, that a song composition is made up of thematic segments and that there is a particular pleasure in the juncture between segments, "pastiche" becomes "medley," with a pleasure in coherence achieved in spite of disjunction. Rather than an incoherent pastiche by a bad poet, we might see here a compelling trace, surviving textually, of performance practice in the early period. This point is well made by Jean-Pierre Diény in his analysis of this poem: "If we were to possess the complete system, we would fly from one motif to another with the same assurance as the poets of yesteryear."[69] In contrast to Diény, I believe that we do have enough pieces to see the coherence here.

---

68. There is a very similar line in Cao Pi's "Weeds on a Large Wall: Ballad" 大牆上蒿行 (Lu Qinli, 396), in which the aristocratic youth, enjoying himself, gestures to heaven to say that he should enjoy himself while he can because he won't be able to look on heaven forever: "Above there are the gray Heavens" 上有滄浪之天.

69. "Si nous possédions le système entier, nous volerions d'un motif à l'autre avec la même assurance que les poètes d'antan" (Diény, *Les dix-neuf poèmes anciens*, 150).

Let us look at the segments and their analogues. Before doing so, we should consider the musical division as given in the "Treatise on Music." *Yan'ge* 豔歌 is a prelude; like some other "preludes" it includes a long "coda," *qu* 趨, beginning with "From youth we have been in conflict" 少小相觸抵.[70] That is, like the more famous "Prelude: O When," this is a two-part composition.

The song begins with the statement of melancholy (that is, if we take the opening six characters together) that conventionally accompanies the encouragement to drink and make merry, as in *Shanzai xing* 善哉行 and *Ximen xing* 西門行. Indeed the phrases on drinking and eating are shared with the *yuefu* "West Gate," "Ximen xing" 西門行: "drink pure ale, / and roast a fat ox" 飲醇酒, 炙肥牛.[71]

Following this introduction we have a version of the "three brothers" segment, closest to that in "Chang'an Has Narrow Lanes," "Chang'an you xiaxie xing" 長安有狹斜行:[72]

大子二千石	The oldest son gets two thousand pecks of grain;
中子孝廉郎	the middle son is a Filial Modest Gentleman;
小子無官職	the youngest son has no office,
衣冠仕洛陽	in cap and gown he serves in Luoyang.

Apart from the variation in line length, the major differences between this passage and "Prelude: O When" are to be found in the rhyming lines.[73] The representation of the youngest son, conventionally a wastrel, is better realized in "Prelude: O When" than in "Chang'an Has Narrow Lanes" (to "serve in cap and gown" suggests that he does indeed have an office). The opening motif of "merrymaking" here is extend to gambling and gallivanting, reminiscent of the scenes of feasting and partying

---

70. "Prelude" is not a particularly good translation for *yan'ge* 豔歌. It is probably a kind of song used for the first and larger part of a performance; we term it prelude only to clarify the sequence with *qu* 趨, which we translate as "coda" and which comes at the end. For an argument about the musical nature of the *yan*, see Piao Yingji, "Cong 'Yange hechang xing' lun Han Wei Jin yuefu shi de jige wenti."

71. Lu Qinli, 269.

72. Ibid., 266.

73. The principle is a simple one: formulae and template lines have to be flexible in rhyming lines, to fit different rhyme words.

in the "Nineteen Old Poems" and some of Cao Zhi's *yuefu*. In one of the conventional sequences of topics, merrymaking leads to a declaration of life's brevity.

The context of "striving hard," *nuli* 努力, deserves some comment. We see it in "Long Song," "Chang ge xing" 長歌行, anthologized in the *Wen xuan*. There it is not explicitly an exhortation to socially advantageous behavior, but could easily be taken as such in the general propriety of that lyric:[74]

| 少壯不努力 | If one does not strive hard in youth, |
| 老大徒傷悲 | one will feel helpless sorrow when old. |

It also occurs on a more explicitly elevated plane in the Su Wu and Li Ling corpus:[75]

| 努力崇明德 | Strive hard to keep your noble virtue lofty— |
| 皓首以爲期 | we will meet again when our hair is white. |

We find it as a general exhortation, as in the *yuefu* above, in "A pair of ducks both flew to the north" 雙鳧俱北飛 in the Su Wu and Li Ling corpus:

| 願子長努力 | I want you to always strive hard, |
| 言笑莫相忘 | and don't forget our laughter together. |

The most famous example is at the end of the first of the "Nineteen Old Poems": "strive hard to eat more" 努力加餐飯, which gives a sense of how general the striving may be. In every case the exhortation marks closure, and in the *yuefu* above it is the closure of a segment.[76]

Up to this point, which is the "prelude," *yan'ge*, we have a nice variation on the feast song. As we move into the *qu* 趨 or "coda," the situation changes to one of conflict and imminent separation. The moment of disjunction when moving between segments involves a certain pleasure, as the reader moves to link the parts. It is easy to construct a narrative here: each of the three brothers has a wife, and the "youngest wife" is always

---

74. Lu Qinli, 262. See the discussion of this motif in relation to the declaration of life's brevity on pp. 178–80.

75. Lu Qinli, 337.

76. A variation can also be seen in the fourth of the "Nineteen Old Poems," where, after the feast and the meditation on life's brevity, the poem enjoins the listener to take action.

the figure of poetic attention. To quote the lines that follow the
passage above from "Chang'an Has Narrow Lanes":[77]

三子俱入室	When the three sons enter the house together,
室中自生光	the chamber fills with light.
大婦織綺紵	The eldest wife weaves figured broadweave,
中婦織流黃	the middle wife weaves the yellow floss,
小婦無所爲	the youngest wife does nothing at all,
挾琴上高堂	zither in arm, she mounts the high hall.
丈人且徐徐	"Be easy, my lord, a while,
調弦詎未央	tuning the chords is not yet done."

Since our youngest son in "Prelude: O When" has been out
carousing, and carousing has led to a declaration of life's
brevity and the importance of striving, it is easy to interpret our
coda as the reproach of the youngest wife. In such a context the
preceding counsel to "strive hard" while he is still young serves
as both a conventional segment closure and a transition to the
next segment.[78]

While this putative narrative unifies the segments, it is no
less true that the poem is linked together by less rational as-
sociations. The topic of conflict at the beginning of the coda
seems surprising in the context of this poem; we wonder where
it comes from. We can explain it as a natural component of our
scenario of a wife trying to make her husband behave himself; it
also appears, however, in the conventional linkage of topics.
Perhaps conflict is a possible association of the topic of
brothers. When there are three (or more) brothers, one of them
always seems to be either poor or in trouble in some way—
though he comes from the same "root" as the others. We might
quote a short anonymous *yuefu*, a version of "Shangliu tian"
上留田行:[79]

---

77. Lu Qinli, 266.

78. The interpretation of the coda as a wife's address to her husband is
made by Huang Jie. Diény rejects this as "pure fantasy." If we can improve on
Diény's remarkably perceptive discussions of these early *yuefu* from the *Song
shu*, it will be in dissociating the components of a theme from a particular
narrative, as in the discussion that follows. The motif of conflict between the
brothers can easily be transferred to a statement of conflict between husband
and wife.

79. Lu Qinli, 288.

出是上獨西門	I went out West Gate alone,
三荊同一根生	three brambles grew from a single root,
一荊斷絕不長	one bramble broke and did not grow tall.
兄弟有兩三人	Brothers there were, two or three,
塊摧獨貧	down and out, one alone is poor.

Here we might consider another version of "Chang'an Has Narrow Lanes," namely, "Cockcrow" 雞鳴. I quote the last part, with more brothers, but also associated with plants that seem bound together:[80]

兄第四五人	Brothers there are, four or five,
皆為侍中郎	all are Attendant Gentlemen.
五日一時來	Every five days they come back once,
觀者滿路傍	and the viewers fill the roadside.
黃金絡馬頭	Gold winds around their horses' heads,
頴頴何煌煌	gleaming and sparkling.
桃生露井上	A peach tree grew by an open well,
李樹生桃傍	a plum tree grew by the peach's side.
蟲來齧桃根	Worms came and gnawed the peach's roots,
李樹代桃殭	but the plum tree collapsed in place of the peach.[81]
樹木身相代	So trees can sacrifice one for the other,
兄弟還相忘	yet brother can still forget brother.

Here we have a clear suggestion of conflict between brothers or one brother failing to help another in time of need. Moreover, scholars have always been puzzled by the opening segment of "Cockcrow," with its suggestion of a wanderer being warned against committing some crime:

雞鳴高樹巔	The cock crows atop a high tree,
狗吠深宮中	a dog barks deep in the compound.
蕩子何所之	Where is the wanderer going?
天下方太平	all the world is now at peace.
刑法非有貸	There is no slackness in the law,
柔協正亂名	the weak reconciled, confusion of names corrected.

---

80. Ibid., 257.

81. These four lines strongly suggest the figuratively political street song (*geyao* 歌謠), such as the last four lines of the street song attributed to Chengdi's reign.

There may be a strong suggestion of the failure of brothers to help one another at the end of "Cockcrow," and the younger brother, given to gambling and carousing in "Prelude: O When," could be considered a "wanderer" (*dangzi* 蕩子, with strong associations of "wastrel"). Law-breaking is hinted at in the opening of "Cockcrow" and clearly implied in a third poem, which is a longer version of the material in the last part of "Prelude: O When." This is "East Gate," "Dongmen xing" 東門行, cited here in the version on the "Treatise on Music."[82]

出東門	I went out East Gate,
不顧歸	not expecting to return.
來入門	I came in the gate,
悵欲悲	full of sorrow.
盎中無斗儲	There is no store of rice in the jar,
還視桁上無懸衣	I look around to no clothes hanging on the rack.
拔劍出門去	I pull out my sword and go out the gate,
兒女牽衣啼	my children tug at my clothes, crying.
他家但願富貴	"Other families just want wealth and station,
賤妾與君共餔糜	but I will share gruel with you,
共餔糜	share gruel with you.
上用倉浪天故	Because of gray Heaven above,
下爲黃口小兒	because of your infant child here below.
今時清廉	These are untroubled times,
難犯教言	you can't violate the rules;
君復自愛莫爲非	You take care of yourself, don't do what is wrong.
今時清廉	These are untroubled times,
難犯教言	you can't violate the rules;
君復自愛莫爲非	You take care of yourself, don't do what is wrong."
行	"I'm going.
吾去爲遲	I've waited too long to be off."
平慎行	"Be careful in what you do;
望君歸	I'll look for you to return."

In "East Gate" we have a poor man, rather than a rich wastrel, but the scene of conflict and a wife's dissuasion is shared with "Prelude: O When."

---

82. Lu Qinli, 269; *Song shu*; *Yfsj* 37. Diény, *Aux origines de la poésie classique*, 126–28; Birrel, *Popular Songs*, 134–37.

Such a multiplication of overlapping texts may be confusing, but if we consider them together, we have a standard situation in narrative theory: we have plot functions and variables. The difference is that in this poetry we never have a complete plot, only different phases. We have three (or two to five) brothers, the youngest of whom is in trouble (either from law-breaking or extravagant behavior or simple bad luck that leaves him poor).[83] What has given critics problems in "Cockcrow" is that there is no specific mention of the younger brother or his being a wastrel or in trouble. Considering these texts as versions of a "story," there doesn't need to be an explicit mention of the younger brother being in trouble: the audience knows it. The other brothers do not help the youngest brother. He has a wife who either tries to reform him or apparently does not, instead playing music for "someone." This is less a "story" than the outline of choices of how to tell a number of possible stories.

What we see in the poems are not stories but pieces, yet enough pieces to construct the variables. In other words, if Poem A shares some material with Poem B, and Poem B shares other material with Poem C, other elements in Poem C may be useful in explaining Poem A, though their only connection lies in the fact that both share material with poem B. This makes sense only if we think of these texts as versions of a repertoire of familiar themes held together by a web of associations. From this point of view, when a listener heard the opening segment on "Cockcrow," warning a wanderer against breaking the law, he would recognize a loose set of themes and topics; when he heard the segment on the brothers, his anticipations would be confirmed. He does not need to have the plea placed in the mouth of the wife. When he hears the final segment on brother failing to help brother, he recognizes something new (at least there is no clear analogue in extant poems): the consequence of failing to heed the warning and the failure of the other brothers to help the youngest.

---

83. Diény (*Aux origines de la poésie classique*, 149) argues that the motif of frequenting the homes of aristocrats is always treated positively; but if we extend the range of our texts beyond the *Song shu yuefu*, this is not necessarily the case. To be the youngest brother is generally a problematic role, and the high life can easily turn negative.

If we treat "Cockcrow" as a self-contained "poem," it presents all the problems of internal coherence that traditional critics have pointed out; if we look at it as one realization of material in a shared repertoire, it holds together quite well. Similarly, as a work that is assumed to postdate "Han *yuefu,*" Cao Pi's "Prelude: O When" may be seen as a pastiche of familiar lines and passages; if, however, we take it as another realization of this same material, it is a very lucid and full version.

An aggregation of topics is not a narrative, though narratives can be produced from such aggregations of topics. The continuity lies in the topics themselves. Specifics can be rearranged. The wife could be someone else's wife, though like the wives of the two elder brothers in "Chang'an Has Narrow Lanes" and its shorter variation, "Meeting," she may be good at sewing. The potential transgression need not be violent, done with sword in hand. The wife may persuade not her husband going off on travels, but the husband who stays at home, who looks with suspicion on her sewing clothes for the wanderer. The component pieces are all present, including the "two or three brothers"; the poet weaves them together into a new story—or into yet another variation of an old story.

豔歌行 Prelude[84]

翩翩堂前燕	Swiftly flitting, swallows before the hall,
冬藏夏來見	out of sight in winter, in summer they appear.
兄弟兩三人	Two or three brothers,
流宕在他縣	roaming free, in another land.
故衣誰當補	Who will mend my old clothes,
新衣誰當綻	who will sew up my new clothes?
賴得賢主人	Luckily we have a gracious hostess
覽取爲我糸/旦	who takes them and patches them for me.
夫婿從門來	Her husband comes in through the gate,
斜柯西北眄	he slouches, and glares to the northwest.
語卿且勿眄	She says, "Husband, do not glare so—
水清石自見	when the water is clear, the stones appear."
石見何累累	The stones appear, how densely strewn,
遠行不如歸	better to go home than travel far.

---

84. Lu Qinli, 273; *Ytxy* 1; *Yfsj* 39. Huang Jie, *Han Wei*, 44–45.

When we have a text whose primary source is *Yutai xinyong*, we need to treat it with a degree of caution, in that the early texts included in *Yutai xinyong* seem to have been often fixed for the tastes of a sixth-century readership. The swallows, figures of sexuality, are also travelers who may come to lodge in someone's dwelling. They appear here only in the opening couplet—though we could easily imagine ten lines on the swallows, followed by the present poem, and concluding with an invocation of blessing on the audience. That is, this is the kind of poem that could be realized in a way very similar to our first version of "Prelude: O When."

There may be "two or three brothers" mentioned; but there seems to be only one wanderer in the rest of the poem, and we know that this must be the youngest brother, who seems to be always associated with possible trouble.[85] Clothing was woman's work and not professionalized, thus the responsibility of family members. For the wanderer clothing represents a problem—a problem here solved by the gracious hostess. We meet this woman in another guise in "Ballad of Longxi" 隴西行; there as here she comes to the margin of respectability by in-teracting with a guest, and by not crossing that margin her virtue is affirmed.[86]

The husband comes upon the scene and is angry and sus-picious. We have seen two prior instances in which the woman speaker tried to persuade the wandering husband; here it seems she is offering a brief persuasion to the suspicious husband at home that nothing is hidden. We may understand the final couplet as being in the voice of the speaker of the poem, in the voice of the husband, or even in the voice of the wife. The reason we include the voice of the wife as a possibility here (producing a discursive twist) is simply because the wife (or "a wife") always tries to persuade the wander to go or come home.

---

85. The encyclopedia fragment from Dunhuang reads *fenju* 分居, "dwelling apart," for *liudang* 流宕, "roaming free" in line 4. This makes it clearer that in this case we have the "poor brother," as in "Shangliu tian."

86. It is tempting to think of this as an issue for itinerant performers, who depended on the goodwill of their hosts and hostesses; it would have been in their interest to praise the kindness of the hostess to the guest but at the same time to reaffirm her propriety.

Mix and Match

Let us return to one of the parting poems from the Li Ling corpus cited earlier: "Once the yellow swan parts for far away." The attentive reader may have noticed something quite peculiar about this poem, beginning with the now familiar motif of birds parting, but closing with the wish that the friends could become a pair of birds flying away together. The return of the yellow swan as the speaker's desired self is all the more remarkable in that the initial image of the yellow swans is presented only to be rejected as a "lower" version of parting, in comparison to the two friends who are "flying dragons." As with the "springtime birds" flying south discussed earlier, one could explain this as poetic ineptness or poetic genius (after the gesture of higher status in the opening, the music provokes such a depth of feeling that the speaker is to be content to be an ordinary bird). The better explanation, however, is the inertia of topics in a theme.

黃鵠一遠別	Once the yellow swan parts for far away,
千里顧徘徊	it looks back and hesitates at a thousand leagues.
胡馬失其群	When the Tartar horse loses its herd,
思心常依依	its longing heart is ever filled with yearning.
何況雙飛龍	Even more so [we], a pair of flying dragons,
羽翼臨當乖	whose wings are on the verge of separating.
幸有絃歌曲	Luckily we have songs and string music
可以喻中懷	which can figure forth our feelings within.
請爲遊子吟	I would have you sing the Traveler's Lay—
泠泠一何悲	how sad its ringing notes are!
絲竹厲清聲	The strings' and pipes' clear notes grow intense,
慷慨有餘哀	in their strong feeling is ample sorrow.
長歌正激烈	Now the Long Songs are urgently stirring,
中心愴以摧	the heart within is depressed and broken.
欲展清商曲	I would perform a tune in the clear Shang mode,
念子不得歸	thinking on how you will not be able to return.
俛仰內傷心	In a moment the heart feels pain within,
淚下不可揮	tears fall, I cannot wipe them away.
願爲雙黃鵠	I wish we were a pair of yellow swans,
送子俱遠飛	I would send you on your way, both flying far.

What has happened here is a compositional process occurring on the margins between elite literary exposition and the common poetic repertoire. We have discussed earlier the element of literary rhetoric in the opening, where standard figures from the poetic tradition are proposed, to be transcended by the elite figure, the "pair of flying dragons." The rhetorical move is continued in a compensatory reversal: "although the pair of flying dragons must feel parting even more intensely than ordinary creatures, we at least have music at the parting feast to give expression to those feelings."

Once the poet has moved to the theme of music, however, he is back in a standard poetic situation, albeit one handled in a peculiar way in this poem. The situation is one in which the traveler hears a singer (or singers), describes the music, and concludes by expressing desire to become a pair of birds and fly off together with some other. The paradigmatic examples are in the fifth and the twelfth of the "Nineteen Old Poems," in both cases with music leading to the wish to fly away as a pair of birds. As we have seen earlier, once a poet enters a standard theme there is an inertia that carries him along, even though the ending may, as here, lead to a position that has a problematic relation to the opening of the poem.

Reading the poems as realizations of a shared repertoire can help explain small details. The fourth of the "Nineteen Old Poems" is a feast poem that leads to the theme of music:[87]

今日良宴會	A fine feast we hold this day,
歡樂難具陳	its pleasures are hard to fully tell.
彈箏奮逸響	Plucked zithers give forth trailing echoes,
新聲妙入神	popular tunes, so fine they belong to the gods.
令德唱高言	One of fine virtue sings forth noble words,
識曲聽其真	those who know song heed its truth.
齊心同所願	Hearts equal, we share the same wish,
含意俱未伸	the sense held back, not fully expressed.
人生寄一世	Man's life sojourns in a single age,
奄忽若飆塵	it fleets by like dust tossed by the wind.
何不策高足	Why not whip on a high-hoofed steed,
先據要路津	be the first to seize the ford.

---

87. Lu Qinli, 330; *Wen xuan* 39. Note that the second couplet is cited under Cao Zhi's name in *Beitang shuchao*. Sui Shusen, *Gushi*, 6–7; Diény, *Les dix-neuf poèmes anciens*, 14–15, 71–77.

無爲守貧賤　　　　Don't stay poor and of low degree,
轗軻長苦辛　　　　struggling and ever bitter.

There are many issues in this poem which we will not address here. Rather, we might simply note the seventh line, in which the listeners "share the same wish." It is easy, perhaps even proper to read that wish as the advice given at the end of the poem. Yet the theme of music commonly leads to a "wish," specifically *yuan* 願, on the part of the speaker to become a bird and fly away with some other of like mind. On the purely verbal level of compositional habit the "wish" recurs here in a truncated form, "not fully expressed." But the unspoken impulse to "go off" returns at the end in a flurry of galloping hooves rather than a flurry of wings.

The pressure of compositional habit can be equally strong in the work of known poets.

曹丕, 清河作 Cao Pi, Written at Qinghe[88]

方舟戲長水　　　　The catamaran sports in the long river,
湛澹自浮沈　　　　in clear, swift currents, it bobs up
　　　　　　　　　　and down.
絃歌發中流　　　　Songs to strings come forth midstream,
悲響有餘音　　　　the moving notes have much resonance.
音聲入君懷　　　　The notes enter your bosom,
悽愴傷人心　　　　dismal, they cause heart's pain.
心傷安所念　　　　The heart feels pain, on what do you
　　　　　　　　　　brood?—
但願恩情深　　　　you want only that love be deep.
願爲晨風鳥　　　　I wish we were the dawnwind hawks,
雙飛翔北林　　　　flying as a pair, soaring in the
　　　　　　　　　　northern woods.

There is no particular singer explicitly here; there is only the music on what appears to be a pleasure outing. Yet once the poet begins describing the musical performance, he seems committed to a sequence of poetic association that leads to true love and the lovers imagined as birds, flying off together. The same sequence appears in the Cao Pi version of "Grand" 善哉行 beginning "In the morning, joy upon joy" 朝日樂相樂. There we find an extended description of music, followed by Cao Pi

---

88. Lu Qinli, 402; *Ytxy* 2. Huang Jie, *Wei Wudi*, 60.

brooding on the danger of excess, followed by the departure of the guests. The poem ends on a peculiar note that requires considerable exegetical ingenuity to link to the preceding section:[89]

比翼翔雲漢	If, wing to wing, they soar in the Milky Way,
羅者安所羈	how can the fowler entrap them?
沖靜得自然	If, empty and calm, one attains the state of nature,
榮華何足爲	how are glory and splendor worthwhile?

What is hard to explain in terms of rational poetic argument is actually a habitual move in conventional sequences of topics. The description of music looks for resolution in two birds flying away together. And those birds do finally make their appearance in this celebratory feast song gone astray.

The desire to become a pair of birds is such a strong verbal habit that the wish can be made even when there is apparently only one person present. There is much uncertain in the short song "The Prince of Huainan" 淮南王: the prince digs a well, drinks the water, and is apparently restored to youth. Youth, however, proves unsatisfying:[90]

揚聲悲歌音絕天	I raise my voice in sad song, the notes break Heaven's heart.
我欲渡河河無梁	I want to cross the river, the river has no bridge;
願化雙黃鵠還故鄉	I want to become a pair of yellow swans and return to my home.
還故鄉	I return to my home,
入故里	I enter my old village,
徘徊故鄉苦身不已	I pace about in my old village, feeling endlessly bitter.
繁舞寄聲無不泰	A flurry of dancers, sounds sent forth, in every way the finest,
徘徊桑梓遊天外	I pace about among the mulberries and roam beyond the heavens.

The song leads to the "wish," *yuan*, to become a pair of birds. Unfortunately there is no other here with whom to form a

---

89. For a complete translation and discussion, see pp. 200–202.
90. Lu Qinli, 276; *Song shu; Jinshu Yuezhi; Yfsj* 54.

"pair." It would have been metrically smoother and more referentially coherent to have omitted the "pair," *shuang* 雙, here; we have no idea who the other member of the swan pair might be in this case. But the line as we have it more perfectly grows out of the repertoire of poetic topics, doubling a bird that should, in this context, be single.

Including the fifth and twelfth of the "Nineteen Old Poems," we have identified above five cases in which the theme of music and/or song leads to the wish to become a pair of birds and fly away together (not including the ambiguous "wish" in the fourth of the "Nineteen Old Poems"). This is yet another example of the association of topics, which can occur in various registers. It occurs in both anonymous verse and poetry by known authors. The question we now want to pose is how those associative links become broken. The topic of becoming a pair of birds does become independent from the experience of music in literary poetry, and it is instructive to look at the way this happens.

The first example is a particularly suggestive one; here we have a musical performance that eventually comes to the very edge of a wish to fly away together. Apparently we begin with a beautiful singer, passing over into the theme of music, with strong counterparts in "Nineteen Old Poems" IV. Then in a separate segment with a new rhyme we have the parted bird seeking its beloved. The poet turns to look on it longingly, but stops just short of the wish to fly away.

曹丕, 善哉行 Cao Pi, Grand![91]

有美一人	There is a person beautiful,
婉如清揚	delicate are her eyelids.
妍姿巧笑	Sensuous form, artful smiles
和媚心腸	soothe and beguile the heart.
知音識曲	One who knows the tone and understands melody
善爲樂方	makes good music.
哀絃微妙	The mournful strings are subtle,
清氣含芳	her clear breath has a sweetness within.
流鄭激楚	Dissolute music of Zheng, the stirring Chu,[92]

---

91. Lu Qinli, 391; *Yfsj* 36. Huang Jie, *Wei Wudi*, 37–38.

92. *Jichu* 激楚 is a kind of dance. The *chu* seems not originally to have been associated with the kingdom of Chu. Here, however, in parallel with *liu Zheng*

度宮中商	play the note *gong*, then strike *shang*.
感心動耳	It stirs the heart and moves the ear,
綺麗難忘	an intricate beauty hard to forget.
離鳥夕宿	The bird, separated, rests for the evening
在彼中洲	on the isle midstream.
延頸鼓翼	It stretches its neck and beats its wings,
悲鳴相求	singing out sadly, seeking.
眷然顧之	With longing I turn to look on it,
使我心愁	making my heart feel grief.
嗟爾昔人	Ah, you person[s] of the past—
何以忘憂	how can I forget my cares?[93]

In "Nineteen Old Poems" V we have the speaker hearing music performed by a woman hidden away high in a building. He stops, is moved by the music, and predictably wishes that they become a pair of birds and fly away. The same moves are here, with a solitary, longing bird being placed in the position of the woman, a bird whose sad cries take the place of the music. We have seen so many pairs of birds as figures for persons attached by love or deep friendship that the appearance of the bird here is hardly surprising. The imagined flight would be a way to "forget cares," but cares win out here.

More often we have the wish to become a pair of birds as an independent topic, detached from the music, but invoked in some variation of the theme of separation. The cues that can invoke it are diverse. In the following case it seems to be the memory of a specific other poem.

徐幹 [/曹丕], 於清河見挽船士新婚與妻別 Xu Gan or Cao Pi,
At Qinghe I Saw a Soldier Boat-Hauler; Recently
Married, He Was Parting with His Wife[94]

與君結新婚	I was recently married to you,
宿昔當別離	after only a night we had to part.
涼風動秋草	Chill winds stir the autumn plants,
蟋蟀鳴相隨	crickets sing, following one another.

流鄭, the "dissolute [music of] Zheng," it is clearly being interpreted as translated above.

93. Wang Fuzhi 王夫之 explains these final lines as: "this has happened since ancient times" 古來有之. Huang Jie, *Wei Wudi*, 38.

94. Lu Qinli, 378; *Ytxy* 2 (attributed to Cao Pi); *Ywlj* 2. Han Geping, *Jian'an*, 347–48; Wu Yun 吳雲, *Jian'an*, 298. Lu argues that this poem is Xu Gan's and that Cao Pi wrote a different one.

冽冽寒蟬吟	Shrilly the cold cicada whines,
蟬吟抱枯枝	the cicada whines, clasping a leafless branch.
枯枝時飛揚	From the leafless branch it soars up betimes,
身體忽遷移	and its body is suddenly shifted elsewhere.
不悲身遷移	I don't feel sad that its body is shifted elsewhere,
但惜歲月馳	I care only how the years and months speed past.
歲月無窮極	The years and months never come to an end,
會合安可知	how will we ever have a meeting?
願爲雙黃鵠	I wish we were a pair of yellow swans,
比翼戲清池	wing to wing, sporting in a clear pool.

We need first to note that although this topic is "literary," insofar as it is a poem based on a circumstance more specific than the general themes of *yuefu* and the "old poems," the specificity is determined only by the title and not by the text itself. Indeed the text is less specific than the similar poem from the Li Ling corpus spoken by a newly married wife to a husband about to set off in the army. This is less a "title" in the later literary sense than a prose note on a circumstance in which a characteristically general "old poem" was (or might have been) used. A poem bound to such a specific circumstance seeks a particular author, but here we have two possible authors offered by the manuscript tradition.

The relationship between the circumstantial title and the generality of the text deserves some comment: in such texts we can see how the generality of the "popular" repertoire might be used in a specific situation. While the individual lines can in very many cases be traced back to the "popular" repertoire, the structure is profoundly different. If we were to organize this poem like "Prelude: O When," we would have an opening segment on the cicada, gradually evoking the human analogy (ll. 3–12); then we would have the human situation in lines 1–2 announced and elaborated into a full segment. Without the music theme, however, we would probably not have the closing wish to be a pair of birds.

How is it then that we have the wish to become two birds? The answer here seems to come from the verbal memory of a specific text that did mention music. In the fifth of the "Nineteen Old Poems," the speaker hears a woman playing music in the upper story of a mansion. He stops and listens. The final part of the poem goes:[95]

不惜歌者苦	I don't care that the singer feels pain,
但傷知音稀	what hurts is that few understand the sound.
願爲雙鴻鵠	I wish we could be two wild swans
奮翅起高飛	to fly with great wingbeats high and away.

What we have in the "Xu Gan" poem seems to be the memory of a specific and unique textual sequence rather than a realization of themes and topics in a repertoire. A couplet pattern ("I don't feel bad about X / I do feel bad about Y") is generating an association of topics in its own right. In this case I believe we can say that the fifth of the "Nineteen Old Poems" is, in some version, older than this poem attributed to Xu Gan or Cao Pi (though the attribution to either should be viewed with great skepticism).

Finally we come to a poem where we can have some faith in authorship and rough dating to the early third century. Here, too, the closing topic of a wish to become two birds is detached from the theme of music.

曹植, 送應氏二首 Cao Zhi, Two Poems
Sending Off Mr. Ying II[96]

清時難屢得	Such clear moments are hard to have often,
嘉會不可常	this splendid gathering will not be forever.
天地無終極	Heaven and Earth have no ending,
人命若朝霜	but man's lifespan is like the frost of dawn.
願得展嬿婉	I want to express my tender love,
我友之朔方	for my friend is going to the northland.
親昵並集送	Kin and intimates all gather to see him off,

---

95. Lu Qinli, 330.

96. Ibid., 454; *Wen xuan* 20. Huang Jie 黃節, *Cao Zijian shi zhu* 曹子建詩注 (Beijing, 1957), 9–10; Nie Wenyu 聶文鬱, *Cao Zhi shi jieyi* 曹植詩解譯 (Xining: Qinghai renmin chubanshe, 1985), 89–90; Zhao Youwen 趙幼文, *Cao Zhi ji jiaozhu* 曹植集校注 (Beijing: Renmin wenxue chubanshe, 1984), 4–6.

置酒此河陽	and we have ale served here on the River's north shore.
中饋豈獨薄	Our feast is indeed no meager one,
賓飲不盡觴	guests drink and do not finish their goblets.
愛至望苦深	Our love is perfect, our hopes terribly deep—
豈不愧中腸	how can it help but shame the heart within?
山川阻且遠	The mountains and rivers are blocked and far,
別促會日長	parting presses on us, the day of our meeting is far off.
願為比翼鳥	I wish we were birds flying wing to wing,
施翮起高翔	spreading pinions to rise, soaring on high.

This poem is rich in topics from the "popular" repertoire (one of which, the figure of blockage, has been discussed earlier). In terms of compositional practice, however, this is much more "literary"; the habitual associations of topics are not followed. The poem is perfectly coherent—indeed probably more coherent than if the standard associations were used—but the coherence comes from a talented writer who is making use of an "old poem" repertoire rather than writing *within* it.

In the Xu Gan poem the closing figure of the birds came from a specific echo of a prior poem; in Cao Zhi's poem it comes from the parting feast. In the poem from the Li Ling corpus we had a parting feast in which music was played, and the music became the theme that suggested the closing wish to become a pair of birds. In the other cases of that closing wish there is music but no parting feast; that is, what determined the closing topic was the description of the music itself rather than a particular situation in which the music was played. Music was generally performed at parties, even though Cao Zhi does not mention it here.

To answer our initial question regarding how topics become independent from associated topics and themes, we have two distinct cases above. In the "Xu Gan" poem we see it happening through a specific verbal echo of a prior text; in Cao Zhi's poem we see it following from a situation in which there surely was music, though music is not mentioned in the poem itself. Implied music is the "trigger" for the image of birds flying off together. For other poets one needed words referring to music; Cao Zhi only needed a situation that implied music. Another way of stating the revolution in the Cao Zhi poem is this: poets who composed from the standard "repertoire" worked with words: they might choose a theme appropriate to the situation, but the poetic structure of words had its own logic.

When Cao Zhi moves from the parting feast to the wish to become a pair of birds, it is indeed a revolution, as subdued as it is profound. He is still using the poetic repertoire and making associations through it; but he is thinking referentially rather than by purely verbal habit. The music that makes one wish to fly off with the beloved or the dear friend is in the situation, but not in the words.

The cluster of themes, topics, and template lines that constitute the poetic "repertoire" remains in the background through the third century and on until the end of the Western Jin. New forces are at work upon this basic material for poetry in the five syllable line. New situations for poetry require a new kind of lines; diction from *fu* and prose are incorporated to mark a higher register.

The Circulation of Themes

We have hitherto been considering only the realization of poetic material in classical poetry. Some of the thematic "material" of classical poetry, however, circulated in a variety of discursive forms. Clearly in the Jian'an certain topics such as "the widow" and military campaigns could be done either in poetic expositions or in classical poetry. Yet there seems to have been other material circulating more widely.

We might begin with two texts we can date with confidence to the Han. They show different forms of treating a theme: a natural tree, cut and fashioned, as a figure for human "talent," *cai* 才／財. The first is a gnomic verse from the *Jiaoshi Yilin*:[97]

梗生荊山	The *pian* tree grows on Jing Mountain,
命制輪班	[Gong]shu Ban is commanded to work it.
袍衣剝脫	Its heavy coat is peeled away,
夏熱冬寒	hot in summer, in winter cold.
飢餓枯槁	Starving and all withered up,
眾人莫憐	no one takes pity on it.

---

97. Wen Yiduo 聞一多, *Yilin jiongzhi* 易林瓊枝, *Wen Yiduo quanji* 聞一多全集 (Beijing: Sanlian shudian, 1968), 4: 142; Chen Liangyun, *Jiaoshi Yilin*, 264. *Geng* 梗 is a mistake for *pian* 楩.

This is characteristic of the *Jiaoshi Yilin* verses, figuratively deploying popular images. In this case the artistry of the famous craftsman Gongshu Ban of Lu is merely a "stripping bare," leaving the tree exposed and suffering.

We have a very different kind of treatment and a very different meaning given the same image in the opening of Lu Jia's 陸賈 chapter "On Material" 資質, which is, for all intents and purposes a loose poetic exposition 賦.[98]

質美者以通爲貴. 才良者以顯爲能. 何以言之. 夫梗柟豫章, 天下之名木也, 生於深山之中, 産於溪谷之傍. 立則爲太山眾木之宗, 仆則爲萬世之用. 浮於山水之流, 出於冥冥之野. 因江河之道, 而達於京師之下, 因斧斤之功, 得其文色. 精捍直理, 密緻博通, 蟲蝎不能穿, 水溼不能傷, 在高柔軟, 入地堅彊, 無膏澤而光潤生, 不刻畫而文章成, 上爲帝王之御物, 下則賜公卿, 庶賤不得以備器械; 閉絕以關梁 . . . 及臨於山阪之阻, 隔於九派之隑, 仆於鬼崔之山, 頓於宦冥之溪, 樹蒙龍蔓延而無間, 石崔鬼巃岩而不開, 廣者無舟車之通, 狹者無步擔之蹊, 商賈所不至, 工匠所不窺, 知者所不見, 見者所不知, 功棄而德亡, 腐朽而枯傷, 轉於百仞之壑, 惕然而獨僵, 當斯之時, 不如道傍之枯楊. 硋硋結屈, 委曲不同. 然生於大都之廣地, 近於大匠之名工, 材器制斷, 規矩度量, 堅者補朽, 短者續長, 大者治鐏, 小者治觴, 飾以丹漆, 斁以明光, 上備大牢, 春秋禮庠, 褒以文彩, 立禮矜莊, 冠帶正容, 對酒行觴, 卿士列位, 布陳宮堂, 望之者目眩, 近之者鼻芳. 故事閉之則絕, 次之則通, 抑之則沈, 興之則揚, 處地梗梓, 賤於枯楊, 德美非不相絕也, 才力非不相懸也, 彼則槁枯而遠棄, 此則爲宗廟之瑚璉者, 通與不通也. 人亦猶此.

> For beauty of material, circulation (*tong*) is most to be valued; for excellence of talent/timber, visibility means success.
>
> How can I explain it?
>
> The *pian* and *nan* and the camphorwood are the most famous trees in the world:
>
> they grow in the deep mountains; they are produced beside stream valleys;
>
> standing, they are the most august of all the trees of large mountains; felled, they are useful for ten thousand ages;
>
> they drift on the currents of mountain rivers; they come out of the mysterious wilderness;
>
> following the course of the Yangzi and Yellow rivers, they arrive near the capital;
>
> then through the accomplishments of the ax and hatchet they are able to display the beauty of their grain-patterns.

---

98. Wang Liqi 王利器, *Xinyu jiaozhu* 新語校註 (Beijing: Zhonghua shuju, 1986), 101–2. I have noted an ellipsis in the text, while Wang reads it as continuous. In the passage 庶賤不得以備器械, I have kept the received text rather than Wang's emendation of 不 to 而.

Fine and resistant, straight of grain, densely textured, widely distributed;

worms and scorpions cannot bore into them; water cannot hurt them;

set up high, they are pliant and flexible; put in the ground, they are firm and hard;

they give off a moist glow without applying oil; their patterns are perfect without being carved;

on the highest level they make things for the use of emperors; on a lower level they are presented to high lords.

commoners cannot use them for vessels and implements. . . .

Blocked by passes and bridges . . .

but when they are blocked by mountain slopes, and cut off by the embankments of the nine reservoirs,

they lie prone on towering mountains, they collapse by dark and obscure creeks;

trees extend spreading vegetation and admit no space [to reach the good trees]; mountains are towering and craggy and do not open a way [to them];

the broadest [ways to them] give no passage to boat or wagon; the narrow [ways to them] have no paths for carrying on foot;

unreached by merchants, unglimpsed by craftsmen,

unseen by those who could recognize them [their worth], unrecognized by those who see them;

the achievement [of being crafted] is lost and their virtue perishes;

they rot and decay and suffer drying up; they roll into hundred fathom ravines,

where, in fear, they lie alone, stiff—

and at a time such as this, they are worse off than a dried up poplar by the roadside.

Lumpy, they bend [poplar roots], in twistiness differing [from the *pian*, *nan*, and camphorwood];

nevertheless they were born in the broad territory of the metropolis, near to the famous workmanship of great craftsmen;

their capacity and timber is determined; they are measured with compass and carpenter's square;

the firm ones mend those with decay; the short add to the length of the long;

from the large parts are fashioned *zun* beakers; from the small parts are fashioned cups;

they are decorated with cinnabar and lacquer, burnished to give off light;

on the highest level they are part of the Great Earth and Grain rite; in spring and autumn they are part of academy ceremonies;

they are commended for their decorative patterns; they vaunt their
dignity in the establishment of rites;

Those with caps and sashes compose their features, and facing wine,
pass the cups;

grandees and gentlemen in their places, spread in array in the palace
hall,

the eyes are dazzled of those who stare at them [poplar wood vessels],
those who draw near then catch the fragrance in the nose.

Thus when something is blocked, it is cut off; when given its proper
position, it gets through;

when it is pressed down, it sinks; when it is lifted up, it rises;

the *pian* and catalpa, by where they grow, are inferior to a dried-up
poplar;

it is not that there is not a great difference in virtue and beauty; it is
not that there is not a great distinction in the strength of tal-
ent/timber;

but the former becomes dead wood, abandoned far in the distance,
while the latter becomes the *hulian* vessel for grain in the ancestral
temple—

this is a question of making it through (*tong*, communication/
circulation) and not.

It is also like this in regard to people.

This is a nice piece of Han rhetoric, which we must imagine was
a kind of oral presentation: the fine timber of the *pian*, the *nan*,
and the camphor tree are not used because they are lost in the
wilderness, while the plain poplar, whose wood is of low quality,
is used in fine ceremonies because it is close at hand.

The "camphor" tree, *yuzhang* 豫章, is also the name of a re-
gion and a mountain. Among the anonymous *yuefu* there is a
"Ballad of Yuzhang Mountain / Camphorwood." Although the
song is filled with lacunae, the outline is clear.

豫章行 The Ballad of Camphorwood
[or Camphorwood Mountain][99]

白楊初生時	When the white poplar first grew,
乃在豫章山	it was right there on Camphorwood Mountain.
上葉摩青雲	Above, its leaves brushed the blue clouds,

---

99. Lu Qinli, 263; *Yfsj* 34. Birrel, *Popular Songs* 61–62.

下根通黃泉	below, its roots reached to the Yellow Springs.
涼秋八九月	In cool autumn, in the eighth or ninth month,
山客持斧斤	a man of the mountains brought an ax.
我口何皎皎	My . . . how gleaming bright,
梯落口口口	hacked away . . .
根株已斷絕	Root and trunk had been broken apart,
顛倒巖石間	it fell over among the rocks of the cliff.
大匠持斧繩	The great craftsman brought ax and saw,
鋸墨齊兩端	with rope and ink he made the two ends even.
一驅四五里	Once it was carried four or five leagues,
枝葉自相捐	the branches and leaves were destroyed.
口口口口口	. . . .
會爲舟船燔	happened to be [burned] for a boat.
身在洛陽宮	My person is in the palace of Luoyang,
根在豫章山	my roots are on Camphorwood Mountain.
多謝枝與葉	Send my regards to my leaves and branches—
何時復相連	when shall we be rejoined again?
吾生百年口	My life, a hundred years . . .
自口口口俱	. . . . together.
何意萬人巧	Who would have thought that the craft of ten thousand
使我離根株	would cause me to be separated, trunk from root?

The first thing we need to point out is that the relation between the ballad and the material represented in Lu Jia's exposition is not accidental; the link may not be direct, but there is a clear link. The common poplar grew plentifully near the capital and is conjoined with *yuzhang* (camphorwood or Camphorwood Mountain) only verbally. As we move from the rhetorician's presentation of two antithetical cases to the lyric voice presenting a single case in the *yuefu*, elements of the antithetical cases are conflated. The common tree (the white poplar) that grew close at hand in Lu Jia is now the tree that grows far away, and the tree that grew far away (the camphor tree) is now the place where the white poplar grows. The rhetorician's argument contrasting the use of what is close at hand with the neglect of what is remote is dropped altogether. If Lu Jia's exposition belongs to a long established tradition of the tree as a figure for talent, shaped to serve as a vessel, the speaking tree of the *yuefu* belongs to Zhuangzi's trees for which cutting destroys their original nature. But the most remarkable conflation is on the purely verbal level: both poplar and camphor are retained as words, the remote "camphorwood" now turned into the remote mountain and the poplar displaced to the wilderness there.

It is possible that the composer of the *yuefu* knew of or had read/heard Lu Jia's exposition; but it seems unlikely that someone with such a direct experience of the original text would conflate its elements in a way that so directly contradicted the original. It seems more likely that there was an intermediary stage in which this became a popular parable, presented either poetically or in rhythmic prose. As is so often the case with the *yuefu* and "old poems," sections drop out and parts become disjoined and rearranged. Arguments are driven by conjunctions of words and images, and not by logic or referential correctness. No one asks why anyone would travel to remote Camphorwood Mountain to cut ordinary white poplar, which can be found nearby. Here the popular material is reassembled as the tree's complaint.

In the next phase the kind of craftsmanship that stirs the tree's complaint in the *yuefu* above is applied to the poetic material itself in another anonymous *yuefu* (which can probably be dated no earlier than the late third century because of the mention of *suhe* incense, an import from the Roman East).

豔歌行 Prelude[100]

南山石嵬嵬	The rocks loom on South Mountain,
松柏何離離	how the pines and cypress are ranged there!
上枝拂青雲	Their upper branches brush blue clouds,
中心數十圍	their trunks are a dozen armspans around.
洛陽發中梁	From Luoyang they needed a central beam,[101]
松樹竊自悲	and the pine felt sorry for itself.
斧鋸截是松	Axes and saws cut this pine,
松樹東西摧	and the pine lay ruined, lying east to west.

---

100. Lu Qinli, 850; *Ywlj* 88; *Yfsj* 39. Huang Jie, *Han Wei*, 45–46; Birrel, *Popular Songs*, 59–60. Although this text is preserved as anonymous, Lu Qinli argues that it is another version of *Fufeng ge* 扶風歌 by Liu Kun. The argument does not seem persuasive to me.

101. Here I generally follow Wen Yiduo's interpretation of *fa* 發. Wen Yiduo, *Yuefu shi jian*, 127.

持作四輪車	They made it into a four-wheeled wagon,[102]
載至洛陽宮	and brought it to the palace in Luoyang.[103]
觀者莫不歎	None who beheld it but sighed,
問是何山材	asking: from what mountain does this timber come?
誰能刻鏤此	Who would be able to carve this?—
公輸與魯班	Gongshu and Ban of Lu.[104]
被之用丹漆	They covered it with cinnabar and lacquer;
薰用蘇合香	they scented it with Suhe-wood fragrance.
本自南山松	Originally it was a pine on South Mountain;
今爲宮殿梁	now it is a beam in the palace hall.

Whoever composed this poem changed the tree to a pine, more appropriate for a beam in the palace. The sequence is roughly the same (including a nearly identical third line). The crude opening of the "Ballad of Camphorwood Mountain" has been replaced by a standard opening pattern of five-syllable-line poetry, with two terms described in partial parallel, with a descriptive compound occupying the first two or last two positions in each line. The second couplet here describes the top and girth rather than the top and roots. The third couplet raises the issue of cutting, as does the third couplet in the ballad.

While roughly retaining the sequence of events, here "Prelude" shifts the message of the poem. Like the poplar on Camphorwood Mountain, the pine "felt sorry for itself"; but it is fine timber, richly carved and adorned, and it ends up as a beam in the palace. Rather than a tree whose nature has been violated, we have a tree that has enjoyed the remarkable good fortune to go from the wilderness to the very center of human civilization.

Poetic "material" circulates, but not just the material: a poem also has a pattern that can be reused with different material. This is what happens in the following anonymous "old poem." We cannot date it, but the writer seems to have known "Prelude." This poem is not about a tree at all; it is about an incense

---

102. Perhaps they moved it by putting wheels under it. Reading 持 for 特 with *Yiwen leiju*.

103. There is a textual problem with this line because it does not rhyme.

104. Gongshu Ban of Lu is actually one person, a famous craftsman of antiquity. There are obvious problems with the rhymes here and in the fifth couplet.

burner. We know that patrons commanded their literary attendants to compose on set topics on the spot; and this seems to be very much the case here. Fortunately for such poets so commanded, extempore composition had conventions that gave the poet time to think: "Everyone be quiet: I'm going to sing about X."[105]

四坐且莫諠	All you guests, stop making noise a while,
願聽歌一言	please listen as I sing a word or two.
請説銅鑪器	Let me tell of the bronze censer,
崔嵬象南山	looming high like South Mountain.
上枝似松柏	Its upper branches are like cypress and pine,
下根據銅盤	its roots below clutch the bronze pan.
雕文各異類	Graven patterns each of a different kind,
離婁自相聯	openwork all connected.
誰能爲此器	Who could make a vessel like this?—
公輸與魯班	Gongshu and Ban of Lu.
朱火然其中	A red fire burns within it,
青煙颺其間	blue smoke wafts through it.
從風入君懷	It goes with the breeze into your bosom,
四坐莫不歡	and all the guests are pleased.
香風難久居	But the scented breeze does not stay long—
空令蕙草殘	it merely causes the melilotus to be consumed.

Rarely do we see the machinery of poetic composition so wonderfully exposed as in this poem. The first couplet is simply filler, setting the rhyme and giving the poet a moment to think. In the third line he continues temporizing, telling us what he is supposed to write about. Censers, also called *boshan lu* 博山爐 ("Bo Mountain censers), were usually in the shape of a mountain (*shan* 山, keeping the rhyme). Thus the poet describes a mountain, indeed South Mountain, using most of the same words as the first line of "Prelude," but in a different order. The memory of "Prelude" lets him know what to say next: trees at the top (pines and cypresses), roots at the bottom. "Chopping" is not applicable here, but he can describe the "carving," followed by the set couplet praising the artisan as "Gongshu and Ban of Lu."

At this point the poet can turn to the specifics of an incense burner (putting "within it" 其中 in parallel to "through it" 其間 is

---

105. Lu Qinli, 334; *Ytxy* 1; *Ywlj* 70; *Cxj* 25.

hardly a sophisticated parallel). Here wood is indeed "put to use." Then, after reworking a line borrowed from Lady Ban's "Poem of Reproach" 怨詩 (出入君懷袖), he adds a filler line ("and all the guests are pleased).

Our purpose in going through the poem in this manner is not to denigrate the skills of an anonymous poet, dead for seventeen hundred years; rather, it is to show how, under the pressure of extempore composition, poets drew on established patterns. It is quite possible that the poet was ingeniously echoing "Prelude" and his listeners would appreciate the way he assimilated it for a new topic; but the observations on compositional technique remain the same, with the only difference being an assumption of self-conscious play shared with the audience.

In this final set of texts we can place the poetics of early classical poetry in something of a continuum, beginning with "material" used in a poetic exposition, conflated to produce a *yuefu* that works by its own logic. That same material is reworked in a relatively literary poem. This last version is transposed as a pure pattern, detached from its original theme, but still held together by a logic of words and phrases.

THREE

Immortals

Here and in the following chapter we will take up a few of the themes used in early poetry. Our interest here is not the intellectual or social historical contexts that might otherwise be of interest in considering such themes, but rather their constitution within a poetic discourse. Discourses of poetry and prose do overlap, but the very few named immortals appearing in early poetry seem to be associated with little of the lore that gathers around them in more specialized Daoist works. In the case of known authors, scholars often try to decide whether the person in question did or did not believe in the immortals.[1] In a textual world of troubled attributions, uncertain dating, and role playing, belief, while it certainly did exist in the historical world of the third century, is a hard thing to verify, particularly in a poetic discourse which invited playing at (and perhaps for the interim "believing") many values.

•

Those who have taken up the cause of public morals in premodern (and indeed modern) China have disapproved of the cult of immortality and the worlds of divine beings that lie on the periphery of the human universe. An interest in the immortals was particularly problematic when it involved rulers. When such an interest spread to a wide range of the literary elite, the entire age was considered fallen from grace, as we saw earlier in Liu Xie's comments on the Wei. Despite such

---

1. We have, for example, Donald Holzman's "Cao Zhi and the Immortals," *Asia Major* 1.1 (1988): 15–57, which weighs texts of skepticism and belief, concluding, as many Chinese scholars have, that he changed his beliefs in the course of his life.

disapproval, interest in the immortals remained an enduring feature of intellectual and literary life for many centuries.

These tainted interests actually covered a broad spectrum, from philosophical reflection on the Way, to the techniques of immortality practiced and professed by adepts (*fangshi*), to local cults, some of which seem to have had religious practices that were distinctly offensive to the political elite. These different ends of the religious spectrum had little to do with each other, and indeed there is little that justifies taking them as a single category ("Daoism") except their refusal to take the orthodox politics of the imperial state as the central issue in life.

Disinterest in orthodox politics is not to imply disinterest in politics altogether. Religious rituals were part of the court; but more important, the end of the Eastern Han saw millenarian Daoist uprisings and a Daoist state in west-central China (under the Five-Pecks-of-Grain sect, *wudoumi* 五斗米, headed by Zhang Lu 張魯) that lasted until 215. Scholars have often puzzled over Cao Cao's Daoist poems, taking them as political allegories or aging disillusionment or mere poetic fun.[2] Daoism, however, was part of contemporary politics in the most direct sense, and a claim of Daoist empowerment was also potentially a political claim. Cao Zhi and his brother may have laughed at the adepts that Cao Cao kept at court,[3] but for a smart politician at the beginning of the third century, this was not essentially different from keeping a group of writers, with the authority of traditional learning.

Quite apart from its politics and formative institutional history in this period, Daoism is a useful way to approach the poetry of the period. With its prescriptions and methods, nascent religious Daoism was supremely technological: certain things were done in a certain order to achieve certain ends (immortality). The poetics of the period, with its structure of topics in a relatively set sequence, was an analogue of Daoism. The poetics of immortality was thus doubly determined.

The theme of immortality is teleological: its end is the acquisition of immortality (or in its negative form, the failure or futility of the attempt). There are, however, some basic vari-

---

2. Jean-Pierre Diény, *Les poèmes de Cao Cao* (Paris: Collège de France, Institut des hautes études chinoises, 2000), 68–71.

3. Donald Holzman, "Cao Zhi and the Immortals," 16–23.

ables that organize topics into two overlapping sub-themes. The first focuses on the acquisition of a drug (the elixir of immortality), or, less commonly, techniques or Daoist mysteries. The core of the second sub-theme is the old "heavenly journey."

In the fullest forms of poems that focus on the drug, the protagonist climbs a mountain, encounters one or more immortals (either old or young, and sometimes riding white deer), and receives the drug from them or is taken to a place where he can acquire it. In some cases the speaker takes the drug himself, but in the most common version he carries the drug back to the mortal world and presents it to his host or a ruler. Thus the account of the acquisition of the drug serves the role of authentication. After having been presented the drug, the host or ruler lives forever, either as a wish or as a claim of fact.

The second variation, the "heavenly journey," may incidentally involve the acquisition of the drug or Daoist mysteries; but that is only a stage in an itinerary. Rather than climbing a mountain and chancing upon immortals, the speaker here usually perfects himself or simply flies up to Heaven. He first goes to Taishan or Kunlun to pay respects to the Queen Mother of the West and her consort, the Eastern Father. He then encounters one of the famous immortals, usually Red Pine, who serves as his guide, taking him around to see the sights of Heaven, usually the stars. There are a number of possible topics here: there may be a heavenly feast with music; he may receive the drug of immortality or magical techniques; he may look back toward his home. In the end, however, like the person who takes the drug in the first variation, he lives forever.

Let us examine the first variation, the transmission of the drug, in a Cao Zhi poem. Rather than transporting the drug back with him, Cao Zhi takes it himself.

曹植, 飛龍篇 Cao Zhi, The Dragon in Flight[4]

晨遊泰山	In the morning I roamed on Mount Tai,
雲霧窈窕	hidden away in the clouds and fog.
忽逢二童	I chanced upon two lads,
顏色鮮好	whose complexion was fresh and fine.

---

4. Lu Qinli, 421; *Yfsj* 64; *Ywlj* 42. Huang Jie, *Cao Zijian*, 105–6; Nie Wenyu, *Cao Zhi shi jieyi*, 294–97; Zhao Youwen 趙幼文, *Cao Zhi ji jiaozhu* 曹植集校注 (Beijing: Renmin wenxue chubanshe, 1984), 397–98.

乘彼白鹿	They were riding upon the white deer,
手翳芝草	their hands were hiding magic fungus.[5]
我知眞人	I knew that they were immortals,
長跪問道	I knelt long and asked of the Way.
西登玉臺	To the west we climbed a terrace of jade,
金樓複道	with golden towers and decks of passageways.
授我仙藥	They gave me an immortal drug,
神皇所造	made by the god.[6]
教我服食	They made me swallow it,
還精補腦	restoring my essence, augmenting my brain.
壽同金石	My lifespan will be the same as metal and stone,
永世難老	never aging for eternity.

The poet begins by going up Taishan, one of the sacred mountains, appropriately hidden in fog. There he meets two immortal lads, though they could just as easily be old men, and the number can vary from one to three. Riding white deer and having magic fungus (*zhi*) in their possession is a clear sign that these are immortals. Recognition is important, however: sometimes the immortal introduces himself as such and sometimes the traveler reads the indications. If the immortal introduces himself, he usually offers knowledge of the mysteries; if the traveler recognizes the figure (or figures) as immortals, as here, he usually asks. They take him to a heavenly palace, where they give him the drug and make him swallow it. Transformed, the speaker lives forever.

The components become predictable in both the sequence of topics and the ways in which those topics can be expanded or contracted. The many poems on this theme under Cao Zhi's name vary greatly in particulars around a stable core. Those who recited, remembered, and copied such poetry had an equal knowledge of legitimate variation. The text as we have it may be exactly as Cao Zhi composed it, but on some level that ceases to matter. We have one possible "rendition." Texts sometimes grew, and more often shrank. Our present version of Cao Zhi's

---

5. The use of *yi* 翳 here is difficult. I have roughly followed Nie Wenyu; Zhao Youwen cites a phrase from the *Xijing fu*: *yiyun zhi* 翳雲芝, "cloud covering *zhi.*"

6. *Ywlj* reads *ke* 可 for *suo* 所, giving *zao* its more expected sense in this context: "One might reach the High God."

collected works has been compiled entirely from anthologies and encyclopedias. This particular version of the poem was preserved in *Yuefu shiji*; and while we can be assured that Guo Maoqian, in the context of Song interest in textual scholarship, copied the text exactly as he had it, the manuscript tradition behind his sources belonged to an age of textual fluidity.

We often think of encyclopedias such as *Yiwen leiju* as giving us "excerpts," which is fair enough when we are given only a couplet or two; but in many cases it might be best to think of these citations as "shorter renditions." We might cite the *Yiwen leiju* "rendition" of Cao Zhi's poem:

晨遊太山	In the morning I roamed on Mount Tai,
雲霧窈窕	hidden away in the clouds and fog.
忽逢二童	I chanced upon two lads,
顏色鮮好	whose complexion was fresh and fine.
乘彼白鹿	They were riding upon the white deer,
手翳芝草	their hands were hiding magic fungus.
西登玉堂	To the west we climbed a hall of jade,
金樓複道	with golden towers and decks of passageways.
投我仙藥	They handed me an immortal drug,
神皇可造	I can now reach the high god.
壽同金石	My lifespan will be the same as metal and stone,
永世難老	never aging for eternity.

This version is two couplets shorter (eliminating the repetition of *dao* 道 as a rhyme word in two consecutive lines) and has some variants, one of which is significant. What we cannot know is whether the *Yiwen leiju* shortened a verse or someone else, knowing the important topics that should be mentioned in this kind of poem, added a couplet on asking for the Way (or the drug) and one on actually taking the drug.

Cao Zhi takes the drug himself; we may here compare the opening segment of an anonymous *yuefu*.[7]

---

7. Although this is one of the more interesting examples of a compound *yuefu*, I refrain from quoting the second segment of "Long Song," a first-person lyric on longing for one's mother, alluding to the *Shijing*. Part of this lyric has been preserved in *Ywlj* as a poem by Cao Pi, "Yu Mingjin zuo" 於明津作, Lu Qinli, 402.

長歌行 Long Song[8]

仙人騎白鹿	An immortal went riding a white deer,
髮短耳何長	his hair was short, and his ears so long!
導我上太華	He led me up Taihua Mountain
攬芝獲赤幢	where I picked magic fungus and obtained a red streamer.[9]
來到主人門	I came to the host's gate
奉藥一玉箱	and offered a jade box of drugs.
主人服此藥	The host swallowed these drugs,
身體日康彊	his body grew daily more healthy and strong.
髮白復更黑	The white of his hair turned black again,
延年壽命長	and extending his years, his span was long.

By habit we translate the immortal (*xianren* 仙人) here as singular, but there could easily be two (or more) of them. The same elements are present though rearranged: rather than climbing a mountain and meeting immortals who lead him to a place where he receives the drug, here the speaker meets an immortal, also riding a white deer, who leads him up the mountain. We know that "magic fungus" (our graceless rendering of *zhi* 芝) is one poetic version of the drug of immortality; in Cao Zhi's poem, it is in the possession of the immortal lads; here it is what is picked. The speaker here may be on a different mountain and not ask for instruction; but in both poems the term "magic fungus" comes first, and the term "drug," *yao* 藥, follows.

We should also note that the ending is essentially the same, the claim of the drug's efficacy. The topic that has been plugged into the sequence is a common one in this type of poem and partially defines it: this is bringing the drug back from the world of the immortals to the mortal host. One way the poem is changed is by variables in the set components (different mountains, different numbers of immortals). Another way the poem is changed is by adding and subtracting topics: the pieces of the Cao Zhi poem are the same, but the topic of the host has been omitted.

---

8. Lu Qinli, 262; *Yfsj* 30. Huang Jie, *Han Wei*, 15–16. Huang Jie also omits the second segment.

9. A *chuang* 幢 was a decorated suspended tube signifying authority. A red one was one of the insignias of a prefect; this obviously presents some problems in the present context.

This already abbreviated version of the theme is given as the first segment of the *yuefu* "Long Song." We should note that the same text (that is, the first segment) is preserved in *Yiwen leiju* as an "old poem," but with one difference: the second couplet is omitted. This version thus has the immortal himself bring the drug to the host. The principle is clear: a certain number of the topics must be present in the right order, but topics can be added or subtracted to fit a situation or a sense of what is right for the textual moment, as in the two renditions of Cao Zhi's "Dragons in Flight."

We can still recognize the theme even in extreme abbreviation. The following anonymous *yuefu* "Grand!" is stanzaic and weaves stanzas on immortals together with other themes. If we read the second and last stanzas together, however, we have all the essential components.

善哉行 Grand![10]

來日大難，	Great hardship in days to come,
口燥唇乾	the mouth parched, the lips dry.
今日相樂	Today we take our pleasure,
皆當喜歡	and we should all be merry.
經歷名山	I passed through all the fabled hills,
芝草翩翩	with magic fungus waving.
仙人王喬	The immortal Qiao the Prince
奉藥一丸	offered me a pill of drugs.
自惜袖短	I regret that my sleeves are too short,
内手知寒	when I draw in my hands I feel the cold.
慚無靈輒	I'm ashamed that I have no Lingche
以報趙宣	to pay his debt to Xuan of Zhao.[11]
月沒參橫	The moon sinks, Shen stretches across sky,
北斗闌干	the northern dipper hangs crossways.
親交在門	Kin and friends are at the gate,
飢不及餐	hungry, not yet having had a chance to eat.

---

10. Lu Qinli, 266; *Song shu*; *Yfsj* 36. Huang Jie, *Han Wei*, 25–26; Diény, *Aux origines de la poésie*, 122–25.

11. Zhao Dun was hunting and found Lingche starving. Zhao Dun gave him food. Later Zhao Dun was to be killed by the ruler of Jin, but one of the palace guards saved his life; the man turned out to be Lingche.

歡日尚少	The days of joy are still too few,
戚日苦多	days of woe, terribly many.
何以忘憂	How can we forget our cares?—
彈箏酒歌	play the zheng and sing drinking songs.
淮南八公	The eight lords in Huainan,
要道不煩	the essential Way brings no bother.[12]
參駕六龍	Just hitch up your six dragons
遊戲雲端	and roam for fun at the edge of clouds.

We do not know who traveled through the mountains and to whom the drug was offered, but we know the speaker occupies the role of host in what is essentially a feast song. The host may have received the drug directly from the immortal or through an intermediary: we have seen both possibilities in the variants of the preceding *yuefu* segment or "old poem." The final stanza does not mention taking the drug, but roaming in the clouds is the consequence of a more permanent solution to mortal cares than drinking and music.

In its use of the stanzaic form to weave together different themes, "Grand!" is almost unique among the early *yuefu*: its closest parallel is Cao Cao's famous "Short Song," which we will return to later.[13] As Diény notes, all these themes belong to the feast; but while a certain kind of coherence is missing, all the *sequences* of themes and topics (apart from the unique third stanza) have parallels elsewhere. The two stanzas on immortals (two and six) may be widely separated, but the sequence is familiar, not simply in the movement from receiving the drug to roaming as an immortal, but on a more specific textual level, as in a couplet of a fragment in the Cao Zhi collection:[14]

教爾服食日精	He had me swallow sun-semen,
要道甚省不煩	the essential Way is quite simple,
	no bother.

Through repetition, sequences of topics and themes can come to seem "natural," even if they are not, from a later perspective,

---

12. Eight immortals were supposed to have visited the Prince of Huainan and have given him the Cinnabar Classic; they then took him up to Heaven in broad daylight.

13. It is generally assumed that "Grand!" is earlier than "Short Song," but this is not necessarily the case.

14. "Cassia Tree: A Ballad" 桂之樹行. Lu Qinli, 438.

"logical." Familiarity has its own logic, and in the context of the poetry of this period, feasting, mortality, patronage, and the quest for immortality all crossed at numerous intersections.

As I suggested at the beginning of the chapter, the cult of immortality was controversial, poetically as well as in public discourse. The celebration of immortality carried with it a negative commonplace that the promise of drugs and immortality was deceptive. This commonplace was deployed briefly in "Nineteen Old Poems" XIII and in Cao Zhi's famous series "To Biao, Prince of Baima," "Zeng Baimai wang Biao" 贈白馬王彪.[15]

虛無求列仙	They seek the immortals where nothing is—
松子久吾欺	Red Pine has long deceived me.

This negative move could also occur within a fully developed poem on the immortals. We will later see Cao Cao doing this with a certain genius. In the current text of "Snapping the Willow," attributed to Cao Pi, the negative move is cruder. The mountain is now an ambiguous "west mountain," rather than the sacred mountains Taishan and Taihua. But the two immortal lads are there nevertheless. After taking the drug, he sprouts wings and flies; but the perspective attained turns to rejection of the immortals and their Way.

曹丕, 折楊柳行 Cao Pi, Snapping the Willow[16]

西山一何高	How high west mountain is!—
高高殊無極	so high, virtually without limit.
上有兩仙童	Up there are a pair of immortal lads,
不飲亦不食	they do not drink and do not eat.
與我一丸藥	They gave me a drug in a pill,
光耀有五色	it glowed with all five colors.
服藥四五日	Four or five days after I swallowed the elixir
身體生羽翼	my body grew wings.
輕舉乘浮雲	I rose lightly riding the drifting clouds,
倏忽行萬億	all of a sudden I had gone millions of leagues.
流覽觀四海	I let my gaze rove over all in the four seas,
茫茫非所識	vast and vague, there was nothing I recognized.

---

15. Lu Qinli, 454.
16. Lu Qinli, 393; *Song shu; Yfsj* 37. Huang Jie, *Wei Wudi*, 46–47.

彭祖稱七百	They claim Peng Zu lived seven centuries,
悠悠安可原	so far, how can one trace it back?
老聃適西戎	Lao Dan went off to the Western Barbarians
于今竟不還	and even now he has never returned.
王喬假虛辭	Qiao the Prince made use of hollow phrases,
赤松垂空言	Red Pine left us empty words.
達人識眞僞	The Perfected Man can tell true from false,
愚夫好妄傳	the fool loves deceptive lore.
追念往古事	I brood on matters in the past—
憒憒千萬端	they're a muddle with thousands of positions.
百家多迂怪	The philosophers are full of absurdities—
聖道我所觀	I will observe the Way of the Sage.

Although this text of "Snapping the Willow" ends up by rejecting the immortals, this is a compound *yuefu*, whose first segment (with a separate rhyme) is a fully developed variation on the theme of receiving the elixir of immortality. *Yiwen leiju* quotes it separately as a "Roaming Immortal" poem, *youxian shi* 遊仙詩. This is one of those cases where we cannot tell whether this is "one poem" or "two poems," set in counterpoint. If we believe this is "a poem composed by Cao Pi," we will describe it as I did above, as a poem in which Cao Pi "rejects the immortals." If, however, it is not the construct of an "author" making an argument, but rather a particular combination of thematically opposite segments, a combination that has been fortuitously preserved (whether that combination was done by Cao Pi or musical specialists), then we have something rather different.

After climbing the mountain, meeting immortals, receiving and taking the drug, and flying off, in the final stage the speaker reaches such heights that he can no longer recognize anything of the sensible world. Behind this moment is a rich history in the poetics of apotheosis, in the "Far Traveling" 遠遊 in the *Chuci* and in Sima Xiangru's "Great Man" 大人賦. This is the fullest realization of religious transfiguration; to claim the achievement of this state is somewhere far beyond a mere worldling's doubt that Peng Zu actually lived seven centuries. There is, indeed, a disjunctive effect as the poet or performer changes rhyme and moves from the sublime to the role of empiricist and skeptic.

If we are reading not an argument in any sense but a poetic medley, we see the shift from affirmation to doubt as something akin to the shift from a major to a minor key in different movements in a musical work. It could be the construct of musicians, but it could just as easily be the construct of an "author"—one who had listened to musicians all his life. Because the second segment is so clearly a negation and rejection of the first segment, the principle of combination is more coherent than in the case of "Long Song" quoted above, where the segment on obtaining and transmitting the elixir is conjoined with a segment on longing for one's mother. Despite this difference, however, in both cases the segments can stand independently.[17]

We see the same movement of reversal in a *yuefu* by Cao Cao, but at the same time the differences from "Snapping the Willow" are striking. It would perhaps be anachronistic to speak of Cao Cao's poetic "style" here in a fully literary sense, but the motives of Cao Cao's court are present. The segments are now long stanzas, the movement between which can be read as a political persuasion of sorts. But the speaker begins in a familiar way, climbing Taihua Mountain to obtain the drug of immortality.

秋胡行 Ballad of Qiuhu II[18]

願登泰華山	I wish to climb Taihua Mountain,
神人共遠遊	to roam afar with the gods.
願登泰華山	I wish to climb Taihua Mountain,
神人共遠遊	to roam afar with the gods.
經歷崑崙山	I would pass by Mount Kunlun,
到蓬萊	and come to the Isle of Penglai,

17. If one reads the second segment of "Snapping the Willow" separately, we have a poem that could fit rather seamlessly into Ruan Ji's "Singing of My Cares." See, for example, "Singing of My Cares" XL.

18. Lu Qinli, 350; *Song shu.* Huang Jie, *Wei Wudi*, 21–23; Diény, *Les poèmes de Cao Cao*, 97–103. The poem has no relation to the Qiuhu story, and the title seems simply to represent the music to which it was performed. We do not know if the association of the lyrics with the title came from Cao Cao's time or was a later court arrangement.

飄颻八極	I would drift around the earth's eight ends,
與神人俱	together with the gods.
思得神藥	I long to obtain the divine drug,
萬歲爲期	to live a span of ten thousand years.
歌以言志	I sing to tell what is on my mind,
願登泰華山	I wish to climb Taihua Mountain.
天地何長久	How long the Earth and Heaven last!
人道居之短	Man's Way is to lodge there briefly.
天地何長久	How long the Earth and Heaven last!
人道居之短	Man's Way is to lodge there briefly.
世言伯陽	People say of Boyang[19]
殊不知老	that he never ever knew old age.
赤松王喬	Red Pine and Qiao the Prince
亦云得道	are also said to have reached the Way.
得之未聞	If they achieved it, they were not heard of,
庶以壽考	perhaps they had great long life.
歌以言志	I sing to tell what is on my mind,
天地何長久	how long the Earth and Heaven last!
明明日月光	Bright is the light of sun and moon,
何所不光昭	their light shines everywhere.
明明日月光	Bright is the light of sun and moon,
何所不光昭	their light shines everywhere.
二儀合聖化	The Two Principles merge in sage transformation,[20]
貴者獨人不	is not man the most noble of all?
萬國率土	In all the land of ten thousand domains
莫非王臣	all are subjects of the king.
仁義爲名	He is famed for Kindness and Right,
禮樂爲榮	he shows his splendor by music and rites.
歌以言志	I sing to tell what is on my mind,
明明日月光	bright is the light of sun and moon.
四時更逝去	The four seasons go off in succession,
畫夜以成歲	days and night create the year.
四時更逝去	The four seasons go off in succession,
畫夜以成歲	days and night create the year.
大人先天	The Great Man anticipates Heaven,
而天弗違	and Heaven does not deviate.
不戚年往	I do not feel sad that the years pass by,
世憂不治	I worry that the age is in turmoil.

---

19. Laozi.
20. The "Two Principles" are Heaven and Earth, *yang* and *yin*.

存亡有命	Life and death are fated,
慮之爲蚩	to worry about it is folly.
歌以言志	I sing to tell what is on my mind,
四時更逝去	the four seasons go off in succession.
戚戚欲何念	What do you brood on so gloomily?—
歡笑意所之	the mind is disposed to merriment.
戚戚欲何念	What do you brood on so gloomily?—
歡笑意所之	the mind is disposed to merriment.
壯盛智惠	The prime of life and sharpness of mind
殊不再來	will not come back again.
愛時進趣	Cling to the moment, go forward and take it,
將以惠誰	for it will show favor to none.
汎汎放逸	Drifting free, letting yourself go
亦同何爲	is also the same as why.[21]
歌以言志	I sing to tell what is on my mind,
戚戚欲何念	what do you brood on so gloomily?

The speaker in Cao Cao's poem says "I wish" to climb the sacred mountain and become an immortal. The term he uses is *yuan* 願, the same verb for wanting and wishing that the speakers in the "old poems" use when they "want" to become a bird and fly away with the imagined beloved. That is, this is a verb of wanting and wishing that does not necessarily imply the possibility of pragmatic fulfillment. The verb more often used in these poems of immortality is *yu* 欲, a "wanting" that is indistinguishable from "intending to" or a simple future tense. Thus we translate later lines in Cao Cao's stanza as "I would pass by Mount Kunlun," rather than "I will pass by Mount Kunlun."

In many of these poems the drug of immortality means that one can live as long as Heaven and Earth. We should then read the *yuan*, the speculative desire for something perhaps impossible, as a context for the beginning of the second stanza: "How long the Earth and Heaven last!" They last too long for man, whose "Way" means only a short stay. Cao Cao could have used a term like *renming* 人命, "man's fate [fated span]" or *rensheng* 人生, "man's life." To use the term "Man's Way" suggests that such a brief lodging is as it should be. The speaker then turns to those who were said to have achieved immortality.

---

21. I have translated this incomprehensible line literally. Various attempts have been made to make sense of it, none of which are natural readings.

Unlike his sons Cao Pi and Cao Zhi and avoiding the conventional topic of the "old poems," Cao Cao does not say this was a deception. He simply says that we don't know—maybe they lived forever.

Rather than the sudden reversal from the poem on immortality to a poem of disbelief, Cao Cao raises doubts about immortality or places understanding beyond human ken. Keeping the tone of visionary grandeur appropriate to a poem on the immortals, the third stanza shifts to a celebration of the cosmos and polity, whose ruler is the agent of "sage transformation." In the space between the Two Principles—the space inhabited by those who hear the song—we have a ruler. Whether Cao Cao means himself or the captive Han emperor we do not know; but Cao Cao loved archaic usages that spoke of the "king," *wang* 王 (in Han usage "prince"). Cao Cao never deposed the Han emperor and never made himself emperor; but he was literally a *wang*, and for all purposes in North China, "the king." Thus: "In all the land of ten thousand domains / all are subjects of the king," echoing the *Shijing* (205).

In the next stanza time is passing, but the king, now as the "Great Man," anticipates Heaven, and Heaven fulfills his anticipations. The "Great Man," *daren* 大人, was the name under which Sima Xiangru had praised Han emperor Wu as flying through the heavens and attaining a state of transcendence: Cao Cao's ruler, in short, has the competence in the divine mysteries of an adept-immortal. A person may want to become an immortal, but in the king one can see Heaven in action. The real issue is that the age is in turmoil; to repair this is the king's work. A desire for more than one's fated span in a world in turmoil is folly. We do not wish to press this stanza too hard, but it does seem to suggest that the best hope for living a longer, though not unlimited span, is to help the king work with Heaven to bring about a well governed (*zhi* 治) world.

Chiding the listener who worries about death and is "gloomy," *qiqi* 戚戚, Cao Cao invites the listener to enjoy himself, to seize the moment, to let himself go. We have come close to the feast poem, with a counterpart in the last couplet of "Nineteen Old Poems" III:

| 極宴娛心意 | Feast to the end, delight the heart, |
| 戚戚何所迫 | why be oppressed by gloomy thoughts? |

The listener should enjoy the moment—though the moment is now framed in political obligation.

In the context of the Daoist strain of politics at the turn of the third century, this is a masterpiece of persuasion, beginning with the theme of immortality framed as a speculative possibility. Cao Cao undercuts the possibility and offers in its place the ruler (or shogun in Cao Cao's case), imbued with the attributes of the Daoist adept-king, but leading the subject away from worry about immortality to concern for the polity and enjoyment of this life.

•

At this point we can turn to a song given under a *yuefu* title that has drawn far more attention than the poem itself. "Dong tao" is either "Dong Flees" (*tao* 逃 "flee") or "Dong's Peaches" (*tao* 桃 "peaches"). One verse given under this title was a song current in the capital in the Zhongping Reign (184–89), preserved in the "Treatise on the Five Phases" by Sima Biao 司馬彪 (240–306), which was later included in the *Hou Han shu*. This verse in the three syllable line, with the repeated refrain "Dong tao," was taken as foretelling the fate of Dong Zhuo, who seized the Han emperor, sacked Luoyang, and moved its population to Chang-an, where he was killed by his subordinates.[22] In this sense the title was understood as "Dong flees."

This reading of the title makes no sense for the song below. The title would, however, make perfect sense if we substituted Dong 東 for Dong 董.[23] Then any listener would think immediately of Dongfang Shuo 東方朔 and the most famous of all stories about peaches, *tao* 桃. In popular legend Dongfang Shuo, a banished immortal and court entertainer in the reign of Han Wudi, stole the immortal peaches that the Queen Mother of the West had given the Emperor.

---

22. Lu Qinli, 212.
23. According to W. South Coblin's sound glosses, the finals of 董 and 東 differ in the Eastern Han; see his *Handbook of Eastern Han Sound Glosses* (Hong Kong: Chinese University Press, 1983). However, as in the ballad *Pingling dong* 平陵東, *dong* 東 rhymes with words that have the same final as *dong* 董. This suggests that they were close enough to sustain a pun between *Dong tao* 東桃, "Dong's peaches," and the topical *Dong tao* 董逃, "Dong flees." Uncommon and extinct double surnames such as Dongfang were often treated as single-syllable surnames in popular usage. Note the variations on Gongshu Ban on pp. 130 and 136.

董逃行 Dongtao Ballad[24]

吾欲上謁從高山	I wanted to pay my respects on high, I went up the high mountain,[25]
山頭危險道路難	the mountaintop was perilous, the road hard.
遙望五嶽端	From afar I gazed on the summits of the Five Sacred Peaks,
黃金烏闕班璘	golden were the turrets, streaked and gleaming,
但見芝草葉落紛紛	and I saw only the leaves falling in a flurry from the magic fungus.[26]
百鳥集來如煙	All the birds come to roost like mist,
山獸紛綸	mountain beasts teeming,
麟辟邪	the unicorn, the averter-of-ill,
其端鶤雞聲鳴	On the summit the kun-fowl were [ ] singing,[27]
但見山獸援戲相拘攀	I saw only the mountain beasts sporting and helping each other along.[28]

---

24. Lu Qinli, 264; *Song shu*, *Yfsj* 34. Huang Jie, *Han Wei*, 18–20; Diény, *Aux origines de la poésie classique*, 119–22.

25. I have kept the text as it is written, though I agree with Wen Yiduo that *cong gao* 從高 should be the common collocation *Song gao* 嵩高, "Mount Song's heights." Wen Yiduo, *Yuefu shi jian*, 128. Mount Song, near Luoyang, was a major sacred site and the home of various immortals. The initial would have been changed by the final "t" in the early medieval pronunciation of the preceding word *ye* 謁. If this seems to contradict line 3, Mount Song, the central of the Five Peaks, is the one earthly place from which one could imagine seeing the other four. Wen and some other commentators take these as the five immortal isles.

26. As Wen Yiduo notes, the "magic fungus" does not have leaves. He suspects the *yeluo* 葉落 is an interpolation.

27. I have kept the original character *duan* 端 in the Chinese text. Looking at the first poem or stanza of Cao Zhi's "Ascent to Heaven" 升天行 (Lu Qinli, 433), we find the line "the soaring kun-fowl sports on the summit" 翔鶤戲其巔. I suspect that *duan* 端 here and in line 3 is a mistake for *dian* 巔, "summit," which is a rhyme word; and in the English translation I have translated it that way. Although *dian* 巔 rhymes with *shan* 山 in the Cao Zhi poem just cited (as it does here), it had a slightly different final that became significantly different in Middle Chinese. The substitution of *duan* 端 would have made a more perfect rhyme. I have not followed Wen Yiduo and Diény here in taking the *qiduan* 其端 as an error for *jiaoduan* 角端, a mythical beast, mentioned in Sima Xiangru's *fu*. As Diény notes, *shengming* 聲鳴 is a problem. Wen Yiduo wants to emend *sheng*, but it is just as possible that a word had dropped out before *sheng*.

28. This is only a guess at what the mountain beasts are doing precisely.

小復前行	I went on a little further,
玉堂未心懷流還	at the Jade Hall the heart yearned to roam around.[29]
傳教出門來	The one who carried instructions came out the gate:
門外人何求	"What does the person outside the gate seek?"
所言欲從聖道	What I said was I wanted to follow the Sages' Way,
求一得命延	that I sought to get my lifespan extended.[30]
敕敕凡吏受言	The decree was to the common clerk to receive these words:[31]
採取神藥若木端	gather the sacred drug at the edge of the Ruo Tree,[32]
玉兔長跪搗藥蝦蟆丸	The Jadewhite Hare kneels long pounding the drug, the Toad's pill,[33]
奉上陛下一玉柈	I offer up to Your Majesty a plate of jade,
服此藥可得神仙	if you take this drug, you will become an immortal.
服爾神藥	He takes the sacred drug,
莫不歡喜	everyone is joyful,
陛下長生老壽	Your Majesty will live long to great old age.
四面肅肅稽首	All around are serious and touch their heads to the ground.
天神擁護左右	The Spirits of Heaven will protect and support you.
陛下長與天相保守	Your Majesty will endure as long as Heaven.

The preceding versions of this theme help us read this poem, with all its obscurities and textual problems. As we will see, the "paying respects on high," *shangye* 上謁, is one of the standard topics in the next theme of the "roaming immortals." The speaker ascends what is probably Mount Song, though that is

---

29. I have thus far seen no satisfactory explanation for the *wei* 未, and have not translated it. It must precede a verb, and there is no verb here. Wen Yiduo believes a character has dropped out.

30. Or, with Wen Yiduo, taking *qiu yi* 求一 as "seeking the One."

31. Wen takes the "common clerk" as the mortal speaker of the poem.

32. I have followed the general preference of editors to read *mu* 木 rather than *shui* 水. The Ruo Tree grows near Mount Kunlun.

33. The Hare and the Toad are denizens of the moon, where the goddess Chang E fled after stealing the elixir of immortality. The Hare pounds the ingredients.

one of the Five Sacred Peaks surveyed in the next couplet. We have the "magic fungus," *zhi* 芝, mentioned first, and the drug, *yao* 藥, later. After a passage on mythical animals, we have a more formal and fuller version of the encounter with the immortals: the speaker comes to a palace of the immortals, requests the secret of long life, and is given permission to "gather" the ingredients for the drug (or a factotum is sent to gather the ingredients). The bureaucratization of the immortal world is very different from the preceding poems and is used to reinforce the point, made in all these poems, that the speaker is an "authorized user" of the drugs of immortality, rather than one who discovers them or makes them on his own.

At this point the speaker shifts to addressing the emperor; that is, he is the mediator who brings the drug back to the human world. The emperor takes the drug and lives forever. We have seen a host or patron before, but this is the first appearance within the poem of an emperor, addressed in court language; and it should remind us that the *yuefu* in the *Song shu* are a court collection.

•

The second variation, the account of a flight through the heavens, can be longer and its parts no less freely expanded or elided. We will begin with an anonymous *yuefu* that stops with an account of the stars. The same final four lines serve as the beginning of the first segment of a compound *yuefu*. If we put the pieces together (as Lu Qinli does), we have a brief but more complete version of the theme.

步出夏門行 Going Out Xia Gate[34]

邪徑過空盧	A narrow lane passes an empty hut,
好人常獨居	a good person lived there ever alone.
卒得神仙道	Finally he achieved the way of gods and immortals,
上與天相扶	and, rising, leaned against Heaven.
過謁王父母	I paid respects to the Royal Father and Mother,[35]
乃在太山隅	that was right in the corner of Taishan.

---

34. Lu Qinli, 267; *Yfsj* 37. Huang Jie, *Han Wei*, 28–29.

35. These are the Royal Lord of the East 東王公 and the Queen Mother of the West 西王母.

離天四五里	Four or five leagues from Heaven,
道逢赤松俱	I met Red Pine and joined him.[36]
攬轡爲我御	Taking the reins he [Red Pine] drove for me
將吾天上遊	and took me roaming through Heaven.
天上何所有	What is there up in Heaven?
歷歷種白榆	white elms planted in clear array.
桂樹夾道生	Cinnamon trees grow lining the road,[37]
青龍對伏趺	the Green Dragon crouches facing them.[38]

We begin with the speaker as a mere mortal, living away from society (the movement between third person and first person is very common). Perfecting himself, he flies up and then, after "paying respects," *ye* 謁, is taken on a tour of the heavens. This tour is "roaming," *you* 遊, the term used later as the normative category of such poetry, "roaming immortals," *you xian* 遊仙.

The poem is picked up in the "Ballad of Longxi," whose human segment celebrates how a wife entertains guests.

隴西行 Ballad of Longxi[39]

天上何所有	What is there up in Heaven?
歷歷種白榆	white elms planted in clear array.
桂樹夾道生	Cinnamon trees grow lining the road,
青龍對伏趺	the Green Dragon crouches facing them.
鳳凰鳴啾啾	The Phoenix sings out *jiujiu*,[40]
一母將九雛	one mother with nine chicks.[41]
顧視世間人	I look back to the world of mortal men—
爲樂甚獨殊	how unique the joy is!
好婦出迎客	The good wife comes out to greet the guest,
顏色正敷愉	her countenance is easy and kind.
伸腰再拜跪	She leans forward, bows and kneels,
問客平安不	asks the guest whether he is comfortable.
請客北堂上	She invites the guest to the north hall
坐客氍㲣毹	and seats him on woolen blankets.[42]

---

36. A famous immortal.

37. Cassia trees, like the white elms in the preceding line, grow in Heaven, produced by the essence of the sun. The "road" is the sun's path.

38. A constellation in the eastern part of the heavens.

39. Lu Qinli, 267; *Ytxy* 1; *Yfsj* 36. Huang Jie, *Han Wei*, 26–28; Birrel *Popular Songs*, 173.

40. A star.

41. The "nine chicks" are a string of stars.

42. Yu Guanying associates this with semi-barbarian Longxi. Yu Guanying, *Han Wei liuchao shixuan*, 31.

清白各異樽	Clear ale and white each in different cups,
酒上正華疏	on the ale's surface the sparkles grow few.[43]
酌酒持與客	She pours the ale and holds it to give to the guest,
客言主人持	the guest says, let the hostess take it.
卻略再拜跪	She draws back, bows, and kneels,
然後持一杯	and only then takes a cup in hand.[44]
談笑未及竟	Before they finish laughing and chatting,
左顧敕中廚	she turns to give orders to the kitchen.
促令辦麤飯	She commands some rough fare to be prepared with all haste,
慎莫使稽留	and warns them not to be long about it.
廢禮送客出	Dropping ceremony, she goes out with the guest,
盈盈府中趨	lovely, as she hurries through the courtyard.
送客亦不遠	She does not go with the guest very far,
足不過門樞	her feet never cross beyond the gate.
取婦得如此	If you can get a wife like this,
齊姜亦不如	even a Jiang of Qi is no match.[45]
健婦持門戶	If a stout wife maintains the gate,
亦勝一丈夫	it is even better than a man.

With the first segment above joined to "Going Out Xia Gate," we have a continuing tour of the constellations, followed by looking back on the mortal world (familiar in accounts of heavenly journeys in prose and poetic expositions), and a declaration of the speaker's joy. As Lu Qinli notes, there are a number of reasons for joining "Going Out Xia Gate" with the first segment of "Ballad of Longxi" (including Li Shan's citation of lines from the latter under the name of the former). The two segments obviously fit together to create a single rendition of a whole. Rather than attempting to decide which is the proper name or whether the combined whole is an independent piece or belongs with the second segment on the good hostess, we might

---

43. This line is extremely problematic and various solutions have been proposed. Lu Qinli emends 正 to 玉. Wen Yiduo takes 疏 as 梳.

44. This and the preceding couplet are in a different rhyme. If we remove them, the woman's behavior is even less decorous.

45. From *Shi* 138, *Hengmen* 衡門: "When you are eating fish, / what need of bream from the River? / When taking a wife, / what need for a Jiang from Qi?" 豈其食魚, 必河之魴? 豈其取妻, 必齊之姜? Jiang was the surname of the Qi ruling house; that is, a noblewoman.

note that the opening segment in the "Ballad of Longxi" is a short rendition, a presentation for readers not essentially different from the "short renditions" we often find in the encyclopedias.

We omitted the second segment of "Long Song" quoted above; here we include the long segment in praise of the good wife. We see a wide range of possible connections between the segments of compound *yuefu*. Sometimes, as in the famous "Mulberries by the Path," "Moshang sang" 陌上桑, the segments are clearly conjoined to produce a single coherent poem. In "Prelude: O When" we saw how the bird segment modulated to set up an analogous case in the human scene of the second segment. In Cao Pi's "Breaking Willow," discussed above, we see antithetical segments conjoined. In "Song of White Hair," "Baitou yin" 白頭吟, to be discussed in a later chapter, we will see how distinct but related thematic segments are interpreted as one poem. Cases like "Long Song" and "Ballad of Longxi" are the far end of the spectrum, in which two unrelated segments are textually performed together. Interpretive ingenuity that tries to make the segments cohere reveals itself as mere ingenuity. What these examples rather tell us is that there was a pleasure in the disjunction of segments and in the movement between them. *Yutai xinyong* often repairs poems; and if it kept this in the present form (without dropped rhymes or troubling textual problems), it was preserving the aura of the old *yuefu*—just as when it fixed the text of "Prelude: O When" but kept the singer's ending.

The laudable behavior of the wife in the second segment so scandalized late imperial critics that they were strongly disposed to take it as satire, beginning with Shen Deqian's 沈德潛 *Gushi yuan* 古詩源, apparently under the assumption that such behavior could not possibly be praised. Li Yindu 李因篤 in his *Hanshi yinzhu* 漢詩音注 tries to explain it as the customs of Longxi, on the frontier.[46] While there is no question such a lyric could possibly have been used satirically in a certain circumstance, it could just as easily have been praise for the good hostess in an era very different from the Ming and Qing.

---

46. Yao Daye 姚大業, *Han Yuefu xiaolun* 漢樂府小論 (Tianjin: Baihua wenyi chubanshe, 1984), 78. Anne Birrel also interprets this as satire.

•

There is no strong reason to suppose that the preceding anonymous *yuefu* are any earlier than Cao Cao's, though they are possibly so. The following version by Cao Cao presents numerous problems in line grouping and rhymes.

曹操, 氣出倡 Cao Cao, Breathe Out I[47]

駕六龍	I hitch up the six dragons[48]
乘風而行	and go, riding the wind.
行四海外	I go out beyond the seas on all sides,
路下之八邦	then my course descends to the eight realms.[49]
歷登高山	I pass through high mountains, climbing them,
臨谿谷	I look down on stream valleys,
乘雲而行	I go riding the clouds.
行四海外	I go out beyond the seas on all sides,
東到泰山	and come to Taishan in the east.
仙人玉女	Immortals and Jade Maidens,
下來遨遊	come down to frolic.
驂駕六龍	They have hitched the six dragons,
飲玉漿	and drink jade liquors.
河水盡	The Yellow River's waters are gone
不東流	and do not flow east.
解愁腹	My sad heart is relieved
飲玉漿	as I drink jade liquors,
奉持行	I carry them as I go.
東到蓬萊山	In the east I come to Penglai Mountain,
上至天之門	and above I reach the gate of Heaven.
王闕下	Beneath the royal gate-towers
引見得入	I am brought in to meet them.
赤松相對	Red Pine faces me.
四面顧望	When I look around on all sides,
視正焜煌	my vision is dazzled with light.

---

47. Lu Qinli, 345; *Song shu*; *Yfsj* 26; Huang Jie, *Wei Wudi*, 3–4; Diény, *Les poèmes de Cao Cao*, 78–84.

48. The "six dragons" are associated with the chariot of the sun, but since we are unsure of the subject when the six dragons return in l. 12, it may simply be a "dragon chariot."

49. That is, to the far lands in the eight directions.

開玉心正興	The Year Star, the Jade Well, and the Heart Star are just rising,[50]
其氣百道至	their vapors reach me by a hundred courses.
傳告無窮閉其口	They inform me of endlessness, of shutting the mouth,[51]
但當愛氣壽萬年	one should cherish one's breath for a life of ten thousand years.
東到海	To the east I come to the sea
與天連	that joins with Heaven.
神仙之道	The Way of gods and immortals
出窈入冥	communicates with the murky and mysterious,
常當專之	one should ever be devoted to it.
心恬澹	The heart is joyous and still,
無所惕欲	there are no lusts or desires,
閉門坐自守	one closes one's gate and preserves oneself,
天與期氣	and Heaven grants a matching breath.
願得神之人	I want to attain to the gods,
乘駕雲車	I ride a carriage of cloud,
驂駕白鹿	I hitch up white deer,
上到天之門	I come to the gate of Heaven above
來賜神之藥	and I am given the drug of the gods.
跪受之	Kneeling, I received it,[52]
敬神齊	showing the gods respect.
當如此	It should be thus,
道自來	and the Way comes on its own.

As we mentioned earlier, critics have often been troubled that a tough-minded general and politician like Cao Cao could have composed poetry on the immortals. Although he may have done so out of personal religious interests (otherwise unknown) or because it was a popular song theme, he could also have composed such poems precisely because he was a tough-minded politician. In this age knowledge of heavenly mysteries was one possible basis for political power. Many of his more orthodox political poems contain an element of persuasion, accrediting himself by comparison to the Duke of Zhou and demonstrating both his public-minded zeal and his eagerness

---

50. In this problematic line I follow Huang Jie. For a fuller discussion and another reading (and punctuation), see Diény, *Les poèmes de Cao Cao*, 83–84.

51. "Shutting the mouth" was a Daoist technique of preserving saliva.

52. Compare Cao Zhi's "I knelt long and asked of the Way" 長跪問道 in "The Dragon in Flight."

to gain adherents. If we take seriously his eagerness for adherents, in the world of the turn of the third century competence in the mysteries would be a persuasive argument for some. Several early sources mention that Cao Cao liked to compose verses, and according to Wang Chen "when he composed new poems, he had them set to instrumental music, and all became musical pieces" 及造新詩, 被之管絃, 皆成樂章.[53] In the political context, this reputation takes on a certain richness: such songs could be performed in the court for visitors with Daoist interests with a full knowledge that Cao Cao composed them.

Let us assume that such songs serve essentially for religious accreditation (perhaps for political ends). To be "accredited" the speaker must claim to have done certain things and experienced certain things. We know that the heavenly traveler must go out beyond the four seas, but he must also go to Taishan, like the speaker in "Going Out Xia Gate," whose lines we will now quote again in sections because they match the sequence in Cao Cao's song. If we do not take Cao Cao's *yuefu* as "later" than the anonymous *yuefu*, it is easier to see how Cao Cao gives a full version, while the five-syllable-line *yuefu* uses bits and pieces.

The first specific place Cao Cao comes to is Taishan:

行四海外	I go out beyond the seas on all sides,
東到泰山	and come to Taishan in the east.

This is also the first place visited by the speaker in "Going Out Xia Gate":

過謁王父母	I paid respects to the Royal Father and Mother,
乃在太山隅	that was right on the corner of Taishan.

Cao flies next to Penglai and then to Heaven, where he meets Red Pine:

上至天之門	and above I reach the gate of Heaven.
王闕下	Beneath the royal gate-towers
引見得入	I am brought in to meet them.
赤松相對	Red Pine faces me.

---

53. Wang Chen 王沈, cited in *San Cao ziliao huibian* 三曹資料彙編 (Beijing: Zhonghua shuju, 1980), 2.

The speaker in "Going Out Xia Gate" also meets Red Pine next, very close to Heaven:

離天四五里	Four or five leagues from Heaven,
道逢赤松俱	I met Red Pine and joined him.
攬轡爲我御	Taking the reins he [Red Pine] drove for me
將吾天上遊	and took me roaming through Heaven.

Cao Cao next sees the stars:

四面顧望	When I look around on all sides,
視正焜煌	my vision is dazzled with light.
開玉心正興	The Year Star, the Jade Well, and the Heart Star are just rising,
其氣百道至	their vapors reach me by a hundred courses.

The third line in the passage above is very problematic; I have followed Huang Jie's interpretation precisely because at this point the heavenly traveler may see various stars, as does the speaker in "Going Out Xia Gate."

The sequence of events is relatively strictly determined, but some variation in the topics is permitted. One may, for example, meet the Queen Mother of the West and her consort, the "Royal Father" or "Eastern Father," on Kunlun rather than on Taishan. Red Pine should be the guide, but the itinerary of stars many be left out. The speaker should, however, declare that he received the magic elixir or certain esoteric secrets. This essential component was omitted in the overlapping anonymous *yuefu* "Going Out Xia Gate" and "Ballad of Longxi." In the following version, the particulars differ but the essential sequence is retained:

曹操, 陌上桑 Cao Cao, Mulberries by the Path[54]

駕虹蜺	I hitched up rainbows,
乘赤雲	I rode russet clouds,
登彼九疑歷玉門	I climbed the Nine Doubts Range and passed through Jade Pass.
濟天漢	I crossed over the River of Stars,
至崑崙	I reached Kunlun,
見西王母謁東君	I met the Queen Mother of the West, and paid respects to the Lord of the East.

---

54. Lu Qinli, 348; *Song shu*; *Yfsj* 28. Huang Jie, *Wei Wudi*, 12–13; Diény, *Les poèmes de Cao Cao*, 73–77.

交赤松	I made a friendship with Red Pine,
及羨門	along with Xianmen Zigao,
受要秘道愛精神	I received the Secret Way, how to hold to spirit's essence.
食芝英	I ate the bloom of the magic fungus,
飲醴泉	I drank from sweet springs,
柱杖桂枝佩秋蘭	I made a cassia branch my staff, and wore autumn orchids at my sash.
絕人事	I cut myself off from mortal affairs,
遊渾元	and roamed in Primal Undifferentiation,
若疾風遊欻飄翩	like the swift winds I roamed, a fleeting flash.
景未移	And before the daylight shifted,
行數千	I had gone several thousand [leagues],
壽如南山不忘愆	long life like South Mountain, not forgetting and not erring.

In place of the general itinerary with which the first "Breathe Out" opens, here we have a shorter but more specific itinerary, from the Nine Doubts Range in the far south to Jade Pass on the northwestern frontiers, and then still farther west to Mount Kunlun. This final stage of the journey requires crossing the Milky Way. In this case Kunlun, rather than Taishan, is the seat of the Queen Mother of the West and her consort, here named as the "Lord of the East," who figures in the "Nine Songs" as a sun god. We have the encounter with Red Pine, receiving the mysteries, eating the magic fungus, and then a flight through the heavens concluding with a declaration of eternal life.

As Diény points out, this version borrows a number of passages and images from the *Chuci*, but these tend to be points where the standard sequence of topics is being elaborated. "Far Roaming," *Yuan you* 遠遊, in the *Chuci* has some pieces of this theme, but "Mulberries by the Path" contains the full set of topics as it had taken shape in early poetics; that is, the *Chuci* imagery lends a literary cachet to what is essentially a poem from the turn of the third century.[55]

---

55. We can see a parallel phenomenon in some of the highly ornamented compositions of the Western Jin toward the end of the third century: when one penetrates beneath the rhetoric, these poets are often following the set sequence of topics in a standard "old poem" theme. The Western Jin fell in 317; and when poetry began to reappear in quantity in the late fourth century, one of

Certain topics could be expanded, but the core components remain in an abbreviated form. In the second "Breathe Out" we have a mountain scene and a musical performance of the immortals; this, in effect, takes the place of the itinerary in the first "Breathe Out" and "Mulberries by the Path." Afterward, however, the speaker roams, visits the Queen Mother of the West on Kunlun, encounters Red Pine, and perhaps (depending on the interpretation) sees the stars.

曹操, 氣出倡 Cao Cao, Breathe Out II[56]

華陰山自以爲大	Huayin Mountain thinks itself grand,
高百丈浮雲爲之蓋	a hundred cubits high, drifting clouds for its cover.
仙人欲來	When the immortals are coming,
出隨風	they come out with the wind,
列之雨	they line up like the rain.[57]
吹我洞簫	I play my panpipes,
鼓瑟琴	strike the zithers,
何闇闇	what harmony of sound!
酒與歌戲	Sporting with wine and singing,
今日相樂誠爲樂	our joy this day is truly joy.
玉女起	Jade maidens rise,
起儛移數時	rise to dance as several hours pass.
鼓吹一何嘈嘈	How loudly sound the pipes and drums,
從西北來時	as they come from the northwest.
仙道多駕煙	In the Way of Immortals they often ride mist,
乘雲駕龍	mount on the clouds, ride dragons,
鬱何蓩蓩	how thickly they throng!
遨遊八極	We roam to the world's eight ends,
乃到崑崙之山	and come to Mount Kunlun,
西王母側	to the side of the Queen Mother.
神仙金止玉亭	To the golden rests and jade pavilions of the gods[58]
來者爲誰	who is it that comes?—

---

the clearest marks of change was the disappearance of the habitual sequences of old topics used when composing by theme.

56. Lu Qinli, 345; *Song shu*; *Yfsj* 26. Huang Jie, *Wei Wudi*, 4–5; Diény, *Les poèmes de Cao Cao*, 85–88.

57. Taking *lie* 列 as it is most commonly used in poetry at this period; cf. *liexian* 列仙. It is unclear whether they are lined up in the rain or as streaming raindrops.

58. Despite ingenious attempts to explain *jin zhi yu ting* 金止玉亭, this is a vexed passage.

赤松王喬	Red Pine and Qiao the Prince,
乃德旋之門	here is the gate to Virtue and the Ring.[59]
樂共飲食到黃昏	We drink and feast joyfully together until dusk.
多駕合坐	Many carriages, seated together,
萬歲長	Ten thousand years!
宜子孫	Have children and grandchildren!

As might be expected, as classical poetry becomes increasingly popular in elite circles in the third century, the strictness of the pattern breaks down. The issue is less literary history here than register and the disposition of certain poets. Even with Fu Xuan in the second half of the third century, however, the central elements are still intact, if almost buried in exuberant description.

傅玄, 雲中白子高行 Fu Xuan, The Ballad of
Bai Zigao in the Clouds[60]

陵陽子	The Master of Lingyang[61]
來明意	had a brilliant intent:
欲作天與仙人遊	he wanted to go roaming with the immortals in Heaven.
超登元氣攀日月	He mounted up over the Primal Vapor, climbed up to the sun and moon,
遂造天門將上謁	he then reached Heaven's Gates, to pay his respects on high.
閶闔闢	The Changhe Gate opened,[62]
見紫微絳闕	he saw the Ziwei Palace and the Crimson Turrets.
紫宮崔嵬	Ziwei Palace loomed,
高殿嵯峨	its high hall was towering,

---

59. This line is variously explained as the "Circle of Virtue" (whatever that might be) or as three stars: Virtue, Circle, and the [Southern] Gate. In this latter explanation, the three stars come to the feast. The inclusion of "ring," *xuan* 旋, does indeed suggest a star name (mentioning various stars is one component of the heavenly journey). I prefer not to ignore the *zhi* 之, and will keep "gate" not as a star name.

60. Lu Qinli, 564; *Yfsj* 63. Jian Changchun 寒長春, Wang Huishao 王會紹, and Yu Xianjie 余賢傑, *Fu Xuan Yin Keng shizhu* 傅玄陰鏗詩注 (Lanzhou: Gansu renmin chubanshe, 1987), 57–59. Bai Zigao is unknown. *Yunzhong* 雲中 can be understood as Yunmeng Marsh, the famous Chu hunting park. I have kept the literal "in the clouds" because of the motif of immortals.

61. An immortal.

62. The Changhe Gate was the gate to Heaven.

雙闕萬丈玉樹羅	for ten thousand yards by the paired turrets, jade trees stood in rows.
童女掣電策	Teenage girls held whips of lightning,
童男挽雷車	teenage boys pulled the Thundercoach.
雲漢隨天流	The Milky Way flowed with the heavens,
浩浩如江河	surging like a river.
因王長公謁上皇	By means of the Senior Prince, I paid my respects to the High God,[63]
鈞天樂作不可詳	"Heaven's Balance" music played, I cannot describe it fully.
龍仙神仙	Dragon immortals and gods
教我靈祕	taught me the magic mysteries.
八風子儀	The Eight Winds and Ziyi[64]
與遊我祥	roamed about with me.[65]
我心何戚戚	Then why was my heart so gloomy?—
思故鄉	I was longing for my home.
俯看故鄉	I looked down at my home,
二儀設張	the Two Principles spread out there.[66]
樂哉二儀	Joyous indeed are the Two Principles,
日月運移	where sun and moon move in their cycles.
地東南傾	The Earth tips to the southeast,
天西北馳	Heaven inclines to the northwest.
鶴五氣所補	Supplemented by the Five Vapors of the crane,[67]
鼇四足所支	supported by the four feet of the Great Tortoise.[68]
齊駕飛龍驂赤螭	Driving flying dragons abreast, with a red kraken as the trace-horse,
逍遙五岳間	I roam freely among the Five Sacred Peaks,
東西馳	speeding east and west,
長與天地並	Lasting as long as Heaven and Earth,
復何爲	what more is there,
復何爲	what more is there?

---

63. The "Senior Prince" or *Wangchanggong* 王長公 is uncertain. *Changgong* 長公 was the term for the eldest prince. I suspect this is a reference to the immortal Qiao the Prince.

64. The Eight Winds are the winds of the eight directions. Ziyi is unknown.

65. I adopt *Yfsj* to take 祥 as 翔. I suspect there is a transposition in this line and it should read: 與我遊翔.

66. The Two Principles are Heaven and Earth.

67. The Five Vapors are the *qi* of the Five Phases. No one knows what the crane is doing here.

68. The Tortoise carries the world on its back.

Here we still have the initial intent to "pay respects on high," *shangye* 上謁, and later "paying respects" to the High God 上皇, replacing the Queen Mother of the West and her consort. As in Cao Cao's *yuefu* there is a preliminary roaming before reaching heaven, which is now a complete palace complex described in some detail. He does not meet Red Pine, but he is introduced by the "Senior Prince" (or Wang Senior), probably the immortal Qiao the Prince (Wangzi Qiao). The speaker is then taught the divine mysteries and goes roaming through the heavens.

At this point there is a sudden shift in tone as the newly made immortal is suddenly "gloomy," *qiqi* 戚戚, the term Cao Cao used when urging his listeners not to worry about mortality. The speaker looks back to his home with longing, and then celebrates the beauties of Earth below. The poem is not fully explicit on this point, but in the end the speaker seems to return to the Earth where he continues to fly about and live the life of an immortal. The movement from Heaven back to Earth should be a return to mortality, a reversal as in Cao Pi's "Snapping the Willow," and in Cao Cao. Here, however, the force of the traditional sequence of topics seems to win out: the speaker must continue roaming and live as long as Heaven and Earth. The poet somehow seems to be able to finish the theme properly, but in the sublunary world.

•

Cao Zhi was working in the context of the shared repertoire, and it affected his work throughout; nevertheless, he took far more liberties with it than most poets.[69] Many of the standard topics appear in Cao Zhi, but some are freely elaborated and the sequences of topics, which have a remarkable consistency elsewhere, are often altered.

---

69. A number of scholars have addressed the issue of Cao Zhi's motives in composing poetry on the immortals. It has been a set topic in Chinese scholarship and criticism on Cao Zhi from the Qing through the present and has been examined in detail by Funatsu Tomohiko 船津富彦 in "Shō Shoku no Yūsenshi ron" 曹植の游仙詩論, *Tōhō bungaku kenkyū*. 13 (1965): 49–65; and by Donald Holzman in "Cao Zhi and the Immortals." Holzman, in particular, draws on prose texts to enrich the picture.

曹植, 五遊詠 Cao Zhi, The Five Wanderings[70]

九州不足步	The Nine Regions are not enough for a stroll,[71]
願得凌雲翔	I wanted to be able to soar up over the clouds.
逍遙八紘外	I roved at ease beyond the Eight Extremes,[72]
遊目歷遐荒	let my eyes roam, crossing the remote wilderness.
披我丹霞衣	I put on my gown of cinnabar-colored cloud-wisps,
襲我素霓裳	I donned my skirt of pale rainbow.
華蓋芬晻藹	My decorated canopy hid me in rich shadow
六龍仰天驤	as my six dragons bounded up toward the heavens.
曜靈未移景	Ere the Radiant Spirit shifted its rays,[73]
倏忽造昊蒼	in a flash I had reached the Celestial Gray.
閶闔啓丹扉	The cinnabar door of Heaven's Gate opened,
雙闕曜朱光	the paired palace towers shone with crimson light.
徘徊文昌殿	I roamed about in the Wenchang Palace,
登陟太微堂	then ascended to Taiwei Hall.[74]
上帝休西櫺	The High God rested by the western casement,
群后集東廂	all the cosmic lords assembled in the eastern loggia.
帶我瓊瑤佩	I wear qiong and yao gems about my waist,
漱我沆瀣漿	and rinse my mouth with a broth of dewy vapors.
踟躕玩靈芝	I paused there, enjoying the magic fungus,
徙倚弄華芳	and lingered, amusing myself with sweet blossoms.
王子奉仙藥	Qiao the Prince offered me immortal drugs,
羨門進奇方	Xianmen Zigao brought me wondrous techniques.

---

70. Lu Qinli, 433; *Ywlj* 78; *Yfsj* 64. Huang Jie, *Cao Zijian*, 80–82; Nie Wenyu, *Cao Zhi*, 276–80; Zhao Youwen, *Cao Zhi*, 400–402. Nie gives the different explanations of the title as roaming over the five peaks, roaming over the five continents, or roaming in the five directions (including up).

71. The "Nine Regions" represented the known world, China.

72. That is, the farthest points in the eight directions.

73. The sun.

74. These are two of three palaces in Heaven.

服食享遐紀	I swallowed them and enjoy a far- reaching span,
延壽保無疆	life extended, I preserve the unbounded.

A review of the preceding poems on immortals will show a remarkable similarity in openings: the poet either begins by climbing a mountain or by just flying off (though we do have "Going Out Xia Gate," where the adept begins by perfecting himself). Cao Zhi, by contrast, begins by finding all China's Nine Regions taken together as too small to walk in. This is hyperbole with precedent. Sima Xiangru said much the same of Han Emperor Wu as the "Great Man" 大人:

宅彌萬里兮	His lodgings filled ten thousand leagues,
曾不足以少留	but they were not enough to stay even a while.[75]

Cao Zhi's seniors, including his father, elder brother, and the Seven Masters, had often alluded to the *Shijing* and worked tags and passages into their poems; they just as frequently made references to old stories and sometimes alluded to the other Classics. Cao Zhi is doing something rather different here. He is, in effect, mixing the heavenly journey of Sima Xiangru's "Great Man" together with the contemporary poem on roaming immortals. Not only does the poem begin with a trope from "The Great Man" not used in early classical poetry, it adopts the confident tone of the heavenly traveler there. In other poems there is sometimes a request or the need for an intermediary; at the very least the visitors to the gods in the preceding poems "pay their respects." Like Han emperor Wu in "The Great Man," Cao Zhi here simply enters the gates of Heaven, and he moves through the palaces of Heaven as a familiar. We do indeed find the word "magic fungus" preceding the word "drug," as in many of the other verses; but Cao Zhi is casually "enjoying," *wan* 玩, and "amusing himself with," *nong* 弄, the numinous plant. We do have two immortals mentioned after the High God: Qiao the Prince and Xianmen Zigao. They bring him the drug and provide magical techniques, but the verbs used (*feng* 奉 and *jin* 進) put these famous immortals in the role of servants or inferiors. The poem ends with the conventional attainment of immor-

---

75. Fei Zhengang 費振剛, Hu Shuangbao 胡雙寶, and Zong Minghua 宗明華, *Quan Han fu* 全漢賦 (Beijing: Beijing daxue chubanshe, 1993), 91.

tality, but the poet has so "raised" his position poetically that he enjoys the ingredients and devices of immortality with all the casualness of an aristocrat walking in his flower garden and being served good pastries.

Here and elsewhere, the influence of poetic exposition (*fu*) and other elite discursive forms appears in Cao Zhi's poetry in the five syllable line. This was very much part of making the low register form into high literature, and it was a process that was intensified in the last part of the third century. Although Cao Zhi still seems quite straightforward in comparison to the poets of the Western Jin, his poetry is filled with both words and topics that are not found in poetry of a lower register.

曹植, 仙人篇 Cao Zhi, The Immortals[76]

仙人攬六著	The immortals take in hand the six-inch slips,[77]
對博太山隅	and, face to face, gamble in the crannies of Taishan.
湘娥拊琴瑟	The Xiang damsels stroke the zithers,[78]
秦女吹笙竽	the daughter of Qin blows the reed organ.[79]
玉樽盈桂酒	Jade goblets brim with cinnamon ale,
河伯獻神魚	The River's Earl presents sacred fish.[80]
四海一何局	This sea-girt world is so confining!—
九州安所如	where can I go in the Nine Regions?
韓終與王喬	Han Zhong and Qiao the Prince[81]
要我於天衢	invite me to join them on Heaven's streets.
萬里不足步	Ten thousand leagues is not enough for a stroll,
輕舉陵太虛	I rise lightly and cross the Great Void.
飛騰踰景雲	Mounting in flight, I pass the sunlit clouds,[82]
高風吹我軀	and the high winds blow my body.

---

76. Lu Qinli, 434; *Yfsj* 64; Huang Jie, *Cao Zijian*, 63–65; Nie Wenyu, *Cao Zhi*, 266–72; Zhao Youwen, *Cao Zhi*, 263–65.

77. These are tallies used in a gambling game.

78. The two goddesses of the Xiang River.

79. This is Nongyu, the daughter of the Duke of Qin, who flew off to Heaven with her husband Xiaoshi.

80. The god of the Yellow River.

81. Qiao the Prince is a familiar figure; Han Zhong was an adept of the time of Qin Shihuang.

82. Huang Jie and subsequent commentators take *jingyun* 景雲 as the "auspicious clouds," *qingyun* 慶雲.

廻駕過紫薇	I turn my carriage and stop by Ziwei Palace,[83]
與帝合靈符	and match the magic tally with that of the god.[84]
閶闔正嵯峨	Heaven's Gates are here looming,
雙闕萬丈餘	paired turrets more than ten thousand cubits high.
玉樹扶道生	Jade trees grow lining the roads,
白虎夾門樞	white tigers on both sides of the gate pivots.
驅風遊四海	Driving winds, I roam the sea-girt world,
東過王母廬	to the east I pass the Queen Mother's cottage.
俯觀五嶽間	I look down among the Five Sacred Peaks,
人生如寄居	where human life is as if but a sojourn.
潛光養羽翼	Hide your light, nourish your wings,[85]
進趨且徐徐	fare forward with slow steadiness.
不見軒轅氏	Have you not seen how the Yellow Emperor
乘龍出鼎湖	rode a dragon out from Cauldron Lake?
徘徊九天上	He roamed about above Heaven's ninth tier,
與爾長相須	with you I will linger forever.

Low register poems on immortals were content to have the Queen Mother of the West and her consort, along with Red Pine and Qiao the Prince, as immortals. Cao Zhi has an entire pantheon, along with details of the world of Heaven and technical terms that are indeed shared with other kinds of works on immortality and the immortals. Behind low register poetry, however, there was a process that was both a sequence of poetic topics and a religious procedure. There is a rudimentary narrative here—he is enjoying an immortal feast, accepts an invitation to fly up to Heaven, and drops by to say hello to the High God—but that narrative is overwhelmed by description.

Where the poet of "Going Out Xia Gate" paid his respects to the Queen Mother of the West and her Consort, "right in the corner of Taishan" 乃在太山隅, Cao Zhi finds immortals gambling. One cannot say that the earlier poems on immortals showed any particular religious awe, but there was sometimes

---

83. One of the three heavenly palaces. I agree with Zhao that the *Yiwen leiju* reading *guo* 過 is correct here, rather than the *Yfsj* reading *guan* 觀.

84. Presumably the tally shows that he is a feudal lord of the god.

85. That is, live hidden away. On becoming an immortal, one grows wings.

a certain exhilaration and wonder; Cao Zhi's immortals exhibit a festive frivolity that is, in many ways, quite appropriate for a world unshadowed by death. They sound like bored aristocratic youths, feeling their surroundings are confining and inviting the speaker to take a walk on Heaven's streets (and although Cao Zhi and his friends might be described as "aristocratic," they were very much shadowed by death).

The world of Heaven was obviously a pleasure to describe, and Cao Zhi describes his itinerary with relish. There is one particularly nice moment when, as he flies over the area of the Five Sacred Peaks (most of inhabited China), he looks down on the mortal world below. And what he sees below him is also the one line in the poem that clearly belongs to the "old poems" and the popular register: in the world below "human life is as if but a sojourn" 人生如寄居. Although the themes of the immortals were themselves also a part of the shared repertoire of early poetry, the difference from the mortal world which they tried to describe was also a poetic difference. Death, separation, and worry dominate much early poetry and provide its most common topics and themes. The world of the immortals was something else altogether, both for poetry and for the imagination.

Cao Zhi has many poems on the immortals. The traces of the shared poetics of the age remain but in fragments. What separates these poems from other early poems on the immortals is something like a "negative capability," the poet's capacity to imagine himself in that world so completely that he can speak from it. Cao Zhi's poetry has almost always been read politically, in reference to his one-time proximity to the throne and the abuse he suffered when the throne went to his older brother. It might be better to read Cao Zhi's poetics politically, as acts of imaginative empowerment where pragmatic empowerment failed.

•

In the final poem we will consider, we have a failed encounter with the immortals. The speaker climbs the mountain, though with none of the joy or exhilaration of the other poems. He is sitting there despondently when three immortals appear and tell him that he can attain the Way. In this case, however, the speaker misses his opportunity and is left behind.

曹操, 秋胡行 Cao Cao, A Ballad of Qiuhu I[86]

晨上散關山	At dawn I went up Sanguan Mountain,
此道當何難	how hard this road was!
晨上散關山	At dawn I went up Sanguan Mountain,
此道當何難	how hard this road was!
牛頓不起	The ox collapsed and did not get up,
車墮谷間	the wagon fell into the valley.
坐盤石之上	I sat upon a boulder
彈五弦之琴	and played a five-stringed zither.
作清角韻	I made the tones of the "Clear Jiao,"[87]
意中迷煩	my mind, confused and troubled.
歌以言志	I sing to state my aims,
晨上散關山	at dawn I went up Sanguan Mountain.
有何三老公	Why have these three old gentlemen[88]
卒來在我傍	come at last to my side?
有何三老公	Why have these three old gentlemen
卒來在我傍	come at last to my side?
負挎被裘	Wearing fur-lined robes on their backs,
似非恆人	they seem not to be ordinary men.
謂卿云何	They say to me: "Why have you,
困苦以自怨	in such misery and feeling ill will,
徨徨所欲	tormented in what you want,
來到此間	come to this place?"
歌以言志	I sing to state my aims:
有何三老公	why have these three old gentlemen come?
我居崑崙山	"We live in the Kunlun Mountains,
所謂者真人	those known as the 'Pure Beings.'
我居崑崙山	We live in the Kunlun Mountains,
所謂者真人	those known as the 'Pure Beings.'
道深有可得	The Way is deep, there is a means to attain it;
名山歷觀	pass through the famous mountains and view,
遨遊八極	roam to the Eight Limits,
枕石漱流飲泉	make rocks your pillow, rinse in currents, drink from springs."

---

86. Lu Qinli, 349; *Song shu*; *Yfsj* 36. Huang Jie, *Wei Wudi*, 20–21; Diény, *Les poèmes de Cao Cao*, 91–96.

87. A musical piece credited to the Yellow Emperor.

88. Lu Qinli prefers this to be a mistake for only one immortal, but such figures often traveled in groups.

沈吟不決	Brooding, I did not decide,
遂上升天	then they rose up to Heaven.
歌以言志	I sing to state my aims:
我居崑崙山	"We live in the Kunlun Mountains."
去去不可追	They kept on going, could not be followed,
長恨相牽攀	I will ever hate how I am pulled and dragged down.[89]
去去不可追	They kept on going, could not be followed,
長恨相牽攀	I will ever hate how I am pulled and dragged down.
夜夜安得寐	How can I sleep from night to night?
惆悵以自憐	I am depressed and pity myself.
正而不譎	[I am] "Upright and not deceitful,"[90]
辭賦依因	relying on poetic expositions,[91]
經傳所過	what he passed through transmitting the Classic;
西來所傳	what is transmitted of his going west.[92]
歌以言志	I sing to state my aims:
去去不可追	they kept on going, could not be followed.

As we learn to recognize those poems that reperform the common themes of poetry, we also can recognize a poem that is quite distinct and without parallel. The poem begins as one might expect, climbing a mountain, indeed the very mountain through whose pass Laozi went west; as one might expect, the speaker encounters immortals. But the tone is wrong from the

---

89. Diény (*Les poèmes de Cao Cao*, 96) offers an excellent discussion of this vexed line. I have not followed his ingenious solution out of the conviction that grammatically the second hemistich must be the object that is hated.

90. The characterization of Duke Huan of Qi in *Analects* XIV.15.

91. This has often been taken as referring to Duke Huan hearing Ning Qi rapping the horns of his ox and singing, after which Duke Huan employed him. *Cifu* 辭賦, translated as "poetic expositions," is not the right term for Ning Qi's song.

92. These lines are very problematic. Commentators usually take them as referring to Duke Huan's campaign against Daxia to the west, transmitted in the Confucian Classics or histories. Von den Steinen's "What he passed through is [found] in classical writings" is the most natural reading for l. 45; though his version of l. 46 ("[In books] coming from the West [stands] what is handed down") is quite far-fetched. Following Balázs, von den Steinen takes these "books coming from the West" as Daoist texts. *Xilai* 西來 often means "going west" rather than "from the west." The appropriate figure in this case would be Laozi, and the "Classic," the *Daode jing*. Diény's explanation (p. 94) is the only one that makes credible sense in the context.

beginning, and it leads the theme astray. Climbing the mountain is hard; the ox collapses; the wagon falls into the valley. This is not an auspicious beginning for an encounter with the immortals, and it understandably leaves the climber in the wrong frame of mind.

At this point the "three old gentlemen" enter, commiserate with our depressed speaker, and offer him the mysteries of the Way and the means to travel without oxcart. The speaker does not seize the opportunity, and the immortals fly back to Heaven.

The final stanza presents serious difficulties of interpretation, but one thing is clear: the speaker is not happy—apparently at the fact that he did not go with the immortals. Considering the delights that poetry insists would follow if he had accepted the immortals' offer, he has reason not to be happy.

Here we seem to have a reference to Duke Huan of Qi, which is the only clear thing about the last four lines apart from the refrain. Unfortunately, the apparent clarity of the reference sets many commentators off in fanciful directions. Diény's alternative hypothesis to explain these lines seems just right and turns on an interesting question:

[Mon récit est] sincère et sans duplicité / [J'en donne pour preuve] l'inspiration des rhapsodies / Les relations des anciennes chroniques / La tradition venue de l'Occident.

[My story is] sincere and without deception / [I offer as proof] the inspiration of poetic expositions / The accounts of ancient chronicles / The tradition that has come from the West.

We might want to change a few things, but the argument is clear and fits the rest of the poem. The interesting question is the four character phrase taken from the *Analects* by which Confucius characterizes Duke Huan of Qi: "upright and not deceitful." Is this an "allusion," as most commentators have understood it, strongly invoking Duke Huan of Qi; or is this a "tag," a resonant phrase from tradition that could be applied in a completely different context? Diény's alternative interpretation, with the speaker claiming himself to be "upright and not deceitful" in his account, treats it as a tag. The true "allusion" then is Sanguan Mountain, through whose pass Laozi went to the west—not necessarily the place Cao Cao once attacked, reenacting the western campaigns of Duke Huan. Allusions in the poetry of this period tend to be to stories. Sanguan Mountain is precisely the place Laozi "passed through" and "transmitted the Classic."

FOUR

Death and the Feast

> They seek the immortals where nothing is,
> Red Pine has long deceived me.
>
> — Cao Zhi, "Presented to
> Biao, the Prince of Baima"

The themes and topics of early classical poetry form a single network of intersections: one theme passes over onto another in predictable ways. There are variables on many levels: in the poetry on immortals the speaker may climb different mountains, meet different gods and immortals; he may swallow the elixir of immortality himself and fly through the heavens, or he may bring it back to the mortal world for the benefit of an earthly ruler or patron. He may, indeed, decide that it is not worthwhile to pursue immortality at all.

The one point on which all agree is that mortal life is short. In the face of that knowledge there are choices. One choice is, of course, to work hard to achieve something in the public realm. This is the burden of "Long Song," *Changge xing* 長歌行, one of the three anonymous *yuefu* included in *Wen xuan* and, not surprisingly, one of the most polished of anonymous *yuefu*.

長歌行 Long Song[1]

青青園中葵	Green, green, the garden's mallows,
朝露待日晞	the dew of dawn will dry with the sun.
陽春布德澤	Bright spring spreads potent moisture,
萬物生光輝	and all things give off a glow.

---

1. Lu Qinli, 262; *Wenxuan* 27; *Ywlj* 42; *Yfsj* 30; Huang Jie, *Han Wei*, 14.

常恐秋節至	But always I fear that autumn will come,
焜黃華葉衰	sere and yellowing, bloom and leaf will decay.
百川東至海	All the rivers go east to the sea,
何時復西歸	when will they turn back west again?
少壯不努力	If one does not strive hard in youth,
老大徒傷悲	when old one will feel helpless sorrow.

Such intimations of mortality can also occur on a specific occasion, as when Chen Lin is out enjoying himself with his friends.

陳琳, 詩 Chen Lin, Poem[2]

節運時氣舒	The season changes, timely weather spreads,
秋風涼且清	the autumn wind is cool and clear.
閒居心不娛	Living at ease, my heart was not happy,
駕言從友生	I got in my carriage, went off with friends.
翱翔戲長流	We rambled, sporting by the long river,
逍遙登高城	we roamed, climbing the high wall.
東望看疇野	I gazed eastward, looking on fields and moors
迴顧覽園庭	then turned to observe the gardens and yards.
嘉木凋綠葉	The green leaves of fine trees were withering,
芳草纖紅榮	the red blooms of sweet flowers perished.[3]
騁哉日月逝	Sun and moon go off in such a rush
年命將西傾	my fated span of years sinks westward.
建功不及時	If one does not achieve great deeds in time,
鐘鼎何所銘	how will cauldrons or bells be inscribed?
收念還寢房	I cease brooding and return to my chamber,
慷慨詠墳經	with strong feeling, I chant the Classics.
庶幾及君在	I hope to reach where my lord is,
立德垂功名	to establish virtue and leave fame of my deeds.

As we will see later in this chapter, on other occasions Chen Lin veers off from the common direction of an established theme. The poem begins as a common Jian'an type, the poem on excursions with friends. But the autumn vegetation stirs dark thoughts and leads him to meditation on his mortality. The

---

2. Lu Qinli, 368; *Ywlj* 28. Han Geping, *Jian'an*, 122–23.
3. As Lu Qinli notes, *xian* 纖 should be *jian* 殲.

solution proposed in "Long Song," to exert oneself, was always available; and Chen Lin resolves to go home and study the Confucian Classics in hope of accomplishing great deeds.[4]

Such virtuous resolution to work hard and make a name for oneself is the path less followed. Whether announced as a commonplace theme from the beginning or called forth, as here, in looking at the autumn scene, the poetic statement of mortality more often leads to seeking the secrets of immortality or to a decision to make merry, dress well, and feast.

We can see the variable, which is the moment of decision, clearly in the following set. We will begin the set with yet another poem on immortals (apparently a fragment), cited under Cao Zhi's name in *Yiwen leiju*.[5]

人生不滿百	Man's life does not last a full hundred years,
戚戚少歡娛	I am gloomy and pleasures are few.
意欲奮六翮	I decide to spread my sixfold wings,
排霧陵紫虛	to brush through fog, cross the purple void.
蟬蛻同松喬	I will shed my husk like Red Pine and Qiao,[6]
翻跡登鼎湖	with flying footsteps rise up at Tripod Lake.[7]
翱翔九天上	I soar about above the nine-tiered heavens,
騁轡遠行遊	my reins gallop as I go roaming afar.
東觀扶桑曜	In the east I view the Fusang Tree aglow;
西臨弱水流	in the west I look down on the Ruo River's flow;
北極登玄渚	to the farthest north, I mount the Black Isles,
南翔陟丹邱	winging south, I climb up Cinnabar Hill.

This is a very standard version of a poem on the immortals, apparently truncated in the middle of the speaker's itinerary

---

4. As we have suggested earlier, these sequences can be done either in expanded or contracted form. For the same sequence in contracted form, see ll. 3–6 in Cao Zhi's "Dew on the Onion-grass" 薤露行 (Lu Qinli, 422).

5. Lu Qinli, 456; *Ywlj* 78. Huang Jie, *Cao Zijian*, 79–80; Nie Wenyu, *Cao Zhi*, 273–75; Zhao Youwen, *Cao Zhi*, 265–66.

6. This is the cicada shedding its husk, a standard image of immortality.

7. Tripod Lake was where the Yellow Emperor rose to Heaven.

through the cosmos. We know how such poems should end, and they should not end with a parallel couplet. What is striking is the commonplace that opens the poem. For all later readers, and no doubt for readers and listeners of the early period, the familiar opening might easily go off in a different direction altogether.

Nineteen Old Poems XV[8]

生年不滿百	Life does not last a full hundred years,
常懷千歲憂	we always worry about living a thousand.[9]
晝短苦夜長	If the daylight is short and the nights are long,
何不秉燭遊	best to go roaming with candle in hand.
爲樂當及時	To make merry we must seize the moment.
何能待來茲	how can we wait for some year to come?
愚者愛惜費	The fool who begrudges spending,
但爲後世嗤	will only be mocked by later ages.
仙人王子喬	Qiao the Prince, the immortal—
難可與等期	it is hard to expect a span like his.

"Cao Zhi," as the imputed speaker in the first poem, does indeed "worry about living a thousand" years (literally, "to harbor in one's heart cares or anxieties about living a thousand"). Chinese poetic language gives us no tense, so we do not know whether the heavenly journey that follows is what he does or what he plans to do in the immediate future. He will "shed his husk like Red Pine and Qiao" the Prince. The speaker in "Nineteen Old Poems" XV has the same desires but no faith in their possibility. For him the alternative is to seize the moment and extend time not to eternity but into the dark of night, "roaming with candle in hand." He calls on his auditors to make merry now, to "spend" both one's mortal time and one's goods. Everyone who hears the poem knows that they are called not to some solitary merriment but to some shared joy, feasting and drinking. This is explicit in the anonymous *yuefu* that incorporates "Nineteen Old Poems" XV.

---

8. Lu Qinli, 333; *Wen xuan* 29. Sui Shusen, *Gushi*, 22–23; Diény, *Les dix-neuf poèmes anciens*, 36–37, 135–140.

9. The late imperial reading of this line is, unsurprisingly, thinking of one's deeds and posterity. Diény accepts Li Shan's citation that this refers to good government. Especially given the use of *sui* 歲, the interpretation above makes the best sense.

西門行 West Gate[10]

出西門	I went out West Gate,
步念之	I paced brooding:
今日不作樂	If I don't make merry today,
當待何時	what moment am I waiting for?
夫爲樂	As for making merry,
爲樂當及時	to make merry we must seize the moment.
何能坐愁怫鬱	Why sit in troubled sadness,
當復待來茲	should we wait for some year to come?
飲醇酒	Drink pure ale,
炙肥牛	roast the fatted ox,
請呼心所歡	call to those your heart enjoys,
可用解憂愁	who can release worries and sadness.
人生不滿百	Man's life does not last a full hundred years,
常懷千歲憂	he worries always about living a thousand.
晝短而夜長	If the daylight is short and the nights are long,
何不秉燭遊	best to go roaming with candle in hand.
自非仙人王子喬	Since I'm not the immortal Qiao the Prince,
計會壽命難與期	it's hard to expect such a long lifespan.
自非仙人王子喬	Since I'm not the immortal Qiao the Prince,
計會壽命難與期	it's hard to expect such a long lifespan.
人壽非金石	Man's lifespan is not of metal and stone,
年命安可期	how can you expect long-fated years?
貪財愛惜費	If you're greedy for goods and begrudge spending,
但爲後世嗤	you'll be only mocked by later ages.

In this context we can recall Cao Cao's "Ballad of Qiuhu" II ("I want to climb Taihua Mountain"), which began with a desire to seek the immortals and closed with an injunction not to worry about how long one will live but, rather, to make merry in the moment. We can see Cao Cao working with the same material and thematic sequences; we can also see Cao Cao adding something quite different: the central praise of kingship that frames the call to pleasure on earth below.

The variables, the choices, are never stable: these are not expressions of firm belief but poetic possibilities that shift back

---

10. Lu Qinli, 269; *Song shu*; *Yfsj* 37. Huang Jie, *Han Wei*, 31–32; Diény, *Aux origines de la poésie classique*, 136–38; Birrel, *Popular Songs*, 89–93.

and forth. There is yet another version of "West Gate" in *Yuefu shiji*; although the same material comes back yet again, it is interesting what has been omitted and added:

出西門	I went out West Gate,
步念之	I paced brooding:
今日不作樂	If I don't make merry today,
當待何時	what moment am I waiting for?
逮爲樂	When it comes to making merry,
逮爲樂	when it comes to making merry,
當及時	we must seize the moment.
何能愁怫鬱	Why be in troubled sadness,
當復待來茲	should we wait for some year to come?
釀美酒	Brew the fine ale,
炙肥牛	roast the fatted ox,
請呼心所懽	call to those your heart enjoys,
可用解憂愁	who can release worries and sadness.
人生不滿百	Man's life does not last a full hundred years,
常懷千歲憂	he always worries about living a thousand.
晝短苦夜長	If the daylight is short and the nights are long,
何不秉燭遊	best to go roaming with candle in hand.
遊行去去如雲除	Go roaming off to the edge of the clouds,
弊車羸馬爲自儲	battered wagon and run-down nag, your store.

It is the "same" poem, but all the lines dismissing the possibility of immortality have been omitted. Instead we have two new lines that conclude the poem, lines whose import at first seems most uncertain. What does it mean to "go roaming off to the edge of clouds"? If this particular text is only one realization of a virtual network of material and associations, then perhaps the ending of the text above was written more clearly elsewhere. Although our extant corpus is extremely limited and has changed through layers of recopying and reuse, we do indeed often find the answers to such problem passages in other poems. In this context we might recall the two final stanzas of a poem quoted earlier, a poem in which feasting and the quest for immortality are not alternative choices, but are woven together. This is the anonymous *yuefu* "Grand!" 善哉行:

歡日尚少	The days of joy are still few,
戚日苦多	days of woe terribly many.

何以忘憂	How can we forget our cares?—
彈箏酒歌	play the zheng and sing drinking songs.
淮南八公	The eight lords in Huainan,
要道不煩	the essential Way brings no bother.
參駕六龍	Just hitch up your six dragons
遊戲雲端	and roam for fun at the edge of clouds.

Although a different word for "edge" is used (the rhymes being different), we see that this roaming is precisely the roaming of the immortals, though here with a "battered wagon and run-down nag" in place of six dragons.[11] If we puzzle about the strange word *chu* 儲, "store" or "accumulation," we might recall the end of the other versions, which warned against being "greedy for goods," *tan cai* 貪財. Perhaps the implications are that these are the only "goods" that remain after the feast, as we see when such extravagant parties are invoked in Zhang Xie's "On History" 詠史, writing of the lords of the Western Han.[12]

揮金樂當年	They distributed gold to have joy in their day,
歲暮不留儲	at year's end no store was left.
顧謂四座賓	Looking round they addressed all the guests:
多財爲累愚	much wealth is encumbrance and folly.

While late in the third century Zhang Xie celebrates expenditure, Ruan Ji had done his own twist on the motif at mid-century. Ruan Ji, characteristically, gives us the aftermath of things.

阮籍, 詠懷 Ruan Ji, Singing of My Cares V[13]

平生少年時	As I used to be as a young man
輕薄好絃歌	I was heedless and loved songs sung to strings.
西遊咸陽中	I roamed west to Xianyang[14]
趙李相經過	and frequented the Zhaos and Lis.[15]

---

11. We find the "nag" in one of Cao Zhi's poems on the immortals, at the beginning of "I Drive My Carriage" 驅車篇 (Lu Qinli, 435), where he drives his nag to Taishan in search of the immortals.

12. Lu Qinli, 744; *Wen xuan* 21.

13. Lu Qinli, 497; *Wen xuan* 22; *Ywlj* 26. Holzman, *Poetry and Politics*, 224.

14. Xianyang, the Qin capital, stands for Chang'an, which in turn stands for Luoyang, the Wei capital.

15. Probably referring to the families of Han Chengdi's women Zhao Feiyan and Li Ping.

娛樂未終極	Before enjoying my pleasures to the fullest,
白日忽蹉跎	the bright sun suddenly slipped away.
驅馬復來歸	I galloped my horse to go back home,
反顧望三河	turned to gaze on the Three River region.[16]
黃金百鎰盡	A hundred pounds of gold were gone—
資用常苦多	the expenses were always terribly great.
北臨太行道	On the north road through the Taihang Range
失路將如何	I lost my way, what shall I do?

Expenditure was part of the theme of the feast: life is short, and hoarding is a waste. Ruan Ji is a poet who often builds on the themes of early poetry, negating them and carrying to a further stage. Here the feast is over, the speaker's fortune is gone, and he turns home, at last losing his way in the mountains.

•

To return to "West Gate," scholarship also has its themes and topics, points that must be examined before one can move on. Ever since, in the world of print culture, different versions were presented side by side, scholars have felt compelled to ask which was the "original" and which, the derivation. Guo Mao-qian, convinced that the *Song shu* versions were the work of Jin musicians, decided that the final version above was the "original." Diény prefers to give priority to the *Song shu* version. The larger "chicken and egg" question is the relation between the *yuefu* versions and the "old poem." In this one instance Diény is even willing to allow that the "old poem" was polished out of the *yuefu* for the *Wen xuan*. This is, of course, not impossible, but it represents a value judgment of priority that misses the point. Any one of the "old poems" could have been incorporated in a *yuefu* or done as a *yuefu*, either a theatrically irregular one like "West Gate" or a regular one; some material preserved as anonymous *yuefu* could not have been done as an "old poem," but much could. Neatness and logical order are not a function of literary history. The theatricality of address in the *yuefu* does

---

16. This probably refers to the area around Luoyang. The "Three River provinces" covered a very large region.

not mean it is earlier or later. When one makes a judgment of priority on these grounds, it is an ideological judgment, not a judgment from historical or textual evidence. Guo Maoqian and many Chinese scholars believed and still believe that there were coherent original poems that were set to music; in the hands of musicians the texts became garbled, illogical, and irregular. This theory persists despite the fact that in the case of the "Treatise on Music," we are talking about the imperial musical establishment, supervised by highly educated ritualists. May Fourth romanticism, with a sympathetic response in European and American scholarly romanticism, believes, on the contrary, that poems begin messy, close to performers or the "folk"; they get neat and logical in the hands of the educated elite. These are ideologies of historical change.

In the versions of the material above, we are talking about variant forms of realization that may possibly have coexisted in the third century; however, these variant forms of realization were later separated into poetry anthologies and collections of musical verse.

•

In "Nineteen Old Poems" XV the meditation on mortality occupies a single couplet, while the remainder of the poem is a call to the feast. In "Nineteen Old Poems" XIII the sequence of themes is exactly the same, but the proportions are reversed.[17]

驅車上東門	I drove my wagon out Upper East Gate[18]
遙望郭北墓	and gaze at the far tombs north of the wall.
白楊何蕭蕭	The white poplars moan in the wind,
松柏夾廣路	pines and cypresses line the wide roads.

---

17. Lu Qinli, 332; *Wen xuan* 29; *Yfsj* 61 (as 驅車上東門行). Sui Shusen, *Gushi*, 19–21; Diény, *Les dix-neuf poèmes anciens*, 32–33, 125–30.

18. Since Upper East Gate was in the walls of Eastern Han Luoyang, this line is commonly used to prove an Eastern Han date for this poem and to contribute to a general argument for an Eastern Han dating for all of the "Nineteen Old Poems." If a poem known to be of a later date refers to "Upper East Gate," then it is simply a literary reference to a place named in the "Nineteen Old Poems." Few seem to appreciate the circularity of such an argument. Perhaps it rests on the assumption that there must be a first usage and that first usage must still exist. If, however, Luoyang's long destroyed Upper East Gate was part of a shared poetic repertoire, then this poem could have been composed later and have used that resonant place-name. It is no less possible that the poem was indeed composed in the Eastern Han before the destruction of Upper East Gate.

下有陳死人	Underneath are men long dead,
杳杳即長暮	fading away into endless twilight.
潛寐黃泉下	They sleep hidden beneath the Yellow Springs,[19]
千載永不寤	never waking once in a thousand years.
浩浩陰陽移	Light and darkness change places in a flooding course,
年命如朝露	our span of years is like morning dew.
人生忽如寄	Man's life is as swift as a sojourn,
壽無金石固	old age, not so firm as metal and stone.
萬歲更相送	For ten thousand years men have seen each other off in turn,[20]
賢聖莫能度	good men and sages cannot cross that span.
服食求神仙	Some swallow herbs to seek the immortals,
多為藥所誤	many have been fooled by such drugs.
不如飲美酒	The best thing is to drink good ale
被服紈與素	and to dress in silks fine and pale.

If one went out Upper East Gate of Luoyang, one saw Beimang 北邙, long the burial ground for the great city.

The meditation on mortality, here extended to dominate the poem, can, as we have seen, lead to the quest for immortality or to the feast. When the choice is made to feast and dress well (the two often go together), one often finds an additional passage specifically rejecting the possibility of seeking the immortals. We see this in "Nineteen Old Poems" XV and we see it here (and if we note that it has been placed last in the sequence of topics in "Nineteen Old Poems" XV, we should note that it is placed earlier when the same material appears in "West Gate").

The figure of roads and paths is useful. The poet comes to a point, often a familiar line like "Life does not last a full hundred years," from which various paths branch out, paths traveled by other poets. Our poet turns down one of those paths and sometimes goes a bit farther or takes a new turn, a turn that will probably be followed by others. In "Nineteen Old Poems" XV the poet sees the tombs, reflects on life's brevity and the world of the dead; then he suggests wearing good clothes and feasting. A poet might go a bit farther along the path that reflects on the world of the dead, where the motif of good clothes and drinking may come back.

---

19. The underworld.
20. That is, accompanying the dead to their tombs.

We come back to a variation on the same opening line. But in this case there are no options: it is too late.

傅玄, 挽歌 Fu Xuan, Bearers' Song[21]

人生尠能百	Human life but rarely lasts to a hundred,
哀情數萬端	sad emotions come from ten thousand sources.
不幸嬰篤病	Unfortunately he is caught by serious illness,
凶候形素顏	signs of doom appear in his pale complexion.
衣衾爲誰施	For whom are gown and coverlet set?—
束帶就闔棺	his belt has gone into the closed coffin.
欲悲淚已竭	He wants to weep, but his tears are gone;
欲辭不能言	he wants words, but he cannot speak.
存亡自遠近	The living and dead are far apart,
長夜何漫漫	the long night lasts on and on.
壽堂閑且長	The funeral hall is quiet, time stretches on,[22]
祖載歸不還	after the ancestral service and the cortege he never returns.[23]

The poetry of the imagined dead became a set type in the third century; the earliest example is attributed to Ruan Yu 阮瑀, one of the Seven Masters of the Jian'an. The speaker begins with a variation on one of the standard opening lines of the feast poem: "[This fine party / this moment] is hard to encounter again" 難再遇. Into the first two positions in the line he puts "life's prime" 丁年. Here the imagined dead cannot feast.

阮瑀, 七哀詩 Ruan Yu, Sevenfold Sorrows[24]

丁年難再遇	Life's prime is hard to encounter again,
富貴不重來	wealth and honor won't come a second time.
良時忽一過	The best of times are suddenly past,
身體爲土灰	and the body becomes dirt and ash.
冥冥九泉室	Dark are the chambers of the Nine Springs,
漫漫長夜臺	stretching on, the Terrace of Endless Night.

---

21. Lu Qinli, 565; *Beitang shuchao* 92. Jian Changchun, *Fu Xuan*, 65–66.

22. The funeral hall is where the corpse is laid out before interment.

23. The *zu* 祖 was the ceremony of worshipping the dead person as an ancestor, carried out in the courtyard; the *zai* 載 was transporting the corpse to the burial ground.

24. Lu Qinli, 380; *Ywlj* 34. Han Geping, *Jian'an*, 369–70; Wu Yun, *Jian'an*, 325–26.

身盡氣力索	The body is gone, spirit's force spent,
精魂靡所能	and the rarified soul can do nothing.
嘉肴設不御	Excellent viands are set out, but I cannot dine,
旨酒盈觴杯	choice ales brim flagons and goblets.
出壙望故鄉	I go out of the tomb-vault and gaze on home
但見蒿與萊	and see only the mugwort and weeds.

The poetic "territory" of the feast and the poetic "territory" of the dead are closely adjacent; the dead try to come back and drink or wear fine clothes but cannot. This poem type has a rich history lasting on to Tao Qian.[25]

The image of roads is attractive because sometimes the poet is literally on the road. He may have been having a hard time, but at a certain moment "cares" explicitly beset him—and then he is on a poetic road that leads to meditation on mortality and to one of the possible resolutions. In the following version of "Grand!" by Cao Pi, the poet does not yearn for immortality, reflect on the dead, or resolve to study the Classics. He is clearly headed in the poetic direction of the feast, but being literally "on the road," it is not an immediate option. He does, however, have good clothes—a "light cape"—and that, along with his fine horse, seems to be enough of the standard topic for the poet to go riding off and enjoy himself.[26]

曹丕, 善哉行 Cao Pi, Good![27]

上山采薇	I climbed the mountain to pick bracken,
薄暮苦飢	toward evening I suffered from hunger.
谿谷多風	In the creek valleys was much wind,
霜露沾衣	the frost and dew soaked my clothes.
野雉群雊	Wild pheasants cried out in their flocks,
猿猴相追	gibbons followed after one another.
還望故鄉	When I turned and looked toward my homeland,
鬱何壘壘	how dense it was in rolling piles.[28]

---

25. See Ikkai Tomoyoshi 一海知義, "*Monzen* banka shi kō" 文選挽歌詩考, *Chūgoku bungaku hō* 12 (1960): 19–48..

26. Cao Pi's fine horse and "light cape" echo *Analects* VI.3, but with none of the possible negative associations.

27. Lu Qinli, 390; *Song shu*; *Wen xuan* 27; *Yfsj* 36. Huang Jie, *Wei Wudi*, 36–37.

28. That is, forested mountains.

高山有崖	The high mountains have their slopes,
林木有枝	the trees in the woods have their branches.
憂來無方	Cares come from I know not where,
人莫之知	no one knows.
人生如寄	Human life is as if a lodging,
多憂何爲	why are troubles so many?
今我不樂	Today I am not happy,
歲月如馳	years and months seem to gallop on.
湯湯川流	The river goes sweeping along,
中有行舟	in it is a moving boat.
隨波轉薄	It turns or runs aground along with the waves,
有似客遊	something like the traveler's wanderings.
策我良馬	I whip my good horse,
被我輕裘	and don my light cape.
載馳載驅	I go galloping and cantering
聊以忘憂	for a while to forget my cares.

Songs like this one preserved under Cao Pi's name are filled with common topics that could lead the poet off in many directions. The figure of the boat swept by the current is a particularly apt one because, at a certain point, the poem is also swept along by the inertia of the theme. Unless we know that wearing nice clothes is a possible poetic consolation against mortality, there is nothing here to explain how galloping about will help him "forget his cares."

Let us say that the poet does not turn down the path to the imagined world of the dead, but rather takes the road to the feast, where he can celebrate his fine clothes and enjoy the carousing that are beyond the reach of the dead. We have been trying to keep "theme" and "topic" apart as distinct levels, but it is not so simple: poets are free to elaborate, and what may have been a simple topic of one or two lines in most poems may become an extended passage in another poem. One important difference does remain: a standard poetic theme invites a sequence of topics that appear often in the corpus; topics, however, are expanded by a rhetoric of exposition found more commonly in prose and poetic expositions. The speaker in "Nineteen Old Poems" XIII is content to simply advise the anxious mortal to drink and dress well. In "Weeds on a Large Wall," attributed to Cao Pi, good clothes and the speaker's sword are lavishly celebrated as an adjunct to the pleasures of entertainment and feasting.

曹丕, 大牆上蒿行 Cao Pi, Weeds on a Large Wall: Ballad[29]

陽春無不長成	In springtime all things grow to fullness,
草木群類隨大風起	then plants and trees of all kinds follow the great wind rising.[30]
零落若何翩翩	Nothing can stop the fluttering as they shed their leaves,
中心獨立一何煢	how lonely the stalks stand by themselves![31]
四時舍我驅馳	The four seasons gallop on, abandoning me,
今我隱約欲何爲	what can I do now in such straits?
人生居天壤間	Man is born to live between Heaven and Earth,
忽如飛鳥棲枯枝	as fleeting as bird perching on withered branch.
我今隱約欲何爲	what can I do now in such straits?
適君身體所服	Suit yourself with things to wear,
何不恣君口腹所嘗	why not taste whatever your mouth and belly like?
冬被貂鼲溫暖	In winter wear the warm sable and squirrel,
夏當服綺羅輕涼	in summer wear light, cool gossamer.
行力自苦	To make myself suffer with effort—
我將欲何爲	why should I do it?
不及君少壯之時	Better when young and strong,
乘堅車策肥馬良	to ride sturdy coaches, whip sleek, fine horses.
上有滄浪之天	Above there are the gray Heavens,
今我難得久來視	but I will not get to look on them long.
下有蠕蠕之地	Below is the Earth that wriggles,[32]
今我難得久來履	but now I will not get to tread on it long.
何不恣意邀遊	Why not please yourself and go roaming,
從君所喜	doing what you delight in?
帶我寶劍	This precious sword that I wear,
今爾何爲自低卬	why now do you swing up and down?
悲麗平壯觀	I am moved by the grand sight of your vigor and flatness,
白如積雪	silvery as the drifts of snow,

---

29. Lu Qinli, 396; *Yfsj* 39. Huang Jie, *Wei Wudi*, 53–55.

30. The autumn wind.

31. This plays on the "stalks" of the plants, which is also the "heart within," *zhongxin* 中心, of a person.

32. "Wriggles" with life.

利如秋霜	sharp as the autumn frost.
駁犀摽首	Horn of unicorn and rhino mark the hilt,
玉琢中央	with jade carved in the middle.
帝王所服	Something worn by an emperor
辟除凶殃	to eliminate evil.
御左右奈何致福祥	When he governs those around him, how can he help but bring good fortune?

吳之辟閭	Wu's sword Pilü,
越之步光	Yue's "Walking Ray,"
楚之龍泉	Chu's "Dragon Spring,"
韓有墨陽	There was Moyang in Han,[33]
苗山之鋌	and the ingots of Miao Mountain.[34]
羊頭之鋼	and the steel of Sheepshead,
知名前代	their fame known in ages past,
咸自謂麗且美	and all were thought lovely and fair;
曾不如君劍良	but none are as good as your sword.
綺難忘	whose fineness cannot be forgotten.

冠青雲之崔嵬	Wear a cap that towers to the blue clouds,
纖羅爲纓	with hat-ribbons of delicate gossamer,
飾以翠翰	ornamented with kingfisher feathers,
既美且輕	beautiful and light.
表容儀	It shows your stylish demeanor,
俯仰垂光榮	above and below shedding splendid light.
宋之章甫	The *zhangfu* cap of Song,
齊之高冠	the tall hats of Qi,
亦自謂美	it is claimed they were lovely,
蓋何足觀	but how are they worth consideration?

排金鋪	Push open the gilded portals,
坐玉堂	sit in the jade hall.
風塵不起	The breeze raises no dust,
天氣清涼	the weather is clear and cool.
奏桓瑟	The huan zither of Qi is played,
舞趙倡	Zhao performers dance,
女娥長歌	the maidens sing long,
聲協宮商	their voices match notes of the melody.
感心動耳	It stirs the heart and moves the ears,
蕩氣回腸	sweeps the breath and turns feelings within.

酌桂酒	Pour the cinnamon ale,
繪鯉魴	offer slices of carp and bream.

---

33. Moyang was a place that produced swords in the ancient state of Han.
34. Miao Mountain was in Chu.

與佳人期爲樂康	Expect to have joy and ease with fair ladies.
前奉玉卮	Lift the jade flagon before you
爲我行觴	and pass the goblet to me.
今日樂不可忘	The joy this day cannot be forgotten,
樂未央	And the joy is not yet exhausted.
爲樂常苦遲	We always wait too late for finding joy,
歲月逝	the years and months pass on,
忽若飛	as swiftly as in flight.
何爲自苦	Why make yourself miserable
使我心悲	and make the heart sad?

This is one of the longest of the non-narrative *yuefu*, but its extensive elaboration is framed within one of the most common sequences of topics in early poetry: (1) life is short, (2) so make merry. When faced with mortality, the speaker has choices. Here as in several earlier examples, in conjunction with his poetic choice the speaker rejects one of the alternatives, in this case working hard: "To make myself suffer with effort—why should I do it?" The second section announces the two primary themes for elaboration: wear good clothes and eat and drink what you like. Following this we have the section praising a sword, then one on nice hats (developing the "clothing" theme), and a feast section on "wine, women, and song," with a coda urging the listener to seize pleasure in the moment.

Some of the Cao Pi attributions are questionable, but there is no reason this poem could not have been composed by him. The rhymes are easy; and rather than matching an existing melody, a poem like this was probably freely improvised to music around a standard theme, while taking into account a sword and hat, of which the singer was particularly proud.

As we suggested above, such fuller development of topics was more common in poetic expositions, *fu*. Here we can find the most extensive third-century descriptions of feasting in "sevens," *qi* 七, such as Wang Can's "Seven Explanations," *Qi-shi* 七釋.[35] Here we have elaborate descriptions of pleasures

---

35. Although this was extensively quoted in commentary and encyclopedia sources, an apparently complete version was preserved in the surviving chapters of the *Wenguan cilin* 文館詞林, compiled by Xu Jingzong 許敬宗 (592–672). Luo Guowei 羅國威, *Ri cang Hongrenben Wenguan cilin jiaozheng* 日藏弘仁本文館詞林校證 (Beijing: Zhonghua shuju, 2001), 130–34.

under various headings (food, clothing, music, etc.) in a tradition extending back to Mei Sheng's "Seven Stimuli," *Qifa* 七發, in the Western Han. The known poets who composed or to whom were attributed these poems and *yuefu* had the verbal resources to do far more rhetorically elaborate work, and evidence suggests that these more elaborate texts were seen as the center of their literary output in the third century. As we have argued above, the interest in their poetry in the five syllable line seems in large measure a function of the growing status of that form of poetry through the fifth century and a new aesthetic capacity to appreciate its relative simplicity and crudeness. That more capacious sense of poetic values, however, did not extend to "Weeds on a Large Wall," which had to await Qing critics to be noticed at all. This is one of those pieces of the manuscript tradition that did not fully surface until *Yuefu shiji* (although *Beitang shuchao* and Li Shan cite lines from the sword passage).

Perhaps because it was itself the primary site of an occasion for song, the feast is one of the least stable themes. Sleeplessness on an autumn night or seeking the immortals were relatively predictable themes; the feast oscillates between pleasure and despair. The mood can change in a moment, as in an untitled poem attributed to Chen Lin in *Yiwen leiju*:[36]

高會時不娛	At a grand gathering for a moment I was not happy,
羈客難爲心	a sojourner cannot keep his spirits up.
愍懷從中發	Dark brooding came from within,
悲感激清音	mournful feelings were stirred by the clear notes.
投觴罷歡坐	I put down my goblet and quit the merry feast,
逍遙步長林	I paced aimlessly through a tall forest.
蕭蕭山谷風	The wind whistled in the mountain valley,
黯黯天路陰	dark above, Heaven's paths lay in shadow.
惆悵忘旋反	Depressed, I forgot to turn back,
歔欷涕霑襟	sobbing, tears soaked the fold of my gown.

36. Lu Qinli, 367; *Ywlj* 28. Han Geping, *Jian'an*, 122–23; Wu Yun, *Jian'an*, 85–86.

A poem like this cannot be explained entirely by the poetics of the age; it is as if a feast poem suddenly turned into one of Ruan Ji's "Singing of My Cares." The speaker begins with a momentary alienation from the mood of the feast. The affect of the music is unpredictable. Here it drives the speaker out to walk alone in the woods at night. Although the poet turns off onto an uncharted poetic road, it still has familiar sign-posts: the first couplet mentions the feast; the second couplet mentions the music; the affect of the music is also mentioned; and the poem ends, as so many poems of the period do, with tears soaking the poet's clothes. Although it has been transposed here into something unfamiliar, there may be one other familiar signpost in Chen Lin's dark banquet poem: the music often inspires the listener with a desire to go off—to gallop away and do something or fly away as a pair of birds. Chen Lin is indeed inspired to go off by the music, and perhaps there is even the memory of the poetic bird when the speaker looks up to specifically "Heaven's paths," now lost in the darkness.

The poet may be in the wilderness, but he is taking some of the familiar turns of the feast poem:

Nineteen Old Poems IV[37]

今日良宴會	A fine feast we hold this day,
歡樂難具陳	its pleasures are hard to fully tell.
彈箏奮逸響	Plucked zithers give forth trailing echoes,
新聲妙入神	popular tunes, so fine they belong to the gods.[38]
令德唱高言	One of fine virtue sings forth noble words,[39]
識曲聽其眞	those who know song heed its truth.[40]

---

37. Lu Qinli, 330; *Wen xuan* 29. Sui Shusen, *Gushi*, 6–7; Diény, *Les dix-neuf poèmes anciens*, 14–15, 71–77.

38. *Rushen* 入神, lamely translated as "they belong to the gods," suggests a quality that is more than earthly or corporeal.

39. This line has caused much controversy, and some commentators have wanted to take it as ironic. *Gao yan* 高言 is not elsewhere used in early poetry, and not commonly in prose. Lu Yun uses it in a letter to Lu Ji to praise the latter's poetic expositions; see Yan Kejun 嚴可均, *Quan shanggu sandai Qin Han sanguo liuchao wen* 全上古三代秦漢三國六朝文 (Beijing: Zhonghua shuju, 1965), 2042.

40. "Knowing the song" is usually having an understanding of the quality and significance of music. Whether the "truth" is in the words or the quality of the music is uncertain.

齊心同所願	Hearts equal, we share the same wish,[41]
含意俱未伸	the sense held back, not fully expressed.
人生寄一世	Man's life sojourns in a single age,
奄忽若飆塵	it fleets by like dust tossed by the wind.
何不策高足	Why not whip on a high-hoofed steed,
先據要路津	be the first to seize the ford.
無爲守貧賤	Don't stay poor and of low degree,
軨軏長苦辛	struggling and ever bitter.

This is one of the finest of the "Nineteen Old Poems," and Chen Lin's verse is a useful foil against which to read it. It begins conventionally, declaring the joy of the feast. Yet even in the commonplace gesture of praise, "hard to fully tell," there is some surplus of feeling that cannot be brought to the surface. In the second couplet, beginning the topic of music, we also see the music somehow slipping out of this world. Both inside the listeners and outside this ordinary world there is something extra. There is something too in the "noble words," not necessarily the surface, but something to be understood and heeded, *ting* 聽, by those who understand.

All that is beneath the surface is summed up in the fourth couplet: listening to the music, all feel and wish the same unspoken thing. Listening to music in other poems often leads to a "wish," *yuan* 願, to fly away; here it seems to be to gallop away—but first the familiar couplet on the brevity of life, with the simile "dust tossed by the wind," like the dust tossed up by the "high-hoofed steed.[42] Chen Lin's poem ends with a statement of misery; "Nineteen Old Poems" IV ends with an injunction not to be miserable. The kinds of statements made are very different, but we cannot help noting that the same issue appears in the same position in each poem.

•

If the feast had some problematic surplus of feeling that could shift from joy over to despair or into some flurry of action, this energy could perhaps be controlled. Those who feel despair

---

41. Despite the poem's explicit reticence on what is wished, Li Shan suggests that they want to become "rich and noble." Diény cites *Lüshi chunqiu* to suggest they might want to find "someone who understands," a *zhiyin* 知音.

42. One might here recall the second version of "West Gate" 西門行 discussed above, in which after the feast and the lines on the brevity of life, the speaker rides off to the "edge of clouds," though apparently an immortal roaming with a "worn out nag" rather than a "high-hoofed steed."

(existential despair not included) could perhaps be convinced that everything was under control and that they could have a place in the order of things and their energy be put to good use. They come as "guests," perhaps travelers or sojourners; the host can convince them that this is a place of order and security and they are welcome to stay.

The feast could thus serve a political function, and its poetry could support that purpose. Cao Cao was not an emperor; Cao Cao was a brilliant warlord contending for power in a world that initially had very many contenders for power. Cao Cao as warlord gathered men like he gathered territory. He was the patron-protector who used his control of the last Han court as effective propaganda: Cao Cao presented himself as the new version of the ancient Duke of Zhou, who had acted as regent for King Cheng. One of the most famous stories about the Duke of Zhou was his favorite: the Duke of Zhou was so eager to gather worthy men that on hearing that a fine guest had arrived, he would spit out his food if eating and wring out his hair if washing it in order to hurry to welcome the person.

曹操, 短歌行 Cao Cao, Short Song[43]

對酒當歌	Facing the ale while singing:[44]
人生幾何	How long does man's life last?
譬如朝露	Liken it to the morning dew,
去日苦多	the days gone by are all too many.
慨當以慷	Melancholy and full of feeling,
憂思難忘	care-filled thoughts, hard to forget.
何以解憂	How can one have release from cares?—
唯有杜康	there is only [the ale of] Du Kang.[45]
青青子衿	"Blue are your lapels,
悠悠我心	ever, ever in my mind."[46]
但爲君故	[Only because of you
沉吟至今	I brood on to this day.][47]

---

43. Li Qinli, 349; *Song shu*; *Wenxuan* 37; *Yfsj* 30. Huang Jie, *Wei Wudi*, 15–17; Diény, *Les poèmes de Cao Cao*, 108–17.
44. Or "Facing the ale one should sing."
45. Du Kang was the legendary inventor of ale and is here metonymic for it.
46. This is a quotation from "Your Lapels" 子衿 from the "Airs of Zheng" in the *Shi*. The blue lapels were associated with students. Apparently Cao Cao is addressing those who consider themselves Confucians.
47. This couplet does not appear in the Li Shan version of the *Wen xuan*.

呦呦鹿鳴	"*Yoo, yoo*, the deer cry out,
食野之苹	eating the flatweed of the wilds.
我有嘉賓	I have splendid guests,
鼓瑟吹笙	strum the zithers, blow the reed-organs."[48]
明明如月	Bright, bright is the moon,
何時可輟	when might it stop?[49]
憂從中來	Cares come from within,
不可斷絕	one may not cut them off.
越陌度阡	Crossing paths, traversing lanes,
枉用相存	you have gone out of your way to call on me.
契闊談讌	Chatting and feasting after long separation,
心念舊恩	the mind thinks on former kindnesses.
月明星稀	The moon is bright, the stars are few,
烏鵲南飛	crows and magpies are flying south.
繞樹三匝	They circle the tree three times around,
何枝可依	on what branch can they find a roost?
山不厭高	The mountain does not tire of being high,
海不厭深	the sea does not tire of being deep.[50]
周公吐哺	The Duke of Zhou spat out what he chewed,
天下歸心	and all the world turned to him.

We cannot easily assume that the anonymous *yuefu* "Grand!," *Shanzai xing* 善哉行, necessarily predates Cao Cao's famous "Short Song"; the two poems do, however, seem related as stanzaic *yuefu* in the four syllable line in which motifs of feasting and patronage are brought together.[51] In "Grand!" mortality and the feast weave back into a poem that ends with an image of immortality. Cao Cao's feast here loses the edge of despair with the promise of drink at the end of the second stanza. As in his "Ballad of Qiuhu" II ("I want to climb Taihua Mountain"), Cao Cao catches his listener's attention with a familiar theme and then carries it off in a new direction.

Much of this poem, Cao Cao's most famous, is either re-formulation of commonplaces or quotation. Perhaps the historical Cao Cao felt the actual sentiments described in the first

---

48. This quotes the first stanza of "The Deer Cry Out," the first of the *Xiaoya* and used in the Eastern Han for welcoming guests.

49. Some texts read *duo* 掇, "to grasp," instead of *chuo* 輟, "to stop."

50. This versifies a proverb.

51. The *Song shu* treats this as a series of eight line stanzas. I am here innocently following the rhyme groups.

two stanzas (or perhaps those sentiments were called up on reformulating the familiar motif); Cao Cao, however, was not someone who would have been bothered by some sense of inauthenticity in converting such sentiments and words to a welcome that was also a political invitation. More to the point, if one is holding a feast and receiving guests, this was the way to invite one's guests to drink. The Cao Cao of public prose was well known for his attempt to prohibit drinking; this is Cao Cao at a different time of life or in a different mood or on an occasion where the role of host had priority.

In the third and fourth stanzas, Cao Cao cites *Shijing*. "Blue are your lapels" is a sartorial way of recognizing the particular guest or guests in question. The person addressed is certainly not a "student," which classical commentary understands as the implication of the "blue lapels"; but this person must belong to one of those families identified with Classical learning. "Guests" with this kind of résumé were often old families (not like most of the upstart Daoists) and sometimes represented local power—though Cao Cao was not averse to taking on literary scholars simply to enhance his prestige. These families of scholars had very much become a social network in the second half of the second century. If the third stanza "recognizes" the guest, the fourth stanza turns to the "proper" feast poetry, a citation from the first of the "Lesser Odes," *Xiaoya*, which was performed at parties that wanted the cachet of elite status. These stanzas not only "recognize" the social standing of the guest, they also identify Cao Cao to the guest as someone who knows the classical forms. The song is a carefully crafted hybrid.

The next stanza returns to the motif of passing time and cares; it does not, however, return to the invitation to drink. Rather, the host continues in the following stanza to politely thank the guests for "going out of their way" to come see the host. Cao Cao defers and assumes a humble position, like the great patrons of the Warring States. The last two stanzas, however, reveal that the politeness was pure fiction: he knows that his guest or guests are not "going out of their way" for a social call; Cao Cao knows they want a place to "roost." Here Cao Cao declares his magnitude, the mountain and the sea that have the capacity for any addition. He concludes as the

Duke of Zhou, welcoming the worthy guest, with the promise that such behavior will eventually bring the whole world to him. The guest is told that he has chosen a patron wisely.

The feast was a way of constituting community; Cao Cao knew this and set himself at the head of such a community, attempting to make a polity out of the horse-riding mob of "Nineteen Old Poems" IV, with each person off to get the best for himself. In Cao Cao's surviving poems we usually have a sense of what he is doing—and what he is often doing is using song for political ends. It seems unlikely that Cao Pi composed all the *yuefu* preserved under his name; some, however, we can easily believe were his. His difference from his father is both his failing and his virtue. The feast poem was a supremely public act; Cao Pi's versions sometimes seem to intend to be public statements, but they can drift in odd directions.

曹丕, 善哉行 Cao Pi, Grand![52]

朝日樂相樂	In the morning, joy upon joy,
酣飲不知醉	we drink ourselves tipsy, without getting drunk.
悲絃激新聲	The sad strings stir popular songs,
長笛吐清氣	the long flutes emit clear breath.
絃歌感人腸	Songs sung to strings touch a man's heart,
四坐皆歡悅	all the guests present are delighted.
寥寥高堂上	Then, in the vast stillness of the great hall,
涼風入我室	a cool breeze enters my chamber.
持滿如不盈	If one maintains things at fullness, without spilling over,[53]
有德者能卒	someone with virtue can bring things to a good end.[54]
君子多苦心	The superior man usually has a long-suffering heart,
所愁不但一	the things that worry him are not one alone.
慊慊下白屋	Modestly he comes out of his plain cottage,
吐握不可失	spitting out his food and wringing his hair, he cannot let anyone escape him.[55]

---

52. Lu Qinli, 393; *Song shu; Yfsj* 36. Huang Jie, *Wei Wudi*, 38–40.

53. The figure of proper measure, "maintaining fullness without spilling over," was a commonplace in ancient and early medieval texts.

54. *Analects* XIX.12 (Zixia speaking): "Is it not the Sage who can both begin things and bring them to a good end?" 有始有卒者, 其惟聖人乎.

55. This is the Duke of Zhou, eager to gather worthy men.

衆賓飽滿歸	When all the guests return, having eaten their fill,
主人苦不悉	the host's troubles are not over.
比翼翔雲漢	If, wing to wing, they soar in the Milky Way,
羅者安所羈	how can the fowler entrap them?
沖静得自然	If, empty and calm, one attains the state of nature,
榮華何足爲	how are glory and splendor worthwhile?

I will not pass judgment on drinking in the morning. The first two stanzas begin with the formulaic congratulations of the singer's coda. There is music and drinking—and human feeling being stirred between the two. There is also the presence of Cao Pi the anxious moralist. We should always retain a degree of skepticism about texts and attributions of early poetry. Sometimes, however, there are moves that are so characteristic of poems attributed to a particular person and so uncharacteristic of third-century poetics as a whole that we can easily believe (belief is cheap) this *is* Cao Pi. Here we find such a move in passing from the pleasure of the feast to an anxiety about excess: "if one maintains things at fullness, without spilling over." The feast indeed tends toward excess. Like his father attempting to prohibit drinking, Cao Pi worries about excess; rather than simply issuing an edict, Cao Pi thinks and versifies: "I'm glad everyone is having a good time; I hope they don't drink too much; the best thing is to stop just before excess; I'm always worried; like my father I want to be the Duke of Zhou in receiving guests, but the guests are all gone and here I am still worrying." Our comic paraphrase of the poem is comic only because it makes the strange twists and turns of the text explicit. When Chen Lin leaves the company of the feasters and writes a poem, there are still common traces of many feast poems. The Cao princes were a singular lot; in contrast to the transmission of other poetry, Cao Cao, Cao Pi, and Cao Rui also had an institutional apparatus to write down extempore composition and preserve it with loving care. I have no idea if Chen Lin wrote the poem attributed to him above; it leaves the conventions of the feast poem, but in a way that could have happened to almost anyone. In the case of Cao Pi's song above the peculiarly anxious process of free association is as persuasively

Cao Pi's own as Cao Cao's masterful sequence of quotation and cliché.

The last four lines of Cao Pi's lyric, however, are something else. We have seen earlier how the feast and the invocation of music may lead to the desire to get away or fly away as a pair of birds (here the "wing to wing"). Having poetically achieved models for the reception and management of guests, why he—or they—should want to fly away is unclear. Since the fowler is the anomalous element, we could put this down to Cao Pi's anxieties about political enemies. However, the inertia of poetic convention may have called to mind these images of flight and transcendence; moreover, these images have been called forth in a moment that previously had no place in the feast tradition, the host's continuing cares after the guests have gone home. If the usual feast song wants to escape death and misery, Cao Pi's song sounds almost as though he wants to escape the oppressive model of the Duke of Zhou's attentiveness (received from Cao Cao) and the constant strains of being a patron.[56]

•

Liu Xie, the famous critic of the Qi and Liang, tends to have rather conservative opinions of particular authors; in one case, however, he goes against what he knows is a consensus in judging Cao Pi to have no less talent than his brother Cao Zhi. Certainly Cao Pi is rarely as polished as his younger brother, but there is a quirkiness in many of his poems that has an attraction all its own. The feast always borders on excess: Cao Pi wants to "hold things at fullness, without spilling over." Cao Zhi is always willing to take the extra step into excess.[57]

---

56. We are content to accept the poem as Cao Pi's, but we cannot but be troubled when a close variation on the ending reappears at the end of the first "An Account of My Aims" 述志 by Xi Kang (Lu Qinli, 488). This suggests that the conclusion was a floating verse, open to reuse. Cao Pi's version seems to appear by the inertia of convention, while Xi Kang's version is more closely integrated with the theme of the poem, escape from the everyday world. A more remote variation occurs in a He Yan 何晏 fragment, "Stating My Aims" 言志, "Swans roamed wing to wing" 鴻鵠比翼遊 (Lu Qinli, 468).

57. For a much fuller discussion of Cao Zhi's feast poems, see Robert Joe Cutter, "Cao Zhi's (192–232) Symposium Poems," *CLEAR* 6 (1984): 1–32.

曹植, 箜篌引 Cao Zhi, Song of the Harp[58]

置酒高殿上	We serve ale in the high hall,
親友從我遊	friends and kindred amuse themselves in my company.
中廚辦豐膳	In the kitchens are prepared rich provisions,
烹羊宰肥牛	simmer mutton and slaughter the fatted ox.
秦箏何慷慨	How strong the feeling from the Qin dulcimer,
齊瑟和且柔	the great zither of Qi is harmonious and gentle.
陽阿奏奇舞	From Yang'e wondrous dances are presented,[59]
京洛出名謳	from Luoyang come famous ballads.
樂飲過三爵	Drinking merrily we exceed the three cups.[60]
緩帶傾庶羞	loosening sashes, we try the full range of assorted delicacies.
主稱千金壽	The host makes toasts of a thousand in silver,
賓奉萬年酬	guests respond, wishing him myriad years.
久要不可忘	One cannot forget old bonds,[61]
薄終義所尤	unfeeling ends are censured by a sense of right.[62]
謙謙君子德	Self-effacing is the virtue of the superior man,
磬折欲何求	but in bowing low, what does he seek?
驚風飄白日	Blasts of wind whirl the bright sun away,
光景馳西流	the light goes racing to the west.

---

58. Lu Qinli, 424, given as 野田黃雀行. *Song shu*; *Wen xuan* 27; *Yfsj* 39. Huang Jie, *Cao Zijian*, 60–62; Nie Wenyu, *Cao Zhi*, 56–62; Zhao Youwen, *Cao Zhi*, 459–62.

59. Yang'e is either a place-name, where Zhao Feiyan, later Han Chengdi's empress, was first indentured, or it is the name of an ancient singer. The place-name provides a more perfect parallel with Luoyang.

60. According to the *Li ji*, a superior person is supposed to withdraw after drinking three cups.

61. *Analects* XIV.13: 久要不忘平生之言 "In old bonds he does not forget what he said earlier in life."

62. The phrase *bo zhong* 薄終 is a problem. Most likely it refers to the old *Shi* adage that while all begin well, few come to a good end (cf. Cao Pi, "Shan zai xing"). In speaking of "old bonds," this is probably "the way things work out in the end." *Bo* is both "stinginess" and "lack of feeling."

盛時不可再	Glorious times will not come again,
百年忽我遭	our hundred years suddenly draw to an end.
生存華屋處	Alive I was kept in splendid rooms,
零落歸山丘	fallen, I return to the mountain and mound.[63]
先民誰不死	Who of our forebears did not die?—
知命復何憂	if one understands fate, what more is there to worry about?

This is a much simpler poem than Cao Pi's. There are snatches of the low register feast song here and there, but as in his poetry on immortals Cao Zhi phrases and organizes materials in a highly independent way, without in the least complicating the elementary message to eat, drink, and make merry because life is short.

With Cao Zhi's literary transformation of the feast song we come to the edge of a new question, which is the elite literary poetry of the Jian'an and its relation to the conventions of lower register poetry.

The Lord's Feast[64]

It is clear from the repertoire of song lyrics from the "Wei" (obviously including the Jian'an Reign of the Han) preserved in the *Song shu* that neither Cao Cao nor Cao Pi objected to low register song being performed for parties in their presence; both seem to have participated in such composition. It may, indeed, have been Cao Cao's somewhat plebeian taste that led to the preservation in the Wei repertoire of many of the anonymous *yuefu*. These *yuefu* come to us through the records of the Jin court repertoire preserved in the *Song shu*. It seems equally clear that the low register poetics we have been describing was familiar to the Seven Masters. Despite these facts, it is also apparent that on certain kinds of occasion, including one designated as a "lord's feast," *gongyan* 公讌 (or 公燕), a poetry in

---

63. Perhaps this is a general reference to tomb mound, though Taishan has been suggested, where the souls of the dead enter the underworld.

64. I adopt here the translation of *gongyan* used by Cutter, "Cao Zhi's (192–232) Symposium Poems." This article treats the "lord's feast" in a broader and fuller context than this present discussion.

a much higher register was expected. Of particular significance is the fact that relatively high register poetry in the five syllable line was expected, rather than the ritual formality of stanzaic poetry in the four syllable line.

We have a few rather clumsy poems in the five syllable line that credibly date from the second half of the second century. These works show the influence of the common poetics, but they are essentially private compositions. Not only are these "lord's feast" poems social works composed in the presence of a community of other writers, they demanded of five-syllable-line poetry a decorum and elevation of register for which no precedent survives. This was a culturally "serious" occasion, and Xiao Tong included four such Jian'an poems in the *Wen xuan*.

Some of the Jian'an poems for lord's feasts may have been written on the same occasion; but the seasons differ often enough to know that this was a repeated occasion for poetry rather than a single party. The host praised is often Cao Pi (though this is uncertain in the poems with a general title), and the poems date from sometime between 208 and 217.

Considering the concluding reference to the Duke of Zhou, it is likely that the surviving Wang Can poem on such an occasion was for a party at which Cao Cao served as host.[65]

王粲, 公讌詩 Wang Can, Lord's Feast[66]

昊天降豐澤	The summery heavens send down enriching moisture,
百卉挺葳蕤	all the plants rise upright, burgeoning.
涼風撤蒸暑	A cool breeze dispels the muggy heat,
清雲卻炎暉	clear clouds make the fiery glow retreat.
高會君子堂	A grand party is held in the gentleman's hall,
並坐蔭華榱	we sit side by side, shaded by decorated beams.
嘉肴充圓方	Excellent viands fill the round and square vessels,
旨酒盈金罍	choice ales brim the golden beakers.
管絃發徽音	Pipes and strings give forth splendid notes,
曲度清且悲	the melody's measure is clear and mournful.

---

65. Although we have seen Cao Pi invoke the model of the Duke of Zhou, Wang Can died before Cao Cao; and it is very unlikely that a poet would have referred to Cao Pi in terms of the Duke of Zhou during Cao Cao's lifetime.

66. Lu Qinli, 360; *Wen xuan* 20. Wu Yun, *Wang Can*, 19–20.

合坐同所樂	Sitting together we share in joy,
但愬杯行遲	complaining only that the cups pass too slowly.
常聞詩人語	I have heard a phrase of the *Shi* poet,
不醉且無歸	of not going home unless drunk.[67]
今日不極歡	If we don't enjoy our pleasure today to the fullest,
含情欲待誰	for whom are we waiting, holding back our feelings?
見眷良不翅	Truly there is no limit to the fond regard I am shown,
守分豈能違	yet how can I err in keeping to my place?
古人有遺言	A phrase comes down from the ancients:
君子福所綏	the gentleman is soothed by his blessings.[68]
願我賢主人	I wish that my worthy host
與天享巍巍	will enjoy towering along with the heavens.
克符周公業	He can match the legacy of the Duke of Zhou,
奕世不可追	not again to be equaled by generations on end.

We have been describing a "shared poetics," one that crossed the later divisions between "poetry" and *yuefu*, a poetics shared by anonymous poetry and poems by known third-century writers. The habitual themes and sequences of topics were very strong and can be seen even in poems that ostensibly set off in new directions. In some other poems Wang Can shows a deep familiarity with these conventions, which seem to guide his poetic associations, as they do in low register poems by anonymous poets. Even though we can see some traces of the low register feast poem here, however, our most striking impression of this poem is its relative independence from all those compositional conventions. This is, in some senses, a truly new poetry, a poetry that works by different rules. When we suggest this, it is in no way to suggest that it supplanted the older poetics; we can see traces of those compositional conventions even among the most elite poets active after the turn of the fourth century. Rather, this was a new order of poetry in the five syllable line, a rhetorical "seriousness" as a form of public deference that acknowledged political power. In this period

---

67. *Shi* 174.
68. *Yuanyang* 鴛鴦 in the *Xiaoya*.

(and throughout medieval and late imperial China) register and poetic structure reflected hierarchy and served to place a poet within a structure of social and political power (which includes a rejection of such a structure). In saying this, we must at the same time point out that this higher register is still relatively simple and comprehensible aurally: when we compare, say, the food and drink couplets here with the long celebrations of exotic delicacies in Wang Can's "Seven Explanations," mentioned earlier, or Cao Zhi's "Seven Openings," *Qiqi* 七啓, we can appreciate that these "lord's feast" poems gesture to a high register without demonstrating erudite rhetorical mastery.

Cao Cao himself might rise at a party and begin a song with the line "Facing the ale while singing." There is no season and no setting; song is repeatable, and these words can be repeated in any season (even the southward flying crows and magpies are sufficiently figurative to show up in any season). This was the prerogative of the host and perhaps of his professional singers. The attendant literary man, by contrast, showed both his own class and his deference to his host by composing a "poem" of a very different sort. He begins with the seasonal setting in summer, balancing Heaven's "sending down," *jiang* 降, with what "rises upright," *ting* 挺, from Earth. The seasonal imagery is replete with associations in the human social order, of enriching grace from above, answered by a "flowering" of plants and words from below. Summer, of course, can be unpleasantly hot, thus the second couplet reassures us of the pleasantness of the weather in nicely parallel lines and high register diction.

Only in the third couplet do we come to the party proper. Lower register poetry would begin with some counterpart of this line: "A grand party is held in the gentleman's hall" 高會君子堂. In contrast to the death-shadowed feast poems, where we are encouraged to translate the presentation of food and drink in the imperative, the poet here is clearly describing and celebrating what is provided; moreover, the high register and the parallelism lend decorum to the feast, even when there is a claim of drunkenness. In "West Gate" we also have parallelism, but it is almost invisible:

飲醇酒	Drink the pure ale,
炙肥牛	roast the fatted ox,

In Wang Can:

嘉肴充圓方	Excellent viands fill the round and square vessels,
旨酒盈金罍	choice ales brim the golden beakers.

We don't know who wrote the first "food and ale" couplet for one of these Jian'an parties, but once in circulation, it became a template couplet for other poets. In "Attending at the Crown Prince's [Cao Pi] Party" 待太子坐詩, Cao Zhi writes:[69]

清醴盈金觴	Clear, sweet ale brims metal flagons,
餚饌縱橫陳	fine foods are arrayed this way and that.

In Cao Pi's "Written in Qiao" 於譙作:[70]

豐膳漫星陳	Sumptuous victuals spread as an array of stars,
旨酒盈玉觴	choice ales brim the jade flagons.

In Cao Pi's poem "Meng Ford" 孟津詩, it becomes:[71]

羽爵浮象樽	Feathered tankards drift with ivory cups,
珍膳盈豆區	precious victuals brim plates on stands.

Indeed, as we read earlier in Ruan Yu's poem, it is just such a feast denied to the dead:

嘉肴設不御	Excellent viands are set out, but I cannot dine,
旨酒盈觴杯	choice ales brim flagons and goblets.

The next couplet takes up music; and apart from the high register term *hui* 徽, "splendid," this couplet is closest to low register poetics. Indeed, in Wang Can's own "Sevenfold Sorrow" II, after walking along the bank and then retiring, there is a familiar move from the common poetics:

獨夜不能寐	Alone at night I cannot sleep,
攝衣起撫琴	I lift robes, get up, and strum the zither.
絲桐感人情	The silk and tung wood stir a man's feelings,
爲我發悲音	on my behalf it gives forth mournful notes.

---

69. Lu Qinli, 450.
70. Ibid., 399.
71. Ibid., 400.

"Silk and tung wood" is metonymic for the zither, like the more common "silk and bamboo," *sizhu* 絲竹, which is metonymic for stringed instruments and woodwinds; the latter poetic metonymy could be varied to *guanxian* 管絃, "pipes and strings." If we combined the third and fourth lines from the Wang Can passage above into a single line and wanted to give it a boost in register by changing the ordinary *bei* 悲, "mournful" (functionally equivalent to "moving"), to a word like "splendid," we would come up with the line:

管絃發徽音　　　Pipes and strings give forth splendid
　　　　　　　　notes,

One should, however, mention that the music is "mournful"; this term is displaced into the following line in Wang Can's poem:

曲度清且悲　　　the melody's measure is clear and
　　　　　　　　mournful.

We might here recall what happened to Chen Lin at the feast:

愍懷從中發　　　Dark brooding came from within,
悲感激清音　　　mournful feelings were stirred by the
　　　　　　　　clear notes.

The "sentiments" in these recurring lines are the same; but more important, the same words recur and the same grammatical patterns. When Cao Pi is having a boating party in "Written at Qinghe" 清河作, the music plays:

絃歌發中流　　　Songs and strings come forth midstream,
悲響有餘音　　　the mournful echoes have lingering notes.

After the couplet on food and drink in Cao Zhi's "Attending at the Crown Prince's Party," quoted above, we have the music couplet.

齊人進奇樂　　　Folk of Qi present rare music,
歌者出西秦　　　singers come from Qin in the West.

It is not simply that line templates recur; we also find the same sequences of topics. In Wang Can's poem above, the couplet on song follows the couplet on food and drink. We have quoted Cao Pi's couplet on food and drink in "Written in Qiao"; the couplet that follows is:

| 絃歌奏新曲 | Strings and song perform new melodies, |
| 游響拂丹梁 | the roaming echoes brush the cinnabar beams. |

We have singers here, so the compound is "strings and song"; the verb in the third position is *zou* 奏, "to perform," rather than *fa* 發, "give forth," or *jin* 進, "present." We have "melodies" rather than "notes." In the first "To the Leader of Court Gentlemen for Miscellaneous Uses [Cao Pi]" 贈五官中郎將詩, Liu Zhen reverses the order of the music and feasting couplets, but the patterns should be familiar:[72]

清歌製妙聲	Clear songs fashion wondrous sounds,
萬舞在中堂	the "dance of the myriad" is here in the hall.
金罍含甘醴	Golden beakers hold sweet ales within,
羽觴行無方	feathered flagons are passed around without set ceremony.

The sequence continues. Wang Can adds a sentiment from the common repertoire, to which is affixed a polite praise of the host:

| 合坐同所樂 | Sitting together we share in joy, |
| 但愬杯行遲 | complaining only that the cups pass too slowly. |

We recall, perhaps, the couplet after the description of music in "Nineteen Old Poems" IV:

| 齊心同所願 | Hearts equal, we share the same wish, |
| 含意俱未伸 | the sense held back, not fully expressed. |

If the couplet from "Nineteen Old Poems" IV has something "held back," *han* 含, as well as something shared (*tong suo* 同所), we might then look again at a couplet that comes soon after in Wang Can's poem:

| 今日不極歡 | If we don't enjoy our pleasure today to the fullest, |
| 含情欲待誰 | for whom are we waiting, holding back our feelings? |

---

72. Ibid., 369.

This is a purely verbal sequence, the same words and phrases repeated in the same order as in "Nineteen Old Poems" IV; the recurring word, however, is in a different topic—indeed, a common one in the feast poem. For example, "Nineteen Old Poems" XV:

| 爲樂當及時 | To make merry we must seize the moment. |
| 何能待來茲 | how can we wait for some year to come? |

Or there is the version of the same lines in "West Gate," which is even closer to Wang Can's lines:

| 今日不作樂 | If I don't make merry today, |
| 當待何時 | what moment am I waiting for? |

Between the couplet that refers to "what is shared" and the couplet on something "held back," Wang Can offers a couplet that refers to the *Shijing*:

| 常聞詩人語 | I have heard a phrase of the *Shi* poet, |
| 不醉且無歸 | of not going home unless drunk. |

After the food couplet and the music couplet, Liu Zhen, in the same poem quoted above, also mentions the issue of going home:

| 長夜忘歸來 | Through the long night we forget to go home, |
| 聊且爲太康 | and for a while there is perfect weal. |

After expressions of gratitude and humility, Wang Can concludes like a professional singer, though the phrasing half-hides the common gesture. I have translated the second line of the couplet literally and awkwardly:

| 願我賢主人 | I wish that my worthy host |
| 與天享巍巍 | enjoy towering along with the heavens. |

The "towering" something that the host is wished is most certainly a life as long as Heaven. We see that same wish at the end of the anonymous *yuefu* "Qiao the Prince" 王子喬:[73]

| 聖主享萬年 | May our Sage Ruler enjoy ten thousand years, |
| 悲今皇帝延壽命 | I am moved that our present Emperor extends his lifespan. |

---

73. Ibid., 262.

In "The Five Wanderings" 五遊詠 Cao Zhi swallows an elixir:

王子奉仙藥	Qiao the Prince offered me immortal drugs,
羨門進奇方	Xianmen Zigao brought me wondrous techniques.
服食享遐紀	I swallowed them and enjoy a far-reaching span,
延壽保無疆	life extended, I preserve the unbounded.

We should note that in these and other cases, *xiang* 享, "enjoy," occupies the third position in the line. In "Dongtao Ballad" 董逃行, the singer ends:

陛下長與天相保守	Your Majesty will endure as long as Heaven.

Or consider the third version of "Breathe Out" 氣出倡:

常願主人增年	We wish the host an increase of years,
與天相守	to last as long as Heaven.

Finally, using resonantly archaic terms, Wang Can praises Cao Cao in his own favorite terms, as the Duke of Zhou.

The "lord's feast" represented (as far as we know) a new situation and a new decorum for poetry in the five syllable line. It was obviously related to the feast song, but, by social necessity, deprived of two of its most important components: the shortness of life and the closing "flight"—into action or to the world of the immortals. These poems sound very different, but not only are there old template lines recurring everywhere, the new patterns of topics and templates become quickly available for reuse by other poets writing for other "lord's feasts." That is, if there is a "new poetry" in the Jian'an, its compositional practice quickly becomes *functionally identical* to the old, low register practice: new sequences of topics and template lines replace old ones. Not all "lord's feast" poems are the same: the most common alternative version is the excursion.[74] But the pattern of Wang Can's version above is a repeated one. The Sui and Tang encyclopedias often quote only passages. When we read the "lord's feast" poem by Ruan Yu given in the *Chuxue ji*, we can tell exactly the point where the compiler of the encyclopedia stopped.

---

74. The excursion poem or the feast on an excursion has very different conventions, but a comparison of such poems shows that they too have conventional topics and templates.

阮瑀, 公讌詩 Ruan Yu, Lord's Feast[75]

陽春和氣動	In bright spring the balmy air stirs,
賢主以崇仁	our virtuous lord honors kindliness.
布惠綏人物	Extending grace, he soothes our gentlemen,
降愛常所親	bequeathing favor, he is constant in his affections.
上堂相娛樂	In the high hall we make merry,
中外奉時珍	seasonal delicacies, domestic and foreign, are served.
五味風雨集	The five flavors gather in a storm,
杯酌若浮雲	goblets of ale are like drifting clouds.

We have every reason to suppose that the next couplet must have been on the music.[76]

"Literary" poetry is created somewhere in between the common low register poetics and a range of discursive forms with considerably more status and requiring far more rhetorical learning and effort. This poetry was a hybrid produced for a court that expected composition in the five syllable line (an expectation for formal occasions that did not come back for several centuries). Its hybridity—the bastard child of true high register composition—may have preserved it, until it found its moment of honor in Xiao Tong, for whom it signified an early dignity in the composition of poetry in the five syllable line.

---

75. Lu Qinli, 380.

76. We have traces that confirm our expectations in such encyclopedia excerpts. The *Taiping yulan* version of Cao Pi's "Summer Day" 夏日詩 (Lu Qinli, 404) has the "food couplet" but not the "music couplet." Only two couplets of the same poem are cited in *Chuxue ji*, including the missing music couplet with the food couplet.

FIVE

Author and Speaker
(dai 代)

The idea of "authorship" was a historical formation in China, as it was in Europe. Since it was a process of formation, "authorship" can mean many things; it must, however, involve a claim that the particular words belong to a specific person and are not merely one possible articulation of a general truth. The words must be presumed to have been composed with that intention, to belong to the person, and they must be repeatable, usually in writing. Authorship, then, is more than a name attached to a book. We can see forms of proto-authorship in the late Warring States theory of Confucius's composition of the *Chunqiu* or philosophers who claimed possession of certain ideas that circulated in books to which their names were attached (even if other writings became attached to the same names).

Although one might like to claim earlier names for "authorship," Sima Qian is perhaps the central figure in the formation of "authorship" in China. For Sima Qian writing became a life project, to which his name was attached and based on which his life was justified. Even if we have a sense of authorship before Sima Qian, it is worth recalling how often we first see these figures as "authors" in the pages of Sima Qian. It is clear, for example, that there was a Qu Yuan legend attached to a corpus of poems before Sima Qian; but, for Sima Qian, Qu Yuan exists as the historical author of written texts that Sima Qian himself read. Qu Yuan is, indeed, an excellent illustration of the problems of early authorship, because he continued to exist as a compositional persona even after Sima Qian made him a literary "author."

"Authorship" in the sense we mean when we speak of Sima Qian consolidated through the last century of the Western Han, but there were other kinds of textual material. There were persona texts, ranging from verse using the persona of Qu Yuan to the posthumous lessons of Zhuang Zhou to the wise things that Confucius should have said (and, on reflection, must indeed have said). There was also much textual material that circulated freely: stories, sayings, ideas, political positions, popular analogies, and probably verses. Such material might have been placed in the mouth of some early figure, but it was not "authored."

It is, perhaps, a testimony to the cultural triumph of "authorship" that, apart from bamboo slips recently excavated, virtually all texts transmitted in the received tradition (apart from the Classics in some sense) come to us attached to some name (or names), even if that name is only Confucius as editor or a Han redactor. By the time of the Eastern Han textual authorship was fully developed in a form that is easily recognizable by our contemporary standards. Certain kinds of texts, texts with "authority," are cited with the name of the book or a writer. There was still, however, material of lesser status that either circulated without names or acquired names circumstantially. We recognize this in much anecdotal material and, I would argue, in much verse. Archaic poetry in the four syllable line was "serious," and authorial attributions of such poetry from the Han on are remarkably stable. This is not necessarily the case of poetry in the five syllable line and other meters. Cao Zhi's collection, for example, surely contained five syllable and irregular poems under his name at the time of its first full compilation, soon after his death. The growth of Cao Zhi's literary collection in the centuries that followed suggests that the authorial name served as a magnet for other texts that were circulating without a name.

We are accustomed to thinking of "authorship" as a historical fact; thus the first question we ask regarding an ascription of authorship is whether it is verifiable, credible, or merely fanciful. Without in any way invalidating this important historical question, it can be sometimes useful to think of the ascription of authorship as a property of a text. Thus when we see a famous version of "I Watered My Horse at a Hole by the Great Wall" ("Yin ma changcheng ku xing" 飲馬長城窟行) given as anonymous "old lyrics" (*guci* 古辭) in the *Wen xuan* and attributed to Cai Yong 蔡邕 in *Yutai xinyong*, the issue may not be deciding if Cai Yong was indeed the author; rather, we might ask what is at stake in these different descriptions ("Cai Yong" or "old lyrics") appended to the title. Since ascribing authorship had long been a positive value, the interesting phenomenon in this case was the possibly positive value of anonymity in poetry, which seems to have been something that happened in the late fifth and early sixth centuries.

Titles (and hence indications of "genre") change with such regularity in different sources that we suspect that early manuscripts often lacked titles: a verse might be an "old poem" or an "old *yuefu*" or acquire specific *yuefu* titles according to the impression or conviction of some compiler. The term *zashi* 雜詩, best translated as "unclassified poems," was probably a Southern Dynasties way of naming poems by known authors without titles; since such poems were often of a predictable range of types, it eventually became a subgenre, a categorical title assigned by poets themselves.[1]

In comparison to titles, ascription of authorship is relatively stable. Even when titles vary, by and large both full texts and passages are cited under the same authors. Although we do have a fair number of cases where a text is cited under different known authors, the majority of cases where there is a question are those in which a poem is given as anonymous or with an author. We can thus see authorship as the most stable "property" of a text, more stable than the title or particular words and challenged only by the cachet of anonymity.

Only in a few cases, such as the Cai Yong attribution of "I Watered My Horse at a Hole by the Great Wall," does ascribed authorship sometimes still win out over claims of anonymity. Anonymity is presumed earlier (and hence more precious). Lu

---

1. It is conceivable that Tao Qian actually entitled some of his poems *zashi*, since these are the earliest examples to appear outside the Liang anthologies. The fact that Tao's "imitations of the old poems" and *zashi* occur toward the end of his collection, as in the *Wen xuan* arrangement, may suggest an early sixth-century redaction.

Qinli still cites "I Watered My Horse" under Cai Yong's name (Lu Qinli, 192), but many anthologies have preferred to consider the poem anonymous. The desire to have only one set of anonymous lyrics for each *yuefu* title has probably kept Chen Lin's name as the author for the other early version (though it is cited as anonymously "old" in *Beitang shuchao*; Lu Qinli, 367).

The extant evidence suggests an early phase in the transmission of poetry in which anonymous texts were gaining authors. We can also see a history of values that resulted in some authors losing their acquisitions. Cao Zhi's present literary collection culls virtually all the verses attributed to his name in anthologies, encyclopedias, and the Li Shan commentary. In some sources, however, he is credited with one of the Nineteen Old Poems and two of the anonymous "old *yuefu*."[2] If modern collections of poetry generally disregard these particular attributions to Cao Zhi, it is not because we know one way or another, but because anonymity is the more attractive claim in these cases. At the same time all the other texts without competing claims are generally accepted as Cao Zhi's works.[3] There is an economy of value at work in belief and disbelief in attributions of authorship, but there are no critical or philological criteria. Authorship, which is usually a positive value, is an unwanted attribute for an anonymous "old poem" or *yuefu*.

Once we delve further into the textual tradition, we find the same phenomenon elsewhere. The anonymous *yuefu* most famously known as "Mulberries by the Path," "Moshang sang" 陌上桑 (among other titles), was clearly well known and had a substantial legacy of variation; it was included in both the "Treatise on Music" of the *Song shu* and the *Yutai xinyong*. Nevertheless, we find a version of the first half, the "prelude" (*yan'ge* 艷歌), included in Fu Xuan's 傅玄 (217–78) collection; this version is so close to the standard anonymous version that it cannot be considered an "imitation" by late third-century standards. Many lines are exactly the same; many lines are

---

2. The "old poem" is "Nineteen Old Poems" IV; Lu Qinli, 330. The *yuefu* are *Junzi xing* 君子行 and *Shanzai xing* 善哉行; Lu Qinli, 263, 266.

3. The authenticity of a range of texts in Cao Zhi's collection has been recognized as a problem; however, collections of Cao Zhi's poems generally include all the more or less complete works (sometimes including the fragments) under his name and often explain them in terms of his life. See Frankel, "The Problem of Authenticity in the Works of Cao Zhi."

within the standard range of textual variation; passages are omitted, which is common; passages are added, which is also common. Seeing the text listed under Fu Xuan's name, scholars read some of the variations as more "literary"; but I have little doubt that if chance had preserved this text as anonymous, it would simply have been given as a variant version of the "same" poem.[4] We should wonder how this could happen, how such a famous anonymous poem could be casually copied under the name of a famous mid-third-century author. Perhaps this was the version as Fu Xuan copied it, exercising the liberties that were the norm in reproducing a text like this; perhaps he was designated the "author" in the age that was assigning authorship to anonymous poems. Only later in the age of literary scholarship and fixed texts that accompanied print culture would the divergences of his "Prelude" be seen as an "imitation," rather than another version of the "same."

In the same vein Cao Pi has a version of "Looking Down from the High Terrace," *Lin gao tai* 臨高臺, the first part of which is identical to the anonymous *yuefu* from the *Naoge*, and the last part of which is a snatch from "Prelude: O When," discussed earlier. One way to understand this is the "mix and match" quality of song traditions. But if reuse and variation is the norm, when that process enters the age of naming authors, versions acquire particular names.

The *Wen xuan* does include some texts under authors we no longer credit, such as the poems by Lady Ban and Li Ling; however, most of its early poetic texts have a rather high degree of credibility. Otherwise we have some reason to be at least slightly skeptical about attributions in other unique sources, compiled from a diverse manuscript tradition that survived into the late fifth century and beyond.

•

The property of authorship is inseparable from acts of valuation; valuation, in turn, gives force to judgments of authenticity, whether the attribution of a text to a particular author is "genuine" or "spurious." The field on which the acts of valuation and judgment occur is an assumed literary historical narrative. If a work is anonymous, it can have value only by being early: it is one thing to say that a poem is by an unknown poet in the

---

4. See Appendix G.

Eastern Han; it is quite another to say that it is an unknown poet of the Jin. The anonymous *yuefu* "Dulu pian" 獨漉篇 (Lu Qinli, 846) would, I suspect, have been included among the canonical anonymous *yuefu* if the musical tradition had not specified that it was Jin.[5] A poem in the Cao Zhi corpus accrues value not only from the name but in being read in the context of Cao Zhi's life, both its known facts and imagined circumstances; if we remove the authorial name, the text becomes less interesting. The first poem in Ruan Ji's "Singing of My Cares" is, as we have seen, a brief and unsurprising treatment of the theme of sleeplessness; attached to Ruan Ji's name and the putative context of his historical moment, it becomes an anthology piece, invested with a richness of putative intentions.

We have a chronological narrative of authors and texts; to destabilize one part threatens to destabilize the whole. The Chinese author cannot "die," as Foucault would have it, if only because, in the context of Chinese poetics, authorship has become a necessary systemic function. Without the contextualizing cultural narrative, replete with authors, many poetic texts become unreadable. Such a claim, however, needs itself to be historicized: this was not necessarily true in all forms at all times.

For more than a millennium the beginnings of Chinese "classical poetry" have been fully historicized. Texts have been assigned to anonymity or authorship, while counterclaims of authorship or anonymity have been disputed, overlooked, or dismissed. From the early fifth century we can see a troubled sense of the "difference" in sets of poems, that they are *zongza*, a "mixed bag," with the admixture usually understood as inauthentic, in the sense of later materials creeping in among "pure" originals. In some cases, however, we find that the literary scholars of the turn of the sixth century were far less certain of authorship or its absence than later scholars.

Although Yan Yanzhi thought the Li Ling corpus was a mixed bag and Zhong Rong thought that the corpus of "old poems" was a mixed bag, it is important to keep in mind that there was an era and a level of manuscript preparation that compiled these two "mixed bags" without apparent qualm. It seems likely

---

5. By contrast, anonymity and a Jin dating is a good thing if a verse belongs to the lineage of short Southern *yuefu*.

that the poems in the Li Ling corpus originally had no titles beyond the attribution of the corpus as a whole (with the Liang anthologists designating some as "To Su Wu," or, ascribing a poem attributed to Su Wu, "To Li Ling"). It was probably from such anonymous and untitled verse collections that some texts acquired the property of authorship, while others simply remained "old," *gu* 古.

Since our sources are mostly much later, it is difficult to understand the situation of the transmission of poetry in the five syllable line in the third and fourth centuries. There were certainly individual literary collections with poems in the five syllable line from the third century, famous poems that made their way into the *Wen xuan*.[6] What generally marks the corpus of "floating" poetry (the "old poems," the Li Ling corpus, and the poems that with less certainty get attached to authors' names) is a lower register of diction. Here we must reiterate that this gives no indication of date, since poetry in a lower register was probably still being composed at the same time Lu Ji was writing five-syllable-line poetry in a very high register.

We cannot know, but we can describe a range in the relation between author and speaker. At one extreme were highly general, often intensely emotional poems that could be uttered in a particular circumstance and become extremely personal. Lack of specificity in the text had a value in inviting reuse in a wide variety of situations. Of these, the "Nineteen Old Poems" and some others survived as anonymous poems. Such survival was made possible by historically locating these poems in the Han, before the full development of poems in the five syllable line by known authors. In this historical location they acquired value by their anonymity.

On the next level toward authorship, there were poems of unknown authorship that seemed appropriate for a certain person to have uttered, a situation alluded to in the fifth of the "Nineteen Old Poems":

---

6. Although *Wen xuan* does include a generous selection of poems in the four syllable line, the partial manuscript of the *Wenguan cilin* recovered in Japan, with numerous poems in the four syllable line not elsewhere preserved, suggests that poetry in the five syllable line had a survival advantage. *Wenguan cilin* is a seventh-century anthology; thus we know that these poems survived into the Tang imperial library. Without very dry climates, however, survival in manuscript culture depends upon continuous and multiple copying.

誰能爲此曲	Who could make such a song?—
無乃杞梁妻	it must be none other than the wife of Qi Liang.[7]

Only the finest line separates the intuition that "it must be none other than" from ascription of a speaker as author. Once such an association is made and the poem is read as being by a particular speaker, a mutually confirming circularity can be created: one has a sense of the person through the poem, and one understands the poem through the person. The link between the fan poem and Lady Ban (to be discussed shortly) is just such a case; the attribution of the poem on Tiying to Ban Gu is similar. The famous parting between Li Ling and Su Wu was a way to ground general texts on parting in the voice of a particular speaker. If the attribution of a series of "old poems" to Mei Sheng never caught on, it is probably because there were no memorable particulars in Mei Sheng's life to which to link the poems.

By the third century we know there was a class of poems later called *daizuo* 代作, in which the author assumed the persona of some historically known character. Often these personae were people in the present (indeed, Lu Ji has a number of extant poems written "on behalf of" contemporaries); sometimes the poet assumed the persona of some historical figure. In poems explicitly designated or recognized as *daizuo* the distinction between "speaker" and "author" is clearest. No one attributes Shi Chong's poem on Wang Zhaojun to Wang Zhaojun herself. In the context of the poetic tradition, however, this is an unstable situation; and if authorship becomes the least bit uncertain, the speaker tends to become identified with the author. This seems to have been the case with the Cai Yan poems. Despite strong indications to the contrary, many scholars still accept the attribution. However, even if no one believes that the speaker is actually the author, poems still adhere to their speakers. Few scholars, I think, still believe that Cao Zhi composed the "seven step poem," given in an anecdote in the *Shishuo xinyu*; but the poem is still included in collections of Cao Zhi's poetry. Cao Zhi is the poem's speaker, and that condition borders on authorship.

---

7. The wife of Qi Liang (or Liang of Qi) was the composer of a zither song. According to the legend accompanying the song, she drowned herself on hearing of her husband's death. The legend has several variations.

Finally, there is a known author, speaking in his own voice, about his own case. Although this situation is sometimes filiated to the historical circumstantiality of the *Shijing*, this is, in fact, a Han phenomenon—or, at the oldest, part of Han interpretation of *Chu ci*. This is a privileged mode in poetry, and its status exerted a pressure on all the other modes of composition and utterance we have described. That is, poems are in search of authors and particularly in search of an author who is speaking about his own case. We find this kind of authorship in some Jian'an poems; indeed, some poems are provided with prefaces or long titles that make the circumstances of their composition highly specific, in ways that can be linked to other texts and believable biographical information. In works credibly linked to known authors we also find the situation discussed in the second level above: that is, we find poems that would seem to have been appropriate to have been composed under some particular known circumstance. Such poems are so intimately linked to that putative circumstance that it becomes part of the way they are understood.

Our concern here is "authorship" as a cultural phenomenon rather than the validity of attribution in particular cases. That some poems acquired authors or moved between authors is beyond question. When part of an anonymous *yuefu* segment reappears in a somewhat different version as a Cao Pi poem, we must conclude either that authorship of an anonymous verse was assigned to Cao Pi or that a Cao Pi poem was reworked into a *yuefu* and the memory of authorship was lost.[8] In either case authorship is as unstable as the text itself, whose phrasing has changed in the two versions and which has either been cut down or expanded.

In almost all cases we cannot decide about authorship any more than we can decide which was the "original" phrasing and length.[9] "Proof" begets "disproof," begetting in turn counterproof, with arguments only very rarely strong enough to finally settle the case. I, too, have my convictions about particular

---

8. Lu Qinli, 262, 402.

9. This is, of course, the consequence of the work appearing in two independent sources. When a work appears in only one source we have no obvious questions to raise about text or authorship—but that is not necessarily a cause for confidence.

cases, which may occasionally emerge; but the more important question is the historical pressure to identify the speaker as the author and to discover a particular speaker-author behind a normative speaker.

The second important question is the way in which prose "contexts" are shaped by the very texts they purport to contextualize. This is closely related to embedding poetry in narrative and anecdote, long characteristic of the Chinese tradition. To recognize that the prose "context" is shaped by the text it contextualizes is to undercut the putative hierarchy of authority, according to which the prose "context" is a stable historical fact against which to read the more elusive and interpretable literary text.

Let us return to the poem we brought up in the introduction, the "Poem of Reproach" 怨詩 (or "Song of Reproach" 怨歌行) attributed to Lady Ban 班婕妤, a court lady of the last third of the first century B.C.[10]

新裂齊紈素	Newly cut, fine plain silk of Qi,
鮮潔如霜雪	fresh and pure as frost or snow.
裁爲合歡扇	It was cut into an acacia-patterned fan,
團團似明月	perfectly round like the bright moon.
出入君懷袖	It goes in and out of your bosom and sleeve,
動搖微風發	stirring in motion, a gentle breeze comes.
常恐秋節至	It ever fears that the autumn will come,
涼飈奪炎熱	and cool gusts will eliminate blazing heat.
棄捐篋笥中	It will be cast away in the storage box,
恩情中道絕	grace and love broken midway.

Lady Ban was the favorite of Emperor Cheng, who later cast her away when he became enamored of the notorious Zhao Feiyan and her sister. The poem thus gains a special weight in the anticipation of Lady Ban's loss of favor. The lady is of use when

---

10. Lu Qinli, 116; *Wen xuan* 27; *Ytxy* 1; *Ywlj* 41, 69; *Yfsj* 42. "Lady Ban" is Ban the *jieyu*, *jieyu* being a harem title. For the Wei dating, see Lu Qinli, *Han Wei liuchao wenxue lunji* 漢魏六朝文學論集, ed. Wu Yun 吳云 (Xi'an: Shanxi renmin chubanshe, 1984), 22–27. We might further note that Cao Zhi does not mention the fan when he writes on Lady Ban in the early third century, virtually unthinkable after the poem was attributed to her. Cao Zhi, "Ban jieyu zan" 班婕妤贊, in Zhao Youwen, *Cao Zhi ji jiaozhu*, 86–87. Wang Shumin, *Zhong Rong*, 147, tries to argue that a reference to wind in Cao Zhi's encomium suggests the fan poem, but this is not persuasive.

the emperor feels the "heat," but she realizes that his passions will eventually cool (autumn) and she may be put aside.

The historical association of the poem with Lady Ban is so strong that, even when the particular attribution to Lady Ban is rejected, scholars want the poem to be delivered in the voice of Lady Ban or, at the very least, in the voice of a court lady currently enjoying the emperor's favor. Such an interpretation is quite plausible. Yet we should here raise an alternative possibility, if only to foreground the weight of history in the interpretation of the poem. Rather than a poem comparing a court lady to a fan, we might well have a poem actually on a fan, implicitly compared to a court lady in the last couplet. Professional poets were indeed called upon to compose on an object from at least the third century, a practice later prefaced as *fude* 賦得, "composed on the assigned topic . . . ."[11] To put it another way, if a third-century poet had been asked to write on a circular fan, the piece above would have been appropriate.

If we bracket the obvious possibility that this is simply a poem on a fan, we have the three levels outlined above: (1) the normative speaker (a favorite court lady anxious about the continuation of imperial favor), (2) Lady Ban as a particular example of such a speaker, and (3) Lady Ban as author. We do not know and (barring an archeological miracle) can never know at which level this poem was first composed. It might even have been composed by Lady Ban—though I would be greatly surprised if this were so. The poem's origin is ultimately less interesting than its historical fate: as the particular court lady anticipates loss of favor, the poem gains favor by authorial attribution to her particular person.

We need to be very careful about the semantic history that links "authorship" and "authority" when working in a Chinese context, where no such semantic link exists.[12] Power, however,

---

11. See the anonymous poem composed on an incense burner, discussed on pp. 137–38. In support of this alternative hypothesis, Lady Ban's poem is sometimes cited in early sources as "Fan Poem," "Shan shi" 扇詩, or "On a Fan," "Yong shan" 詠扇.

12. The Chinese term for an "author" is *zuozhe* 作者, a "maker," exactly parallel to the etymology of "poet." The question of being a "maker" in the Chinese tradition was a very complex one; for the debates surrounding this issue, see Michael Puett, *The Ambivalence of Creation: Debates Concerning*

is clearly an issue here: the fan owner / emperor has the power to put away the fan/favorite. The poem acknowledges such power and resists it. The cleverness of a poem composed around the central figure of the fan is one of the things that argue for a third-century date. Not only is the woman the fan, the fan is figured with an "acacia" pattern, *hehuan* 合歡, which is also the "union of lovers," a pattern of circles that suggests union, as does the roundness of the moon, to which the fan is also compared. The fan produces "breeze" or "wind," *feng* 風, which is also the term for song and implicit criticism.

Those with royal power may treat their subjects—whether generals, courtiers, or court ladies—as mere implements, to be taken up and discarded according to their immediate usefulness. Han Xin, a famous general in the service of Liu Bang, the founder of the Han, was said to have commented that when the birds are gone, the good bow is discarded. People who are treated as mere tools by a person with power may speak back in protest, to instill shame and gratitude for past service. The issue is not how the court lady is like a fan, but how she is *not* like a fan: the comparison creates a disjunction.[13]

The invitation to read the poem in the voice of a court lady has very much to do with the implicit differential of power. The subservience of the speaker's position is clear when we contrast it with the lines in "Song of White Hair" 白頭吟, which convey essentially the same sentiment:[14]

| 願得一心人 | I want a man with a single heart, |
| 白頭不相離. | who will not leave me when the hair is white. |

"Poem of Reproach" anticipates the man's desertion not simply before the fact, but when favor is still new—for the fan is made of silk "newly cut." The speaker attempts to forestall desertion, to create sympathy and shame and thus to achieve the permanence expressed as a direct wish in "Song of White Hair." Thus the speaker's helplessness and passivity in "Poem of Reproach" are the counterpart of a veiled persuasive intent in

---

Innovation and Artifice in Early China (Stanford: Stanford University Press, 2001).

13. If we take the poem as actually about a fan, the humanization is merely clever, as is the anonymous poem on the incense burner.

14. Lu Qinli, 274.

the face of imperial power. It is no accident that the "Song of White Hair" is attributed to Zhuo Wenjun as speaker-author, addressing her fickle husband, Sima Xiangru: the poem's greater directness invites an attribution to a lower position in the social order.

In *yuefu* it is well known that misery is coming; the response is a desperate and shadowed pleasure in the present. In the "Poem of Reproach" there is no interval of pleasure, only a fear that the autumn will come (l. 7), a constant anxiety that seeks to forestall the anticipated future. We might note that the seventh line of "Poem of Reproach" also occurs in the "Long Song," "Changge xing" 長歌行, included in the *Wen xuan*, which also has the marks of elite composition.[15] There, in place of despair at fate and the call to pleasure, we have a concluding injunction to work hard in youth. The anxious and continuous anticipation of autumn seems to facilitate forms of resistance.

Figural displacement and concealment are often associated with women and women's motives in the elite tradition or with disempowered courtiers who figure themselves as women. As Lady Li hides her face, ruined by sickness, behind the covers and refuses to see Han emperor Wu, our putative Lady Ban hides her face, withered by anticipated aging, behind the figure of a fan—and hiding the face is, of course, another use of the fan. One version of woman is as the perfectly natural being, who feels strongly and speaks directly. The other version, particularly associated with court women (and with courtiers), links them to hidden motives and figural displacement. Direct power lies with the figure of authority; he may keep the fan or put it away. The object of such power can only respond indirectly, attempting to control not what the authority figure does but what he *wishes* to do.

Let us return to the term *dai* 代: "to replace," "to put in place of," which is the operative term in *daizuo*, the "persona poem." The woman speaks in the place of the fan; the poet speaks in the place of the woman. The circular fan as the image of the circular moon and a ground marked with circle patterns of *he-huan*, stands "in place of" the interlocked union of lovers. The alternative title is "Song of Reproach" ("Yuan ge xing" 怨歌行), a title that could be prefaced with *dai*, "To 'Song of Reproach.'"

---

15. Ibid., 262.

Unless a particular *yuefu* is the putative "original," all versions are *dai*, replacements of words for an old song, often long forgotten.

The *yuefu* writer puts his words in place of the old words of a song—whether he knows those old words or not—just as the writer of the persona poem puts his words in place of the unknown or never spoken words of some past figure. These two usages of *dai* share a common principle: the poet does not necessarily write for himself: though happy, he may feign sadness for the sorrow of some historical figure in the past or for the sad mood of some earlier song. Feigning had not yet become the problematic inauthenticity that it was later to become. Yet the growing anxiety about feigning is what presses the speaker to be taken as the author.

•

We might consider the way in which an imputed speaker can control the interpretation and textual evolution of a poem even in a case in which the attribution is apparently rejected. The *Xijing zaji* 西京雜記 includes an anecdote about the Western Han poet Sima Xiangru; when Sima Xiangru took a woman from Maoling as his concubine, his wife Zhuo Wenjun composed the "Song of White Hair," "Baitou yin" 白頭吟, to break off with him.[16] Dating the *Xijing zaji* is a matter of perpetual controversy, but at the very least we can say that this is the earliest mention of this title, probably in the third or early fourth century.

We cannot be certain if the version of "Song of White Hair" known to the compiler of *Xijing zaji* was the same as one of the two current versions or overlapped with them, but since the opening stanza of the current versions speaks of infidelity and a desire to break off a relationship, it seems likely that this part, at least, was known. The title next appears in a note by Wang Sengqian 王僧虔 in his *Jilu* 技錄 from the mid-fifth century, quoting the first line, but without the attribution to Zhuo Wenjun. Both of our current versions are given as anonymous: the earliest is found in the *Song shu*, then another version, perhaps half a century later, included in the *Yutai xinyong*.

---

16. Ge Hong 葛洪, *Xijing zaji quanyi* 西京雜記全譯 (Guiyang: Guizhou renmin chubanshe, 1993), 115.

We noted earlier that the attribution of "Poem of Reproach" to Lady Ban probably occurred in the mid-third century, roughly the same period when the "Song of White Hair" was attributed to Zhuo Wenjun. This invites the question why the attribution to Lady Ban endured, while the attribution to Zhuo Wenjun fell away (though was never quite forgotten). The most likely answer is the primary venue of preservation. "Poem of Reproach" is found in the *Wen xuan* and *Yutai xinyong*, but not in the *Song shu* (though it was often later quoted as a *yuefu*). "Song of White Hair," by contrast, seems to have come into the "poetry" sphere from musical compilations. In citing secular lyrics the *Song shu* includes only anonymous poems and poems by Cao rulers or princes. (It does include poems commissioned for ritual occasions by officials.) To note Zhuo Wenjun as the author of "Song of White Hair" would have been the sole exception and therefore inappropriate.[17] The *Yutai xinyong*, usually inclined to welcome any attribution to a known author, seems to accept the authority of the *Song shu* in this case. Let me first quote the two versions side by side.

白頭吟 Song of White Hair[18]

Yutai xinyong	*Song shu*
皚如山上雪	晴如山上雪
皎若雲間月	皎如雲間月
聞君有兩意	聞君有兩意
故來相決絕	故來相決絕
	平生共城中
	何嘗斗酒會
今日斗酒會	今日斗酒會
明旦溝水頭	明旦溝水頭
躞蹀御溝上	蹀躞御溝上
溝水東西流	溝水東西流
	郭東亦有樵
	郭西亦有樵
	兩樵相推與
	無親爲誰驕

---

17. This leads to the possibility that the term "old lyrics," *guci* 古辭, as used in the *Song shu*, may not imply a judgment of anonymity, as it was later understood.

18. Lu Qinli, 274; *Song shu*; *Ytxy* 1; *Yfsj* 41. Huang Jie, *Han Wei*, 48–51; Diény, *Aux origines de la poésie classique*, 155–61; Birrel, *Popular Songs*, 154–58.

凄凄復凄凄　　　　　凄凄重凄凄
嫁娶不須啼　　　　　嫁娶亦不啼
願得一心人　　　　　願得一心人
白頭不相離　　　　　白頭不相離
竹竿何嫋嫋　　　　　竹竿何嫋嫋
魚尾何簁簁　　　　　魚尾何離簁
男兒重意氣　　　　　男兒欲相知
何用錢刀爲　　　　　何用錢刀爲
　　　　　　　　　　齗如馬噉箕
　　　　　　　　　　川上高士嬉
　　　　　　　　　　今日相對樂
　　　　　　　　　　延年萬歲期

Below I will translate the *Song shu* version, with the verses omitted from the *Yutai xinyong* version in italics. Note that there are some other differences in phrasing.

白頭吟 Song of White Hair

晴如山上雪　　Clear like snow on the mountain,
皎如雲間月　　shining like the moon among clouds.
聞君有兩意　　I have heard you have feelings for another
故來相決絕　　and I come to break off with you.
平生共城中　　*Our lives spent in the same city,*
何嘗斗酒會　　*when have we ever met over a jug of ale?*
今日斗酒會　　This day we meet over a jug of ale,
明旦溝水頭　　tomorrow morning, by the waters of the moat.
蹀躞御溝上　　Slowly pacing by the royal moat,
溝水東西流　　the moat's waters flow off east and west.
郭東亦有樵　　*East of the town there is a woodsman,*
郭西亦有樵　　*west of the town there is also a woodsman.*
兩樵相推與　　*The two woodsmen each defer to the other,*
無親爲誰驕　　*without kin, to whom can one show off?*
凄凄重凄凄　　Dreary, ah so dreary,
嫁娶亦不啼　　in marrying one does not weep.
願得一心人　　I want someone with a faithful heart,
白頭不相離　　never separating until hair turns white.
竹竿何嫋嫋　　How the bamboo pole sways!
魚尾何離簁　　how the fishtails swish to and fro!
男兒欲相知　　When a man wants someone to love,
何用錢刀爲　　what use is coin and cash?
齗如馬噉箕　　*Munching, the horse chews its straw,*
川上高士嬉　　*by the river fine gentlemen sport.*
今日相對樂　　*This day we have pleasure together,*
延年萬歲期　　*may your years extend to ten thousand.*

When we have different versions like this, we may argue either that the *Yutai xinyong* represents the "original poem," with the *Song shu* version arranged by musicians for performance (as Guo Maoqian conventionally does), or that the *Song shu* version is the base text, with the *Yutai xinyong* modifying it to produce a version more acceptable as "poetry" in the sixth-century sense (Diény's argument). As we argued briefly in regard to "Prelude: O When?" and elsewhere, we have many small indications that the latter is the case.[19] If we understand this as *Yutai xinyong* reworking the *Song shu* version for form and sense, the removal of the third couplet is necessary: it has no corresponding rhyme and makes no immediate sense in the context. The quatrain on the two woodsmen was a clear candidate for exclusion, as were the lines on the straw-munching horse, the sporting gentlemen, and the singer's benediction on the audience.

There is, however, a more profound way in which *Yutai xinyong* has turned a "*yuefu*" into a "poem." In this we can see the shadow of Zhuo Wenjun still cast over the verse, even though it is given as anonymous. If we put the *Yutai xinyong* version out of our minds and look at the *Song shu* version as simply another *yuefu*, a performance text, we would be strongly inclined to read it as a compound *yuefu*. This is essentially what Diény has so finely done, and my argument essentially follows his with some small modifications. For a compound *yuefu* we would take the final segment beginning with the line "Dreary, ah so dreary" 淒淒重淒淒. This is clearly recognizable as one standard opening template. Segments of a compound *yuefu* are essentially autonomous, combined perhaps circumstantially, perhaps by habit. If we read the final segment independently, without putting it in the context of the separation in the opening, we have a poem on a woman (or possibly a man) wanting to get married; we may keep the closing couplets or not.

淒淒重淒淒	Dreary, ah so dreary,
嫁娶亦不啼	but in marrying one does not weep.
願得一心人	I want someone with a faithful heart,

---

19. In the present case the addition of a couplet that does not rhyme makes no sense in arranging a text for musical performance; it makes sense only through some form of imperfect transmission, oral memory or textual.

白頭不相離	never separating until hair turns white.
竹竿何嫋嫋	How the bamboo pole sways!
魚尾何簁簁	how the fishtails swish to and fro!
男兒欲相知	When a man wants someone to love,
何用錢刀爲	what use is coin and cash?
齕如馬噉箕	*Munching, the horse chews its straw,*
川上高士嬉	*by the river fine gentlemen sport.*
今日相對樂	*This day we have pleasure together,*
延年萬歲期	*may your years extend to ten thousand.*

These lines make far more sense this way than trying to reconcile them with the opening scene of parting. The imagery of fishing is a standard figure of courtship. In the aesthetics of *yuefu* the quatrain on the woodsmen introduces the motif of loneliness and possibly seeking "kin," and it punctuates the medley of moods.

Diény further divides the first part into the opening four lines, on breaking a relationship, and the following six lines on a parting—not one of the sort that occurs in breaking a relationship. His argument here is quite persuasive. Perhaps the earliest "Song of White Hair" was only the opening four lines, a short song like the anonymous "Song of the Harp," "Kunghou yin" 箜篌吟,[20] or "The Fierce Tiger," "Menghu xing" 猛虎行.[21] What we see then in the *Song shu* version is the opening song compounded with other short snippets. The ground of such combination may be, as Diény suggests, musical or the conventions of performance; however, such repeated performances create an aesthetic of words in their own right.

We do not demand unity of compound *yuefu*; the "Ballad of Longxi" can cheerfully combine a scene of wandering in Heaven with a wife receiving guests. "Song of White Hair," however, has been more commonly read in the *Yutai xinyong* revision, unified by the presumption of a single speaker breaking off with her beloved: this is the shadow of Zhuo Wenjun in the poem. The *Yutai xinyong* makes a small textual change: instead of "in marrying one does not weep" 嫁娶亦不啼, it reads: "in marrying one should not weep" 嫁娶不須啼. In the context of the putative breakup of the couple, this suggests that she does indeed weep, but that to weep is not right. The lines on wanting someone

---

20. Lu Qinli, 255.
21. Ibid., 287.

with a "faithful heart" and growing old with that person—
perfectly straightforward in a poem on seeking a mate—take on
a new psychological depth as a failed wish, something the
speaker "had wanted."[22] The fishing passage, standard in
courtship lyrics, becomes peculiar. And one line of the final
couplet is changed to the famous form in which it has been
known ever since, often understood out of context—in context
it is open to various interpretations:

男兒重意氣	A man values real spirit/In a man real spirit is valued
何用錢刀爲	what use is coin and cash?

However we read this, it is a very different statement from a
"man wanting someone to love," more appropriate for a court-
ship poem.

What was apparently once a compound *yuefu* with disparate
segments has been turned into a persona poem unified by a
single speaking voice; even if later readers did not believe the
poem was by Zhuo Wenjun, it was in a form in which they could
see how it might have been uttered by Zhuo Wenjun.

•

We may turn now to a pair of long poems in which there is
no question who the speaker is, a speaker who unifies the
poem without textual modification and interpretive ingenuity.
Here the question is rather whether the speaker is indeed the
author.

Cai Yan 蔡琰 was the daughter of the great Eastern Han in-
tellectual and literary figure Cai Yong 蔡邕 (A.D. 132–92). In the
wars on the disintegration of the Han, she was captured and
sent to the Xiongnu. She bore children there, then was ran-
somed by Cao Cao and returned to China; she had to leave her
children among the Xiongnu and had no immediate family sur-
viving when she returned. Cao Cao had her married, and it is
from this phase of her life that the poems are presented. The
poem does, indeed, have a core of historical truth, but it was
also a wonderful story, with immense resonance. We often

---

22. Not just the shadow of Zho Wenjun makes the opening speaker a woman;
the line on "having feelings for another" implies a woman speaker, as in the
nearly identical line in "There Is Someone I Love" 有所思: "I heard you loved
another" 聞君有他心.

cannot disentangle historical fact from historical romance, and in China historical romance often became history. Thus Cai Yan entered Fan Ye's *History of the Latter Han (Hou Han shu)*, compiled in the mid-fifth century. And the story reappeared with two versions of a poem, one in the five syllable line and one in a "Chu song" meter. The differences between the two versions are largely generic. We know that there was an "Independent Biography of Cai Yan," "Cai Yan biezhuan" 蔡琰別傳, in circulation later; such a title strongly suggests historical romance. The "Independent Biography" may have been Fan Ye's source, or it may have been elaborated from Fan Ye's biography.

As speaker/author of "Poem of Reproach," Lady Ban particularizes a text that is in itself categorical; that is, the poem could be spoken by any young woman enjoying the favor of a man, though literary convention strongly disposes us to take the speaker as a harem favorite. By contrast, Cai Yan is clearly the speaker of "Poem of Grief": she tells the "Cai Yan story" with its particular details. The point of greatest scholarly debate has been whether the speaker is also the author. Although I agree with Hans Frankel that neither of the two versions is actually by Cai Yan, this remains a point that cannot be definitively proven.[23]

These two versions of "Poem of Grief" are unique as the earliest extant long first-person narratives in verse, and they are unique as two radically different metrical treatments of the same material. Their uniqueness, however, is probably a function of the venue of their survival in the *Hou Han shu* from the mid-fifth century. If there were other such poems (as there probably were), they lay outside the world of "poetry" as conceived in the following century.

The history of the reception of the versions of "Poem of Grief" should be a flag warning us of how taste and generic norms selected and excluded materials. These poems survive only because they were included in a standard history, and the nearly complete silence about them in literary sources gives us an indication of the fate of poems that were not favored. Neither version of "Poem of Grief" is included in the *Wen xuan* or *Yutai xinyong*, nor is Cai Yan mentioned in *Wenxin diaolong* or *Shipin*.

---

23. Hans H. Frankel, "Cai Yan and the Poems Attributed to Her," *CLEAR* 5 (1983): 133–56.

Considering the easy availability of the text in the *Hou Han shu* and the diligence of Qi and Liang scholars in gathering and commenting on early poetry, this absence is significant.[24] The version in the five syllable line is cited only in the *Wen xuan* commentary (once) and in *Taiping yulan*, but not in the Sui and Tang encyclopedias.[25] While her story was well known and circulated with the poems in the "Independent Biography," the earliest literary mention of the poems after the *Hou Han shu* is a favorable comment attributed to Su Shi in *Zhuzhuang shihua* 竹莊詩話.[26] Most later comments on Cai Yan concentrated on the even later "Eighteen Stanzas of the Tartar Reed Flute," "Hujia shibapai" 胡笳十八拍, rather than on the versions of "Poem of Grief."[27] The "Poem of Grief" does not begin to commonly appear in anthologies of pre-Tang poetry until the mid-eighteenth century, although it has now become one of the most famous of all early poems and is included in every anthology. The two versions of "Poem of Grief" are the most recent additions to the canon of early classical poetry, although they are among the earliest to enter the textual record.

蔡琰, 悲憤詩 Cai Yan, attrib., Poem of Grief [28]

漢季失權柄	In the last days of Han authority failed,
董卓亂天常	Dong Zhuo threw Heaven's norms into turmoil.
志欲圖篡弑	His plans were to kill and usurp the throne,
先害諸賢良	so first he harmed all good and worthy men.
逼迫遷舊邦	He forced folk to move to the old capital land,
擁主以自彊	holding the ruler to make himself strong.

---

24. The absence of this poem, in a woman's voice, from the *Yutai xinyong* is particularly striking; the *Yutai xinyong* did include long poetic narrative.

25. The *Cai Yan biezhuan* is cited as a source for passages from the Chu song version in *Beitang shuchao* 111 and *Yiwen leiju* 44. The relation between the *biezhuan* and the biography that appeared in the *History of the Latter Han* is uncertain.

26. He Wen 何汶, *Zhuzhuang shihua* 竹莊詩話 (Beijing: Zhonghua shuju, 1984), 19–20.

27. Lu Qinli, 201. The "Eighteen Stanzas of the Tartar Reed Flute" are of uncertain date, perhaps Tang.

28. Lu Qinli, 199; *Hou Han shu*, 2801–3.

海內興義師	From all the world over rose a loyalist army
欲共討不祥	to unite and punish that ill-omened man.
卓眾來東下	Dong Zhuo's hordes descended on the east,
金甲耀日光	metal armor gleamed in the rays of the sun.
平土人脆弱	The people of the plains were weaker,
來兵皆胡羌	the troops that came were all Hu and Qiang.
獵野圍城邑	They coursed the wilds, surrounded the cities,
所向悉破亡	wherever they went, all were destroyed.
斬截無孑遺	They butchered and beheaded, left not one person behind,
尸骸相撐拒	corpses were propped up against one another.
馬邊懸男頭	Men's heads were strung from the horses' sides,
馬後載婦女	women and girls, brought behind the horses.
長驅西入關	In a long march we went west into the Passes,
迥路險且阻	the long route was dangerous and blocked.
還顧邈冥冥	When I looked around, it was remote and dark,
肝脾為爛腐	my liver and spleen were crushed by this.
所略有萬計	Those captured were counted in ten thousands,
不得令屯聚	they could not gather them all.
或有骨肉俱	Sometimes flesh and blood got together,
欲言不敢語	wanting to talk, but not daring to speak.
失意幾微間	If they were dissatisfied in the least,
輒言斃降虜	they would always say: "Slay the captives,
要當以亭刃	We should let you meet the blade,
我曹不活汝	we are not going to let you live."
豈復惜性命	We did not care about our lives anymore,
不堪其詈罵	we couldn't bear their curses.
或便加箠杖	Sometimes they would flog us,
毒痛參並下	pain and misery were endured together.
旦則號泣行	At dawn we walked on, crying out and weeping,
夜則悲吟坐	at night we would sit, moaning in sorrow.
欲死不能得	If someone wanted to die, she could not get to,
欲生無一可	wanting to live, there was nothing she could do.
彼蒼者何辜	O Heaven, what fault have I committed?—
乃遭此厄禍	to meet such trouble and calamity.

邊荒與華異	The frontier wilds are different from China,
人俗少義理	there is little propriety in their customs.
處所多霜雪	Where I lived there was much frost and snow,
胡風春夏起	nomad winds rose in spring and summer.
翩翩吹我衣	They blew my clothes flapping,
肅肅入我耳	whistling, they entered my ears.
感時念父母	Stirred by the times, I thought on my parents,
哀歎無窮已	my sorrowful sighs never ceased.
有客從外來	Whenever a visitor came from the outside,
聞之常歡喜	I would always be delighted to hear of it.
迎問其消息	I would greet him and ask of the news,
輒復非鄉里	but time and again he was not from my home.
邂逅徼時願	I chanced to be blessed by a wish of the times,[29]
骨肉來迎己	my own flesh and blood came to meet me.
己得自解免	I had been released myself,
當復棄兒子	but I had to abandon my children.
天屬綴人心	Natural relations are bound to a person's heart,
念別無會期	I brooded on parting, never to meet again.
存亡永乖隔	We would be separated forever in life and death,
不忍與之辭	and I could not bear to take leave of them.
兒前抱我頸	My son came forward and embraced my neck
問母欲何之	and asked: "Where are you going, mother?
人言母當去	People say that you have to go away,
豈復有還時	that you certainly will never return again.
阿母常仁惻	Mother has always been gentle and caring,
念何更不慈	I wonder how you can now be so unkind.
我尚未成人	I am not yet fully grown,
奈何不顧思	how can you not show concern for me?"
見此崩五內	Hearing this made my organs fail within me,
恍惚生狂癡	I was confused and felt foolish and mad.
號泣手撫摩	Weeping, I caressed him with my hand,
當發復回疑	I was due to set out, then turned back unsure.
兼有同時輩	There were also others of my own age
相送告離別	who sent me off and said their goodbyes.

---

29. That is, she was ransomed.

慕我獨得歸	They envied how I alone got to return,
哀叫聲摧裂	shouting in woe, their voices were shattering.
馬爲立踟躕	Because of this, the horses stood hesitating,
車爲不轉轍	because of this, the carriage did not roll.
觀者皆歔欷	Those watching all heaved sighs,
行路亦嗚咽	those on the road also groaned.
去去割情戀	Going farther on, I cut away yearning,
遄征日遐邁	I went swiftly, daily getting ever farther.
悠悠三千里	On and on for three thousand leagues,
何時復交會	when would we ever meet again?
念我出腹子	I brood on the sons that came from my womb,
胸臆爲摧敗	because of this my breast is shattered.
既至家人盡	Arriving, I found that my family was gone,
又復無中外	once again I had no blood relations or in-laws.
城郭爲山林	Cities and towns had become mountain forests,
庭宇生荊艾	yard and room grew with thorns and moxa.
白骨不知誰	White bones—I didn't know whose they were—
從橫莫覆蓋	lay scattered around, none of them covered.
出門無人聲	When I went out the gate, no human voices,
豺狼號且吠	the wild dogs and wolves howled and barked.
煢煢對孤景	In isolation I faced my solitary shadow,
怛吒糜肝肺	distressed wailing ground down liver and lungs.
登高遠眺望	Climbing a high place, I gazed afar,
魂神忽飛逝	my spirit and soul suddenly flew off.
奄若壽命盡	Swiftly my life was gone,
旁人相寬大	those around me encouraged me to take it easy.
爲復彊視息	Once again I forced myself to look and breathe,
雖生何聊賴	yet though I lived, what had I to rely on?
託命於新人	I entrusted my life to a new husband,
竭心自勖厲	I did my utmost and exerted myself.
流離成鄙賤	Carried off, I became defiled,
常恐復捐廢	I was ever in fear of being cast off again.
人生幾何時	How long does human life last?—
懷憂終年歲	I will feel grief to the end of my years.

蔡琰, 悲憤詩 Cai Yan, attrib., Poem of Grief

嗟薄祜分遭世患 Alas for my ill fate,　born in a time
　　of troubles,

宗族殄分門户單 my kindred were wiped out,　of my
　　family I was alone.

身執略分入西關 I was seized and taken　out through
　　the Western Passes,

歷險阻分之羌蠻 I went through hardship and peril　to go
　　to the Qiang and Man.

山谷眇分路漫漫 Mountain valleys remote,　the journey
　　stretched on and on,

眷東顧分但悲歎 I looked back east with longing,　but only
　　could sadly sigh.

冥當寢分不能安 In darkness one should sleep,　but I could
　　get no rest;

饑當食分不能餐 in hunger one should eat,　but I could
　　not dine.

常流涕分眥不乾 Ever shedding tears,　eye sockets never dry,

薄志節分念死難 feeble in my resolve,　I thought dying
　　was too hard,

雖苟活分無形顏 though I got by with my life,　I was left
　　without honor.

惟彼方分遠陽精 That place　is far from the sun,

陰氣凝分雪夏零 Yin vapors congeal,　snow falls in summer.

沙漠壅分塵冥冥 The desert is blocked off,　darkened by
　　the dust,

有草木分春不榮 there are plants and trees,　they do not
　　bloom in spring.

人似獸分食臭腥 The people are like beasts,　they feed on
　　stinking meat,

言兜離分狀窈停 their language goes *douli*,　their appearance
　　is *yaoting*[?].

歲聿暮分時邁征 The year comes to its end,　the seasons
　　move ahead,

夜悠長分禁門扃 the nights grow long,　I am locked behind
　　barred doors,

不能寢分起屏營 I cannot get to sleep,　I rise and pace
　　restlessly.

登胡殿分臨廣庭 I go in the Tartar's great hall,　I look out
　　on the broad courtyard,

玄雲合分黯月星 black clouds merge,　hiding the moon
　　and stars,

北風厲分肅泠泠 the north wind is harsh,　severe and chill.

胡笳動兮邊馬鳴	Hu reed flutes sound, the frontier horses neigh,
孤雁歸兮聲嚶嚶	the lone goose returns, its voice goes *yingying*.
樂人興兮彈琴箏	The musicians rise, they pluck zithers and zheng,
音相和兮悲且清	the notes blend in harmony, mournful and clear.
心吐思兮胸憤盈	The heart produces longing, the breast swells with wrath,
欲舒氣兮恐彼驚	I want to give it vent, but I fear they will be alarmed,
含哀咽兮涕沾頸	so I hold back mournful sobs, tears soak my neck.
家既迎兮當歸寧	My family came to get me, I was to return to my home,
臨長路兮捐所生	on the verge of the long journey I abandoned those I had born.
兒呼母兮啼失聲	My son called to his mother, he wept so he could not speak,
我掩耳兮不忍聽	I covered my ears, I could not bear to listen.
追持我兮走煢煢	He came after me holding on, he rushed on lonely,
頓復起兮毀顏形	All at once I set off again, to the ruin of my dignity.[30]
還顧之兮破人情	Looking back at him would break a person's heart,
心怛絕兮死復生	heart's utmost misery, to the point of death.

Even if we do not identify Cai Yan as speaker of the "Poem of Grief" with the author, the versions of the poem still seem to come from a relatively early period. The version in the five syllable line can be dated from the first phrase, "In the last days of Han," *Han ji* 漢季, indicating that the Han has ended, which in turn places it after the death of Cao Cao. It begins with a verse epitome of the civil war between Dong Zhuo and his adversaries, which finds close parallels in some of Cao Cao's *yuefu*, such as the opening of "Dew on the Scallions" 薤露:[31]

---

30. 毀顏形 should mean "ruins my looks," but since earlier (l. 11) the compound in inverse form clearly means "having no face [sense of shame] left," it seems best to take it that way here.

31. Lu Qinli, 347.

惟漢二十世	In the twentieth generation of the Han,
所任誠不良	those trusted with power were truly not good.
沐猴而冠帶	Bathed monkeys in caps and sashes,
知小而謀強	short on sense and strong on plots.

In contrast to the "last days of the Han," we see here how a poet refers to the Han when the Han is still alive, albeit in its death throes. Likewise we read in Cao Cao's "The Land of the Dead" 蒿里行:[32]

| 關東有義士 | East of the passes were loyalist troops, |
| 興兵討群凶 | an army raised to quell a host of monsters. |

This can be compared to Cai Yan's:

| 海內興義師 | From all the world over rose a loyalist army, |
| 欲共討不祥 | to unite and punish that ill-omened man. |

This same bare narrative style, an epitome of history, can be seen in some verses in a six syllable line attributed to Kong Rong 孔融 in the *Guwen yuan*:[33]

漢家中葉道微	In the middle of its generations the Way of the House of Han diminished,
董卓作亂乘衰	Dong Zhuo took advantage of decline to foment turmoil.
僭上虐下專威	He usurped the ruler's place, terrorized the commons, and took all authority to himself,
萬官惶布莫違	The officials quaked in fear and none thwarted him,
百姓慘慘心悲	the peasants were miserable and felt grief.

Such bare versification of narrative can also be seen in the inscription on the Fei Feng stele.[34]

Such a bare narrative style disappears from elite poetry by the end of the third century. We may contrast the opening of the "Poem of Grief" above with the opening of an admitted persona poem (*daizuo*) by Shi Chong 石崇 (249–300) on Wang Zhaojun, leaving the court to be married to the Xiongnu ruler:[35]

---

32. Ibid.
33. Ibid., 197.
34. Ibid., 176.
35. Ibid., 643.

我本漢家子	I was born of a Chinese family,
將適單于庭	to be sent to the camp of the Shanyu.
辭訣未及終	Before I had finished taking my leave,
前驅已抗旌	the vanguard had already raised their flags.
僕御涕流離	The driver's tears were streaming,
轅馬爲悲鳴	the horses on the shaft called out sadly for me.

The smoothness of the style and the figures of "sympathy" mark a very different era in poetry in the five syllable line.

The "Chu song" version is generally considered inferior (and thus its authenticity is suspect). The "Chu song" style was commonly used in embedded verse within narrative, though usually for a shorter lyric outburst. Here, used as a narrative meter, it suffers in comparison with the five syllable line version both by its tendency to elaborate moments of greatest pathos and by the inherent limitations of the form, with its three syllable hemistich, each hemistich being a single predicate. We can see clearly that it was composed at a time when the topics and templates of five-syllable-line poetry were already well established. The three syllable hemistich could easily be filled with the second part of a five syllable line. Thus when "the nights grow long" 夜悠長, we can anticipate the line that follows: she "cannot get to sleep" 不能寢 and "rises and paces restlessly" 起屏營.

The "Chu song" version is not without its fine points, especially the scene in which Cai Yan stares out of the palace in the dark, with black clouds covering the stars, the wind howling, horses whinnying, and the reed flutes moaning. The culminating moment is her parting from her children, after which this version breaks off.

家既迎兮當歸寧	My family came to get me, I was to return to my home,
臨長路兮捐所生	on the verge of the long journey I abandoned those I had born.
兒呼母兮啼失聲	My son called to his mother, he wept so he could not speak,
我掩耳兮不忍聽	I covered my ears, I could not bear to listen.
追持我兮走煢煢	He came after me holding on, he rushed on lonely,

頓復起兮毀顏形	All at once I set off again, to the ruin of my dignity.
還顧之兮破人情	Looking back at him would break a person's heart,
心怛絕兮死復生	heart's utmost misery, to the point of death.

Here the five-syllable-line version shows its strength as a form with a capacity for narrative. The son here does not simply call out and weep as in the "Chu song" version: he addresses his mother.

己得自解免	I had been released myself,
當復棄兒子	but I had to abandon my children.
天屬綴人心	Natural relations are bound to a person's heart,
念別無會期	I brooded on parting, never to meet again.
存亡永乖隔	We would be separated forever in life and death,
不忍與之辭	and I could not bear to take leave of them.
兒前抱我頸	My son came forward and embraced my neck
問母欲何之	and asked: "Where are you going, mother?
人言母當去	People say that you have to go away,
豈復有還時	that you certainly will never return again.
阿母常仁惻	Mother has always been gentle and caring,
念何更不慈	I wonder how you can now be so unkind.
我尚未成人	I am not yet fully grown,
奈何不顧思	how can you not show concern for me?"
見此崩五內	Hearing this made my organs fail within me,
恍惚生狂癡	I was confused and felt foolish and mad.
號泣手撫摩	Weeping, I caressed him with my hand,
當發復回疑	I was due to set out, then turned back unsure.

The speaker in the "Chu song" version simply knows not to look back; here she is torn and hesitates. The five-syllable-line version also includes parting from the other, less lucky captives and her return to find only ruin and the rest of her family dead. We also learn of her remarriage and her anxiety that she will be cast off because of her "defilement." The poem comes to a finale with the "old poem" convention "How long does human life last?" and the concluding statement of sorrow.

Elements of the "old poem" repertoire occur throughout, both on a straightforward level and in a relatively high register.

When carried off to Central Asia, traveling was hard, and we get a variation on a standard line in "the long route was dangerous and blocked" 迥路險且阻 (cf. 道路阻且長 in the first of the "Nineteen Old Poems"). When leaving her children behind, we have the common "old poem" theme of separation from kin: the first of the "Nineteen Old Poems" measures that interval somewhat hyperbolically as "more than ten thousand leagues apart" 相去萬餘里; Cai Yan goes "on and on for three thousand leagues" 悠悠三千里 (cf. the Fei Feng stele: 相去三千里 "three thousand leagues apart"). The first of the "Nineteen Old Poems" notes the increasing distance, "daily ever farther apart" 相去日已遠; Cai Yan repeats the sentiment in a higher register, "I went swiftly, daily getting ever further" 遄征日遐邁. The first of the "Nineteen Old Poems" asks if the pair will meet again (會面安可知); Cai Yan has simply "when would we ever meet again" 何時復交會.

Beyond the general case of separation from kin, abandoning one's own child had a special resonance, how the historical turmoil of the disintegration of the Han could disrupt even the firmest family bonds. This was, of course, also the focus of attention in Wang Can's first "Sevenfold Sorrows" 七哀詩, in which a mother, fleeing from Chang'an, abandons her baby. Both poems also have that other marker of broken families, the white bones left unburied.

In the end the reason why the two versions of "Poem of Grief" were so thoroughly excluded from the domain of poetry for so long remains a mystery. Although we do have the much longer "Old Poem: On Behalf of the Wife of Jiao Zhongqing" 古詩爲焦仲卿妻作 included in *Yutai xinyong* (very dubiously attributed to the Jian'an, and certainly Southern Dynasties in its current form), that poem too went largely unnoticed until much later ages. Perhaps it was simply a prejudice against long narrative poems, which seem to have been a continuous popular tradition.

•

At some point prior to the early fifth century a corpus of poems on parting and separation became associated with the failed Western Han general Li Ling 李陵, who surrendered to the Xiongnu and lived out much of his life among them. The famous scene of his meeting with and parting from the Han envoy

Su Wu 蘇武 is given in the *Han shu* and already shows that the historical event, whatever its basis, had been romanticized.[36] This was a topic that invited persona composition, as can be seen in the song in the biography and in the famous letters, of uncertain date, supposedly exchanged between the two men.[37] A Li Ling collection in two scrolls survived in the *Sui shu* "Bibliography."

Yan Yanzhi 顏延之 (384–456) already doubted the authenticity of the collection, calling it a "mixed bag" and suspecting "false attribution." He did not, however, necessarily reject all the poems ("not all were composed by Ling" 非盡陵製). In the crucial period from the late fifth century through the first four decades of the sixth century Li Ling's authorship came to be generally accepted, and he was often treated as the first "author" of poetry in the five syllable line. (Mei Sheng, to whom some of the "old poems" were attributed, was earlier, but he was not made the first "author" in accounts of the form.)

At some point the absurdity of linking two scrolls of poems by one person to a single occasion must have become apparent. There in the land of the Xiongnu Li Ling is extemporizing one poem after another to Su Wu, who must, at some point, have grown impatient in his double role as recipient and probable scribe. The peculiarity of such a situation would have been increased, if one considers that, according to Zhong Rong, these were the first poems in the five syllable line. The absurdity of the situation was mitigated somewhat by transferring some of the poem to Su Wu, addressing Li Ling.[38]

Apart from the situation of parting there is nothing in these poems to link them specifically to the story of Li Ling and Su Wu; at the same time there is nothing to forbid linking them with the historical occasion (if one of the most famous is in the voice of a woman about to part from her husband setting off to the wars, it could be read as figurative). The collection also contained poems of separation as well as the moment of parting,

---

36. *Han shu*, 2464–65.

37. *Wen xuan* 41. As Suzuki points out (*Kan Gi*, 329), the material in the letters overlaps with the poems, a phenomenon we will also see in the Qin Jia poems and letter.

38. As Lu Qinli (336–37) points out, in the Liang some of the poems in the corpus came to be attributed to Su Wu. See also Lu Qinli, *Han Wei*, 5–8.

and it is interesting to note that the *Wen xuan* did not include these when it made its selection (they have been preserved primarily in the *Guwen yuan*).

In Jiang Yan's "Poetic Exposition on Hard Feelings" 恨賦, we have a scene of Li Ling and his parting from Su Wu:[39]

至如李君降北	When Li Ling surrendered to the North,
名辱身冤	his reputation was shamed, his person felt the injustice.
拔劍擊柱	He drew his sword and struck a column,
弔影慚魂	lamenting his shadow, shamed before his soul.
情往上郡	His feelings went to Shangjun [Han frontier commandery];
心留鴈門	his heart lingered at Wild Goose Gate.
裂帛繫書	He tore silk and tied a letter [to a wild goose],
誓還漢恩	vowing to return the grace shown him by the Han.
朝露溘至	The dawn dew suddenly came;
握手何言	they [Li Ling and Su Wu] clasped hands, what more was there to say?

Jiang Yan also included a Li Ling imitation on his "Various Forms," a set of imitations of earlier poetic style composed in the late fifth century. Despite the uniqueness of the situation (no less than Cai Yan parting from her children born among the Xiongnu), it could frame a normative parting poem and make that parting the normative type for all partings.

李陵/蘇武 Li Ling/Su Wu, attrib.[40]

攜手上河梁	We hold hands stepping onto the River bridge,
遊子暮何之	where will the traveler go at dusk?
徘徊蹊路側	We hesitate here by the path side,
恨恨不能辭	with sad looks, we cannot take our leaves.
行人難久留	The traveler cannot linger long,
各言長相思	we each say that we will always think of each other.

---

39. *Wen xuan* 16.
40. Lu Qinli, 337; *Wen xuan* 29 (as Su Wu); *Ywlj* 29; *Cxj* 18.

安知非日月	How do we know we are not like sun and moon,
弦望自有時	having our own phases of halved and full?[41]
努力崇明德	Strive hard to reverence your noble virtue—
皓首以爲期	we will meet again when our hair is white.

Although the Xiongnu were not well known as bridge builders, the "River bridge" came to represent the parting of Li Ling and Su Wu; there are no other limiting specifics in this or any other poems in the corpus to situate this poem historically, geographically, or personally. The particularity of the putative speaker and author here can be assumed, but it quickly dissolves into a normative grammar of any parting: we are here, but it is hard to part; the traveler must go, but we will always think of each other, and someday we may meet again. The clearest variable comes in the parting injunction: "Strive hard to reverence your noble virtue." This is not one of those Chinese lines that translate happily. "Be good!" is too short to fill a line and rather comic in poetry, but it carries, however ineptly, the social sense of the line. The poem is remembered and has a beauty, but it is the beauty of "auld lang syne," framed by a historical narrative.

If the poem above could have reasonably been imputed to the occasion of Li Ling's parting from Su Wu, some of the other poems in the corpus, while among the finest of early parting poems, do not quite fit, nor are they easily susceptible to a figurative reading. This suggests that a critic like Zhong Rong or a critical anthologist like Xiao Tong did not compare the details of the poem too strongly against the imputed circumstance:

李陵/蘇武 Li Ling/Su Wu, attrib.[42]

骨肉緣枝葉	Flesh and blood are connected as branches and leaves,
結交亦相因	those who form ties also depend on one another.
四海皆兄弟	Since all in the sea-girt world are brothers,[43]
誰爲行路人	who is a traveler on the road?

---

41. Though the poem refers to "sun and moon," obviously the moon alone is intended; the half-moon is separation, and the full moon, union.

42. Lu Qinli, 338; *Wen xuan* 29 (as Su Wu); *Ywlj* 29 (as Su Wu).

43. Paraphrasing a famous passage from *Analects* XII.4.

況我連枝樹	Even more so we, trees whose branches have grown together—
與子同一身	you and I share the same body.
昔爲鴛與鴦	Before we were the mandarin duck and drake,
今爲參與辰	now we will be like the stars Shen and Chen.[44]
昔者常相近	Before we were always close to each other,
邈若胡與秦	[now] as remote as Turkestan and Qin.
惟念當乖離	Thinking on how we would have to separate,
恩情日以新	our feelings of affection were daily renewed.
鹿鳴思野草	"The deer cry out," thinking of the plants of the moor—[45]
可以喻嘉賓	this can serve as a figure for a fine guest.
我有一尊酒	I have a goblet of ale,
欲以贈遠人	I want to give it to the one going far.
願子留斟酌	I would have you stay and pour
慰此平生親	to console our lifetime of closeness.[46]

Although the first part of the poem concerns distinctions of relationships, the relationship between the speaker and the person addressed here is not quite clear. The relation between friends becomes as strong as ties of blood, and, citing the *Analects*, becomes a relation between brothers. But if we thought the speaker was referring to his relationship to the person leaving, we soon realize in line 4 that this is a consolation for the traveler: wherever he goes, he will find such "brothers." Although Xiao Tong places this poem in the mouth of Su Wu, it is, in fact, Su Wu who is leaving, while Li Ling is staying. (The Tang Wuchen 五臣 commentator Zhan Xian 張銑 solves this by having Su Wu parting from his brothers.)

Next we have the highly rhetorical *kuang* 況, "even more," which is used in another poem in the Li Ling corpus but not generally in low register poetry. The *kuang* gestures to argument, and we read this as: you will find "brothers" wherever you go, and even more so am I your "brother," not of the "branch and leaf" type, but like two different trees whose branches grow together. "Sharing the same body" seems to be

---

44. Shen is a star that appears in the west, while Chen appears in the east; taken together they are common figures for the greatest degree of separation.

45. *Shi* 161.

46. *Xu* 敘 is a common variant for 慰.

carrying this apparently male-male relationship a bit far, but when we come to the figure of the mandarin ducks, we have a standard figure for man and wife—and we are no longer sure if this is a wife addressing a departing husband or two friends who are like "man and wife." We suspect, as seems to have been the case with the "old poems," a user could interpret the poems as he pleased and hear the parts he chose to hear.

In the context of the parting between Li Ling and Su Wu, the cliché "as far apart as Turkestan and Qin" becomes quite literal and no longer deserving the "as," *ruo* 若. The parting in this poem is one between people who have been together a very long time, which also does not fit the Su Wu and Li Ling case. The speaker then gestures to the *Shi* "The deer cry out," the standard poem for welcoming guests to a party, offering the standard interpretation in a form that sounds like he is repeating what he learned in school. Again, the speaker is taking only the part he wants (*duanzhang quyi* 斷章取義), a reference to a "guest," which is not entirely appropriate for a pair who "share the same body." At last we have the speaker urging the traveler to drink and stay a bit longer.

Although this famous poem is memorable in its pieces, it cannot bear the scrutiny that its gestures to rhetorical argument invite. It is read vaguely, against a general idea of parting and the parting feast, historically instantiated in the parting of Li Ling and Su Wu. In contrast to the generality of the first poem we cited, this poem works by multiple specificities, vaguely pointing in different directions.

•

As we saw in the first chapter, the old attributions of parting poems to Li Ling and "Poem of Reproach" to Lady Ban left large lacunae in the history of poetry in the five syllable line before the Jian'an Reign. These lacunae troubled several critics writing accounts of poetry in the form. Lacunae can be productive: in the early sixth century poems began to emerge to fill the void. We have some reason to be skeptical of the attributions of poems to the Eastern Han, most of which come from *Yutai xinyong*, an anthology of dubious fidelity to its sources.

Yutai xinyong anthologized four poems by one Qin Jia 秦嘉 (fl. 147) and a piece by his wife Xu Shu responding to him. Zhong Rong's preface to the *Gradations of Poetry* mentions only

Ban Gu's "Poem on History" in what he sees as a troubling gap between Lady Ban and the Jian'an; in the main body of the work, however, he apparently includes Qin Jia and Xu Shu in his middle category. We say "apparently" because Zhong Rong's comments are ambiguous and may refer only to Xu Shu.[47] Zhong Rong's comments are as follows:

夫妻事既可傷, 文亦悽怨. 二漢爲五言者, 不過數家, 而婦人居二. 徐淑敍別之作, 亞於團扇矣.

When there is something that causes pain in relations between a man and wife, the texts composed are also sad and filled with reproach. Only a few have written in the five syllable line in the Han, and two of these are women. Xu Shu's composition on parting is inferior to the poem on the round fan [Lady Ban's poem].

An innocent reading of Zhong Rong's comment strongly suggests that he is writing only about Xu Shu. However, three of the four *Yutai xinyong* poems under Qin Jia's name are in the five syllable line and are far more attractive than Xu Shu's poem, essentially a poem in the four syllable line with a *xi* 兮 placed in the third position of every line. Thus readers have been very much disposed to understand Zhong Rong's comments as referring to Qin Jia *and* his wife.

In fact, the *Sui shu* "Bibliography" mentions a short collection only under Xu Shu's name.[48] It might indeed seem that Zhong Rong included this peculiar variant of a four syllable line in order to fill in his lacuna of Han writers in the five syllable line.

徐淑, 答秦嘉詩 Xu Shu, Answering Qin Jia[49]

妾身兮不令	My person is not good,
嬰疾兮來歸	encumbered by sickness, I have gone home.
沉滯兮家門	I lie bedridden in my family's gates,
歷時兮不差	with passing time I do not mend.

---

47. In the current version the heading reads: 漢上計秦嘉嘉妻徐淑詩, which by the doubling of the "Jia" 嘉 makes reference to both Qin Jia and his wife. If, however, there is only one "Jia," the entry would refer just as unambiguously only to Xu Shu. Doubling a character is one of the easiest changes to make in a text, and I suspect this was done for "clarity" once the Qin Jia poems were in circulation.

48. *Sui shu*, 1059.

49. Lu Qinli, 188; *Ytxy* 1.

曠廢兮侍覲	Helpless, I have to give up serving and seeing you,
情敬兮有違	in affection and respect I have missed the mark.
君今兮奉命	You now have received a command
遠適兮京師	and go afar to the capital.
悠悠兮離別	Long will be our separation,
無因兮敘懷	I have no means to give account of my feelings.
瞻望兮踴躍	I gaze afar, leaping with joy,
佇立兮徘徊	I stand long, faltering.
思君兮感結	Longing for you, responses take shape within,
夢想兮容暉	in dream I envisage the glow of your face.
君發兮引邁	You set forth, faring on,
去我兮日乖	leaving me farther away each day.
恨無兮羽翼	I feel bad that I do not have wings
高飛兮相追	to fly high and go after you.
長吟兮永歎	I chant long and give drawn-out sighs,
淚下兮沾衣	tears fall and soak my clothes.

We cannot know when this poem was composed—it might even be from the Eastern Han. We can, however, be reasonably certain that this is the poem that Zhong Rong had in mind in the entry in *Gradations of Poetry*. From the entry it also seems that Zhong Rong did not know of the Qin Jia poems; indeed they may not have been composed yet.

Here we should note a series of letters supposedly exchanged between Qin Jia and Xu Shu, preserved through quotation in anthology sources and in a Dunhuang manuscript.[50] These probably made up the bulk of the single scroll attributed to Xu Shu in the "Bibliography" of the *Sui shu* (the Xu Shu letters are clearly the centerpiece; the Qin Jia letters are rudimentary). Like the famous Li Ling letter included in the *Wen xuan*, these are certainly persona compositions. Here, as with Li Ling and Su Wu, we have a parting scene, supplied with letters and poem(s). Unlike the case of Li Ling, however, we have no early historical source for the story. Qin Jia is not mentioned in the *Hou Han shu*, and it is hard to imagine why Fan Ye would have left him and Xu Shu unmentioned if their collected correspondence and poems had been in wide circulation in the

---

50. Yan Kejun, *Quan Hou Han wen* 66.2b–3a, 96.8b–10a.

mid-fifth century.[51] The letters are mentioned in the first two "Lover's Union" "Hehuan shi" 合歡詩, attributed to Yang Fang 楊方 in the early Eastern Jin; but these are also *Yutai xinyong* poems.[52] When Jiang Yan wrote his series of imitations in the last part of the fifth century, he imitated neither Qin Jia nor Xu Shu; we can understand why he would not have imitated the Xu Shu poem, since it is not true five-syllable-line poetry; but he certainly would have imitated the Qin Jia poems if he had known of them. Thus we can suspect that the core of this material was produced no earlier than the second half of the fifth century and the Qin Jia poems, perhaps no earlier than the early Liang.

If the poem attributed to Xu Shu above was the one known to Zhong Rong, we can ascertain several things. By the early sixth century it was known that Qin Jia served as a local "deputy to the capital" and that his wife was sick in her natal home and did not have the chance to see him off: these are things that can be known from Xu Shu's letters and her poem. Xu Shu's piece was an answering poem. What was needed were poems to which Xu Shu's poem was the answer.[53] These were apparently discovered or supplied by the first part of the sixth century—significantly increasing the number of Eastern Han poems in the five syllable line.

秦嘉, 贈婦詩三首 Qin Jia, fl.147, attrib., To His Wife (three poems)[54]

Jia served as commandery deputy to the capital. His wife Xu Shu had returned to her home with a debilitating illness and he could not have a face-to-face parting with her. He sent her these poems.

I

人生譬朝露	Human life may be likened to morning dew,
居世多屯蹇	our dwelling in the world is full of adversity.
憂艱常早至	Grief and trouble always come too soon,
歡會常苦晚	joyous meetings are always terribly late.

---

51. Fan Ye was particularly fond of such occasions of pathos.

52. Lu Qinli, 860; *Ytxy* 3; *Yfsj* 76. One hesitates at wholesale suspicion of *Yutai xinyong* attributions unattested elsewhere, but the production of persona poems that passed from persona to authorship is precisely the question we are considering.

53. With the attribution of some of the poems of the Li Ling corpus to Su Wu, we might note the interest in constructing poem exchanges.

54. Lu Qinli, 186; *Ytxy* 1.

念當奉時役 I brood on how I had to accept timely service,
去爾日遙遠 and daily I grew farther from you.
遣車迎子還 I sent a carriage to bring you back;
空往復空返 it went off empty, and empty it returned.
省書情悽愴 When I read your letter, my heart felt sore,
臨食不能飯 facing my food I could not eat.
獨坐空房中 I sat alone in the empty room,
誰與相勸勉 with no one else to encourage me.
長夜不能眠 The whole night long I could not sleep,
伏枕獨展轉 I tossed and turned alone on my pillow.
憂來如循環 Grief comes like following a ring—
匪席不可卷 [my heart] "not being a mat, it cannot be rolled up."[55]

II

皇靈無私親 August spirits have no favoritism:
爲善荷天祿 doing good, one receives Heaven's recompense.
傷我與爾身 But I am pained that I and you personally,
少小罹煢獨 from youth have suffered solitude.
既得結大義 Since we were able to form the Great Bond,[56]
歡樂苦不足 pleasure and joy has been woefully inadequate.
念當遠離別 I brood on our being parted by great distance,
思念敘款曲 I yearn to give account of the secrets of the heart.
河廣無舟梁 The river is broad, no boat or bridge,
道近隔丘陸 the way is short, but we are separated by hill and highland.
臨路懷惆悵 Setting out on the road, I felt despair;
中駕正躑躅 in mid-course, I hesitated.
浮雲起高山 Drifting clouds rise from the high mountains,
悲風激深谷 gloomy winds stir the deep valleys.
良馬不廻鞍 The good horse does not turn back with its saddle,
輕車不轉轂 the light carriage does turn its wheels around.

---

55. A line from "Cypress Boat" 柏舟 in the *Shijing*.
56. That is, marriage.

針藥可屢進	The acupuncture needle and medicines may be often applied,
愁思難爲數	but sorrowful thoughts are hard to count.
貞士篤終始	The true gentleman is stalwart to the end,
思義可不屬	can our love not continue?

III

肅肅僕夫征	Swiftly the groom fares onward,
鏘鏘揚和鈴	tinkling the harmonious yoke bells resound.
清晨當引邁	In the clear dawn I must set off,
束帶待雞鳴	I tighten the sash and await the cockcrow.
顧看空室中	Looking back into the empty chamber,
髣髴想姿形	I vaguely envision your form.
一別懷萬恨	Once parted, I feel thousands of piques,
起坐爲不寧	rising and sitting, I am made uneasy by this.
何用敘我心	How can I give an account of my heart?
遺思致款誠	I send my longing and express my sincerity.
寶釵好耀首	The precious hair clasp gleams well on the head,
明鏡可鑒形	the polished mirror can reflect the form.
芳香去垢穢	Sweet scents get rid of foul odors,
素琴有輕聲	the plain *qin* has a delicate tone.
詩人感木瓜	The speaker in the *Poems* was stirred by the quince;
乃欲答瑤瓊	he wanted to respond with jade and *qiong* gems.[57]
愧彼贈我厚	I am ashamed at the generosity of the other's gift,
慚此往物輕	and am embarrassed at the triviality of these things I send.
雖知未足報	Though I know they are inadequate to repay,
貴用敘我情	they are valuable in expressing my feelings.

From the first poem we know that at least one of Xu Shu's letters already existed when this poem was composed. The more interesting question is whether the second of the Qin Jia letters to Xu Shu had already been written and was included in the collection; if that letter was part of the collection, then the poet here is simply versifying part of it in the third poem.

---

57. These and the lines that follow refer to "Quince" 木瓜 in the *Shijing*.

Here we have a nice case of author and persona, one that would slide over into forgery only through an intention to deceive. The Chinese term, however, was *bu* 補, "to fill in a gap"—a gap both in the poems that inspired Xu Shu's answer and more generally in absent Eastern Han poems in the five syllable line. This seems to have been an ongoing process: *Yutai xinyong* includes another poem to Xu Shu, this one in a four syllable line; in other sources we have two short poems on a wedding in the four syllable line and some other fragments. We cannot tell if these were composed in the persona of Qin Jia or were attributed to him as the "name" under which to place poems on marriage. As the literary scholars of the Qi and Liang organized the textual remains of early poetry and gave an account of it, they probably repaired much that seemed to their eyes imperfect and filled in more than a few gaps.

•

We have seen both poems composed for the particular circumstances of a particular speaker and the imputation of a speaker-author as a way to read less specific poems. We might now take up a case in which the imputation of authorship lends a level of depth to the reading of a poem, though the author is not the "speaker" in the sense of the preceding poems.

We know that sometime after the publication of the *Song shu* in 488 Lu Jue 陸厥 (472–99) took issue with Shen Yue's account of the history of euphony in poetry; and in the course of his argument he mentioned a "poem on history," *yong shi* 詠史, attributed to Ban Gu 班固 (A.D. 32–92). Ban Gu is placed in the lowest category of Zhong Rong's *Gradations of Poetry* on the basis of this poem, which Zhong Rong characterizes as "having lines that stirred [his?] sighs" 有感歎之詞. Although there are fragments from other poems that sound like "poems on history" in *Beitang shuchao* and *Taiping yulan*, the only complete "poem on history" is found in Li Shan's commentary to the *Wen xuan* and Zhang Shoujie's 張守節 *Shiji zhengyi* 史記正義, also from the Tang. The exclusion of this poem from the Liang anthologies and Sui and Tang encyclopedias, despite its early date and the eminence of its imputed author, is striking.

The poem retells the story of Tiying 緹縈, the daughter of Chunyu Yi, the Director of the Imperial Granaries in Qi. In the reign of Han Wendi, Chunyu Yi was charged with a serious offense and placed under arrest to await punishment. On being arrested, he complained to his daughters that he had no son to come to his aid. His youngest daughter, Tiying, followed him to the capital and sent a letter to the emperor, offering herself to die in her father's place. On reading the letter, Wendi was moved and ordered Chunyu Yi's release.

班固, 詠史 Ban Gu, On History[58]

三王德彌薄	The three kings' virtue grew increasingly thin,
惟後用肉刑	only then were flesh-cutting punishments used.
太蒼令有罪	The Director of Granaries was charged with a crime
就逮長安城	and was arrested in Chang'an.
自恨身無子	He was bitter that he had no sons of his own,
困急獨煢煢	in his urgent distress he felt helpless and alone.
小女痛父言	His youngest daughter was pained by her father's words,
死者不可生	those who die cannot be brought back to life.
上書詣闕下	She went to the palace gates to present a letter to the throne,
思古歌雞鳴	thinking of antiquity, she sang "Cockcrow."[59]
憂心摧折裂	Her anxious heart was breaking,
晨風揚激聲	and she raised the stirring sounds of the "Dawnwind Hawk."[60]
聖漢孝文帝	Emperor Wen of the Sagely Han
惻然感至情	felt pity, stirred by her intense feeling.
百男何憒憒	A hundred male children would be in such a muddle,
不如一緹縈	no match for a single Tiying.

---

58. Lu Qinli, 170. See Holzman, "Les premiers vers pentasyllabiques datés dans la poésie chinoise," 88–92.

59. "Cockcrow" 雞鳴 in the *Shi* makes reference to the "blueflies," figures for slanderers who present virtue as wrong. The implication is that her father has been falsely slandered.

60. "Dawnwind Hawk" 晨風 in the *Shijing* in the Mao version. "Dawnwind Hawk" is taken as criticizing Duke Kang of Qin for rejecting virtuous ministers; the "Three Schools" seem to be in basic agreement.

The first couplet establishes the moment in historical culture in which the narrative occurs, while the last couplet celebrates Tiying's virtue; the intervening couplets retell the narrative in a straightforward epitome fashion, showing modest erudition through allusion to the *Shijing*. Particularly the final couplet offering judgment is characteristic of poetic narratives of old stories, both in "poems on history" and *yuefu*.

It is not entirely beyond the reach of possibility that this poem could have been composed by Ban Gu; however, our first reliably datable versions of this type of poem do not appear until the early third century, the period when we begin to have general confidence in attributions. If we make the assumption that the poem was later attributed to Ban Gu, then we can ask why Ban Gu—not a name that commonly attracted the attribution of poems—was chosen.

The answer comes from Ban Gu's biography: Ban Gu died in prison and had a sister in the palace. In this context this piece of undistinguished verse, surviving in the flotsam and jetsam of the manuscript tradition, suddenly became interesting, with Ban Gu implicitly lamenting his own situation through historical parallel. By acquiring the property of an "author" the poem gains the most common kind of value in the Chinese poetic tradition: someone writing about his own case, writing about something that mattered to him personally through a parallel historical case. Only in this way can this poem be understood as having "lines that stirred sighs."

•

Even if an author only tells a story, if the story echoes back on the author's own case, as with Ban Gu, it can become an integral part of reading the poem.

曹植, 野田黃雀行 Cao Zhi, Brown Sparrow in
Wild Fields: A Ballad[61]

高樹多悲風	In tall trees the gloomy winds are heavy,
海水揚其波	the sea waters raise their waves.
利劍不在掌	If you don't have a sharp sword in hand,
結友何須多	what need to have many friends?

---

61. Lu Qinli, 425; *Yfsj* 39. Huang Jie, *Cao Zijian*, 98–99; Nie Wenyu, *Cao Zhi*, 79–83; Zhao Youwen, *Cao Zhi*, 206–7.

不見籬間雀	Have you not seen the sparrow in the hedge?—
見鷂自投羅	it saw the sparrow hawk and threw itself in the mesh.
羅家得雀喜	The fowler was delighted getting the sparrow,
少年見雀悲	but the young man saw the sparrow and felt sad.
拔劍捎羅網	He drew his sword and swept it through the net of mesh,
黃雀得飛飛	and the brown sparrow got to go flying off.
飛飛摩蒼天	It flew and flew until it brushed the gray sky,
來下謝少年	then came down and thanked the young man.

I do not want to dispute the attribution to Cao Zhi of this now famous poem; nevertheless, we should point out that the earliest primary source of the poem is the *Yuefu shiji* (another poem to the same *yuefu* title is given in *Song shu*). This *yuefu* is included in the current version of Cao Zhi's "Collected Works," but the "Collected Works" were recompiled entirely from anthology sources and citations; thus this poem was almost certainly taken from *Yuefu shiji*. This poem was not anthologized earlier or quoted in any of the Tang encyclopedias or Li Shan's commentary. Perhaps Guo Maoqian found it in an old edition of Cao Zhi's "Collected Works"; we do not know where he discovered it. Not to put too much of a point on it, Cao Zhi died in 232, and this poem did not surface until the turn of the twelfth century. The earlier existence of most Cao Zhi poems appearing fully for the first time in *Yuefu shiji* is confirmed by prior citations and references; that is not the case here.

The theme was an old one: we find it in the *Jiaoshi Yilin* of the Western Han:[62]

雀行求粒	A sparrow went looking for food,
誤入網罟	it mistakenly entered the fine-meshed net.
賴仁君子	By the grace of a kindly gentleman,
復脫歸室	it got away and went back home.

---

62. Chen Liangyun, *Jiaoshi Yilin*, 248.

In the *yuefu* this core motif has been complicated and drama-tized, with the general aphorism in the opening adding another level of complication to the parable.

The poem was not much noticed until Wang Fuzhi 王夫之 (1619–92) anthologized it in his *Gushi pingxuan* 古詩評選, calling it one of the two Cao Zhi *yuefu* that were still worth reading.[63] Later in the Qing the poem received more attention. A bit later Chen Zuoming 陳祚明 in his *Caishutang gushi xuan* 采菽堂古詩選 (1706) suggested that Cao Zhi was comparing himself to the sparrow.[64] The essential change came with Zhu Qian's 朱乾 *Yuefu zhengyi* 樂府正義, which noted that "he is feeling sad himself that his friend is in difficulty and doesn't have the strength to save him" 自悲友朋在難, 無力援救.[65] This makes the particulars of the poem best fit the case of an author speaking of his own situation. Zhang Yugu 張玉穀 in the *Gushi shangxi* 古詩賞析 adds some nuance, saying that because he doesn't have enough power, he has to fail a friend who had hoped to be saved by him.[66] Since several of Cao Zhi's closest friends were killed for their association with him after Cao Pi took the throne, the particulars for such a general putative case are well known.

Cao Zhi's friend Ding Yi 丁儀 had hoped to put Cao Zhi on the throne as Cao Cao's heir, and when Cao Cao considered doing this, Ding Yi urged the case. When Cao Zhi's brother Cao Pi took the throne instead, he wanted Ding Yi to commit suicide. Ding Yi was incapable of doing so and eventually he was thrown into prison and executed. Read from Cao Zhi's perspective in this context, the poem becomes very powerful; there is acute awareness of one's helplessness: if one does not have the power to help one's friends in a time of need, one should not make friends. The sense of helplessness is resolved by a parable of a young man who does have the sword to save the trapped bird. Because he may not openly protest the execution of Ding Yi and his brother (also Ding Yi 丁翼), he speaks figuratively. There are some loose ends: what does the "sparrow hawk" represent? Nevertheless, once the poem has found an author and cir-

63. *San Cao ziliao huibian*, 166.
64. Ibid., 188.
65. Ibid., 198.
66. Ibid., 210.

cumstances in the author's life that animate it, that frame is so crucial to understanding the poem that it becomes virtually part of the text—as canonical Chinese poetry has generally been accompanied by commentary around the text. Now it is this version of "Brown Sparrow in Wild Fields: A Ballad," rather than the long feast poem under the same title included in the *Song shu* and *Wen xuan*, that is included in anthologies.

It ceases to matter that the poem appears in the textual record remarkably late, under an author whose collection was notoriously filled with dubious attributions. And if we are persuaded by the ascription of authorship, it does not matter that we have no idea when in Cao Zhi's life the poem was composed. The poem has found its place in a great cultural narrative.

SIX

Imitation

The term *ni* 擬, usually translated as "imitation," does not appear in its literary sense until the second half of the third century.[1] It first occurs in several works by Fu Xuan 傅玄 (217–78) and became more widespread in the next generation, most famously in Lu Ji's imitations of the "old poems."[2] In these third-century usages and through the middle of the fifth century, *ni* referred to the imitation of a specific work rather than of an author.[3] Since most literary work in the period was based on reformulating shared material or emulating prior texts, we might ask what particular quality made an imitation "*ni*"? That is, if we use the term "imitation" in its broad, modern sense, why are some imitations "*ni*," while others are not?

We do have a general term "imitating the old" (*nigu* 擬古), perhaps from the late fourth century or as late as the sixth.[4]

---

1. An apparent exception is "Imitating Linked Pearls" 擬連珠 by Ban Gu, a fragment preserved in the *Yiwen leiju*. Even if the title is original, this is clearly not a "literary imitation" of a prior text: "Linked pearls" had not yet become a genre, and the title may be explicitly figurative, a series of gemlike aphorisms "resembling linked pearls." Cf. Fu Xuan's "Preface to 'Linked Pearls'" 連珠序, which gives Ban Gu as the first author. *Ywlj* 57.

2. Although the titles of poems were freely changed, the appearance in a single period of a number of poems by different authors preserved in different sources does suggest the general use of the term beginning in a specific age.

3. As mentioned previously, titles were particularly open to variation. Although there are several later cases where passages from third-century *yuefu* were cited with *ni* before the title, the use of *ni* before *yuefu* titles does not seem to have come into common use until the fifth century at the earliest.

4. Since the term "poem," *shi* 詩, was commonly appended to poem titles, we do not know how to parse the title *ni gu shi* 擬古詩, whether it is a "poem imitating the old" or "imitating the old poems." From the Eastern Jin usages, particularly Tao Qian's, *ni gu shi* did not seem to have the particular anony-

Otherwise, the term is fairly consistently used through the fifth century only for "imitating" specific titles.[5] By the late fifth century we are no longer sure if precedent poems under such titles actually existed or the imitator is simply choosing a typical title.[6] Imitating (*ni*) an earlier poem, moreover, did not mean stylistic imitation of that poem—not until the late fifth century, when we see the growth of literary historical consciousness and the complex mapping of period and authorial style. When Bao Zhao imitated the first of Ruan Ji's "Singing of My Cares" in the mid-fifth century, he was still following the older practice of rewriting the precedent text line by line in a more elevated register. Ruan Ji's "In the night I could not sleep" 夜中不能寐 becomes "The water-clock reached midpoint, I could not rest" 漏分不能臥. When Jiang Yan did his imitations of poets at the end of the fifth century, he was clearly trying to capture both period style and authorial style; at the same time, he no longer followed the earlier practice of couplet-by-couplet imitation.

We could call the third-century practice of *ni* "thematic imitation," but close comparison between the handful of extant imitations and "originals" reveals that *ni* is much more: for the most part, imitation means to rewrite an original in a higher register. That is, *ni* is one particular and specialized version of the various forms of recreating shared poetic material; and among these forms it is the only one that is specifically textual, responding to what is presumed to be a *fixed prior text*. *Ni* is also the only form of using prior poetic materials that

---

mous "old poems" as understood in the Qi and Liang in mind. It is possible, however, that this title was used by later editors for certain of Tao's untitled poems—after the meaning of *ni* had broadened.

5. The exception is Xie Lingyun's "Imitations of the Collection in Ye," which sounds like it is imitating a group of poems—though no such group of poems is known to exist. In contrast to other *ni*, no specific titles are named for the individual authors (though we can see sections of known poems in these imitations). For an extensive discussion of imitation and persona poetry in the *Yezhong ji*, see Mei Jialing, *Han Wei Liuchao wenxue xinlun: nidai yu zengda pian*, 5–92. Here we can see *ni* beginning to broaden with the imitation of only a specific prior passage.

6. Jiang Yan seems to be using categorical titles, though in some cases he is imitating particular known poems. When generally imitating someone's "style," *ti* 體, which we begin to find in the mid-fifth century, terms of "imitation" like *xue* 學 and *xiao* 效 are used.

requires consistent *difference* from its source text: one of its primary rules is avoiding verbal repetition in the important words in the line.

We can thus think of *ni* as a formalized extension of earlier poetics. In earlier poetics we had a freely recreated sequence of topics around a shared theme, with the topics arranged in a more or less determined sequence; there was variation in the articulation of these conventional topics, but these articulations were often very similar and sometimes identical. As *ni* appears in the late third century, the topics and their sequence become fixed in some particular prior text, and the difference of variation becomes a requirement for every significant word and phrase. Variation should, moreover, articulate a hierarchy of registers, so that the later text is always "higher." The figure of poetic "social mobility" seems to have been precisely what was at stake, as poetry in the five syllable line aspired to literary legitimacy.

Ni was used in a wide range of nonliterary ways from the Eastern Han through the Jin; one of the most common of these usages was *niji* 擬跡, "to follow the traces/footsteps" of some predecessor. This is a particularly suggestive usage in that it reminds us that "imitation" was not of some vague, general quality, but rather of specific "traces." Imitation of a prior text couplet by couplet is indeed "following the traces" of the predecessor text. Since this kind of imitation largely continued through the first part of the fifth century, these works can tell us much about the older texts whose traces they were following; specifically, from these "imitations" we can see how the texts they followed resemble or differ from the texts we now have.

Only a small number of complete *ni* survive from the third century. We have fragments of Fu Xuan's "imitations" of the *Heaven Questions* (*Tian wen* 天問) and *Calling Back the Soul* (*Zhao hun* 招魂) from the *Chuci*. His complete imitation of Zhang Heng's "Fourfold Poems of Sorrow" 四愁詩 (Lu Qinli, 573) is indeed line by line, as is the set by Zhang Zai 張載 in the next generation (Lu Qinli, 742). When Pan Yue claims to have "imitated" Cao Pi's *Poetic Exposition on the Widow* 寡婦賦, it may be difficult to believe that such a long piece followed Cao Pi's original line by line; but then Cao Pi's original survives only as a fragment.

The most important examples of "imitation" are found in Lu Ji's imitations of the "old poems" (including the imitation of one "old poem" not included in Xiao Tong's "Nineteen Old Poems").[7] We have thirteen of these, of which eleven recast the original, couplet by couplet, in a higher poetic register.[8] In some of these eleven we find additional couplets in the anonymous original or in the imitation. In two cases the order of couplets seems to have been transposed. The interesting question is how we interpret the divergences here. A liberal notion of *ni* would allow the imitator some latitude in working with the original. An alternative hypothesis is that Lu Ji was working with versions of the "old poems" that were slightly different from those that survived in the manuscript tradition in the early sixth century.

This second hypothesis gives us some confidence, otherwise unwarranted, that close versions of at least eleven of our "Nineteen Old Poems" were circulating in something very much like their present form in the last part of the third century. This same hypothesis, however, leads to the conclusion that Lu Ji knew a completely different version of "Nineteen Old Poems" IX and had a significantly different version of the most famous of all, the first poem. We must here stress that even if Lu Ji had slightly or significantly different versions from our current texts of the "Nineteen Old Poems," this does not mean that the current versions are necessarily later. We know from evidence preserved in the later manuscript tradition that a degree of textual variation was the norm, and we can reasonably guess that these popular anonymous poems were continually changing while in circulation. The Lu Ji "imitations," rather, show that in the case of the "old poems," at least, the degree of variation was already limited.[9]

---

7. For another recent discussion of these poems, see C. M. Lai, "The Craft of Original Imitation: Lu Ji's Imitations of the Han Old Poems," in *Studies in Early Medieval Chinese Literature and Cultural History*, 117–48.

8. We may have a hint that *ni* implied using a higher register than the original in Fu Xuan's preface to his imitation of Zhang Heng's "Fourfold Poems of Sorrow." There Fu Xuan describes the Zhang Heng set by saying: "their form is small and common" 體小而俗. "Common" or "vulgar," *su* 俗, was a distinctly pejorative term and not something to be imitated. The antithesis of *su* was *ya* 雅, roughly translated as "elegant," which would be the term that would best characterize a more elevated register.

9. We must, of course, also consider the degree to which the texts of the "old poems" were stabilized by the famous imitations.

In many cases Lu Ji's imitations provide a small "textbook" of examples of elegant variation in late third-century poetics. Sometimes we even see Lu Ji answering a prior line with a perfect parallel, as if original and imitation formed a parallel couplet. For "Whirling gusts rise, shaking the land" 迴風動地起 (XII), Lu Ji answers, "The falling dews descend, filling the heavens" 零露彌天墜. The parallelism answers "wind" 風 with "dew" 露, giving the common compound "wind and dew." "Heaven" ("heavens") parallels "Earth" ("land"); "descending" matches "rising."

Everywhere we see "elevation" of register: if the old poem has "the four seasons" 四時 (XII), Lu Ji offers the metonymic "hot and cold [weather]" 寒暑. If the four seasons merely "keep on changing" 更變化, Lu Ji's changing temperatures "creep up on one another" 相因襲. If, on hearing a woman play music, the speaker in the "old poem" rather baldly "wish[es] we could be two wild swans" 願爲雙鴻鵠 (V), Lu Ji rather "long[s] to ride the feathers of the homeward swan" 思駕歸鴻羽.

What the Lu Ji "imitations" give us is something invaluable: a very precise late third-century reading of some of the "Nineteen Old Poems." We will begin with the twelfth poem.

Nineteen Old Poems XII[10]

東城高且長	The eastern wall is high and long,
逶迤自相屬	winding off continuously
迴風動地起	Whirling gusts rise, shaking the land,
秋草萋已綠	the autumn plants are rich and green.
四時更變化	The four seasons keep on changing,
歲暮一何速	how swiftly comes the year's end.
晨風懷苦心	The dawnwind hawk harbors a bitter heart,
蟋蟀傷局促	the crickets lament how hard pressed they are.[11]
蕩滌放情志	Set your mood and aims free, sweeping along—
何爲自結束	why constrain yourself?

---

10. Lu Qinli, 332; *Wen xuan* 29; *Ytxy* 1 (as Mei Sheng). Sui Shusen, *Gushi*, 18–19; Diény, *Les dix-neuf poèmes anciens*, 30–31, 117–25.

11. These lines are commonly understood as referring to *Shi* 132 ("Dawnwind Hawk" 晨風) and 114 ("Cricket" 蟋蟀), respectively. The interpretation of the lines is reconfigured to match the Mao understanding of these poems. See Appendix F.

燕趙多佳人	There are many fair women from Yan and Zhao,
美者顏如玉	the most beautiful have complexions like jade.
被服羅裳衣	They are clothed in gossamer skirts and gowns,
當戶理清曲	at their doors they practice clear melodies.
音響一何悲	How sad the music's echoes are—
絃急知柱促	from the high-pitched strings one knows the pegs are set tight.
馳情整巾帶	Passions gallop, I straighten kerchief and sash,
沉吟聊躑躅	brooding, I pause there awhile.
思爲雙飛燕	I wish we could be a pair of swallows in flight,
銜泥巢君屋	mud in beaks to make a nest in your roof.

The main point of Qing and modern scholarly contention in this poem is its unity. The poem presents no serious problem of coherence, but scholars have noticed a break between lines 10 and 11. The sense of a break comes from long experience of early poetry: lines 9 and 10 are a common form of poetic conclusion, while line 11 is an opening template ("at place X there is much Y," using "much," *duo* 多, in the third position of the five syllable line). The Qing scholar Zhang Fengyi 張鳳翼 first offered the speculation that this was indeed two poems mistakenly joined together because they shared the same rhyme.[12] Ji Yun used the Lu Ji imitation in his response, noting that Lu treated it as a single poem. Diény offers the suggestion that seems to be the correct one: poem conjoins segments, as we find in *yuefu*.[13]

Lu Ji's imitation is followed by the juxtaposition of the original and imitation side by side.

---

12. Quoted in Sui Shusen, *Gushi*, 18.

13. Diény, *Les dix-neuf poèmes anciens*, 123. While Diény draws a valid conclusion, we must object to his formulation of the insight: that the author of the poem is "imitating" the shifts of *yuefu*. This presumes a historical sequence. Diény compares the shift between segments here to the third of the "Nineteen Old Poems"; however, we might note that passages of the third poem are cited in *Beitang shuchao* as "old *yuefu*."

陸機, 擬東城一何高 Lu Ji, Imitating
"How high the eastern wall is"[14]

西山何其峻	How high west mountain looms!—
層曲鬱崔嵬	in tiered bends it swells towering.
零露彌天墜	The falling dews descend, filling the heavens,
蕙葉憑林衰	the melilotus leaves decay in the woods.
寒暑相因襲	Cold and heat creep up on one another,
時逝忽如頹	the seasons go off swiftly as if tumbling down.
三閭結飛轡	The Master of the Three Clans ties his flying reins,[15]
大耋嗟落暉	octogenarians sigh at the setting sunglow.
曷爲牽世務	Why be drawn by duties of the age?—
中心若有違	my heart within feels like it has missed something.
京洛多妖麗	In Luoyang there are many beguiling beauties,
玉顏侔瓊蕤	jade faces, the like of alabaster flowering.
閑夜撫鳴琴	On calm nights they strum zithers,
惠音清且悲	their gentle notes, clear and mournful.
長歌赴促節	Their long songs move to the urgent rhythm,
哀響逐高徽	mournful echoes follow the high-set strings.
一唱萬夫歎	Singing once, a thousand sigh;
再唱梁塵飛	singing again, the dust flies on the rafters.[16]
思爲河曲鳥	I long to be those birds by the river's bends,
雙游灃水湄	swimming as a pair by the shores of the Feng.

東城高且長	西山何其峻
逶迤自相屬	層曲鬱崔嵬
迴風動地起	零露彌天墜
秋草萋已綠	蕙葉憑林衰

---

14. Lu Qinli, 688; *Wen xuan* 30; *Yutai xinyong* 3. Hao Liquan 郝立權, *Lu Shiheng shi zhu* 陸士衡詩注 (Beijing: Renmin wenxue chubanshe, 1958), 48.

15. Qu Yuan, whose title was "Grand Master of the Three [Royal] Clans" of Chu. Li Shan suggests that this refers to the line in the Li Sao: 總余轡乎扶桑 "I gathered my reins together at the Fusang Tree." Thus this line would refer to sunrise and the following line, to sunset.

16. These are commonplaces for music that is popular and excellent.

四時更變化	寒暑相因襲
歲暮一何速	時逝忽如頹
晨風懷苦心	三閭結飛轡
蟋蟀傷局促	大耋嗟落暉
蕩滌放情志	曷爲牽世務
何爲自結束	中心若有違
燕趙多佳人	京洛多妖麗
美者顏如玉	玉顏伴瓊蕤
被服羅裳衣	閑夜撫鳴琴
當户理清曲	惠音清且悲
音響一何悲	長歌赴促節
絃急知柱促	哀響逐高徵
馳情整巾帶	一唱萬夫歎
沉吟聊躑躅	再唱梁塵飛
思爲雙飛燕	思爲河曲鳥
銜泥巢君屋	雙游灃水湄

We should first note that Lu Ji uses a different "title," which is to say a version of the first line different from that in the *Wen xuan* version given above.[17] This is no accident, since Lu Ji's opening line "imitates" (*ni*) the title as he gives it in the title of the imitation, rather than the current version. This should alert us to the probability that while the text we now have is more or less the one Lu Ji used, there were still likely many differences in the particular phrasing of lines.[18]

Lu Ji's acts of "imitation" often clarify what is ambiguous or problematic in the original. Commentators have gone to some length to explain the fourth line: "autumn plants are rich and green." The description seems inappropriate for autumn vegetation; the fact that commentators have gone to these lengths to show that it is indeed appropriate testifies to the problem. The word *qi* 萋 (written 凄) can mean "bleak," but in combination with "green" it describes lush vegetation. Diény cites a line

---

17. The *Yutai xinyong* gives the title / first line as it occurs in the current version of the "Nineteen Old Poems." Since the *Yutai xinyong* is a text that was much tampered with in later periods, it is hard to say what its original reading was.

18. We must allow even the third-century "imitator" some latitude; nevertheless, it is hard not to notice that the second line of the "old poem" elaborates the "long," the element omitted in Lu Ji's version of the original. On a speculative level, in the version of the "old poem" that Lu Ji knew the second line may have been different and stressed height.

by Lu Ji's contemporary Zhang Xie 張協, from the first of his "Unclassified Poems": "plants in the yard are rich and green" 庭草萋以綠 (Lu Qinli, 745). This is also an autumn poem, and the line here may be a textual memory of this particular "old poem." This gives us some confidence that Lu Ji was imitating the line as we now have it. Lu Ji, however, refashions the line to produce a more conventional image of autumn vegetation: "the melilotus leaves decay in the woods" 蕙葉憑林衰 (using the high register locator verb *ping* 憑, "to rest upon").

The third couplet is an exemplary case of *ni*, in which each hemistich of each line is recast with a synonym or paraphrase in a higher register. The creatures from the natural world in the fourth couplet have been replaced by human beings, including Qu Yuan. The rhetorical move here is homologous to the elevation in lexical register: the "low" creature is replaced by human beings who by quality (Qu Yuan) or age hold an exalted position.

In the fifth and final couplet of the first segment Lu Ji transposes the order and eliminates the marker of poetic closure; the shift that troubled a number of Qing critics is here softened—though Lu Ji keeps the opening template in the following couplet. The lexical elevation of register is commonly accompanied by more explicitly elite concerns. The speaker in the old poem felt generally hampered: "why constrain yourself?" 何爲自結束. Lu Ji's constraints are explicitly those of public service: "Why be drawn by duties of the age?" 曷爲牽世務 (substituting the usual interrogative *he* 何 with the archaic interrogative *he* 曷, phonologically distinct from *he* 何 in the third century).

The second segment follows the current "old poem" very closely, except in the penultimate couplet, where there is perhaps too much passion for Lu Ji:

馳情整巾帶	Passions gallop, I straighten kerchief and sash,
沉吟聊躑躅	brooding, I pause there a while.

Lu Ji instead continues the music motif, only implying the powerful effect on the listener:

一唱萬夫歎	Singing once, a thousand sigh;
再唱梁塵飛	singing again, the dust flies in the rafters.

Driven less by the habits of the repertoire than the particular text he is imitating, Lu Ji comes at last to the wish to become a pair of birds. What happens to the *shuang* 雙 ("pair") is worth noting. In the surviving examples that belong to the old compositional repertoire, *shuang* should directly modify the birds. Lu Ji's revision omits the *shuang*, but displaces it to the line that follows (exactly the same displacement occurs in Lu Ji's imitation of the fifth of the "Nineteen Old Poems").

Lu Ji's procedures in "imitation" are obvious and relatively consistent. They give us a clear sense of what marked distinctions in register, and from that sense we can measure the "old poem" against the imitation. We cannot always be certain that the current version of an "old poem" was the exact text Lu Ji knew, but in a majority of cases it is relatively clear whether Lu Ji's "original" was essentially the same as our current text or different.

•

The case of the second of the "Nineteen Old Poems" is an excellent example of an imitation that confirms that our present text is the one Lu Ji had.

Nineteen Old Poems II[19]

青青河畔草	Green, green, the grass by the river;
鬱鬱園中柳	in the garden the willows are thick and full.
盈盈樓上女	Lovely, the girl in the upper story,
皎皎當窗牖	bright, she stands at the window.
娥娥紅粉粧	Beautiful, made up in red rouge,
纖纖出素手	she puts out her pale hand, so slender.
昔爲倡家女	She used to be a girl of a singer's family,
今爲蕩子婦	now she is the wife of a wastrel.
蕩子行不歸	The wastrel travels and does not come home,
空牀難獨守	an empty bed is hard to keep alone.

陸機, 擬青青河畔草 Lu Ji, Imitating
"Green, green, the grass by the river"[20]

| 靡靡江蘺草 | Wind-ruffled, the river grasses, |
| 熠燿生河側 | gleaming fresh, they grow by the river's side. |

---

19. Lu Qinli, 329; *Wen xuan* 29; *Ytxy* 1 (as Mei Sheng); *Ywlj* 32; *Cxj* 19. Sui Shusen, *Gushi*, 3–4; Diény, *Les dix-neuf poèmes anciens*, 10–11, 59–62.

20. Lu Qinli, 687; *Wen xuan* 30; *Ytxy* 3; *Ywlj* 32. Hao Liquan, *Lu Shiheng*, 45.

皎皎彼姝女	Bright is that fair maiden,
阿那當軒織	lithe and graceful, she weaves by the window rail.
粲粲妖容姿	Sparkling are her beguiling features,
灼灼美顏色	richly radiant, her lovely complexion.
良人遊不歸	Her husband roams and does not return,
偏棲獨隻翼	she roosts isolated, a single wing alone.
空房來悲風	To her empty room comes a gloomy wind
中夜起歎息	and at midnight she rises and gives a sigh.

青青河畔草	靡靡江蘺草
鬱鬱園中柳	熠燿生河側
盈盈樓上女	皎皎彼姝女
皎皎當窗牖	阿那當軒織
娥娥紅粉粧	粲粲妖容姿
纖纖出素手	灼灼美顏色
昔為倡家女	良人遊不歸
今為蕩子婦	偏棲獨隻翼
蕩子行不歸	空房來悲風
空牀難獨守	中夜起歎息

Lu Ji has retained the sequence of descriptive compounds at the beginning of the first six lines, the most striking formal feature of the poem and one that probably accounts for its textual stability. We note, however, that while the "old poem" uses only descriptive compounds that repeat the same syllable, Lu Ji has made two into descriptive compounds whose syllables rhyme, but do not repeat (*dieyun*); likewise he has varied the pattern of the second line so as not to repeat the grammar of the first line. We can assume that variation to avoid monotony was already part of a high poetic register, and in some basic ways *ni* imitation was an exercise in variation.

The second kind of "elevation" that Lu Ji works on the "old poem" is to clean up its dubious morality. The woman in the "old poem" is putting on makeup, a distinctly inappropriate activity for a woman whose husband is away; even worse, she is doing it by the window where she can be seen. Lu Ji's beauty has to be visible, but she is attending to more appropriate womanly tasks by weaving. Lu Ji's woman does not stretch out her hand. The woman in the "old poem" comes from a dubious social background, a "singer's family," and her husband is a "wastrel," *dangzi* 蕩子, at very best a man who does not stay home when he should. The husband in Lu Ji's poem is referred to more positively as *liangren* 良人, her husband, or literally her "goodman." Finally, the wife in the "old poem" has trouble keeping an empty bed; Lu Ji's wife has an "empty room" and wakes in sad but decent solitude, sighing in the night. Lu Ji has in mind someone like the unmarried girl of Cao Zhi's "The Beauty" 美女篇:[21]

佳人慕高義	The fair woman aspires to one of great virtue,
求賢良獨難	seeking a worthy man is truly uniquely hard.
眾人徒嗷嗷	In vain the crowd murmurs in distress,
安知彼所觀	how can they understand how she looks on things?
盛年處房室	In life's prime she stays in her chambers,
中夜起長歎	at midnight she rises and gives a long sigh.[22]

In the account of literary history that took shape in the Qi and Liang, the higher poetic register that appeared in the Western Jin was sometimes viewed as the beginning of a frivolous ornamentation that was morally suspect. In the Western Jin itself, however, the higher register seems to have embodied a strong sense of class difference, linked not only to learning but to the moral values of the elite.

We can see the difference between *ni* in Lu Ji's sense and its looser meaning toward the middle of the fifth century by looking at the version by the Liu-Song prince Liu Shuo (431–53).[23] He maintains the theme and the ten-line length, but the couplets no longer match as closely as Lu Ji's. Furthermore, the avoidance of repeated patterns in poetic rhetoric had become so habitual that Liu Shuo seems unable to bring himself to use six descriptive compounds in a row:

劉鑠, 擬青青河畔草 Liu Shuo, To
"Green, green, the grass by the river"[24]

| 淒淒含露臺 | Chill is Dewy Terrace, |
| 蕭蕭迎風館 | gloomy, the Lodge to Receive the Wind.[25] |

---

21. Lu Qinli, 431.

22. Ibid., 431–32.

23. According to the *Nan shi* Liu Shuo wrote over thirty imitations of early poetry. *Nan shi*, 395.

24. Lu Qinli, 1215; *Ytxy* 3.

25. Even though these are given as if they are names, neither are clearly identified, although Han Wudi built a Palace to Receive the Wind.

思女御櫺軒	The longing woman serves at the grillwork railing,
哀心徹雲漢	her mournful heart penetrates the Milky Way.
端撫悲絃泣	With purpose she brushes the sad strings weeping,
獨對明燈歎	alone she faces the bright candle sighing.
良人久徭役	Her husband has long been away in service,
耿介終昏旦	with pure resolution she spends dawn to dusk.
楚楚秋水歌	Bitter, that song of autumn waters,
依依採菱彈	full of fond longing, the ditty on picking water chestnuts.[26]

Lu Ji had elevated the woman of the poem from singer status to respectability; Liu Shuo raises her even higher by placing her in a palatial setting. In the second couplet, which locates the woman in some visible part of the building, Lu Ji was compelled to repeat the straightforward locator of the original, *dang* 當, "to be at." Liu Shuo wants to raise the register without using one of the high register locators that imply "leaning on," which could be taken as slovenly literal in the present context; he comes up with the rather excessive *yu* 御, "serves at." Lest she seem still too earth-bound, her misery rises up all the way to the stars. The third couplet of the original has the woman applying makeup and extending her hand; Lu Ji has already busied her hands with wifely weaving and uses this couplet simply to describe her beauty. Liu Shuo uses the woman's hand for a more aristocratically expressive purpose, brushing the strings of a zither. Although we do find the theme of song and performance in the anonymous originals, it particularly fascinated the poets of the fifth and early sixth centuries. After the fourth couplet, in which the husband is declared absent, Liu Shuo ends the poem with a parallel couplet, naming kinds of music and their affect. More than anything else in the poem, this displacement of the concluding statement of sorrow, which we see in Lu Ji's poem, marks the fifth century. Instead of having the woman rising at night and sighing, the poet names different tunes, merely implying her emotions through their associations.

---

26. This was a Southern Dynasties song-type.

From roughly the same period as Liu Shuo, Bao Linghui, Bao Zhao's sister, also maintains the ten lines but shows a similar liberty.

鮑令暉, 擬青青河畔草 Bao Linghui, Imitating
"Green, green, the grass by the river"[27]

褭褭臨窗竹	Swaying gracefully, the bamboo by the window,
藹藹垂門桐	shadowing, the tung tree at the gate's edge.
灼灼青軒女	Radiant, the girl at the blue balcony,
泠泠高臺中	fresh and chill on the high terrace.
明志逸秋霜	Her bright aims leave behind the autumn frost,
玉顏豔春紅	jade complexion, gorgeous as springtime red.
人生誰不別	In human life who does not know parting?—
恨君早從戎	yet she hates that he had to go off on campaign so early.
鳴絃慚夜月	Singing strings are shamed by the night moon,
紺黛羞春風	her red and black brows are embarrassed by the spring breeze.[28]

It seems likely that either Bao Linghui knew of Liu Shuo's version or vice versa (or, perhaps, there was a whole series of such imitations that no longer survive). In the third couplet Liu Shuo's "her mournful heart penetrates the Milky Way" matches Bao Linghui's "her bright aims leave behind the autumn frost," and neither have precedent in the anonymous version or in Lu Ji's imitation. Likewise, Bao Linghui also uses the motif of music in the final couplet. Later imitations often become less useful for reflecting the textual state of the original because they can develop their own traditions and echo one another.

At some point we must stop and acknowledge that we have these imitations primarily through the *Wen xuan* and *Yutai xinyong*, rather than through the chance survivals of commentary and the encyclopedias. The early sixth century was the era that canonized the anonymous "old poems." If Lu Ji's "imitations" contributed to the canonization process, anthologizing subsequent imitations confirmed it. In the same way the

---

27. Lu Qinli, 1313; *Ytxy* 4.
28. A carmine was used as well as black in painting brows.

Wen xuan is largely responsible for the supporting materials that contributed to the canonization of the Jian'an "moment." Countless poetic expositions were overlooked, but Xiao Tong provided his selection of the materials in the *Lunwen* 論文 chapter of Cao Pi's *Dianlun* 典論, which focused on the Jian'an Masters.[29] It was Xiao Tong who preserved for us the famous letters of Cao Pi and Cao Zhi, commenting on the Jian'an "moment." And it was Xiao Tong who ignored some of Xie Lingyun's best landscape poems to include Xie's "Imitations of the Collection at Ye," which can be considered valuable only as a tribute to the Jian'an. If in reading pre-Tang literature we keep coming back to the "old poems" and Jian'an, that is, in part, the result of continuing (or renewed) interest in the third through fifth centuries; but it is also, in part, the motives of sixth-century anthologists who documented their importance.

Early fifth-century imitators generally retain the number of lines, though they sometimes exercise the freedom to vary the topic. Thus when Lu Ji also uses the same number of lines, it is sometimes hard to tell if the imitators are imitating the "old poem" or Lu Ji's imitation. When Lu Ji's lines vary, we can get an indication. For "Nineteen Old Poems" III, we have a Lu Ji imitation with an additional couplet and a Bao Zhao imitation with the same number of couplets as the "old poem." The close adherence of both imitations to the original suggests that Bao Zhao and Lu Ji had essentially the same "old poem," but Lu Ji's version was one couplet longer.[30] Bao Zhao, however, permits himself a liberty: he is uninterested in describing the wonders of the city and suggests looking for beautiful girls instead.

Nineteen Old Poems III[31]

青青陵上柏	Green, green, cypress on mound,
磊磊澗中石	scattered around, stones in a ravine.[32]

---

29. The fragments preserved in Yan Kejun suggest that the original version included more on Han authors.

30. By Bao Zhao's time Xie Lingyun's poetry anthology would have already been in circulation. It is an unprovable speculation that our current versions of the "old poems" came to us through that widely circulated anthology.

31. Lu Qinli, 329; *Wen xuan* 29. Sui Shusen, *Gushi*, 4–5; Diény, *Les dix-neuf poèmes anciens*, 12–13, 62–70.

32. *Leilei* 磊磊 (translated as "scattered around") is the quality of an area covered with small rocks, as one does indeed find in a stream bed. English unfortunately has no appropriate descriptive other than "stony" or "rocky."

人生天地間　Man is born between Heaven and Earth,
忽如遠行客　he goes swiftly, like a traveler far
　　　　　　　　from home.

斗酒相娛樂　With a gallon of ale we make merry,
聊厚不爲薄　let it be thick ale, not the thin.[33]
驅車策駑馬　Speed the wagon, whip on the nag,
游戲宛與洛　to go have fun in Wan and Luo.
洛中何鬱鬱　How Luoyang teems with people,[34]
冠帶自相索　men with caps and sashes seek out
　　　　　　　　one another.

長衢羅夾巷　Long avenues set with narrow alleys,
王侯多第宅　with many mansions of princes and counts.
兩宮遙相望　The two palaces face one another afar
雙闕百餘尺　with twin turrets rising more than a
　　　　　　　　hundred feet.

極宴娛心意　Feast till the end, delight the heart,
戚戚何所迫　why be oppressed by troubled thoughts.[35]

陸機, 擬青青陵上柏 Lu Ji, Imitating
"Green, green, cypress on mound"[36]

冉冉高陵蘋　Burgeoning, the bin plant on the high ridge,
習習隨風翰　wings moving with the gentle breeze.
人生當幾時　Just how long does human life last?—
譬彼濁水瀾　liken it to ripples in muddy water.
戚戚多滯念　Troubled, many concerns linger in me,
置酒宴所歡　I serve ale and feast those I love.
方駕振飛轡　Teams side by side, the flying reins shake,
遠游入長安　we travel far, into Chang'an.
名都一何綺　How finely wrought is that famed metropolis,
城闕鬱盤桓　its wall-towers well up magnificently!
飛閣纓虹帶　Soaring pavilions, strung with rainbow
　　　　　　　　sashes;
層臺冒雲冠　tiered terraces, capped by covering clouds.

---

33. This line is open to a variety of interpretations. "Thick" and "thin" can describe the depth of human relationships as well as ale.

34. *Yuyu* 鬱鬱 (translated as "teems with people") describes something thickly packed (unexpressed feelings, willow leaves). I have added "with people" because of the following line, but it can also refer to the buildings of the great city.

35. It is ambiguous whether this is merely an injunction not to worry or implies that the person addressed is indeed troubled.

36. Lu Qinli, 688; *Wen xuan* 30. Hao Liquan, *Lu Shiheng*, 47.

高門羅北闕	High gates are ranged by the northern turrets,
甲第椒與蘭	the chief mansions, Pepper and Orchid.[37]
俠客控絕景	Men-at-arms rein in faster-than-light chargers,
都人騁玉軒	people of the great city hitch up jade coaches.
遨遊放情願	Roaming freely, we follow our mood and desires—
慷慨爲誰歎	overcome by feeling, for whom does one sigh?

鮑照, 擬青青陵上柏 Bao Zhao, Imitating
"Green, green cypress on mound"[38]

涓涓亂江泉	In streaming trickles, springs cut across the river's current,
綿綿橫海煙	continuous, the mist driving across the sea.
浮生旅昭世	This life adrift is as a sojourner in a glorious age,
空事歎華年	I spend time in vain sighing over my flowering years.
書翰幸閒暇	Fortunately having leisure for book and pen,
我酌子縈絃	I will pour, you wind the strings,[39]
飛鑣出荊路	A flying horse-bit sets out on the roads of Jing,
鶩服指秦川	the galloping charger to the right heads for the streams of Qin.
渭濱富皇居	The Wei's shores are rich in imperial dwellings,
鱗館匝河山	lodges like scales encompass the rivers and hills.
輿童唱秉椒	Lads in coaches sing of holding pepper in the hand,[40]
櫂女歌采蓮	girls at the oar sing songs of picking lotus.
孚愉鶯閣上	There is pleasure up in the simurgh towers,
窈窕鳳楹前	secluded beauty before the phoenix pillars.

---

37. Pepper and Orchid are from the Li Sao, figures of the emperor's favorite ministers.

38. Lu Qinli, 1298; Huang Jie 黃節, *Bao Canjun shi zhu* 鮑參軍詩注 (Beijing: Zhonghua shuju, 1972), 132–33.

39. *Yingxian* 縈絃 should mean winding up the zither strings and not having them strung. We expect this to be turning up the strings to tune them in order to play, though it may be in preparation for the travel that follows.

40. As a gift for a loved one.

娛生信非謬　　To delight in this life is truly no error,
安用求多賢　　what point in seeking to be very virtuous.

青青陵上柏	冉冉高陵蘋	涓涓亂江泉
磊磊澗中石	習習隨風翰	綿綿橫海煙
人生天地間	人生當幾時	浮生旅昭世
忽如遠行客	譬彼濁水瀾	空事歎華年
斗酒相娛樂	戚戚多滯念	書翰幸閒暇
聊厚不爲薄	置酒宴所歡	我酌子縈絃
驅車策駑馬	方駕振飛鸞	飛鑣出荊路
游戲宛與洛	遠游入長安	驚服指秦川
洛中何鬱鬱	名都一何綺	渭濱富皇居
冠帶自相索	城闕鬱盤桓	鱗館匝河山
長衢羅夾巷	飛閣纓虹帶	[輿童唱秉椒]
王侯多第宅	層臺冒雲冠	[櫂女歌采蓮]
兩宮遙相望	高門羅北闕	[孚愉鶯閣上]
雙闕百餘尺	甲第椒與蘭	[窈窕鳳楹前]
	俠客控絕景	
	都人騁玉軒	
極宴娛心意	邀遊放情願	娛生信非謬
戚戚何所迫	慷慨爲誰歎	安用求多賢

Bao Zhao's avoidance of some of the obvious variations used by Lu Ji suggests that he knew both the "old poem" and Lu Ji's version and that the principle of difference in variation could encompass earlier imitations of the same original as well as the original itself.

Lu Ji clearly enjoyed showing his rhetorical superiority, but in some basic way he was still very close to the poetic world of the "old poems." Rhetorical flourishes seemed neither a challenge nor a delight to Bao Zhao; by the fifth century ornamented diction was commonplace, and Bao Zhao's imitation here is plain in comparison to many of his poems—though still far more "elevated" than Lu Ji. Indeed, one of Bao Zhao's striking characteristics is his fascination with "popular" poetry and the poetic past, a fascination that in many ways set the stage for the appreciation of the more straightforward early poetry at the end of the century.

Bao Zhao opens brilliantly with images of liquid currents and wind-driven mist over water, which resolves into the required motif of life's brevity in the second couplet. We are, however, clearly in a world very different from that of Lu Ji or the speaker of the old poems: life is still short, but Bao Zhao's brief life is set in a "glorious age," which means he has leisure. The moments of pleasure that must be seized in early poetry come to Bao Zhao as good fortune. He has leisure for writing—for "book and pen," *shuhan* 書翰. We should pause here, in that the subsequent pleasures described (and indeed prescribed by the model text) are anything but bookish. Writing may, however, be the context for pleasure, in that the kind of utter indulgence described may be achieved only textually and by returning to imitate a poem of two or three centuries earlier.

Perhaps the most profound difference between Bao Zhao and the earlier poems may be in the closing. The speaker or the listener in the old poem is in danger of sinking into gloom and depression. Taking pleasure in the moment is the alternative; it is the means of holding depression at bay. For Bao Zhao, however, the alternative to pleasure is "seeking to be very virtuous." The Liu-Song was not, practically speaking, a very safe age; Bao Zhao himself was eventually killed in an army uprising. But here I think we can see that there was the illusion of a world in order—the "glorious age" of the third line is mere politeness, but the absence of the desperation that one finds in early poetry is something more profound. It may be that this underlying sense of security (however unjustified) that appeared in the fifth century was the precondition for a fascinated return to early poetry, with its images of a society torn apart and no one "at home."

•

The sixth of the "Nineteen Old Poems" and the anonymous "Orchid and duruo grow in spring light" 蘭若生春陽 (not included in Xiao Tong's "Nineteen") also match Lu Ji's imitations line by line. In many cases, such as the fifth of the "Nineteen Old Poems," however, there are slight divergences between our current versions of the poems and the Lu Ji imitations, suggesting that Lu Ji knew a slightly different version.

Nineteen Old Poems V[41]

西北有高樓	To the northwest stands a high tower
上與浮雲齊	whose top is level with drifting clouds,

---

41. Lu Qinli, 330; *Wen xuan* 29; *Ytxy* 1 (as Mei Sheng). Sui Shusen, *Gushi*, 7–9; Diény, *Les dix-neuf poèmes anciens*, 16–17, 78–86.

交疏結綺窗	its windows are meshed with latticework,
阿閣三重階	with eaves all around, three flights of stairs.
上有絃歌聲	From above came song and the sound of a harp
音響一何悲	whose echoes were sad as they could be.
誰能爲此曲	And who could sing a song like this?—
無乃杞梁妻	it must be someone like Qi Liang's bride.
清商隨風發	The clear *shang* mode came out with the wind,
中曲正徘徊	and then faltered, mid-melody;
一彈再三歎	once she strummed, then sighed again,
慷慨有餘哀	impassioned and filled with melancholy.
不惜歌者苦	I don't care that the singer feels pain,
但傷知音稀	what hurts is that few understand the sound.
願爲雙鴻鵠	I wish we could be two wild swans
奮翅起高飛	to fly with great wingbeats high and away.

陸機, 擬西北有高樓 Lu Ji, Imitating
"To the northwest stands a high tower"[42]

高樓一何峻	How the high tower looms above!—
迢迢峻而安	far above, looming and steady.
綺窗出塵冥	Its meshed windows emerge from the darkening dust,
飛陛躡雲端	its soaring stairs stride to the edge of clouds.
佳人撫琴瑟	A fair woman strokes a zither,
纖手清且閑	her delicate hand is pure and idle.
芳氣隨風結	Her fragrant breath concludes with the breeze,
哀響馥若蘭	and the mournful echoes are as redolent as orchids.
玉容誰能顧	Who can look on her marble features?—
傾城在一彈	the ruin of cities lies in a single plucking of the strings.
佇立望日昃	I stand long, gazing on the sun's declination,
躑躅再三歎	pausing uncertain, I sigh repeatedly.
不怨佇立久	I don't resent standing there so long,
但願歌者歡	I want only that the singer feel joy.
思駕歸鴻羽	I long to ride the feathers of the homeward swan,
比翼雙飛翰	and wing to wing, we will fly as a pair.

---

42. Lu Qinli, 688; *Wen xuan* 30; *Ytxy* 3. Hao Liquan, *Lu Shiheng*, 49.

西北有高樓　　　　　　高樓一何峻
上與浮雲齊　　　　　　迢迢峻而安
交疏結綺窗　　　　　　綺窗出塵冥
阿閣三重階　　　　　　飛陛躡雲端
上有絃歌聲　　　　　　佳人撫琴瑟
音響一何悲　　　　　　纖手清且閑
誰能為此曲
無乃杞梁妻
清商隨風發　　　　　　芳氣隨風結
中曲正徘徊　　　　　　哀響馥若蘭
一彈再三歎　　　　　　玉容誰能顧
慷慨有餘哀　　　　　　傾城在一彈
　　　　　　　　　　　佇立望日昃
　　　　　　　　　　　躑躅再三歎
不惜歌者苦　　　　　　不怨佇立久
但傷知音稀　　　　　　但願歌者歡
願為雙鴻鵠　　　　　　思駕歸鴻羽
奮翅起高飛　　　　　　比翼雙飛翰

Lu Ji does not imitate the fourth couplet and adds another couplet after the sixth in the original. The fourth couplet, speculating on the kind of person that could play such music, is indeed anomalous in the corpus of anonymous old poems—and, as we have seen, anomalous moves are not common in this early poetry. It further disrupts the description of the music that is continuous in the Lu Ji version. The possibility that this particular couplet might not have been in Lu Ji's version is of some interest: without this couplet the "old poem" has a stranger and a woman, whose music expresses some undefined sadness; the stranger concludes that he would like to fly away with her. We should not read too much into the additional couplet in question, but Qi Liang's wife, on hearing of her husband's death, composed a zither song before committing suicide. In a very light way this speaks to the ethical issues that might otherwise be at stake in the poem, like the ethical issues that were very much at issue in the second of the "Nineteen Old Poems." That is, on a less explicit level than Lu Ji's imitations the couplet in our current version of the "original" "raises" the ethical tone of the poem.

Lu Ji's additional couplet is also interesting, in that it uses both hemistiches of the first line of the sixth couplet in the original (一彈再三歎). The "old poem" is ambiguous as to whether the person sighing and feeling pain is the woman or the listener; Lu Ji's imitation clarifies this and makes it explicit.

Lu Ji also "fixes" the most striking and problematic couplet of the original:

| 不惜歌者苦 | I don't care that the singer feels pain, |
| 但傷知音稀 | what hurts is that few understand the sound. |

Lu Ji wants to keep the rhetorical contrast and indeed finds something for the first line that the speaker need not feel bad about:

| 不怨佇立久 | I don't resent standing there so long, |
| 但願歌者歡 | I want only that the singer feel joy. |

The closing wish to become a pair of birds is retained, recast in a high register.

•

The evidence of Lu Ji's imitations is valuable for understanding the "old poems" at an early phase; the evidence is, however, often ambiguous and open to very different interpretations. In his imitation of the seventh of the "Nineteen Old Poems," "The bright moon's rays are gleaming" 明月皎夜光, Lu Ji has one couplet more than the original.

Nineteen Old Poems VII[43]

明月皎夜光	The bright moon's rays are gleaming,
促織鳴東壁	the crickets sing by the eastern wall.
玉衡指孟冬	The Jade Yoke points to early winter,
眾星何歷歷	how clear are the hosts of stars!
白露霑野草	White dew soaks the wild plants,
時節忽復易	and the season has suddenly changed once more.
秋蟬鳴樹間	Autumn cicadas sing among the trees,
玄鳥逝安適	the swallows go off to where?
昔我同門友	Friends of the same circle long ago
高舉振六翮	have risen high, beating their sixfold wings.
不念攜手好	With no care for our fondness, once holding hands,
棄我如遺跡	they abandoned me like tracks left behind.

---

43. Lu Qinli, 330; *Wen xuan* 29. Sui Shusen, *Gushi*, 10–11; Diény, *Les dix-neuf poèmes anciens*, 20–21, 90–96.

南箕北有斗	In the South the Sieve, the North has the Dipper,
牽牛不負軛	the ox of burden bears no yoke.[44]
良無盤石固	Truly lacking the firmness of boulders,
虛名復何益	what gain comes from an empty name?

陸機, 擬明月皎夜光 Lu Ji, Imitating
"The bright moon's rays are gleaming"[45]

歲暮涼風發	At year's end a chill wind rises,
昊天肅明明	the vast heavens are bright and stern.
招搖西北指	The Flarer star points northwest,[46]
天漢東南傾	the River of Stars pours over to the southeast.
朗月照閑房	The bright moon shines in an idle room,
蟋蟀吟戶庭	the crickets hum within the yard.
翻翻歸鴈集	Winging, the migrating wild geese roost,
嘒嘒寒蟬鳴	chittering, the cold weather cicadas sing.
疇昔同宴友	Friends with whom I shared feasts long ago
翰飛戾高冥	have flown with their wings to the high, dark skies.
服美改聲聽	Robed in finery, they have changed what they listen to,
居愉遺舊情	dwelling in cheer, they abandoned what they used to feel.
織女無機杼	The Weaver Woman lacks loom or shuttle;
大梁不架楹	the Great Beam rests on no column.[47]

明月皎夜光	歲暮涼風發
促織鳴東壁	昊天肅明明
玉衡指孟冬	招搖西北指
眾星何歷歷	天漢東南傾
白露霑野草	
時節忽復易	
	朗月照閑房
	蟋蟀吟戶庭
秋蟬鳴樹間	翻翻歸鴈集
玄鳥逝安適	嘒嘒寒蟬鳴

---

44. This couplet reworks images from *Shi* 203, *Dadong* 大東 (*Xiaoya*), on constellations that do not perform the functions of their names. Thus it is a figure of "name," *ming* 名, without "substance" or "fact," *shi* 實.

45. Lu Qinli, 689; *Wen xuan* 30. Hao Liquan, *Lu Shiheng*, 50.

46. The seventh star of the Northern Dipper, here probably referring to the Dipper as a whole.

47. See note 44 to this chapter.

昔我同門友　　　　疇昔同宴友
高舉振六翮　　　　翰飛戾高冥
不念攜手好　　　　服美改聲聽
棄我如遺跡　　　　居愉遺舊情
南箕北有斗　　　　織女無機杼
牽牛不負軛　　　　大梁不架楹
良無盤石固
虛名復何益

Commentators on the "old poem" have spilled much ink on the apparent astronomical error of the Jade Yoke constellation indicating the first month of winter in a poem obviously and explicitly set in autumn, not to mention the clarity of the stars conjoined with bright moonlight. In a poetics that has spring birds flying south and lets the sun wax and wane along with the moon, we should perhaps not worry too much about such imprecision. We certainly do not need to appeal to ancient calendars. This was not a referential poetics; and in the context of the third century or earlier (as opposed to the sanctity of the *Wen xuan*) the offending stellar configuration could change with the mood of the reciter. It may be sheer chance that we have the present line.[48]

The autumn scene leads to the departure of the swallows, which allows the transition to former friends who no longer care for the speaker, having "flown off" on high. At this the speaker reworks the images of constellations from "Great East" 大東 in the *Shijing*, as the traditional images of things whose behavior does not match their name; in the same way his "friends" do not behave as friends should.

There are several peculiar things about Lu Ji's imitation. Most of the couplets match very closely. Lu Ji's title renders the opening line of the current version correctly, so we can assume that our current version of the first couplet was also his. His imitation is within a normative range of variation, describing

---

48. One resists the history of argument around such a line at the risk of seeming unscholarly. Still, the immense attention granted to the referential problem here is a function of the canonization of the "Nineteen Old Poems." Referential inconsistencies in other poems of the age are ignored. Other poems are permitted to be clumsy or to have been garbled in transmission. Canonicity can be oppressive, requiring that the poems bear more weight of scrutiny than they can sustain.

the atmosphere of late autumn on the edge of winter. The second couplet is an even more exact reworking of the original and gets the correct stellar configuration.

In the third couplet, however, Lu Ji replaces the original couplet on dew and the changing seasons with a couplet on moonlight and the cries of insects, the exact pairing of topics in the opening couplet of the original version. There are several possible explanations for this. One possibility is that he is "correcting" the *taxis* of the original, just as he raises the register. Instead of opening with a couplet on Heaven (moon) and Earth (crickets), then moving to Heaven and then to Earth again, he opens with a scene of Heaven and then brings the focus down to Earth in the third couplet. By the late Southern Dynasties and the Tang, the original order would have been more correct, with the second couplet developing the first line and the third couplet developing the second line; but this was not yet the case in Jin poetic rhetoric. It is, of course, also possible that the third couplet in Lu Ji's original had yet another "moonlight and insect cries" couplet. Whatever the explanation, the pressure of an original clearly led Lu Ji to something he would have avoided without the constraints of *ni* imitation: he gives two couplets in sequence both with the cries of insects.

The rest of the poem follows the original very closely, consistently raising the register. Lu's version does not, however, have a couplet matching the final couplet of the original, which draws the obvious lesson from the names of constellations. Lu Ji's ending, as it stands, is quite unusual in elite poetics of the Western Jin; and unless we take this as a particularly bold move on Lu Ji's part, we must conclude that the version he knew also ended abruptly. This should not surprise us. As admired as these anonymous verses must have been, they still probably had a degree of variability, permitting expansion or contraction in a particular rendition. The anonymous *yuefu* "Going Out Xia Gate," in its current version, also ends abruptly with just such a parallel couplet:

天上何所有	What is there up in Heaven?
歷歷種白榆	white elms planted in clear array.

桂樹夾道生	Cinnamon trees grow lining the road,
青龍對伏趺	the Green Dragon crouches facing them.

The "Ballad of Longxi" opens with these same lines and continues them. Anyone would recognize that an ending such as the one above was not a "full" version, but verses could be performed or transcribed in pieces.

As for "Nineteen Old Poems" VII, it would have been quite natural for another version or some later reciter or scribe to add the final couplet and draw the appropriate lesson.

Chasing Phantoms: The First of the "Nineteen Old Poems"

As we suggested earlier, eleven of Lu Ji's thirteen imitations correspond either exactly or mostly with the current versions. This is a strong statistical argument for assuming that in the two cases where the imitations do not match the current versions Lu Ji was working with texts that looked quite different from our current versions. If we add all the other examples of *ni* through the mid-fifth century, "imitations" that follow known originals couplet by couplet, the probability is stronger still. We will have to grant the possibility that in these two cases Lu Ji was simply demonstrating "creative liberty"; that is an argument that cannot be refuted any more than it can be proven. Even those who would argue for Lu Ji's "creative liberty" should at the same time acknowledge that there may have been versions of the "old poems" in the late third century that were quite different from the versions used by anthologists of the early sixth century.

It was not uncommon for different poems to have the same first line. Thus when we compare Lu Ji's imitation of "Nineteen Old Poems" IX, "There is a rare tree in my yard" 庭中有奇樹, with the anonymous version and find them very different, we need not be surprised: Lu Ji was probably reading a different "original" that used the same opening line.

The case of the first of the "Nineteen Old Poems" is far more complex: The first line (of course), the "animal couplet" in the middle, and the end match; there are also lines that match here and there; but as a whole the imitation does not match the anonymous "old poem" that we have.[49] To attempt to reconstruct the "original" poem that Lu Ji imitated would be a vain and foolish enterprise. To look for the parallels and sequences of topics *as if* seeking to reconstruct an original, however, can give us insight into the poetics of the "old poems." When we add the third-century counterparts of our current version of "Nineteen Old Poems" I, we get a fuller sense of the intricacy of links, themes, and variations at work.

We can begin with the current version of the first of the "Nineteen Old Poems," perhaps the most famous piece in all early classical poetry.

Nineteen Old Poems I[50]

行行重行行	On and on, on and on,
與君生別離	parted from you in life.
相去萬餘里	We are more than ten thousand leagues apart,
各在天一涯	each at a different edge of the sky.
道路阻且長	The road between is blocked and long.
會面安可知	how can we meet face to face?
胡馬依北風	The nomad horse leans to the north wind,
越鳥巢南枝	the bird of Yue nests on the southward branch.
相去日已遠	We grow daily farther apart,
衣帶日已緩	my belt gets daily looser.
浮雲蔽白日	Drifting clouds block the bright sun,
遊子不顧返	the traveler does not look to return.
思君令人老	Longing for you makes me old,
歲月忽已晚	the years and months are suddenly late.
棄捐勿復道	Drop it! say no more!
努力加餐飯	try your best to eat more.

---

49. We know of a couplet cited as an anonymous "Walking Out Xia Gate" 古步出夏門行 that begins with the same first line as the anonymous version and continues: "the bright sun draws near the western hills" 白日薄西山 (Lu Qinli, 290). The same texts are commonly cited as *yuefu* or as an "old poem," and this could be another "old poem" version; but the second line matches neither the current "old poem" nor the Lu Ji imitation. There is a Liu Shuo poem given as an imitation of "Nineteen Old Poems" I in *Yutai xinyong*, but given as simply *Nigu* 擬古 in *Wen xuan*. This poem is two couplets longer than the anonymous poem, and overall matches neither Lu Ji's version nor the anonymous version.

50. Lu Qinli, 329; *Wen xuan* 29; *Ytxy* 1 (as Mei Sheng); *Ywlj* 29. Sui Shusen, *Gushi*, 1–3; Diény, *Les dix-neuf poèmes anciens*, 8–9, 49–59.

陸機, 擬行行重行行 Lu Ji, Imitating
"On and on, on and on"[51]

悠悠行邁遠	Ever onward, my journeying goes far,
戚戚憂思深	dismal, my troubled thoughts deepen.
此思亦何思	And what thoughts are these thoughts?—
思君徽與音	I think on your excellence and repute.
音徽日夜離	Separated day and night from your excellence and repute,
緬邈若飛沈	far asunder, as one flying and the other underwater.
王鮪懷河岫	The royal paddlefish longs for the grotto by the river;[52]
晨風思北林	the dawnwind falcon thinks of the northern forests.
遊子眇天末	The traveler is faint at the end of the horizon,
還期不可尋	and a date for return cannot be sought.
驚飆褰反信	Sudden gusts snatch up the returning messenger,[53]
歸雲難寄音	one cannot send word by homing clouds.
佇立想萬里	I stand long, envisioning thousands of leagues away,
沈憂萃我心	and brooding cares gather in my heart.
攬衣有餘帶	I feel my clothes, there is extra length in the sash;
循形不盈衿	I trace my form, it does not fill the gown's folds.
去去遺情累	Going farther off, I leave the entanglements of feeling,
安處撫清琴	and reside in peace, stroking the clear zither.

行行重行行	悠悠行邁遠
與君生別離	[戚戚憂思深]
相去萬餘里	[此思亦何思]
各在天一涯	[思君徽與音]
道路阻且長	[音徽日夜離]
會面安可知	[緬邈若飛沈]

---

51. Lu Qinli, 685; *Wen xuan* 30; Hao Liquan, *Lu Shiheng*, 42.

52. Legend has it that the paddlefish entered the Yellow River by coming through a grotto that connected with rivers and lakes in the South. See David Knechtges, *Wen xuan* (Princeton: Princeton University Press, 1982), 1: 252–53. The point here is that the paddlefish, once in the Yellow River, longs for the grotto that links it to the South from whence it came.

53. In this period *xin* 信 should mean messenger: perhaps this is a figurative usage for the clouds in the following line or for birds.

胡馬依北風　　　　　　　王鮪懷河岫
越鳥巢南枝　　　　　　　晨風思北林
相去日已遠，

　　　　　　　　　　　　遊子眇天末
　　　　　　　　　　　　還期不可尋
　　　　　　　　　　　　驚飆褰反信
　　　　　　　　　　　　歸雲難寄音
　　　　　　　　　　　　佇立想萬里
　　　　　　　　　　　　沈憂萃我心
衣帶日已緩　　　　　　　攬衣有餘帶
　　　　　　　　　　　　循形不盈衿

浮雲蔽白日
遊子不顧返
思君令人老
歲月忽已晚
棄捐勿復道　　　　　　　去去遺情累
努力加餐飯　　　　　　　安處撫清琴

Fame and canonicity carry weight. To lighten that burden we should keep in mind that, so far as we know, this poem became the "first" of the "Nineteen Old Poems" only in the *Wen xuan* selection and arrangement. Xiao Tong may have followed the sequence of Lu Ji's imitations in this positioning of the "original," but Lu Ji's other imitations in the *Wen xuan* do not follow the same sequence in which Xiao Tong gives the anonymous originals.

Let us suggest as a hypothesis that Lu Ji was imitating a poem that began "On and on, on and on," a poem that shared some lines with the current version but was different in what was included and in the arrangement. The compositional practice that produced the anonymous poems (both our present version and the version that Lu Ji imitated) involved the recombination and reformulation of common topics around a set theme. This gives us some hope that in the remnants of that poetic tradition, we can perhaps find some of the pieces that made up Lu Ji's version.

The version of "On and on, on and on" that we have as the first of the "Nineteen Old Poems" is a perfect piece of poetry and fully deserves its canonical status. I do not, however, believe it is a "Han" poem in the sense of being a fixed text—though the pieces that constitute it probably originated in the Eastern Han.

As a poem it is a fortuitous or gifted realization of a common theme.

If we were not trying to read Lu Ji's poem as an imitation of the first "Nineteen Old Poems" and were simply trying to find what text he was imitating, we would have no difficulty at all locating the source for the opening passage. I will first quote the entire poem, then compare the opening passages in the first segment.

[蔡邕], 飲馬長城窟行 [Cai Yong], I Watered
My Horse at a Watering Hole by the Great Wall[54]

青青河邊草	Green, green, the grass by the river,
綿綿思遠道	on and on, I long for him on the far road.
遠道不可思	The one on the far road may not be longed for—
宿昔夢見之	last night I saw him in dreams.
夢見在我傍	I saw him in dreams at my side;
忽覺在他鄉	I suddenly woke, he was in a different land.
他鄉各異縣	In a different land, each in another place,
展轉不可見	I toss and turn and cannot see him.
枯桑知天風	The leafless mulberry knows heaven's wind;
海水知天寒	the sea's waters know heaven's cold.[55]
入門各自媚	Whoever comes in the gate is sweet to his own,
誰肯相爲言	no one is willing to talk to me.
客從遠方來	A traveler came from far away
遺我雙鯉魚	and gave me a pair of carp.[56]
呼兒烹鯉魚	I called to the boy to boil the carp
中有尺素書	and inside there was a letter.
長跪讀素書	I knelt down and read the letter,
書中竟何如.	and what was it like in the letter?—
上有加餐食	At first it said to eat more,
下有長相憶	then it said, I love you always.

青青河邊草	悠悠行邁遠
綿綿思遠道	戚戚憂思深
遠道不可思	此思亦何思
宿昔夢見之	思君徽與音
夢見在我傍	音徽日夜離

---

54. Lu Qinli, 192; *Wen xuan* 27 (as "old lyrics"); *Ytxy* 1; *Ywly* 41; *Yfsj* 38.
55. Cf. the same pattern in an anonymous *yuefu* quoted in *Tpyl*: 天寒知被薄, 憂思知夜長 (Lu Qinli, 294).
56. That is, a letter case in the shape of a fish.

忽覺在他鄉　　　　　緬邈若飛沈
他鄉各異縣
展轉不可見
枯桑知天風　　　　　王鮪懷河岫
海水知天寒　　　　　晨風思北林
入門各自媚
誰肯相為言

Except for Lu Ji's first line, which reformulates the first line of the current "old poem," lines 2 through 6 of "I Watered My Horse" could serve perfectly as the "originals" for Lu Ji's reworking in a higher register; the opening lines of the current version of the first of the "Nineteen Old Poems" do not match Lu Ji's lines. Lu Ji even retains the repetitions in "I Watered My Horse" that link lines together, which is not proper in elite Jin poetics and is uncommon in anonymous *yuefu* and old poems.[57] This relatively long series of linked phrases marks this version of "I Watered My Horse" as clearly as the long series of descriptive compounds at the beginning of lines marks "Nineteen Old Poems" II (which begins with the same opening line as "I Watered My Horse").[58]

"I Watered My Horse" is another *Wen xuan* text and as canonical as "On and on, on and on." Before we can snatch out its opening, we need to dismantle the poem. This version of "I Watered My Horse" is a compound *yuefu*, each of whose two segments fortuitously begins with a line that also begins one of the "Nineteen Old Poems." The first segment, "Green, green, the grass by the river," is essentially the same opening as that of the second of the "Nineteen Old Poems" discussed above: there a woman longs for an absent beloved (and seems to invite a stranger to her bed); here a woman longs for an absent beloved. The second segment, beginning "A stranger came from a faraway place," is the same opening as "Nineteen Old Poems" XVIII, where a woman also receives a message from the absent beloved. The same theme appears as a segment in "Nineteen Old Poems" XVII, in a form even closer to the segment in "I

---

57. Cf. the version of "I Watered My Horse" by Fu Xuan; Lu Qinli, 556. This clearly imitates part of the present version, but takes off in other directions. Lu Ji echoes the pattern of repetitions without duplicating them exactly, as he did in the imitation of "Nineteen Old Poems" II.

58. This should be distinguished from repeated phrases linking "stanzas" (or poems in a set), as in Cao Zhi's "For Biao, Prince of Baima" 贈白馬王彪.

Watered My Horse." Like "Nineteen Old Poems" XII, "I Watered My Horse" is an excellent example of one form of segmented composition in which the first theme leads smoothly into the second theme to make one continuous poem.

We might be tempted simply to graft lines 2–6 of "I Watered My Horse" onto the corresponding lines of "On and on, on and on" to produce the beginning that Lu Ji imitated. Thematically this would present no problem; but here, however, we encounter a problem of rhymes. "I Watered My Horse" opens with three "rhyming couplets" (AA, BB, CC), while "On and on, on and on" uses "couplet rhyme" (AB, CB, DB).[59] We should add that although it uses couplet rhyme, "On and on, on and on" changes rhyme midway. Following elite practice, Lu Ji's imitation uses couplet rhyme but carries the whole poem through on a single rhyme. We can be reasonably certain that Lu Ji is "upgrading" his original with respect to rhyming practice; we don't know, however, whether his original used rhyming couplets or passages in couplet rhyme.

We do know one thing for certain: *hang* 行 does not rhyme with *dao* 道; if "I Watered My Horse" is the obvious model for the opening and if the first line of the original must be "On and on, on and on" (*hanghang chong hanghang* 行行重行行), then either the last word of the second line must be revised to rhyme with *hang* or the last word of the fourth line must be changed to produce couplet rhyme.[60]

Let us assume, for the sake of argument, that the version of "On and on, on and on" that Lu Ji knew began with some variation on the material that opens "I Watered My Horse," with a woman longing for the absent beloved. Considering the couplet on the "royal paddlefish" and "dawnwind hawk" in Lu Ji's imitation, it is likely that his version of the "original" was continued by the images of the "nomad (*hu*) horse" and the "Yue bird," as in the current version. What then of the rest?

---

59. "I Watered My Horse" also uses couplet rhyme later.

60. *Hang* is a common and easy rhyme, and indeed the rhyme used in ll. 5–6 of "I Watered My Horse." I adopt the reading *hang* for 行, rather than the predominant modern reading *xing*, because *hang* is almost always required when it is used as a rhyme word in third-century poetry.

Lu Ji's fifth couplet looks as if it goes with the current version:

遊子眇天末　　　The traveler is faint at the end of
　　　　　　　　　　the horizon,
還期不可尋　　　and a date for return cannot be sought.

Here, perhaps, "I Watered My Horse" can give us inspiration. Possibly the version Lu Ji knew used rhyming couplets. We can, indeed, match Lu Ji's lines by taking a sequence of two rhyming lines out of the first part current version (ll. 4, 6):

各在天一涯　　　Each at a different edge of the sky,
會面安可知　　　how can we meet face to face?

We cannot say that these are the actual sources for Lu Ji's imitation, but if we juxtapose our imagined original with Lu Ji's lines, we find something perfectly consistent with Lu Ji's process of imitation elsewhere (including sometimes keeping one ordinary word in the same position in a line, in the second line of our couplet):

各在天一涯　　　　　　　遊子眇天末
會面安可知　　　　　　　還期不可尋

Lu Ji's following couplet on the failure to send a message in the clouds calls to mind the centrality of the letter in "I Watered My Horse." It has no counterpart in our current version of "On and on, on and on," though the clouds do appear there as blocking the sun.

Messages are a very common topic in the theme of separation, even though they do not appear in the current version of "On and on, on and on." There are essentially three poetic situations of "messages." There is the "gift-message to be sent": the plant or sprig plucked by a woman and sent to the beloved ("Nineteen Old Poems" VI, IX). There is the "message received": it is usually brought when "A traveler came from far away" 客從遠方來, the situation in "I Watered My Horse" (as well as "Nineteen Old Poems" XVII and XVIII). The final situation is the "message sent that can't get through (or its arrival is unknown)." This is clearly the situation in Lu Ji's imitation and perhaps in his original. The failed message is carried by a cloud or bird messenger, attested first in the Jian'an poets and a poem in the Li Ling corpus.

李陵 Li Ling, attrib.[61]

有鳥西南飛	A bird went flying southwest,
熠熠似蒼鷹	shining brightly, like the gray hawk.
朝發天北隅	At dawn it set out from a nook north of the heavens,
暮聞日南陵	in the evening it was heard on a hill south of the sun.[62]
欲寄一言去	I wanted to send word,
託之牋綵繒	I put it on a note of brightly colored silk.
因風附輕翼	With the wind I attached it to its wings,
以遺心蘊蒸	to send the feelings that swell in my breast.
鳥辭路悠長	The bird took its leave, the journey was long,
羽翼不能勝	its wings were unable to bear it up.
意欲從鳥逝	I wanted to go off following the bird,
駑馬不可乘	but my worn-out horse could not be mounted.

Perhaps the most famous example of the failed bird messenger is in the last part of Cao Zhi's first "Unclassified Poem" 雜詩:[63]

孤鴈飛南游	A lone goose roams southward in flight,
過庭長哀吟	as it passes my yard, it gives a long sad cry.
翹思慕遠人	My thoughts take wing, loving the person afar,
願欲託遺音	and I want to entrust it [goose] with word.
形影忽不見	Its outline is suddenly not to be seen,
翩翩傷我心	its swift wing-beats wound my heart.

The cloud messenger of Lu Ji's imitation appears in Cao Pi's second "Banquet Poem" 燕歌行.[64]

鬱陶思君未敢言	With pent-up feeling, I long for you and dare not speak,
寄聲浮雲往不還	I send word by the floating clouds, they go and don't return.

We therefore can suspect that a message was dispatched in the version of "On and on, on and on" that Lu Ji knew.

---

61. Lu Qinli, 339; *Guwen yuan* 4.
62. "South of the sun," Rinan 日南, was also the name of a Han commandery.
63. Lu Qinli, 456; *Wen xuan* 29.
64. Lu Qinli, 394; *Song shu*; *Ytxy* 9; *Yfsj* 32.

The couplet that follows in Lu Ji's imitation is a statement of longing and misery, which is common enough, though a specific example of this sequence of topics is hard to place in lower register poetry:

| 佇立想萬里 | I stand long, envisioning thousands of leagues away, |
| 沈憂萃我心 | and brooding cares gather in my heart. |

Although this is not the closing, it looks like a closing couplet. The sequence of topics, however, begins to become familiar. Let us consider one of the most innocuous of the "Nineteen Old Poems":

Nineteen Old Poems VI[65]

涉江採芙蓉	I crossed the river to pick lotus,
蘭澤多芳草	many fragrant plants in the orchid bog.
采之欲遺誰	When I pick them, to whom will I give them?—
所思在遠道	the one I love is far away.
還顧望舊鄉	He turns to look, gazing toward his home,
長路漫浩浩	the long road stretches on through the vastness.
同心而離居	Hearts as one, yet living apart:
憂傷以終老	worry and pain through old age.

Here we have the love-gift or message, the gazing, the accumulation of pain, and old age. In the Lu Ji imitation of "On and on, on and on" we have the message, the gazing, and the accumulation of pain. In the current anonymous version of "On and on, on and on" we have the gazing (phrased negatively, "the traveler does not look to return") and the mention of old age. As we often find in early poetics, a sequence of recurring words (or synonyms) is repeated, even when the statements made around those words change.

The final part of Lu Ji's imitation circles back to match the current version. The couplet on the loosening sash in Lu Ji's imitation matches the line in the anonymous poem, and Lu Ji's conclusion is a characteristic transformation of the "old poem" closing.

If all this has grown too intricate, let me try to tell a story, assuming that we can rearrange the order, change the gender,

---

65. Lu Qinli, 330; *Wen xuan* 29; *Ytxy* 1 (as Mei Sheng); *Ywlj* 29.

and choose alternatives. A man and a woman are separated. Their relationship is undefined, though they long for one another. They do not exist in the ordinary geography of China with place-names; they exist in an abstract two-dimensional geography of the interval that separates them. We do not know why the traveler travels; we know only that he travels by necessity and would go home if he could. From the perspective of each, the other is beyond the horizon.

The woman dreams of the man one night—or, as we will see, she simply envisages his appearance. When she wakes, she finds she is alone. Or perhaps, from the intensity of her longing, "in the night she cannot sleep." She picks plants to send to him. He tries to send a message by bird or cloud, but unsuccessfully. Perhaps he only gazes toward home, his vision blocked by cloud. Perhaps a traveler passes by, going toward his home; he gives him a letter to take to his beloved. He is growing thinner from longing, his clothes hanging looser on his body; he knows that she must be experiencing the same. Longing makes a person old. In the letter—or simply the implied message in the closing—he says: "I will love you always; try to eat more."[66]

•

We have pieces of this narrative in our current anonymous version of "On and on, on and on," in Lu Ji's imitation, and in "I Watered My Horse." None of them have all the parts and variations of the narrative, but when we put them together and add other poems on separation, the sequences are obvious and often repeated. If Lu Ji was "imitating" a version of this story that differs from our current version, we can find the current version scattered throughout a set of poems attributed to the first part of the third century. [67] Consider the first poem of the set "Chamber Thoughts" 室思 of Xu Gan 徐幹:[68]

---

66. The exegetes try to make the current version of "On and on, on and on" close with the speaker's resolution to eat more himself and cease longing; this is possible, but seems rather warped, however little he may hope to return. "Eat more" is the message appropriate to send to the beloved.

67. I have no confidence in the textual integrity of poems anthologized in *Yutai xinyong*, but the reader is welcome to take this as evidence of the existence of the received version of "Nineteen Old Poems" I in the early third century.

68. Lu Qinli, 376; *Ytxy* 1. Han Geping, *Jian'an*, 351–52.

沉陰結愁憂	Sunken in shadow, trouble and sorrow form,
愁憂爲誰興	on whose account do sorrow and cares arise?
念與君生別	I think on being parted from you while alive,
各在天一方	each of us in a different corner of the sky.
良會未有期	There is no time set for a happy meeting,
中心摧且傷	My heart is shattered and wounded within.
不聊憂飡食	I am listless and too worried to eat,
慊慊常飢空	I am unsatisfied and ever starving.
端坐而無爲	I sit up straight and do nothing
髣髴君容光	and vaguely see your bright appearance.

Setting aside the rhetorical beginning couplet and reserving the final couplet for future consideration, the middle couplets of this poem are virtually a synopsis of the current "Nineteen Old Poems" I. If some of the topics are missing, the opening lines of the second poem fill them in.[69]

峨峨高山首	Looming, the top of the high mountain,
悠悠萬里道	lasting on, the thousand league road.
君去日已遠	You go off daily farther away,
鬱結令人老	the swelling feeling makes one old.

The third poem adds the clouds, which, as suggested above, tend to be failed messengers (ll. 1–6):[70]

浮雲何洋洋	How billowing are the drifting clouds!—
願因通我辭	I want to use them to send my words.
飄颻不可寄	They are whirled on and I cannot send word by them,
徙倚徒相思	I linger, helplessly longing for you.
人離皆復會	When people are separated they always meet again,
君獨無返期	you alone have no date for return.

Of course, the poor woman longs so intensely for her beloved that she cannot sleep, which brings us to the fourth poem of the series, discussed earlier in the set of poems on sleeplessness.[71]

What is of particular interest, however, is the closing of the first poem: "I sit up straight and do nothing / and vaguely see

---

69. Lu Qinli, 376; *Ytxy* 1. Han Geping, *Jian'an*, 351–52.
70. Lu Qinli, 376; *Ytxy* 1. Han Geping, *Jian'an*, 351–52.
71. See pp. 77–91.

your bright appearance." Although Xu Gan's is a waking vision versus a dream (with "bright appearance," *rongguang* 容光, being a standard high register term for physical appearance), this version shares the appearance of the beloved as a consequence of longing with "I Watered my Horse."

青青河邊草	Green, green, the grass by the river,
綿綿思遠道	on and on, I long for him on the far road.
遠道不可思	The one on the far road may not be longed for—
宿昔夢見之	last night I saw him in dreams.
夢見在我傍	I saw him in dreams at my side;
忽覺在他鄉	I suddenly woke, he was in a different land.

Even though Lu Ji may have been working with a different version of "On and on, on and on," it is still, in a deeper sense, all "one poem."

•

By observing the kinds of transformations Lu Ji performed on his originals, we can measure our "originals" as the "traces" in which he walked (*niji* 擬跡). When we do this, we find that these "old poems" had more or less stabilized by the end of the third century—but only "more or less." We can also strongly suspect that Lu Ji had a version of "On and on, on and on" different from the one that survived into the Qi and Liang. The version that did survive is itself old and a remarkable work—we may even be glad that it survived rather than Lu Ji's version. Triangulating an imaginary space between Lu Ji's imitation and the current version, we can see how low register texts were still changing shape in the late third century. While we can never find the poem Lu Ji imitated, we can find all the pieces that could have been imitated and the sequences that linked such pieces together.

Appendixes

APPENDIX A

Yuefu *as a Generic Term*

Here we will review the evidence for the use of the term *yuefu* as a kind of verse, rather than an institution. In the pre-Tang period the institutional meaning of the term is by far the most common usage, both in reference to the Western Han "Music Bureau" proper and, in elegant anachronism, to later court musical establishments.

Many scholars (Suzuki Shūji, Masuda Kiyohide, Joseph Allen) note the appearance of the term in Zhi Yu's 摯虞 *Wenzhang liubie lun* 文章流別論, composed around the turn of the fourth century. Since this may be the only case in which *yuefu* is associated with five-syllable-line poetry before the mid-fifth century, it is important to comment on the particular form of the textual fragments of the *Wenzhang liubie lun*. We should first note that many modern versions of Zhi Yu's comments on poetry are based on Yan Kejun's text in the *Quan Jin wen*. Although Yan Kejun presents his citation as based on the *Yiwen leiju*, it is in fact a composite of *Yiwen leiju* and *Taiping yulan* citations; in one case the *Taiping yulan* citation is rather drastically changed—and that case happens to be the one involving the five syllable line and *yuefu*. The proper versions can be found in Deng Guoguang's *Zhi Yu yanjiu*.[1]

The *Yiwen leiju* citation (which Deng identifies as the "General Discussion of Letters" 總論文章) has a general discussion of poetry followed by examples of different line lengths in the

---

1. Unfortunately Deng's fourteenth note in his chapter 12 is missing, just at the point where we would hope he might explain the rather striking differences in the standard version. See Deng Guoguang 鄧國光, *Zhi Yu yanjiu* 摯虞研究 (Hong Kong: Xueheng chubanshe, 1990), 185.

Shijing. The *Taiping yulan* citation (identified by Deng as the "Separate Discussions of Genres" 分論文體) gives exactly the same phrasing with the same *Shijing* lines, but adds a comment on where they are used in later poetry. The first question we must ask is whether these are indeed two distinct sections of the *Wenzhang liubie lun,* or (1) the *Yiwen leiju* gave an abbreviated version of the passage, or (2) the *Taiping yulan* has added early notes to the main text as if those notes were the main text.

We have reason to suspect the *Taiping yulan* quotation because the first example says "the four syllable line of the *Shi*" 古詩之四言者 and cites a four syllable line. The line is, however, incorrectly cited: it is actually a three syllable line, cited and identified as such in the *Yiwen leiju* version. The appended comment on the verse's later application is: "This was often used in the Han Songs for the Suburban Sacrifice and Ancestral Temple" 漢郊廟歌多用之. Since those songs are in lines of both three and four syllables, this doesn't tell us much.

Next come lines of five, six, and seven syllables. Here let me put the *Taiping yulan* citation side by side with Yan Kejun's version (omitting the *Shijing* lines cited).

Taiping yulan	Yan Kejun
五言者, 樂府亦用之	于俳諧倡樂多用之
六言者, 樂府亦用之	樂府亦用之
七言者, 於俳諧倡樂世用之	于俳諧倡樂世用之

In each version one comment is repeated (and perhaps the use of *yi* 亦 gives some weight to the *Taiping yulan* version). The long and short of it is that in the *Taiping yulan* version poetry in the five syllable line is used in *yuefu,* while in Yan Kejun's version it is used by professional singers in bantering.

Allen is presumably referring to the *Taiping yulan* version when he observes that the context suggests that in using the term *yuefu* "the reference is to the 'ballad' type of literature, not the 'hymn' type."[2] If so, the six syllable line must be the "hymn type"—though which hymns is uncertain. But if that is the case, why, in discussing the three (or four) syllable line did Zhi Yu specify "Songs for the Suburban Sacrifice and Ancestral Temple" rather than *yuefu*—since those songs were the su-

---

2. Allen, *In the Voice of Others,* 48–49.

preme examples of verse explicitly linked with the Han institution of the *Yuefu*. This is all the more the case because the term *yuefu* is otherwise exclusively used to refer to the court musical establishment, either of the Han or on the Han model. The further question is whether *yuefu* here means a genre (a kind of poetry) or an institution.

When we come to a textual problem like this, we should acknowledge the source in trying to trace the history of the use of the term *yuefu*; at the same time, we should not base a historical narrative on it, tracing the use of the term to describe poetry in the five syllable line to the turn of the fourth century. It is a solitary case and a textually very troubled case.

•

The first case in which we find the term *yuefu* clearly used for a kind of poetry is a century and a half after Zhi Yu: in a preface Bao Zhao (d. 466) uses the term "*yuefu* poem," *yuefu shi* 樂府詩, to refer to a poem by Fu Xuan 傅玄 (217–78), the "Tortoise and Crane Piece" 龜鶴篇.[3] This Bao Zhao "imitates," *ni* 擬, in a poem in the five syllable line entitled "Pine and Cypress Piece" 松柏篇. We do not know whether the term *yuefu shi* is Bao Zhao's own description of the piece, a category that had entered the manuscript collection of Fu Xuan before Bao Zhao, or was a category originally used by Fu Xuan. We note that poems with titles ending in *pian* 篇 also characterize those poems in the *Wen xuan* categorized as "*yuefu* poems."[4]

When *ni* is used in a title, it is always followed by the title of the poem imitated. Perhaps used here in a discursive preface, it had a looser sense, since Bao Zhao's poem does not have the same title as the poem he supposedly "imitated." By the ordinary rules of *ni*, Fu Xuan's now lost original would have had to have been in the five syllable line and line for line as long as Bao Zhao's poem. Perhaps, however, with a looser, discursive sense of *ni*, these norms would not have applied. Bao Zhao's poem is

---

3. Lu Qinli, 1264–65. Fu Xuan has an extant *Fangge xing* 放歌行 (Lu Qinli, 557) that begins with a reference to the "holy tortoise," *linggui* 靈龜, but there is no crane nor does it bear any resemblance to Bao Zhao's poem.

4, In the third century, *pian* 篇 probably still retained something of its earlier sense as a text on a bundle of bamboo slips. The transfer of this term to something like a "chapter" is comprehensible. How and when the term came to be applied to poems that were very short by *pian* standards is an issue deserving some study.

quite different from the other poems of his now classified as
yuefu; and the "tortoise and crane" of the Fu Xuan original are
auspicious creatures, associated with longevity. Without Bao
Zhao's imitation—which is certainly not a ritual *yuefu*—the title
of Fu Xuan's lost *yuefu* alone would suggest ritual *yuefu*. That
is, the first clear usage of *yuefu* to refer to a type of poetry comes
from one known author imitating another known author, on a
theme and under a title which is quite distinct from the kind of
poetry usually later classified as *yuefu*. Nevertheless, we can
say that the term is used to describe a kind of poetry at least by
the mid-fifth century.

The next clearly generic use of the term is noted by Anne
Birrel, in which Shen Yue uses *yuefu* to describe some of the
compositions of Shen Liang 沈亮.[5] Here again it is listed well
separated from poetry and in between two ritual genres; this
strongly suggests that even though it is being used in a generic
sense, a kind of ritual hymn is meant. As is well known, Shen
Yue does not use the term *yuefu* in the "Treatise on Music."

The first extensive treatment of *yuefu* as a named category
can first be found in *Wenxin diaolong* at around the turn of the
sixth century, where Liu Xie devotes an entire chapter to it, in
the broad sense of poetry associated with music. He uses the
term as the counterpart of "poetry," but he treats it as generi-
cally distinct. Although Liu Xie is clearly thinking of ritual
music as the normative form, his version clearly included "lit-
erary *yuefu*" and was broad enough to encompass the anony-
mous verses now considered "Han *yuefu*," though nowhere
does he distinctly indicate such material. As we move into the
sixth century, the term had come into fairly common use and
was broad enough to encompass almost the full range of verse
we now classify as early *yuefu*. In Ren Fang's 任昉 *Wenzhang
yuanqi* 文章緣起 *yuefu* is described in the following terms: "They
are the old Poems" *gu shi ye* 古詩也.[6] This probably means that
it belongs to the tradition of the *Shijing*, though we cannot en-
tirely discount the possibility that he was identifying *yuefu* with
the anonymous "old poems." However, *yuefu* is listed in the

---

5. Birrel, *Popular Songs and Ballads*, 7; *Song shu*, 2452.
6. Ren Fang 任昉, *Wenzhang yuanqi zhu* 文章緣起注 (rpt. Taibei: Guangwen
shuju, 1970), 37.

middle of a long list of genres, far away from forms of "poetry" in various line lengths, which begin the list of genres. Zhong Rong nowhere discusses *yuefu* in his *Gradations of Poetry*, but his inclusion of Cao Cao, all of whose works were in the song tradition, suggests that he saw literary *yuefu* at least as a subset of poetry.

The question is whether there was a broad notion of "poetry" that included *yuefu* or whether "poetry" and *yuefu* were seen as distinct things. The evidence suggests that anonymous song material—both the early material and more recent Southern songs—were not initially significant to the literary scholars in thinking of *yuefu* as a literary genre. The collocation "*yuefu* poems," *yuefu shi* 樂府詩, was probably the earliest use, referring to *yuefu* by known authors. The term *yuefu* alone probably was a possible term for ritual song, extended to "song" as a general concept in Liu Xie. In the *Wen xuan* we see the first evidence of inclusion of anonymous song within the scope of "belles lettres"; Xiao Tong includes very few of these, perhaps influenced by the archaic cachet of anonymity that surrounded the "old poems." Xiao Tong clearly treats them as a subset of "poetry," and he places his three anonymous pieces at the beginning of a chronological set of *yuefu* by known authors, just as he places the "Nineteen Old Poems" at the beginning of a chronological set of "unclassified poems," *zashi* 雜詩. That is, anonymous *yuefu* are brought in to serve as the anonymous origins of a literary form based on the established model of the "old poems." Here, for the first time, we see anonymous *yuefu* positioned within the literary lineages by which sixth-century critics understood their literary past.

This move seems to have opened the way for subsuming anonymous *yuefu* within the larger category of "poetry"— though the separate bibliographical tradition of musical specialists continued. We have no confidence as to how closely our current version of *Yutai xinyong* 玉臺新詠 matches its sixth-century form, but here—in a collection specifically of *yong* 詠, "songs"—*yuefu* and "poetry" appear side by side. Anonymous "old poems" are followed by anonymous *yuefu* at the beginning; the sub-lineages of the *Wen xuan* are gone, and the two groups together represent the "beginnings" of classical poetry.

Here we might recall Liu Xie's term of praise for the anonymous "old poems": they are "direct without being uncouth," *zhi er bu ye* 直而不野. As received texts, it seems that anonymous *yuefu* were often "uncouth," *ye* 野. For a "terrace of jade," *yutai* 玉臺, such "uncouth" verses needed some polish.

•

We have become so accustomed to the broad category of *yuefu* that it is worth remembering that it was once much smaller and more specialized. The "Bibliography" in the *Sui shu* lists many titles of collections of musical verse, a number of which are clearly ritual music and songs for court feasts. *Yuefu* is a common term in such titles, but we cannot date most of these works. We are left with only imperfect negative evidence: collections in this category that have known pre-sixth-century compilers do not use the term *yuefu*.

The *Sui shu* "Bibliography" does, however, include one interesting and suggestive anomaly that wonderfully confuses the issue. We have a list of categories of "records of song lyric and dance" 歌辭舞錄; here we have a series of types of music, many of which are now considered as subcategories of *yuefu*. In the third place in this list, however, we have a category called *yuefu*: "fife and drum songs, *qingshang* songs, *yuefu*, feast music, high pregnancy-seeking rites, kettle-drum music, bell music, etc., ten types" 鼓吹, 清商, 樂府, 讌樂, 高禖, 鞞, 鐸等歌辭舞錄, 凡十部.[7] We do not know the provenance of this list; its existence, however, is a valuable reminder that these terms had scattered histories that we no longer understand.

We know that *yuefu* was a particular Western Han institution that came to be used to describe court musical establishments, particularly those charged with providing ritual music. In that sense it came to describe a subset of lyrics to music, which were more broadly preserved in a tradition of manuscripts, conceived as a distinct kind of material, but not commonly known as *yuefu*. Sometime, probably in the latter part of the fifth century, the term *yuefu* was gradually extended to the full range of verse in that musical tradition, and it is in this sense that we see Liu Xie using the term. Because verse in the musical tradition had always overlapped with poetry, *yuefu* became the term for such poetry. Generic categories were fluid.

---

7. *Sui shu*, 1085.

As the literary record was being reviewed and categorized around the turn of the sixth century, *yuefu* came to be used as a blanket term for a loose assortment of poetic texts, covering much of the range of the current generic term. It also became a standard term used in the titles of collections of song materials. When, however, we look at the way passages are cited in encyclopedia and commentarial sources from the seventh and early eighth century, we can see that *yuefu* was not yet a stable generic term, either to distinguish a body of texts from *shi* or to describe texts associated with music.

APPENDIX B

The Musical Traditions

I have in my possession a number of CDs of "Tang music." I can enjoy these with a good-humored knowledge that any relation to the Tang Dynasty is purely fanciful. I have Pickens's reconstructions of Tang music based on speeding up Japanese court music to melodies that sound like the sound track for an *Arabian Nights* film. I believe that it is not at all impossible that Tang music actually sounded like this, but I do not believe this *is* "Tang music."

•

Nowhere is the scholarship on early classical poetry more intricate and frustrating than in trying to sort out the *yuefu* lineages of transmission of tune titles and their various categories—through the early musical sources preserved in the head-notes of *Yuefu shiji*, through the *Yuezhi* of the *Song shu*, and in various other sources. This is not scholarship for the fainthearted; and if I reviewed it properly here, this appendix would be many times longer than the book to which it is appended. Scholars who are not in the least fainthearted—such as Suzuki Shūji, Masuda Kiyohide, and Wang Yunxi—have thoroughly mined the sources for what is there. To attempt to reproduce them would be mere epitome. I have struggled with the primary sources and the arguments of scholars of those sources without finding the information for which I was searching. This is an exemplary case of how the sources set boundaries for questions which become all too absorbing in their own detail and whose endless problems easily direct the scholar's attention away from some very basic and essential issues.

The pre-Tang sources that we use to reconstruct the history of early musical poetry (*yuefu*) are concerned primarily with titles and taxonomies, and perhaps with song traditions. We can guess what instruments were in vogue in the court in a certain period. We do not, however, know some other things that are very important. We do not know the extent to which song lyrics were committed to writing. We also do not know when song lyrics were committed to writing. Scholars are often willing to believe that if they have an early mention of a title and sometimes of a first line, there is continuity between the piece mentioned and a later textual manifestation of lyrics under that title. But the tradition is always composing new lyrics to old titles, reworking lyrics, reusing first lines, and "filling in" what is missing. We want to know how we received the texts we have, whether those texts appear in the early sixth-century *Song shu* or in the *Yuefu shiji*, from the turn of the twelfth century. Perhaps the first line of the "Song of White Hair," "Baitou yin" 白頭吟, attested by its name and first line around the turn of the fourth century, belongs to an old Han ditty—and if we can believe the first line, we can probably believe the first four lines. Already we have compounded a "perhaps" and a "probably," conditional on the "perhaps." But, as Diény has shown and we will recapitulate in a different way, the longer poem preserved in the *Song shu* is a composite of different segments. What reason do we have to believe this particular confection of segments belongs to the Han? If we had a clear tradition of texts known to contain lyrics, we might believe. But we know musicians and musical scholars were always reworking things. We know the tradition of the title and the first line (only dating from the turn of the fourth century); but we have no idea from when and how we have the text we have. Perhaps it is indeed an old Han mix; perhaps it is the way the poem was performed in the fifth century. It doesn't matter aesthetically for the text we have, with its wonderful leaps of theme. But it is not a text around which we can tell a historical story of *yuefu*—even though Shen Yue names it specifically as a Han "street song." He knows probably only a little better than we do the origins of the version he has.

We are looking for lines of transmission not of lore but of texts. In a note attached to the "Lyrics for the Three Modes in the *Qingshang*" (清商三調歌詩), Shen Yue specifically notes: "These were past lyrics compiled/collected and put to use by Xun Xu" 荀勗撰舊詞施用者. What does *zhuan* 撰 mean here: does it mean he "wrote them down" or that he "selected" (*xuan* 選) them? Note that this is *jiuci* 舊詞 rather than *guci* 古詞: these are lyrics from the recent past. Xu Xun (d. 289) was a central figure in the musical establishment of the Western Jin and is credited in the "Bibliography" of the *Sui shu* with a work called *Lyrics for Jin Banquet Music, Jin yanyue geci* 晉讌樂歌辭. A title like this is reassuring because it specifies the "lyrics," *geci* 歌辭. We assume these are texts—though we do not know which texts. Does this mean that Shen Yue has a textual source for the lyrics in this section? If it does mean this, what does that imply for the other sections where there is no such note?

We like book titles that specify "lyrics," *geci* 歌辭, because many of the works in the tradition of musical poetry are called *lu* 錄, "records." We suppose that a relatively long work like Zhijiang's *Gujin yuelu* 古今樂錄 of the sixth century must have contained actual texts as well as taxonomical discussions and traditions, but the important works by Zhang Yong and Wang Sengqian from the mid-fifth century, also called "records," may have been only notes on titles, taxonomy, and sometimes first lines (the Wang Sengqian *Jilu* is recorded in only one scroll, which suggests from citations in the *Yuefu shiji*, via the *Gujin yuelu*, that we must have most, if not all of it, as pure "records" of titles and taxonomy).

Classical Chinese is nothing if not imprecise. Often when the *Gujin yuelu* cites a passage from Wang Sengqian, we see the closing phrase: "it is now not transmitted" 今不傳 or "now not sung" 今不歌. We have no way of knowing if this is part of Wang Sengqian's quotation from the mid-fifth century or Zhijiang's comment from the mid-sixth century (Suzuki takes these as Zhijiang's comments, but that is only a supposition; if the texts existed in Shen Yue's day, why did he not include them?). "Not now transmitted" seems to clearly indicate that they have neither the words nor the music; "now not sung" might mean that they had the words but not the music, or it might be functionally the equivalent of "not transmitted." It is important to note that these lost pieces belong to numbered sets under a certain musical heading and that versions of some members of those sets have survived. Can this mean that an earlier musical specialist copied down some lyrics but not others? Given the impulse to completeness on the part of scholars in the musical tradition, this is inconceivable. The obvious conclusion confirms our supposition above: these musical works are lists and lore, not including the texts.

Where then do the texts come from? When a musical specialist notes that a song is "not now transmitted," he may be matching a list with received texts in some other source. It is also possible that he has no text and is matching his list against the pieces still included in a performance repertoire. We have so much information; we wish just once one of the musical specialists had told us from where the texts came.

As for the music itself we know even less. There is remarkably little indication that these scholars, whom I have been calling "musical specialists," were much concerned with what we would consider essential information about the music itself (except instrumentation). Their focus was on textual lore and tradition. When we see the note that a certain piece was "now not sung," we can infer that some pieces were still sung—but the actual musical relation between third-century practice and mid-fifth-century practice is beyond speculation. There was a musical notation system, but we do not know how widely it was used or how well it was understood beyond the circle of professional performers. Like most musical notation systems prior to the increasingly specific Western notation system of the last four centuries, it did not have enough information to perform a piece without a teacher. Our best guess is that there was considerable musical drift between the third and the mid-fifth century. The textual "musical specialists," limited by human memory (and its vagaries), would have had no way to judge how accurately music from two centuries earlier was preserved.

The relationship between music and text is notoriously elusive, even when we have a stable text and a relatively precise notation for the music. We do not know enough to begin to address this question. We cannot even answer the simpler and more basic questions: what was sung when and under what circumstances? We can assume court traditions that either were continuous (which is not to say that the music remained stable) or claimed continuity. The most we can say is that a certain body of texts, now called *yuefu*, were associated with the idea of music, and that such an association welcomed the possibility of performance. We can assume that Cao Cao's songs were musically performed in his court around the turn of the third century; we can guess that those traditions continued to be performed by professionals for an uncertain period in special court venues. Whether or not Cao Cao's songs still could be performed by the early sixth century, it seems clear that for entertainments the more recent "Songs of Wu," performed by choruses of local girls, were preferred.

APPENDIX C

Anthologies and Poetry in the Five Syllable Line

We tend to retrospectively grant poetry in the five syllable line an importance that it probably did not possess before the early decades of the fifth century. "Poetry," *shi* 詩, as a category did have a certain canonical weight; but we should try to look past the favor of fifth- and sixth-century poets, critics, and anthologists, who imitated, commented on, and anthologized earlier poetry in the five syllable line. When we do so, we find both that up to the early fifth-century poetry was not a focus of interest and that poetry in the four syllable line was just as favored and sometimes more so. The practice of the five syllable line seems strongly tied to members of the Cao family and their courts; the form continued through the Jin, but with a new preference for the four syllable line in group composition.

Certainly poetry in the five syllable line was preserved in the collected works of individuals; but when we look at the two collections from the third century that were not reconstituted from anthology and encyclopedia sources, the collections of Xi Kang and Lu Yun (setting aside the poetry collection of Ruan Ji), we find very different proportions of poetry in the four and five syllable line from elsewhere. About half of the poems in Xi Kang's collection are in the four syllable line, and most of Lu Yun's are four-syllable-line poems. This may be, in part, the result of the peculiarities of these particular poets; but it reminds us of the degree to which our general impression of poetry in the period may be highly influenced by later preferences. The remnants of the immense *Wenguan cilin* 文館詞林 happen to include *juan* covering poetry in the four syllable line; pieces preserved there remind us how much was overlooked in poets now known for their five-syllable-line poetry. As we mentioned in Chapter 1, of the 104 entries in the chapter "Learning / Belles-Lettres," "Wenxue" 文學, in the *Shishuo xinyu*, only four touch on poetry in the five syllable line. Poetic expositions and prose are far more often mentioned. This gives us some indication of the small role played by poetry in the five syllable line in the imagined literary life of the fourth and early fifth century. Of those four entries, only two—the entry with Cao Zhi's famous "seven-step poem" and the entry on the "old poems"—treat poetry that would later become part of the canon.

We might here amplify our comments on anthologizing poetry in the five syllable line. Despite the immense uncertainties in looking at lists of lost books, we can learn a few things of use. The "Bibliography" of the *Sui shu* is a problematic source, mingling later works with a Liang bibliography. The "Bibliography" groups works by categories and seems to try to arrange works chronologically within a category. Wei Zheng 魏徵 (580–643) may not have known the author or date of some works, but we assume he was following the order of his sources.

Sometimes people comment on the richness of pre-Tang anthologies now lost; much was indeed lost, but some of this "richness" may be in some part an illusion, particularly before the late fifth century. Again there is much that we do not know, but we have some hint of the instability of manuscript culture, even over a relatively short span.

The case of the anthology of poetry in the five syllable line attributed to Xun Chuo 荀綽, the *Gujin wuyanshi meiwen* 古今五言詩美文 in five scrolls, is a vexed one. There was a Xun Chuo who was the grandson of the famous Xun Xu 荀勗 (d. 289) and an eminent Jin intellectual in his own right. This Xun Chuo died at the beginning of the fourth century. Unlike the Xie Lingyun anthology, Xun Chuo's anthology is not attested elsewhere. Not only is this anthology listed after the Xie Lingyun anthology, it is listed immediately after another anthology without attribution of authorship entitled *Unclassified Poems of the Two Jins, Er Jin zashi* 二晉雜詩. It is unclear whether this anthology is also intended to be credited to Xun Chuo; if so, we have a serious anachronism, since Xun Chuo died in the Yongjia Reign, before the founding of the Eastern Jin. What makes this particularly interesting is a historical work under Xun Chuo's name that also suggests the Eastern Jin or later. It may be that there were two Xun Chuos: the earlier and more famous figure who wrote on offices, and a later, more obscure figure who was conflated with the former. Not only does the "Bibliography" tend to favor chronological sequences within types and sub-types, but types of works, once established, tend to have a continuous lineage. If the *Gujin wuyanshi meiwen* were a poetry anthology of the turn of the fourth century, it would stand unique and alone, more than a century earlier than the next datable poetry anthology likely to contain poetry in the five syllable line. One cannot help suspecting that it was later, while allowing the possibility that it might be the earliest anthology of poetry in the five syllable line and an important source for early poetry.

The famous poet Xie Lingyun 謝靈運 (385–433) is credited with an anthology of poetry known simply as *Shi ji* 詩集 in fifty scrolls; there is an expansion in one hundred scrolls later in the fifth century, another hundred-scroll work of the same title attributed to Yan Jun 顏峻, and another work of the same title in forty scrolls attributed to Song Mingdi (r. 465–72). It is possible that these are all different anthologies, but then we see another shorter anthology, *Shi ji chao* 詩集鈔, in ten scrolls by Xie Lingyun, apparently the same work that appears again under the title of *Zashi chao* 雜詩鈔, also attributed to Xie Lingyun, in ten scrolls in the Liang. Then there is another ten-scroll *Shi chao* 詩鈔 without a compiler listed and noted as "lost." Then we have another anthology attributed to Xie Lingyun called *Shi ying* 詩英 in nine scrolls. By its placement directly after the *Shi ying* (as a sub-entry), we may suppose that Xiao Tong's *Wenzhang yinghua* 文章英華 in thirty scrolls is an expansion of Xie Lingyun's *Shi ying* (despite the apparently more general title, the *Wenzhang yinghua* is listed in poetry anthologies), but a few entries later we find a *Gujin shiyuan yinghua* 古今詩苑英華 in nineteen scrolls attributed to Xiao Tong.

We might conclude from this and other evidence that many anthologies were lost, which is, of course, true. We might, however, also conclude that manuscripts, particularly of popular material such as poetry, were often changing size in the course of recopying, either supplemented or excerpted at will. In many cases the works do not seem to have formal "titles" but are simply brief descriptions of the content. It is possible that Xie Lingyun compiled four different anthologies of different sizes and with different names, but it seems far more likely that the Xie Lingyun anthology circulated under different titles in various sizes, with another editor sometimes claiming credit when Xie's anthology was expanded. That is, what looks like a "bibliography" may in fact be a library "catalogue" of manuscripts, with no two being exactly alike.

Literary anthologies do have an ancestor, and it is given pride of place (apart from the *Chu ci*) in the *Sui shu* bibliography: this is the *Wenzhang liubie* 文章流別 from the turn of the fourth century, discussed in Chapter 1. There were other anthologies of roughly the same period, but Zhi Yu's was the most influential. A fragment of Li Chong's 李充 (fl. mid-fourth century) *Hanlin* 翰林 is quoted as praising the poetry in the five syllable line of Ying Qu 應璩 (190–252), and the "Bibliography" lists a presumably Jin commentary on Ying Qu by Ying Zhen 應貞, presumably an act of family pride. We have other general literary anthologies before the *Wen xuan*, and it is reasonable to assume that poetry in the five syllable line was gradually represented ever more fully.

When we turn to anthologies specifically of poetry, we find only two listed before the Xie Lingyun anthologies: the *Ji ya pian* 集雅篇 in five scrolls with no date given and the *Jing-gongtang song* 靖恭堂頌 in one scroll from the Jin. We have no idea what the former was, but the term *ya* 雅 would probably not have been used in an early anthology of poetry in the five syllable line. The latter seems to have been a collection specifically of "hymns," *song* 頌, since several other collections of *song* are appended to it. *Song* by this period were in the four syllable line.

The variations on the Xie Lingyun anthology suggest its popularity in the fifth century; on the level of pure speculation, Xie, during his second period in the imperial library, would have had access to the trove of manuscripts brought back by Liu Yu from his northern campaign, and this may have considerably extended the corpus of earlier poetry that was available in the South; Xie's poetry anthology could then have been responsible for the dissemination of this material. We do see a striking growth in the interest in earlier poetry and imitations in the mid-fifth century.

We have a valuable critical comment on Xie's anthology by Zhong Rong in the "Preface" to the *Gradations of Poetry*: "When it comes to Xie Lingyun's collection [anthology] of poems, he just took whatever poem he happened on" 至於謝客集詩, 逢詩輒取. Lack of discrimination was a common complaint among Qi and Liang critics, but we should understand it not in purely aesthetic terms, but also in regard to judgments of authenticity, as in Zhong Rong's complaint that the full collection of anonymous old poems was a "mixed bag," *zongza* 總雜, a term which, as we will see, is connected to judgments about false attributions. Xie's large collection, alternatively expanding and shrinking in subsequent copying, may have simply uncritically drawn from manuscripts available in the early fifth century.

Following the set of anthologies appended as sub-entries to Xie Lingyun's original anthology, we have an anthology with a title of particular interest for our concerns: the *Gu shi ji* 古詩集 in nine scrolls, given without a compiler. We should clearly not take this as a compilation dedicated to anonymous "old poems"; for a work of this size the scope of "old" clearly must extend well later than the Han.

We can follow no clear bibliographical trail on how the anonymous "old poems" passed from the third century to the literary men of the late fifth and early sixth century. Our *Shishuo xinyu* anecdote suggests they were common knowledge among the elite at around the turn of the fifth century; but that is the only evidence before a spate of imitations in the mid-fifth century. We know that the imperial library in the early Eastern Jin was vastly reduced from what had existed in the Wei; it must have been gradually supplemented from private sources. We can reasonably suspect that Xie Lingyun's anthology played an important role in disseminating early poetry; and considering his interest in the Seven Masters of the Jian'an, their poems were probably included.

As we mentioned in the main text, the most significant categorical fact in the "Bibliography" is the clear division between poetry anthologies and collections of lyrics for music (except for one anthology called *Gu yuefu* 古樂府 in eight scrolls, out of sequence). There is a remarkably extensive corpus of collections in the musical tradition, though many are clearly ritual collections. Studying old music (meaning the traditions) was an activity with some cachet, as can be seen in the introduction to the "Yuezhi" of the *Song shu*. Considering the number of these collections, we need to reflect on two facts: first, that Zhong Rong does not include anonymous *yuefu* in his *Gradations of Poetry*, and second, that Liu Xie gives them a separate chapter, where he treats ritual pieces and *yuefu* by known authors, but makes no clear reference to the anonymous "old *yuefu*." Liu Xie does express much disapproval of popular song, which may include the old *yuefu*; but this seems unduly harsh for texts that were so carefully conserved by so many reputable scholars.

APPENDIX D

"As Performed by the Jin Musicians"

In "Contre Guo Maoqian: à propos des deux versions de certains poèmes des Han et des Wei," Jean-Pierre Diény has presented a thorough comparison of the paired versions of *yuefu* given in *Yuefu shiji* as "original lyrics" and "as performed by the Jin musicians."[1] He has made a long and convincing argument why the *Song shu* versions are the older texts. I am in complete agreement with him, and in the following appendix, I would like to supplement and reinforce his argument with a brief consideration of variation in manuscript culture and a return to one of the texts he discusses, *Man'ge xing* 滿歌行, to consider some of the points he raises and some others in the context of compound *yuefu*.

The issue is this: a number of the *yuefu* from the *Song shu* are given with variant versions in the *Yuefu shiji* 樂府詩集. There the *Song shu* version is marked by Guo Maoqian "as performed by the Jin musicians," *Jin yue suo zou* 晉樂所奏, while the alternative version is often given as the "original lyrics," *ben ci* 本辭. Since the *Song shu* versions often have incongruous passages, irregular lines, transpositions, and loan characters, this has led to the widely accepted belief that the "original lyrics" were changed for the requirements of music, changed by musicians who were less than fully literate and less than fully careful in their transcriptions. The fact that the lyrics in the "Treatise on Music," *Yuezhi* 樂志, of the *Song shu* represents the conser-

---

1. *T'oung Pao* 85, nos. 1–3 (1999): 65–113.

vation efforts of some of the best scholars of several centuries in a long tradition should be taken into consideration.

If we look at this from the point of view of a manuscript tradition, we have in the *Song shu* a reasonably reliable text from the beginning of the sixth century, carefully conserved because it became the standard history of a dynasty; as we have discussed elsewhere, it represents a highly conservative tradition of musical scholarship, committed to presenting texts as they were received. In the *Yuefu shiji* we have a book from six centuries later. Guo Maoqian, its compiler, had access to a range of sources for musical poetry (*yuefu*) whose origins and transmission are uncertain. We do not know who first made the distinction between "original lyrics" and lyrics "as performed by the Jin musicians," but it is a judgment made only when scholars began to collect and compare versions. It has the appearance of an ideological rather than a historical judgment, a way to explain the textual mess and poetic inconsistencies of the *Song shu* materials.

I would like to look at one of the less popular of the anonymous *yuefu*, where I think we can clearly see that the difference between the two versions makes sense only as an imperfect attempt on the part of the so-called original lyrics to regularize, repair, and provide consistency to a text in the *Song shu*.

This argument is based on a premise that is developed more fully in the main body of this work and is shared by many scholars in the field: that performance and compositional practice commonly joined independent segments to produce a "complete" work. Sometimes those segments are tightly integrated; sometimes they are close enough that interpreters have been able to integrate them; and sometimes the segments are incongruous.

Below I am going to discuss the *Man'ge xing* 滿歌行, "Full Song." First I will give the two versions, followed by a translation of the *Song shu* version.

Song shu	*Yuefu shiji* "original lyrics"
爲樂未幾時 遭世儉巇 逢此百離	爲樂未幾時 遭時儉巇 逢此百罹

零丁荼毒	零丁荼毒
愁懣難支	愁苦難爲
遙望辰極	遙望極辰
天曉月移	天曉月移
憂來闐心	憂來塡心
誰當我知	誰當我知
戚戚多思慮	戚戚多思慮
耿耿不寧	耿耿殊不寧
禍福無刑	禍福無形
唯念古人	惟念古人
遜位躬耕	遜位躬耕
遂我所願	遂我所願
以茲自寧	以自寧
自鄙山棲	自鄙棲棲
守此一榮	守此末榮
莫秋冽風起	暮秋烈風
西蹈滄海	昔蹈滄海
心不能安	心不能安
攬衣起瞻夜	攬衣瞻夜
北斗闌干	北斗闌干
星漢照我	星漢照我
去去自無他	去自無他
奉事二親	奉事二親
勞心可言	勞心可言
窮達天所爲	窮達天爲
智者不愁	智者不愁
多爲少憂	多爲少憂
安貧樂正道	安貧樂道
師彼莊周	師彼莊周
遺名者貴	遺名者貴
子熙同戱	子遐同遊
往者二賢	往者二賢
名垂千秋	名垂千秋
飲酒歌舞	飲酒歌舞
不樂何須	樂復何須
善哉照覩日月	照視日月
日月馳驅	日月馳驅
轗軻世間	轗軻人間
何有何無	何有何無
貪財惜費	貪財惜費
此何一愚	此一何愚
命如鑿石見火	鑿石見火
居世竟能幾時	居代幾時

但當歡樂自娛　　　爲當懽樂
盡心極所熙怡　　　心得所喜
安善養君德性　　　安神養性
百年保此期頤　　　得保遐期

滿歌行 Full Song[2]

爲樂未幾時	Making merry does not last long,[3]
遭世嶮巇	I have encountered perilous times.
逢此百離	I have met all manner of misfortune,
零丁荼毒	isolated and in wretchedness,
愁懑難支	this sad bitterness is hard to endure.
遙望辰極	I gaze at the Pole Star afar,
天曉月移	the heavens turn morning, the moon shifts.
憂來闐心	Worries come, filling the heart,
誰當我知	who will understand me?
戚戚多思慮	Gloomy and with many cares,
耿耿不寧	I am restless and not at peace.
禍福無刑	No signs of good or ill fortune.[4]
唯念古人	I brood on that man of old,[5]
遜位躬耕	who declined position and plowed for himself.
遂我所願	I would achieve that which I wish
以兹自寧	and by this bring myself peace.
自鄙山棲	I despise lodging in the mountains,[6]
守此一榮	stuck in this paltry flourishing.[7]
莫秋冽風起	Late autumn's fierce winds rise,
西蹈滄海	to the west I fared on the gray seas,
心不能安	my heart is unable to be at rest.
攬衣起瞻夜	I lift my clothes, rise and look at the night,
北斗闌干	the Northern Dipper is stretched out on the sky.

---

2. In the *Yuefu zhengyi* 樂府正義, Zhu Qian 朱乾 interprets man 滿 as men 懣, "depressed." Although this is possible, the motive seems to be to make the title match the tone of the poem.

3. Huang Jie in his notes cites the commonplace line: "Making merry one must seize the moment" 爲樂當及時. This is perhaps what is intended here.

4. This line is in the *Song shu* version, but not in the alternative version in *Yuefu shiji*. I take 刑 as 形, the "signs" that let one know what is coming.

5. This is the recluse Xu You, who fled when Yao offered him rule of the empire.

6. The alternative text reads 棲棲 for 山棲, giving a very different sense: "I despise this restlessness of mine."

7. Zheng Wen offers a nice explanation for "paltry flourishing": a small salary.

星漢照我	The River of Stars shines on me,
去去自無他	I will go off myself and nothing other.
奉事二親	Serving both one's parents,
勞心可言	in this the heart toils, needless to say.
窮達天所爲	Failure and success are made by Heaven,
智者不愁	the wise person does not grieve,
多爲少憂	many worry for a few things.
安貧樂正道	Be at rest in poverty, delight in the right Way,
師彼莊周	I will take Zhuang Zhou as my teacher.
遺名者貴	One who leaves behind a name is noble,
子熙同遊	a fellow-traveler with Zixi.[8]
往者二賢	Those two worthies of bygone times,
名垂千秋	their names last a thousand years.
飲酒歌舞	Drink ale, have song and dance—
不樂何須	why wait anymore for joy?
善哉照觀日月	Grand! Look at the sun and moon shining,
日月馳驅	the sun and moon go speeding by.
轗軻世間	Struggling hard in the world of men,
何有何無	whatever is had, whatever is lacking.
貪財惜費	Greedy for goods and begrudging expense—
此何一愚	how foolish this is!
命如礱石見火	Fate is like grinding stone, seeing the spark—
居世竟能幾時	how long, after all, can we live in the world?
但當歡樂自娛	We should just have pleasure and make merry,
盡心極所熙怡	let the heart enjoy fully what delights it.
安善養君德性	Rest in goodness, nourish your virtuous nature,
百年保此期頤	preserve this span of a hundred years.

The two versions are, indeed, remarkably close. The most obvious difference is how irregular lines in the *Song shu* version are replaced by regular lines where possible in the "original lyrics." The one case in which a four syllable line has been expanded is II.2, where it serves to parallel a five syllable line that could not be easily reduced to four syllables. (Indeed, both

---

8. Zixi is unidentified. The alternative version reads Zixia 子遐, also unknown. I have retained the *Yfsj* reading 遊.

of the five syllable lines retained, I.1 and II.1, are hard to compress.) A dropped rhyme is corrected (IV.7) and a transposition of characters (V.8). There are also numerous small changes of wording that make better sense in the "original lyrics."

Unfortunately the poem as a whole doesn't make a great deal of sense, rambling from complaints to a decision to follow Daoist quietude and live in poverty, to a call to drink, make merry, and spend what one has. Some of those little changes of wording, moreover, produce differences that would seem rather important to later readers. For example, the last couplet in the *Song shu* version reads:

安善養君德性	Rest in goodness, nourish your virtuous nature,
百年保此期頤	preserve this span of a hundred years.

In the "original lyrics" this becomes:

安神養性	Giving rest to the spirit and nourishing nature,
得保遐期	one can preserve a far-reaching lifespan.

"Goodness," *shan* 善, becomes the phonologically close "spirit," *shen* 神. "Virtue," *de* 德, is dropped to shorten the line. The "hundred-year" lifespan, a full but normal mortal life, becomes a "far-reaching lifespan," *xia qi* 遐期, strongly suggesting immortality. The *Song shu* message is: enjoy yourself, be good, and live out your mortal life. The message of the alternative version is: practice techniques of Daoist self-cultivation, and you will become an immortal.[9]

The *Song shu* version has something else: unlike the "original lyrics," it is divided into stanzas and designates the last stanza as a *qu* 趨, a "coda." That is, this final section is not the song "proper," but rather something added. In the *Song shu* lyrics many codas are thematically independent. We might then look at the final stanza of the *Song shu* version separately:

---

9. For the clear opposition between immortality and "preserving a hundred-year span," see the last lines of Cao Pi's "Written at Lotus Pool" 芙蓉池作 (Lu 400).

飲酒歌舞	Drink ale, have song and dance—
不樂何須	why wait anymore for joy?
善哉照覩日月	Grand! Look at the sun and moon shining,
日月馳驅	the sun and moon go speeding by.
轗軻世間	Struggling hard in the world of men,
何有何無	whatever is had, whatever is lacking.
貪財惜費	Greedy for goods and begrudging expense—
此何一愚	how foolish this is!
命如鑿石見火	Fate is like grinding stone, seeing the spark—
居世竟能幾時	how long, after all, can we live in the world?
但當歡樂自娛	We should just have pleasure and make merry,
盡心極所熙怡	let the heart enjoy fully what delights it.
安善養君德性	Rest in goodness, nourish your virtuous nature,
百年保此期頤	preserve this span of a hundred years.

This is a version of a very familiar song-type, the feast poem, without the least incongruity.[10] Moreover, with this stanza removed, the main body of song also becomes coherent, lamenting the world and resolving to follow a life of Daoist quietism (with no hint of the quest for immortality other than lasting fame). Thrown together, they make a satisfying sequence, in which the private lament and ascetic resolve are answered by the voice of the community, urging the listener to enjoy the life he has. We find a similar sequence in Cao Cao's "Ballads of Qiuhu" II, in which the quest for immortality is answered by a closing feast segment (see pp. 149–53).

From this point of view, the final stanza makes sense only as a "coda," *qu*, which plays against and need not continue the main body of the song. In the "original lyrics" we see this independent segment regularized to try to produce a "single poem," with the ending changed to reconcile it with the strong Daoist motifs in the main stanzas. We can see the process with particular clarity here because the attempt to create a single "poem" fails so badly.

---

10. Cf. Suzuki, *Kan Gi*, 408.

We see this same process at work in other *Song shu* texts that have alternative versions, especially those preserved in *Yutai xinyong*. When we see other, smooth *yuefu* texts that have no *Song shu* version, we perhaps have cause to wonder what their sources looked like.

APPENDIX E

Examples of the Topic "Human Life Is Brief"

This set is reproduced from Suzuki Shūji, *Kan Gi shi no kenkyū*, pp. 364–72.

人生要死, 何爲苦心.	屬王骨歌, *Han shu* biography
人生行樂耳, 須富貴何時.	楊惲, 拊缶歌
人生天地間, 忽如遠行客.	"Nineteen Old Poems" III
人生寄一世, 奄忽若飆塵.	"Nineteen Old Poems" IV
人生非金石, 豈能長壽考.	"Nineteen Old Poems" XI
人生忽如寄, 壽無金石固.	"Nineteen Old Poems" XIII
人生無幾時, 顛沛在其間.	*Gushi, Yutai xinyong*
人生一世間, 貴與願同俱.	"Li Ling"
人生不滿百, 常懷千歲憂.	西門行
人生譬朝露, 居世多屯蹇.	Qin Jia, "To His Wife" I
人生幾何時, 懷憂終年歲.	Cai Yan, 悲憤詩
人生有何常, 但患年歲暮.	Kong Rong, 雜詩 I
人生圖嗣息, 爾死我念追.	〃 II
人生自有命, 但恨生日希.	〃 II
對酒當歌, 人生幾何,	
譬如朝露, 去日苦多.	Cao Cao, 短歌行
人生欲寄, 多憂何爲.	Cao Pi, 善哉行
人生居天壤間, 忽如飛鳥棲枯枝.	〃 大牆上蒿行
人生各有志, 終不爲此移.	Wang Can, 詠史詩
人生實難, 願其弗與.	〃 贈蔡子篤詩
人生一世間, 忽若暮春草.	Xu Gan, 室思
人生處一世, 去若朝露晞.	Cao Zhi, 贈白馬王彪 V
俯觀五嶽間, 人生如寄居.	〃 僊人篇
人生不滿百, 歲歲少歡娛.	〃 遊僊
日月不恆處, 人生忽若遇.	〃 浮萍篇
人生有所貴尚, 出門各異情.	〃 當事君行

Without the phrase 人生 . . .

生年不滿百, 常懷千歲憂.	"Nineteen Old Poems" XV
人壽非金石, 年命安可期.	西門行
天德悠且長, 人命一何促.	
百年未幾時, 奄若風吹燭.	怨詩行
鑿石見火, 居代幾時.	滿歌行
天地何長久, 人道居之短.	Cao Cao, 秋胡行
騁哉日月逝, 年命將西傾.	Chen Lin, 遊覽詩 II
天地無期竟, 民生甚局促.	
為稱百年壽, 誰能應此錄.	Liu Zhen, 詩
民生受天命, 漂若河中塵.	
雖稱百齡壽, 孰能應此身.	Ruan Yu, 怨詩
天地無終極, 人命若朝露.	Cao Zhi, 送應氏詩 II
天地無窮極, 陰陽轉相因.	
人居一世間, 忽若風吹塵.	Cao Zhi, 薤露篇
天地無窮, 人命有終.	Cao Rui, 月重輪行

Suzuki Shūji's examples are all drawn from the Han and Wei. When these old topics are carried over into the Eastern Jin and later, they are often expanded. One famous example can be seen in the opening of Tao Qian's first "Unclassified Poem" (*Zashi* 雜詩), slightly shifting the predicate of "Human life is . . ." from brevity to helplessness.

人生無根蒂	Human life has no root or stem,
飄如陌上塵	wind-tossed like dust on the lanes,
分散逐風轉	coming apart as it whirls with the wind,
此已非常身	this body with no permanence.

Although avoiding the higher lexical register of late fourth- and early fifth-century poetry, this is characteristic of the copiousness of the later tradition. In the case of Tao Qian's poem the functional role of the *rensheng* topic is identical to what it had been in many earlier "old poems" and *yuefu*, but it takes up more of the poem's "space."

Shijing *Echoes in the*
"Old Poems": A Case

In "Nineteen Old Poems" XII we have the following couplet:

晨風懷苦心	The dawnwind hawk harbors a bitter heart,
蟋蟀傷局促	the crickets lament how hard-pressed they are.

These lines are commonly understood as referring to two *Shijing* poems, "Dawnwind Hawk" 晨風, *Shi* 132, and "Cricket" 蟋蟀, *Shi* 114, respectively. The nature of this couplet allows us to pose questions about the use of the *Shijing* in the "old poems." We cannot answer these questions definitively, but exploring them can be fruitful.

Let us begin by setting some parameters for our inquiry. First, we know that some of the "old poems" do make reference to the *Shijing* in no ambiguous way. In "Nineteen Old Poems" VII, for example, we read:

不念攜手好	With no care for our fondness, once holding hands,
棄我如遺跡	they abandoned me like tracks left behind.
南箕北有斗	In the South the Sieve, the North has the Dipper,
牽牛不負軛	the ox of burden bears no yoke.
良無盤石固	Truly lacking the firmness of boulders,
虛名復何益	what gain comes from empty name?

The middle couplet of our citation reworks images from *Shi* 203, "Dadong" 大東 (*Xiaoya*), on constellations that do not perform the functions of their names. Thus the three couplets taken together function almost like a scholastic exercise in "application": we have a current situation, the citation (or reworking) of a *Shijing* passage, and a generalization that interprets the *Shijing* passage in such a way that it applies to the current situation. In its scholastic usage, it is reminiscent of the use of the *Shijing* in the Li Ling corpus:

鹿鳴思野草	"The deer cry out," thinking of the plants of the moor—[1]
可以喻嘉賓	this can serve as a figure for a fine guest.

We see that same series of images of the stars from "Dadong" echoed in "Nineteen Old Poems" X:[2]

迢迢牽牛星	Far, far is the Oxherd Star,
皎皎河漢女	bright, the woman in the River of Stars.
纖纖擢素手	She lifts a pale and slender hand,
札札弄機杼	click-clack, she dallies at loom and shuttle.
終日不成章	In a whole day she completes no piece,
泣涕零如雨	her tears are falling like rain.
河漢清且淺	The River of Stars is shallow and clear,
相去復幾許	how far apart are they?
盈盈一水間	Across the brimming stream,
脈脈不得語	gazing with longing, unable to speak.

The passage in question describes the constellation of three stars known as the Weaver Woman, the subject of the poem above, who meets with her lover, the Oxherd constellation, only once a year. That legend, the theme of "Nineteen Old Poems" X, is not in "Dadong" (the last lines of the fifth and first lines of the sixth stanza):

跂彼織女	Straddling is the Weaver Woman,[3]
終日七襄	in a whole day she crosses seven stages.[4]
雖則七襄	But though she crosses seven stages,
不成報章	she completes no full unit.[5]

---

1. *Shi* 161.

2. Lu Qinli, 331; *Wen xuan* 29; *Ytxy* 1 (as Mei Sheng); *Ywlj* 4; *Cxj* 4.

3. *Qi* 跂, "straddling," describes legs spread and the configuration of the three stars.

4. Seven stages of the sky.

5. Playing on her name as the Weaver Woman, she completes no section of cloth.

In the context of "Dadong," this passage serves exactly the same function of the Sieve, Dipper, and Ox (Oxherd) in "Nineteen Old Poems" VII: the stars have "empty names" and do not perform the functions proper to them. Although the Weaver Woman in "Nineteen Old Poems" X is not performing her weaving duties, the reason is not the issue of "empty name," but because she is distracted by longing for the Oxherd constellation. That is, this is not a scholastic usage of the *Shijing* poem, but a "tag," a phrase detached from the standard interpretation of the poem—even though it is based on elementary knowledge of the poem. If one reads just the surface level of the original *Shijing* context into this usage (that is, "empty name" as pejorative), one is misreading.

At a still further remove from a *Shijing* source, in Chapter 2 we discussed "The road is blocked and long" 道路阻且長 from "Nineteen Old Poems" I. The "source" is "Jianjia" 蒹葭 (*Shi* 129): *dao zu qie chang* 道阻且長. This is a phrase that may have originally been expanded from the *Shijing* line, but it circulates in five syllable poetry on its own, without any reference to the *Shijing*.

Our first parameter is thus that some of the "old poems" show knowledge of the *Shijing*, but there is a range of usage, from scholastic reference to a poem with its interpretation to a verbal tag to a phrase that has a separate life without reference to a *Shijing* source. For clarity, let us cite again the couplet with which we began:

晨風懷苦心　　The dawnwind hawk harbors a bitter heart,
蟋蟀傷局促　　the crickets lament how hard-pressed
　　　　　　　　they are.

Our second parameter is that these creatures are part of the natural world, consistent with that described in the poem. Reference to the *Shijing* is not needed here, as it is in the passage on the stars in "Nineteen Old Poems" VII. The dawnwind hawk and the crickets appear in the corpus "old poems" independently, in ways that would be very awkward to explain in reference to the *Shijing* poems to which they lend their names.

Before examining our couplet with reference to these two parameters, we need to add one essential qualification: while on the whole the corpus of "old poems" shares a common poetics, we have no reason to assume that these come from the same period or that their poets (along with those responsible for all the variations they may have passed through) belonged to the same class or educational level.

From Li Shan on through modern times Chinese commentators have generally assumed that the poets they were studying possessed the learning, the libraries, and the leisure for study that those commentators themselves enjoyed. If the commentator reads in a book something that looks like a source for a passage he is studying, then the poet must have read the same book and have remembered it. This may not necessarily be the case.

In the Eastern Han and third century, as now, knowledge of the *Shijing* existed on a gradient from scholars to students who had studied the Classic at various levels, to those who knew of it in bits and pieces. This was particularly true of this period when many moderately educated people often specialized in one Classic or another and had only a "popular" knowledge of other Classics. Everyone with any education knew that "The Deer Cry Out," "Lu ming" 鹿鳴, was to be performed at banquets. It seems likely that the passage on the constellations with the "empty names" in "Dadong" was also known. This is not to say that everyone knew all the poems of the *Shijing* with their Mao (or Sanjia) interpretations. Here we should mention one other phenomenon: throughout the medieval period (through the Tang) it is very common to find references made to the *Shijing* made in a "naive" way; that is, taking a passage as it would be understood from the surface of the words rather than as those words were interpreted by Mao or the scholastic tradition that built upon him. We often do find reference to the *Shijing* that shows a scholastic education in the Classic, but we just as often find bits and pieces of the *Shijing* appearing in less learned ways.

•

Let us now consider our first parameter, the way in which our couplet might be grounded in the *Shijing*. We will quote the first stanzas from the two poems in question.

Shi 132

鴥彼晨風　　　Swiftly flies the dawnwind hawk,
鬱彼北林　　　dense is the northern wood.

未見君子	Not having seen my lord,
憂心欽欽	my careworn heart is troubled.
如何如何	How is it? how is it?
忘我實多	truly he greatly forgets me.

According to the "Lesser Preface" this is directed against Duke Kang of Qin, for expelling virtuous ministers.

Shi 114

蟋蟀在堂	Cricket in the hall
歲聿其莫	the year draws to its end.
今我不樂	If we don't take our joy now,
日月其除	the days and months will pass us by.
無已大康	Yet let not pleasure go too far,
職思其居	just think upon your stations;
好樂無荒	delight should not get out of hand,
良士瞿瞿	the well-born man is circumspect.

According to the "Lesser Preface" this is directed against Duke Xi of Jin, whose excessive frugality caused him to fail in proper ceremony. Thus the folk of Jin are here urging him to take pleasure in a timely and moderate fashion.

•

Few scholars suspect that the possible *Shi* echoes imply political criticism. But there are two points of verbal overlap that could support reading the "old poem" lines in relation to the *Shijing*. The dawnwind hawk "harbors a bitter heart" 懷苦心 for reasons we do not know; in "Dawnwind Hawk," we have a "careworn heart" 憂心. Second, the couplet just before the couplet cited in "Nineteen Old Poems" XII reads:

四時更變化	The four seasons keep on changing,
歲暮一何速	how swiftly comes the year's end.

This has a parallel in "the year draws to its end" 歲聿其莫 in "Cricket." This second case, however, is a weak one, since mentioning year's end is commonplace and naturally linked to autumnal crickets.

•

The evidence from early poetry strongly suggests that both images could be used without reference to the *Shijing*. Ban Gu's "On History" has Tiying reciting the "Dawnwind Hawk" to Han Wendi, but the bird is generally tied to an autumn scene. When the speaker in "Nineteen Old Poems" XVI (an autumn poem) says:[6]

亮無晨風翼	Truly I have not the dawnwind hawk's wings:
焉能凌風飛	how can I fly up over the wind?

we might relate it to the longing for one's lord in the *Shijing* poem. But the image functions in a similar way in a parting poem in the Li Ling corpus:[7]

欲因晨風發	I would like to set off with the dawnwind hawk
送子以賤軀	and see you on your way in person.[8]

The element of longing for someone is often present, as in another poem from the Li Ling corpus.[9]

晨風鳴北林	The dawnwind hawk cries out in the northern woods,
熠燿東南飛	gleaming brightly, it flies southeast.
願言所相思	I want the one I am longing for,
日暮不垂帷	at twilight I don't draw down the bed-curtain.

And the bitterness is often present, as in our couplet:[10]

寒風吹我骨	A cold wind blows over my bones,
嚴霜切我肌	harsh frosts cut into my flesh.
憂心常慘戚	My care-filled heart is always miserable,
晨風爲我悲	the dawnwind hawk grieves for me.

In Cao Pi the dawnwind hawk even becomes the imagined bird with whom the speaker will fly off as a pair:[11]

心傷安所念	When the heart feels pain, on what does one brood?—
但願恩情深	one wants only that love be deep.
願爲晨風鳥	I wish we were the dawnwind hawks,
雙飛翔北林	flying as a pair, soaring in the northern woods.

---

6. Lu Qinli, 333.
7. Ibid., 337.
8. I have emended Lu Qinli's 軀 to 軀 in the translation.
9. Lu Qinli, 340.
10. Ibid., 341.
11. Ibid., 402.

In an odd transformation in Ruan Ji's "Singing of My Cares" LXVIII, it becomes the bird on which the speaker will fly off to Heaven.

In another poem from the Li Ling corpus, the dawnwind hawk even appears in parallel with the crickets, as markers of the autumn scene, but leading to longing:[12]

爍爍三星列	Gleaming, the Three Stars in a row,
拳拳月初生	curving, the new moon appears.
寒涼應節至	The cold arrives, responding to the season,
蟋蟀夜悲鳴	the crickets sing sadly by night.
晨風動喬木	The dawnwind hawk stirs in the tall trees,
枝葉日夜零	branches shed their leaves day and night.
遊子暮思歸	The traveler at twilight longs to go home,
塞耳不能聽	he blocks his ears and cannot listen.

In the case of the image of the dawnwind hawk, I think we can conclude that it picked up associations from the context of its use in the *Shijing* stanzas; but except in the case of the Ban Gu poem, where it is used as a *Shijing* poem rather than a bird, it does not carry the Mao interpretation along with it. Rather, those associations of bitter longing adhere to the image of the dawnwind hawk and contribute to its various transformations in poetic usage.

The cricket is a marker of autumn in the *Shijing* poem that takes its name from the insect, and it occurs elsewhere in the *Shijing* as a marker of autumn. Here the problem is that the cricket *is* a strident marker of autumn in the natural world, quite apart from classical reference. It appears as such in poetry, sometimes echoing other *Shijing* usages, but only as a mark of autumn. It is "hard-pressed" in our couplet, by the lateness of the year, but it would be overreading to link that to the excessive frugality of Duke Xi of Jin or even to the restraint of the banqueters.

---

12. Ibid., 339.

APPENDIX G

Imitations, Retellings,

and Renditions

Sometimes one's argument runs so counter to that of a fellow scholar that it is necessary to return to the evidence and consider it in detail. Joseph Allen's "From Saint to Singing Girl: The Rewriting of the Lo-fu Narrative in Chinese Literati Poetry" begins with an extended comparison of the anonymous *yuefu* commonly known as "Mulberries by the Path," "Moshang sang" 陌上桑, and a text included under Fu Xuan's 傅玄 name in *Yuefu shiji* 28, "Prelude," "Yan'ge xing" 豔歌行.[1] In his comparison Allen treats the Fu Xuan version as a highly self-conscious conservative and literary transformation of popular material. Indeed most Chinese and Japanese scholars who have touched on this poem treat it as an "imitation."

This is an issue that deserves some reconsideration. The Fu Xuan version does leave out certain lines of the "original" and includes others, but one point made by Allen needs to be clarified from the outset. According to Allen, "The largest single deletion in Fu Hsüan's poem is Lo-fu's celebrated description of her husband, which occurs in the last eighteen lines of the original" (329). This would, indeed, be a major deletion. We need, however, to look at the *Song shu* source, which is entitled "Prelude: Luofu Ballad," "Yan'ge Luofu xing" 豔歌羅敷行.[2] Here the verse is divided into three stanzas (*jie* 解), with a note at the end: "First there is the prelude; afterward there is a coda" 前有

---

1. *HJAS* 48, no. 2 (1988): 321–61.
2. *Song shu Yuezhi jiaozhu*, 250.

豔辭曲, 後有趨. That is, the last eighteen lines are not part of the "Prelude" proper, and in a *yuefu* like this they may well have been added later. They do indeed make a dramatic response to the governor; but we must note that, in contrast to the first two stanzas that mention Luofu's name repeatedly, the "coda" does not mention Luofu even once. Since these are supposed to continue her words, that is understandable. We should, however, entertain the possibility that the final segment was added later, perhaps even a different verse added to the Luofu ballad. And if that is the case, Fu Xuan's "Prelude" worked with the "prelude" and omitted nothing at the end.

We should also address the question of Fu Xuan. Most of his *yuefu* show up for the first time in *Yuefu shiji*, though a few do have encyclopedia citations. Since there remain a substantial number of encyclopedia citations without complete poems, we must conclude that Guo Maoqian had either a shortened version of the Fu Xuan collection or drew from a *yuefu* collections with a substantial representation of Fu Xuan pieces.

Let us now do a simple thing. Let us forget that Fu Xuan is a "literati" poet and that his name is attached to "Prelude." Let us forget that encyclopedia quotations are supposed to be "excerpts." Let us say simply that we have a number of versions of this Luofu story and set them side by side. (I omit the *Yutai xinyong* version, which is based on the *Song shu* version; most of its variants also appear in the *Yiwen leiju* and *Chuxue ji* versions.

Song shu	Fu Xuan, "Prelude"	*Yiwen leiju*	*Chuxue ji*
日出東南隅	日出東南隅	日出東海隅	日出東南隅
照我秦氏樓	照我秦氏樓	照我秦氏樓	照我秦氏樓
秦氏有好女	秦氏有好女	秦氏有好女	秦氏有好女
自名爲羅敷	自字爲羅敷	自名爲羅敷	自言名羅敷
羅敷善蠶桑		羅敷喜蠶桑	羅敷善採桑
採桑城南隅		採桑城南隅	採桑城南隅
青絲爲籠系		青絲爲籠繩	青絲爲籠繩
桂枝爲籠鉤		桂枝爲籠鉤	桂枝爲籠鉤
頭上倭墮髻	首戴金翠飾	頭上綵墮髻	頭上髮墮髻
耳中明月珠	耳綴明月珠	耳中明月珠	耳中明月珠
緗綺爲下裙	白素爲下裙	緗綺爲下裙	緗綺爲下裙
紫綺爲上襦	丹霞爲上襦	紫綺爲上襦	紫綺爲上襦
行者見羅敷			觀者見羅敷

下擔捋髭須			下擔捋髭鬚
少年見羅敷			少年見羅敷
脫帽著帩頭			脫帽著幞頭
耕者忘其耕			耕者忘其犁
鋤者忘其鋤			鋤者忘其鋤
來歸相怒怨			來歸相喜怒
但坐觀羅敷			但坐觀羅敷
	一顧傾朝市		
	再顧國爲虛		
	問女居安在		
	堂在城南居		
	青樓臨大巷		
	幽門結重樞		
使君從南來	使君自南來	使君從南來	使君從南來
五馬立踟躕	駒馬立踟躕	五馬立踟躕	五馬立踟躕
使君遣吏往	[遣吏謝賢女]	使君遣吏往	
問是誰家姝		問是誰家姝	
秦氏有好女			
自名爲羅敷			
羅敷年幾何			
二十尚不足		二十尚未然	
十五頗有餘		十五頗有餘	
使君謝羅敷	遣吏謝賢女	使君謝羅敷	
寧可共載不	豈可同行車	寧可共載不	
羅敷前置辭	斯女長跪對	羅敷前致詞	
使君一何愚	使君言何殊	使君一何愚	
使君自有婦	使君自有婦	使君自有婦	
羅敷自有夫	賤妾有鄙夫	羅敷自有夫	
	天地正厥位		
	願君改其圖		
東方千餘騎		東方千餘騎	
夫婿居上頭		夫婿居上頭	
何用識夫婿		何用識夫婿	
白馬從驪駒		白馬從驪駒	
青絲繫馬尾		青絲繫馬尾	
黃金絡馬頭		黃金絡馬頭	
腰中鹿盧劍		腰中鹿盧劍	
可值千萬餘		可值千萬餘	
十五府小史		十五府小史	
二十朝大夫		二十朝大夫	
三十侍中郎		三十侍中郎	
四十專城居		四十專城居	

為人潔白晳
鬤鬤頗有鬚
盈盈公府步
冉冉府中趨
坐中數千人
皆言夫婿殊

為人潔白晳
鬤鬤頗有鬚
盈盈公府步
冉冉府中趨

Allen notes that, in contrast to the omission in the Fu Xuan version, "In 'Mo-shang sang' her beauty virtually stops men in their tracks (ll.13–20)" (331). Yet the same omission is made in *Yiwen leiju* (and in the *Yutai xinyong* and *Chuxue ji* versions, they are "watching," *guan* 觀, not "walking," *hang* 行). Fu Xuan leaves off the "coda," but so does *Chu xueji*. The most interesting issue is the omission of mulberry picking, which may indeed be significant. In conjunction with the locked gates of her dwelling, this is quite consistent with third-century elite practice, which we have seen in Lu Ji, taking women who are seductively exposed and hiding them or putting them to womanly work (though such hiding of women also occurs in low register poetry). The same is true of the polite self-reference (*jianqie* 賤妾) and phrases like "worthy girl," *xiannü* 賢女). This may help us historicize Allen's surprise that even later poetry mentioned her sericultural activities (329). Later poetry in the Southern Dynasties, far more "elite" than Fu Xuan, was fascinated by the exposure of women to men's gaze, particularly women of less than elite status.

Then we might turn to Fu Xuan's "additions." "Mulberries by the Path" is a text that first appears in history at the beginning of the sixth century, with the designation that it is "old."[3] Fu Xuan's poem does not appear in history until the turn of the twelfth century; but if we believe the attribution, it comes from the mid-third century. This is not to suggest that Fu Xuan's poem is earlier; but considering the way the text kept changing shape, even after its relative stabilization in the *Song shu* and *Yutai xinyong*, it seems at least a strong possibility that in Fu Xuan's time the text did not look the same way it looked in the *Song shu*. Much had happened to books and traditions in that interval. The verses without counterparts in the *Song shu* ver-

---

3. The title is mentioned much earlier, but we cannot know how much the *Song shu* text resembled the song through its early history.

sion are "additions" only if we take the *Song shu* version as a fixed standard.

While I disagree with many of Allen's points that supposedly show "literati" revision of "Mulberries by the Path," I do agree that the omission of mulberry-picking and some details of phrasing show traces of late Wei and Western Jin sensibilities. I think these traces are far lighter than Allen suggests.

All this is to take us to the main point, which is: What is this piece by Fu Xuan? Our terminology, based in a scholarly culture of print culture in which texts are "intellectual property," divides textual production into exact reproduction and imitation or variation. As we have seen throughout this book (to be confirmed by a cursory glance at Lu Qinli), in early manuscript culture there is exact reproduction only for texts with strict protocols demanding exact reproduction (like the Classics). Other texts are always changing size and shape, proportional to their distance from "seriousness." And "Mulberries by the Path," except as preserved text in the imperial musical repertoire and then part of an accepted history, was far from seriousness.

This text is clearly not an "imitation" in the sense of *ni* 擬. It violates *all* the rules of *ni*. If the *Song shu* version is the "original," the Fu Xuan version omits lines, adds lines, reproduces more than half of its lines exactly or almost exactly, and only in the case of two lines (豈可同行車 and 斯女長跪對) could we limply suggest that they were rewritten in a higher register. If this is not *ni*, then is this a "thematic imitation" (a free literary rewriting of the same materials)? Again I think we must answer negatively. We have some excellent examples of Fu Xuan rewriting texts for which we have other versions, and nowhere is so much of the poem the same as the other version.

Jean-Pierre Diény is, I believe, closer to the truth when he says that Fu Xuan is not imitating but rewriting, "purging a song judged to be imperfect."[4] This, however, presumes that "Mulberries by the Path" was then the fixed text in exactly the form we have it now. This is not impossible, but it is an assumption that should be examined. If, however, "Mulberries by

---

4. Jean-Pierre Diény, *Pastourelles et magnarelles: essai sur un thème littéraire chinoise* (Geneva: Librairie Droz, 1977), 113.

the Path" always changes when it is written down, then this is a version with a known transcriber, a version that betrays the interests of that transcriber. This is, in effect, Diény's interpretation framed with a different set of assumptions.

It is not a quibble to say that this is a "version" of the *yan'ge* of the Luofu story, another "version" of which went into the *Song shu*. This version shows the traces of elite poetics (as do a great many of the texts preserved as "anonymous" and "old"); the version in the *Song shu* shows fewer such traces. To believe that Fu Xuan's version derives from the *Song shu* is an ideological assumption that there is originally a pure "folk poetry" to which literati do things. It is no less possible that Fu Xuan wrote down this long version of a snatch of song preserved with a rudimentary story, an old title "Mulberries by the Path"; through his important role in the imperial musical establishment, his version became part of the court repertoire, where it was popularized, with some pieces cut and some added—most important, the "coda" necessary for a full suite. I am not advocating this scenario of reverse filiation; I am simply suggesting that it is just as likely as Fu Xuan "changing" the present text. It is far better to think of song material appearing in different versions, each one appropriate for its venue.

•

We actually have a far better case from which to consider Fu Xuan's level of "literary" transformation (as well as the "literary" level of "Mulberries by the Path," a remarkably smooth piece). Zuo Yannian 左延年 was a member of the imperial musical establishment around the mid-third century, a generation older than Fu Xuan, who also became an important figure in the musical establishment. The name Yannian indicates a professional performer. Under his name a remarkable text has been preserved in the *Yuefu shiji*. It is as good an example as we have of low register ballad style in the third century, and we can use it as a touchstone against which to read other texts. By comparison many of the texts that might seem "folkish" begin to appear rather polished.

左延年, 秦女休行 Zuo Yannian (early to mid-third century),
Ballad of Qin's Maid Xiu[5]

始出上西門	When first I went out Upper West Gate,
遙望秦氏廬	I gazed afar on the house of the Qins.[6]
秦氏有好女	The Qins have a lovely daughter,
自名爲女休	she calls herself Maid Xiu.
休年十四五	Xiu was fourteen or fifteen,
爲宗行報讎	when she went to carry out a revenge for her family line.[7]
左執白楊刃	In her left hand she held a Baiyang blade,
右據宛魯矛	her right hand rested on a Wanlu spear.
讎家便東南	The enemy's home was to the southeast,
仆僵秦女休	he lay stiff before Qin's Maid Xiu.
女休西上山	Maid Xiu went west up the mountains,
上山四五里	up the mountains four or five leagues.
關吏呵問女休	The officer at the pass shouted and questioned Maid Xiu,
女休前置辭	Maid Xiu came forward and told her story.
平生爲燕王婦	I used to be wife of the Prince of Yan,
於今爲詔獄囚	now I'm a prisoner by royal command.
平生衣參差	I used to dress in fine colored clothes,
當今無領襦	now I don't have even a jacket.
明知殺人當死	Well I know that one must die for murder,
兄言快快	my big brother's words were troubled,
弟言無道憂	my younger brother worried that I had done wrong.
女休堅詞爲宗報讎	Maid Xiu stoutly maintains she has taken revenge for her family,
死不疑	she will die without wavering.
殺人都市中	They kill people in the capital market,
徼我都巷西	they transfer me west of the capital's lanes.
丞卿羅東向坐	Ministers and grandees are lined up sitting facing east,
女休悽悽曳梏前	Maid Xiu, miserable, comes forward dragging her chains.
兩徒夾我	Two fellows stand on either side,
持刀刀五尺餘	holding swords, swords that are more than five feet long.

---

5. Lu Qinli, 410; *Yuefu shiji* 61; Huang Jie, *Han Wei*, 191. Bits and pieces were preserved in *Beitang shuchao* and *Taiping yulan*.

6. *Taiping yulan* reads *lou* 樓 for *lu* 廬. This is a better rhyme, and formulaic.

7. Either she is taking revenge in a generational blood-feud or acting on behalf of the lineage. Note that this is for her own bloodline.

刀未下	But before the sword falls,
瞳朧擊鼓赦書下	there is a faint beating of drums as the pardon is given.

Although Huang Jie tries to explain the rhymes at the end, the last part seems garbled and more like a prose summary to end a ballad poorly remembered.

We have discussed how poetry could expand and contract. The narrative here is an excellent example: it is epitome. Many parts not only could be more fully elaborated, some parts beg elaboration. We have the impression of a listener jotting down lines (perhaps of a performance). The opening is, of course, essentially the same as that of "Mulberries by the Path."

In the Fu Xuan poem we can see a literary re-creation in the full sense. It shares no lines with the Zuo Yannian version and elaborates at expected points. It is nothing at all like the alternative version of "Mulberries by the Path." No one, however, could call this a high register poem. Comparison with Lu Ji's *yuefu* shows how plain the narrative style is.

傅玄, 秦女休行 Fu Xuan, The Ballad of Qin Nüxiu[8]

龐氏有烈婦	The family Pang had a heroic wife,
義聲馳雍涼	her virtue's fame sped through Yong and Liang.
父母家有重怨	Her parents suffered accumulated grievances,
仇人暴且彊	their enemy was violent and strong.
雖有男兄弟	Though she had male brothers,
志弱不能當	they were weak-willed, not up to the task.
烈女念此痛	The heroic woman brooded on this pain,
丹心爲寸傷	and her true heart was minutely wounded.
外若無意者	Outside she seemed to have nothing planned,
內潛思無方	but hidden within, her thoughts were boundless.
白日入都市	In broad daylight she entered the capital market,
怨家如平常	her enemy was as he usually was.
匿劍藏白刃	Her hidden sword had its silver blade concealed,
一奮尋身僵	one strike lay his body flat on the ground.

---

8. Lu Qinli, 563; *Yfsj* 61; Jian Changchun, *Fu Xuan*, 53.

身首爲之異處	She made his body and head be in different places,
伏尸列肆旁	and she lay the corpse by the execution ground [in the market].
肉與土合成泥	His flesh and the dirt combined into a mud,
灑血濺飛梁	and his spattered blood sprinkled the soaring rafters.
孟氣上干雲霓	Her fierce spirit passed through clouds and rainbows above,
仇黨失守爲披攘	while her enemy's clique lost heart and submitted to her.
一市稱烈義	The whole marketplace acclaimed her righteous daring,
觀者收淚並慨忙	those who watched stopped their tears and were strongly moved.
百男何當益	What advantage serves a hundred males?—
不如一女良	they are no match for the excellence of one woman.
烈女直造縣門	The heroic woman went straight to the county office gate,
云父不幸遭禍殃	she said that unfortunately her father had met with disaster.
今仇身以分裂	Today his enemy's body has been cut to pieces,
雖死情益揚	though he is dead, his mood will increasingly be uplifted.
殺人當伏法	When you kill someone, you must submit to the law,
義不苟活贖舊章	righteousness does not permit one to stay alive illicitly and thus ruin the old statutes.
縣令解印綬	The county magistrate undid the ribbon with his seal [to resign]—
令我傷心不忍聽	"It causes me to feel pain and I cannot bear to obey."
刑部垂頭塞耳	The head of the Board of Punishments hung his head and stopped his ears—
令我吏舉不能成	"It causes me to be unable to fully carry out official action [against her]."
烈著希代之績	Her heroism shows merit rarely seen in the world;
義立無窮之名	her righteousness establishes endless renown.

夫家同受其祚	Her husband's family all received good fortune from her;
子子孫孫咸享其榮	children and grandchildren all enjoyed the fruits of her glory.
今我作歌詠高風	Now I make this song to sing of her noble qualities;
激揚壯發悲且清	to spread word of her bold venture, moving and pure.[9]

The story of Qin Nüxiu is here linked to that of Zhao Eqin 趙娥親, married to Pang Zixia 龐子夏. Her father was killed by the local warlord Li Shou, and in 179 she assassinated Li. She turned herself in to the yamen, but was pardoned. Details of this story do not match the ballad.

---

9. Jian Changchun suggests that this should be 壯髮, the hair hanging down over the forehead.

Reference Matter

Selected Bibliography

The following abbreviations are used in the notes to the text:

Ywlj   Ouyang Xun, *Yiwen leiju* 藝文類聚.
Cxj   Xu Jian, *Chuxue ji* 初學記.
Yfsj   Guo Maoqian, *Yuefu shiji* 樂府詩集.
Ytxy   Xu Ling, *Yutai xinyong* 玉臺新詠.
Tpyl   *Taiping yulan* 太平御覽.

Allen, Joseph. "From Saint to Singing Girl: The Rewriting of the Lo-fu Narrative in Chinese Literati Poetry." *Harvard Journal of Asiatic Studies* 40 (1989): 321–61.

———. *In the Voice of Others: Chinese Music Bureau Poetry.* Ann Arbor: University of Michigan Center for Chinese Studies, 1992.

Balazs, Etienne. "Ts'ao Ts'ao, zwei Lieder." *Monumenta Serica* 2 (1936–37): 410–20.

Birrel, Anne. *Popular Songs and Ballads of Han China.* London: Unwin Hyman, 1988.

Cao Xu 曹旭. *Shipin jizhu* 詩品集注. Shanghai: Shanghai guji chubanshe, 1994.

Chen Liangyun 陳良運. *Jiaoshi Yilin shixue chanshi* 焦氏易林詩學闡釋. Nanchang: Baihuazhou wenyi chubanshe, 2000.

Coblin, W. South. *A Handbook of Eastern Han Sound Glosses.* Hong Kong: Chinese University Press, 1983.

Connery, Christopher. *The Empire of the Text: Writing and Authority in Early Imperial China.* Lanham, MD: Rowman & Littlefield, 1998.

Cutter, Robert Joe. "Cao Zhi's (192–232) Symposium Poems." *CLEAR* 6 (1984): 1–32.

Deng Guoguang 鄧國光. *Zhi Yu yanjiu* 摯虞研究. Hong Kong: Xueheng chubanshe, 1990.

Diény, Jean-Pierre. *Aux origines de la poésie classique en Chine: étude sur la poésie lyrique à l'époque des Han.* Leiden: E. J. Brill, 1968.

———. "Contre Guo Maoqian: à propos des deux versions de certains poèms des Han et des Wei." *T'oung Pao* 85, nos. 1–3 (1999): 65–113.

———. *Les dix-neuf poèmes anciens*. Paris: Presses universitaires de France, 1963.

———. *Les poèmes de Cao Cao*. Paris: Collège de France, Institut des hautes études chinoises, 2000.

———. *Pastourelles et magnarelles: essai sur un thème littéraire chinoise*. Geneva: Librairie Droz, 1977.

Egan, Charles H. "Were Yüeh-fu Ever Folk Songs? Reconsidering the Relevance of Oral Theory and Balladry Analogies." *CLEAR* 22 (2000): 31–66.

Fei Zhengang 費振剛, Hu Shuangbao 胡雙寶, and Zong Minghua 宗明華. *Quan Han fu* 全漢賦. Beijing: Beijing daxue chubanshe, 1993.

Frankel, Hans H. "Cai Yan and the Poems Attributed to Her." *CLEAR* 5 (1983): 133–56.

———. "The Problem of Authenticity in the Works of Cao Zhi." In Chan Ping-leung et al., eds., *Essays in Commemoration of the Golden Jubilee of the Fung Bing Shan Library (1932–1982)*. Hong Kong: Hong Kong University Press, 1982, 183–201.

Fu Gang 傅剛. *Zhaoming wenxuan yanjiu* 昭明文選研究. Beijing: Zhongguo shehui kexue chubanshe, 2000.

Funatsu Tomohiko 船津富彦. "Shō Shoku no Yūsenshi ron" 曹植の游仙詩論. *Tōhō bungaku kenkyū* 13 (1965): 49–65.

Ge Hong 葛洪. *Xijing zaji quanshi* 西京雜記全釋. Guiyang: Guizhou renmin chubanshe, 1993.

Guo Maoqian 郭茂倩. *Yuefu shiji* 樂府詩集. Beijing: Zhonghua shuju, 1979.

Guoyu 國語. Shanghai: Shanghai guji chubanshe, 1978.

Han Geping 韓格平. *Jian'an qizi shiwenji jiaozhu yixi* 建安七子詩文集校注譯註. Changchun: Jilin wenshi chubanshe, 1991.

Han shu 漢書. Beijing: Zhonghua shuju, 1962.

Hao Liquan 郝立權. *Lu Shiheng shi zhu* 陸士衡詩注. Beijing: Renmin wenxue chubanshe, 1958.

Holzman, Donald. "Cao Zhi and the Immortals." *Asia Major* 1, no. 1 (1988): 15–57.

———. "Immortality-Seeking in Early Chinese Poetry." In Willard J. Peterson, Andrew Plaks, and Ying-shu Yü, eds., *The Power of Culture: Studies in Chinese Cultural History*. Hong Kong: Chinese University Press, 1994, 103–18.

———. *Poetry and Politics: The Life and Works of Juan Chi (A.D. 210–263)*. Cambridge: Cambridge University Press, 1976.

———. "Les premiers vers pentasyllabiques datés dans la poésie chinoise." *Mélanges de sinologie offerts à Monsieur Paul Demieville*. Paris: Presses universitaires de France, 1974, 77–116.

Hou Han shu 後漢書. Beijing: Zhonghua shuju, 1965.

Hu Zhiji 胡之驥. *Jiang Wentong ji huizhu* 江文通集彙注 (1598). Beijing: Zhonghua shuju, 1984.

Huang Jie 黃節. *Bao Canjun shi zhu* 鮑參軍詩注. Beijing: Zhonghua shuju, 1972.

———. *Cao Zijian shi zhu* 曹子建詩注. Beijing: Renmin wenxue chubanshe, 1957.

———. *Han Wei yuefu feng jian* 漢魏樂府風箋. Hong Kong: Shangwu yinshuguan, 1961.

———. *Ruan bubing Yonghuai shi zhu* 阮步兵詠懷詩注. Beijing: Renmin wenxue chubanshe, 1957.

———. *Wei Wudi Wendi Mingdi shi zhu* 魏武帝文帝明帝詩注. Beijing: Renmin wenxue chubanshe, 1958.

Ikkai Tomoyoshi 一海知義. "*Monzen* banka shi kō" 文選挽歌詩考. *Chūgoku bungaku hō* 12 (1960): 19–48.

Itō Masafumi 伊藤正文. "Ō San shi ronkō" 王粲詩論考. *Chūgoku bungaku hō* 20 (1965): 28–67.

Jian Changchun 蹇長春, Wang Huishao 王會紹, and Yu Xianjie 余賢傑. *Fu Xuan Yin Keng shizhu* 傅玄陰鏗詩注. Lanzhou: Gansu renmin chubanshe, 1987.

Jin shu 晉書. Beijing: Zhonghua shuju, 1974.

Knechtges, David. "Culling the Weeds and Selecting Prime Blossoms: The Anthology in Early Medieval China." In Scott Pearce et al., eds., *Culture and Power in the Reconstitution of the Chinese Realm, 200–600.* Cambridge: Harvard University Asia Center, 2001, 200–241.

———. "Han Wudi de fu" 漢武帝的賦. *Disanjie guoji cifuxue xueshu yantaohui lunwenji* 第三屆國際辭賦學學術研討會論文集 (December 1996): 1–14.

———. *Wen xuan or Selections of Refined Literature,* vol. 1, *Rhapsodies on Metropolises and Capitals.* Princeton: Princeton University Press, 1982.

Kroll, Paul W., and David R. Knechtges. *Studies in Early Medieval Chinese Literature and Cultural History: In Honor of Richard B. Mather and Donald Holzman.* Provo, Utah: T'ang Studies Society, 2003.

Lai, C. M. "The Craft of Original Imitation: Lu Ji's Imitations of the Han Old Poems." In Paul W. Kroll and David Knechtges, eds., *Studies in Early Medieval Chinese Literature and Cultural History: In Honor of Richard B. Mather and Donald Holzman.* Provo, Utah: T'ang Studies Society, 2003, 117–48.

Liu Yiqing (Liu I-ch'ing). *A New Account of Tales of the World.* Trans. Richard B. Mather. Minneapolis: University of Minnesota Press, 1976.

Lu Qinli 逯欽立. *Han Wei liuchao wenxue lunji* 漢魏六朝文學論集. Ed. Wu Yun 吳雲. Xi'an: Shanxi renmin chubanshe, 1984.

———. *Xian-Qin Han Wei Jin Nanbeichao shi* 先秦漢魏晉南北朝詩. Beijing: Zhonghua shuju, 1983.

Lu Yun 陸雲. *Lu Yun ji* 陸雲集. Ed. Huang Kui 黃葵. Beijing: Zhonghua shuju, 1988.

Luo Guowei 羅國威, ed. *Ri cang Hongrenben* Wenguan Cilin *jiaozheng* 日藏弘仁本文館詞林校證. Beijing: Zhonghua shuju, 2001.

Masuda Kiyohide 增田清秀. *Gafu no rekishiteki kenkyū* 樂府の歷史的研究. Tokyo: Sōbunsha, 1975.

Mather, Richard B. *The Poet Shen Yüeh (441–513): The Reticent Marquis*. Princeton: Princeton University Press, 1988.

Mei Jialing 梅家玲. *Han Wei Liuchao wenxue xinlun: nidai yu zengda pian* 漢魏六朝文學新論: 擬代與贈答篇. Taibei: Liren shuju, 1997.

Nakatsuhama Wataru 中津濱涉. *Gafu shishū no kenkyū* 樂府詩集の研究. Tokyo: Kyōko shoin, 1970.

Nan shi 南史. Beijing: Zhonghua shuju, 1975.

Nie Wenyu 聶文鬱. *Cao Zhi shi jieyi* 曹植詩解譯. Xining: Qinghai renmin chubanshe, 1985.

Ong, Walter J. *Orality and Literacy: The Technologizing of the Word*. London: Methuen, 1982.

Ouyang Xiu 歐陽修. *Ouyang Xiu quanji* 歐陽修全集. Rpt., Taibei: Shijie shuju, 1963.

Ouyang Xun 歐陽詢 (557–641). *Yiwen leiju* 藝文類聚. Taibei: Wenguang chubanshe, 1974.

Pearce, Scott, et al., eds. *Culture and Power in the Reconstitution of the Chinese Realm, 200–600*. Cambridge: Harvard University Asia Center, 2001.

Pu Yingji 朴英姬. "Cong 'Yan'ge hechang xing' lun Han Wei Jin yuefu shi de jige wenti" 從豔歌何嘗行論漢魏晉樂府詩的幾個問題. *Zhongguo wenhua yuekan* 193 (November 1995): 103–23.

Puett, Michael. *The Ambivalence of Creation: Debates Concerning Innovation and Artifice in Early China*. Stanford: Stanford University Press, 2001.

Ren Fang 任昉. *Wenzhang yuanqi zhu* 文章緣起注. Rpt., Taibei: Guangwen shuju, 1970.

San Cao ziliao huibian 三曹資料彙編. Beijing: Zhonghua shuju, 1980.

Song shu 宋書. Beijing: Zhonghua shuju, 1974.

Steinen, Diether von den. "Poems of Cao Cao." *Monumenta Serica* 4 (1939–40): 125–81.

Su Jinren 蘇晉仁 and Xiao Lianzi 蕭煉子. *Song shu Yuezhi jiaozhu* 宋書樂志校注. Ji'nan: Qi Lu shushe, 1982.

Sui shu 隋書. Beijing: Zhonghua shuju, 1973.

Sui Shusen 隋樹森. *Gushi shijiushou jishi* 古詩十九首集釋. Beijing: Zhonghua shuju, 1955.

Suzuki Shūji 鈴木修次. *Kan Gi shi no kenkyū* 漢魏詩の研究. Tokyo: Taishūkan shoten, 1967.

Taiping yulan 太平御覽. Sibu congkan, 3d series. Rpt., Taibei: Shang-wu yinshuguan, 1980.

Wang Ching-hsien. *The Bell and the Drum: Shih Ching as Formulaic Poetry in the Oral Tradition*. Berkeley: University of California Press, 1974.

Wang Liqi 王利器. *Xinyu jiaozhu* 新語校註. Beijing: Zhonghua shuju, 1986.

Wang Shumin 王叔岷. *Zhong Rong Shipin jianzheng gao* 鍾嶸詩品箋證稿. Zhongguo wenzhe zhuankan. Taibei: Zhongyang yanjiuyuan, Wen-shizhe yanjiusuo, 1992.

Wen Yiduo 聞一多. *Wen Yiduo quanji* 聞一多全集. 4 vols. Beijing: San-lian shudian, 1968.

Williams, Gary Shelton. "A Study of the Oral Nature of the Han *Yüeh-fu*." Ph.D. dissertation, University of Washington, 1973.

Wu Yun 吳雲. *Jian'an qizi ji jiaozhu* 建安七子集校註. Tianjin: Tianjin guji chubanshe, 1991.

Wu Yun 吳雲 and Tang Shaozhong 唐紹忠. *Wang Can ji zhu* 王粲集注. Henan: Zhongzhou shuhua she, 1984.

Xiao Tong 蕭統. *Wen xuan* 文選. Shanghai: Shanghai guji, 1986.

Xu Jian 徐堅 (659–729). *Chuxue ji* 初學記. Beijing: Zhonghua shuju, 1962.

Xu Ling 徐陵. *Yutai xinyong* 玉臺新詠. Beijing: Zhonghua shuju, 1985.

Yan Kejun 嚴可均. *Quan shanggu sandai Qin Han Sanguo Liuchao wen* 全上古三代秦漢三國六朝文. Rpt. Beijing: Zhonghua shuju, 1965.

Yao Daye 姚大業. *Han Yuefu xiaolun* 漢樂府小論. Tianjin: Baihua wenyi chubanshe, 1984.

Yu Guanying 余冠英. *Han Wei Liuchao shixuan* 漢魏六朝詩選. Beijing: Renmin wenxue chubanshe, 1978.

———. "Yuefu geci de pincou he fen'ge" 樂府歌辭的拼湊和分割. In idem, *Han Wei Liuchao shi luncong* 漢魏六朝詩論叢. Beijing: Zhonghua shuju, 1962, 26–38.

Yu Jiaxi 余嘉錫. *Shishuo xinyu jianshu* 世說新語箋疏. Shanghai: Shang-hai guji chubanshe, 1993.

Yu Yuan 郁沅 and Zhang Minggao 張明高. *Wei Jin Nanbeichao wenlun xuan* 魏晉南北朝文論選. Beijing: Renmin wenxue chubanshe, 1996.

Zhan Ying 詹鍈. *Wenxin diaolong yizheng* 文心雕龍義證. Shanghai: Shanghai guji, 1989.

Zhao Youwen 趙幼文. *Cao Zhi ji jiaozhu* 曹植集校注. Beijing: Renmin wenxue chubanshe, 1984.

Zheng Wen 鄭文. *Han shi xuanjian* 漢詩選箋. Shanghai: Shanghai guji chubanshe, 1986.

Index

Harvard East Asian Monographs
(*out-of-print)

Harvard East Asian Monographs

Harvard East Asian Monographs

Harvard East Asian Monographs

Harvard East Asian Monographs

203. Robert S. Ross and Jiang Changbin, eds., *Re-examining the Cold War: U.S.-China Diplomacy, 1954–1973*

204. Guanhua Wang, *In Search of Justice: The 1905–1906 Chinese Anti-American Boycott*

205. David Schaberg, *A Patterned Past: Form and Thought in Early Chinese Historiography*

206. Christine Yano, *Tears of Longing: Nostalgia and the Nation in Japanese Popular Song*

207. Milena Doleželová-Velingerová and Oldřich Král, with Graham Sanders, eds., *The Appropriation of Cultural Capital: China's May Fourth Project*

208. Robert N. Huey, *The Making of 'Shinkokinshū'*

209. Lee Butler, *Emperor and Aristocracy in Japan, 1467–1680: Resilience and Renewal*

210. Suzanne Ogden, *Inklings of Democracy in China*

211. Kenneth J. Ruoff, *The People's Emperor: Democracy and the Japanese Monarchy, 1945–1995*

212. Haun Saussy, *Great Walls of Discourse and Other Adventures in Cultural China*

213. Aviad E. Raz, *Emotions at Work: Normative Control, Organizations, and Culture in Japan and America*

214. Rebecca E. Karl and Peter Zarrow, eds., *Rethinking the 1898 Reform Period: Political and Cultural Change in Late Qing China*

215. Kevin O'Rourke, *The Book of Korean Shijo*

216. Ezra F. Vogel, ed., *The Golden Age of the U.S.-China-Japan Triangle, 1972–1989*

217. Thomas A Wilson, ed., *On Sacred Grounds: Culture, Society, Politics, and the Formation of the Cult of Confucius*

218. Donald S. Sutton, *Steps of Perfection: Exorcistic Performers and Chinese Religion in Twentieth-Century Taiwan*

219. Daqing Yang, *Technology of Empire: Telecommunications and Japanese Expansionism, 1895–1945*

220. Qianshen Bai, *Fu Shan's World: The Transformation of Chinese Calligraphy in the Seventeenth Century*

221. Paul Jakov Smith and Richard von Glahn, eds., *The Song-Yuan-Ming Transition in Chinese History*

222. Rania Huntington, *Alien Kind: Foxes and Late Imperial Chinese Narrative*

223. Jordan Sand, *House and Home in Modern Japan: Architecture, Domestic Space, and Bourgeois Culture, 1880–1930*

224. Karl Gerth, *China Made: Consumer Culture and the Creation of the Nation*

225. Xiaoshan Yang, *Metamorphosis of the Private Sphere: Gardens and Objects in Tang-Song Poetry*

226. Barbara Mittler, *A Newspaper for China? Power, Identity, and Change in Shanghai's News Media, 1872–1912*

227. Joyce A. Madancy, *The Troublesome Legacy of Commissioner Lin: The Opium Trade and Opium Suppression in Fujian Province, 1820s to 1920s*